JasperReports 3.5

for Java Developers

Create, design, format, and export reports with the world's most popular Java reporting library

David R. Heffelfinger

BIRMINGHAM - MUMBAI

JasperReports 3.5 for Java Developers

First published: August 2009

Production Reference: 1050809

Published by Packt Publishing Ltd.
32 Lincoln Road
Olton
Birmingham, B27 6PA, UK.

ISBN 978-1-847198-08-2

www.packtpub.com

Cover Image by Parag Kadam (paragvkadam@gmail.com)

Credits

Author
David R. Heffelfinger

Reviewers
Allan Bond
BalaKishore G. Pamarti
T. David Hoppmann, Jr
Thomas M. Ose

Acquisition Editor
Douglas Paterson

Development Editor
Amey Kanse

Technical Editor
Ishita Dhabalia

Copy Editor
Sanchari Mukherjee

Editorial Team Leader
Gagandeep Singh

Project Team Leader
Priya Mukherji

Project Coordinators
Ashwin Shetty
Neelkanth Mehta

Indexer
Hemangini Bari

Proofreaders
Jade Schuler
Laura Booth

Production Coordinator
Adline Swetha Jesuthas

Cover Work
Adline Swetha Jesuthas

About the Author

David Heffelfinger is the Chief Technology Officer of Ensode Technology, LLC, a software consulting firm based in the greater Washington DC area. He has been professionally designing and developing software since 1995. David has been using Java as his primary programming language since 1996, and has worked on many large scale projects for several government and commercial clients, including IBM, Verizon, the US Department of Homeland Security, Freddie Mac, Fannie Mae, and the US Department of Defense.

David is the author of *Java EE 5 Development Using GlassFish Application Server* and *Java EE 5 with NetBeans 6 and JasperReports For Java Developers*, both by Packt Publishing.

David has a Masters degree in Software Engineering from Southern Methodist University. David is the Editor in Chief of Ensode.net (`http://www.ensode.net`), a web site about Java, Linux, and other technology topics.

I would like to thank everyone who has helped to make this book a reality. I would like to thank the Development Editor, Amey Kanse; the Project Coordinators, Ashwin Shetty and Neelkanth Mehta; the Technical Editor, Ishita Dhabalia; the Acquisition Editor, Douglas Paterson, and everyone else at Packt Publishing for giving me the opportunity to update this book.

I would also like to thank the Technical Reviewers Allan Bond, BalaKishore G. Pamarti, David Hoppmann, and Thomas M. Ose for their insightful comments and suggestions.

Additionally, I would like to thank Teodor Danciu, JasperSoft, and all the JasperReports contributors for creating an outstanding reporting library.

Finally, I would like to thank my wife and daughter for putting up with the long hours of work that kept me away from the family.

About the Reviewers

Allan Bond is a software developer who has been active in the IT industry for 10 years. His primary focus is the development of both frontend and backend systems using Java and related technologies. He has worked and consulted for a variety of organizations ranging from small businesses to Fortune 500 companies, and government agencies. Allan holds a Masters degree in Information Systems Management from Brigham Young University.

BalaKishore G. Pamarti is working in St. Jude Children's Research Hospital's Clinical Informatics Department as a Programmer Analyst for the past five years. It's a non-profit organization supporting all the software systems in the patient care area. Before joining St. Jude, BalaKishore did his Masters in Engineering Technology at the University of Memphis and a Bachelors from the JNTU College of Engineering, Hyderabad in Civil Engineering.

He lives with his wife and they both love hiking and exploring new places!

T. David Hoppmann, Jr is the DBA and lead report developer for Monolith Software Solutions, an open source business intelligence and data warehousing solution for restaurateurs. He graduated from the College of Charleston in his hometown of Charleston, SC with degrees in Computer Science and Computer Information Systems. He is also an active member of the Charleston, SC Linux Users Group (CSCLUG).

Thomas M. Ose has been actively involved in computer and Information Technologies for the past 30 years. He has seen computer and software trends and technology mature over various industries including manufacturing, office automation, and communication sectors. Over the years, Thomas has been a programmer, consultant, and manager for various industries, and has become proficient in many languages and disciplines including C, C++, C#, PHP, JAVA, XML, and UML. He prides himself at always learning something new and developing applications and solutions at the cutting edge of technology and the industry. Thomas is currently the President of his own consulting company, Ose Micro Solutions, Inc. specializing in electronic B2B, G2B system for the Uniform Commercial Code and Business Registration systems for state and local governments. For his solutions, he utilizes PHP, JAVA, and C# to provide web service and browser-based solutions using XML to file regulatory documents at state and local governments. He has developed many national standards in this area and spoken at numerous trade conventions.

Table of Contents

Preface

If you want to create easily understood, professional, and powerful reports from disordered, scattered data using a free, open source Java class library, this book on JasperReports is what you are looking for. JasperReports is the world's most popular embeddable Java open source reporting library, providing Java developers with the power to create rich print and web reports easily.

JasperReports allows you to create better looking reports with formatting and grouping, as well as adding graphical elements to your reports. You can also export your reports to a range of different formats, including PDF and XML. Creating reports becomes easier with the iReport Designer visual designing tool. To round things off, you can integrate your reports with other Java frameworks, using Spring or Hibernate to get data for the report, and Java Server Faces or Struts for presenting the report.

This book shows you how to get started and develop the skills to get the most from JasperReports. The book has been fully updated to use JasperReports 3.5, the latest version of JasperReports. The previously accepted techniques that have now been deprecated have been replaced with their modern counterparts in this latest version. All the examples in this book have been updated to use XML schemas for report templates. Coverage of new datasources that JasperReports now supports has been added to the book. Additionally, JasperReports can now export reports to even more formats than before, and exporting reports to these new formats is covered in this new edition of the book.

The book steers you through each point of report setup, to creating, designing, formatting, and exporting reports with data from a wide range of datasources, and integrating JasperReports with other Java frameworks.

What this book covers

Chapter 1, *An Overview of JasperReports*, introduces you to JasperReports and how it came to be. It gives you an insight to JasperReports' capabilities and features, and also an overview of the steps involved in generating reports using JasperReports.

Chapter 2, *Adding Reporting Capabilities to Java Applications*, teaches you how to add reporting capabilities to your Java applications. You will have your development and execution environment set up to successfully add reporting capabilities to your Java applications by the end of this chapter.

Chapter 3, *Creating Your First Report*, shows you how to create, compile, and preview your first report in both JasperReports' native format and web browser. It also briefs you about the JRXML elements corresponding to different report sections.

Chapter 4, *Creating Dynamic Reports from Databases*, continues with report creation, exploring how to create a report from the data obtained from a database. It also teaches you to generate reports that are displayed in your web browser in the PDF format.

Chapter 5, *Working with Other Datasources*, uses datasources other than databases, such as empty datasources, arrays or collections of Java objects, Maps, TableModels, XML, CSV files, and custom datasources to create reports, enabling you to create your own datasources as well.

Chapter 6, *Report Layout and Design*, gets you creating elaborate layouts, by controlling report-wide layout properties and styles, dividing the report data into logical groups, adding images, background text, and dynamic data to the reports, conditionally printing the report data, and creating subreports.

Chapter 7, *Adding Charts and Graphics to Reports*, takes you to more appealing reports by showing how to take advantage of JasperReports' graphical features and create reports with graphical data like geometric shapes, images, and 2D and 3D charts.

Chapter 8, *Other JasperReports Features*, discusses the JasperReports features that lets you create elaborate reports, such as displaying report text in different languages, executing Java code snippets using scriptlets, creating crosstab reports, running a query with the results of a different query, adding anchors, hyperlinks, and bookmarks to the reports.

Chapter 9, *Exporting to Other Formats*, demonstrates how to export reports to the formats supported by JasperReports, such as PDF, RTF, ODT, Excel, HTML, CSV, XML, and plain text and how to direct the exported reports to a browser.

Chapter 10, *Graphical Report Design with iReport*, helps you get your hands on a graphical report designer called iReport, so that you can design reports graphically, and also, using iReport's graphical user interface.

Chapter 11, *Integrating JasperReports with Other Frameworks*, explains how to integrate JasperReports with several popular web application frameworks and ORM tools, such as Hibernate, JPA, Spring, JSF, and Struts.

What you need for this book

To use this book, you will of course need JasperReports. This is freely downloadable from `http://www.sourceforge.net/projects/jasperreports`.

JasperReports has its own requirements for proper and successful functioning: Java Development Kit (JDK) 1.4 or newer (`http://java.sun.com/javase/downloads/index.jsp`), a recent version of ANT (`http://ant.apache.org/`), and iReport (to visually design reports) (`http://jasperforge.org/plugins/project/project_home.php?projectname=ireport`). Any operating system supporting Java can be used (any modern version of Microsoft Windows, Mac OS X, Linux, or Solaris).

Who this book is for

If you are a Java developer who wants to create rich reports for either the Web or print, and you want to get started quickly with JasperReports, this book is for you. No knowledge of JasperReports is presumed.

Conventions

In this book, you will find a number of styles of text that distinguish between different kinds of information. Here are some examples of these styles, and an explanation of their meaning.

Code words in text are shown as follows: "The `<queryString>` element is used to embed a database query into the report template."

A block of code is set as follows:

```
<path id="classpath">
  <pathelement location="./" />
  <pathelement location="${classes.dir}" />
  <fileset dir="${lib.dir}">
    <include name="**/*.jar" />
  </fileset>
</path>
```

When we wish to draw your attention to a particular part of a code block, the relevant lines or items are set in bold:

```
<band height="20">
  <staticText>
    <reportElement x="20" y="0" width="200" height="20"/>
    <text>
      <![CDATA[If you don't see this, it didn't work]]>
    </text>
  </staticText>
</band>
```

Any command-line input or output is written as follows:

```
$ ant
Buildfile: previewReportDesignXML.xml

viewDesignXML:
```

New terms and **important words** are shown in bold. Words that you see on the screen, in menus or dialog boxes for example, appear in the text like this: "clicking the **Next** button moves you to the next screen."

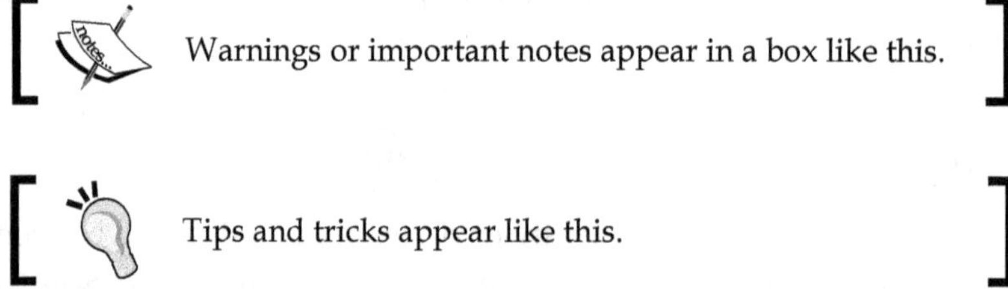

Warnings or important notes appear in a box like this.

Tips and tricks appear like this.

Reader feedback

Feedback from our readers is always welcome. Let us know what you think about this book—what you liked or may have disliked. Reader feedback is important for us to develop titles that you really get the most out of.

To send us general feedback, simply send an email to `feedback@packtpub.com`, and mention the book title via the subject of your message.

If there is a book that you need and would like to see us publish, please send us a note in the **SUGGEST A TITLE** form on `www.packtpub.com` or email `suggest@packtpub.com`.

If there is a topic that you have expertise in and you are interested in either writing or contributing to a book on, see our author guide on `www.packtpub.com/authors`.

Customer support

Now that you are the proud owner of a Packt book, we have a number of things to help you to get the most from your purchase.

Downloading the example code for the book

Visit `http://www.packtpub.com/files/code/8082_Code.zip` to directly download the example code.

The downloadable files contain instructions on how to use them.

Errata

Although we have taken every care to ensure the accuracy of our content, mistakes do happen. If you find a mistake in one of our books—maybe a mistake in the text or the code—we would be grateful if you would report this to us. By doing so, you can save other readers from frustration, and help us to improve subsequent versions of this book. If you find any errata, please report them by visiting `http://www.packtpub.com/support`, selecting your book, clicking on the **let us know** link, and entering the details of your errata. Once your errata are verified, your submission will be accepted and the errata added to any list of existing errata. Any existing errata can be viewed by selecting your title from `http://www.packtpub.com/support`.

Piracy

Piracy of copyright material on the Internet is an ongoing problem across all media. At Packt, we take the protection of our copyright and licenses very seriously. If you come across any illegal copies of our works, in any form, on the Internet, please provide us with the location address or web site name immediately so that we can pursue a remedy.

Please contact us at `copyright@packtpub.com` with a link to the suspected pirated material.

We appreciate your help in protecting our authors, and our ability to bring you valuable content.

Questions

You can contact us at `questions@packtpub.com` if you are having a problem with any aspect of the book, and we will do our best to address it.

1
An Overview of JasperReports

In this chapter, along with an overview of JasperReports, we explain its capabilities and features. Here is a brief outline of the topics we will cover in this chapter:

- A brief history of JasperReports
- What JasperReports is and what it can do for us
- The JasperReports open source license
- The features of JasperReports
- JasperReports' class library dependencies
- The steps required to generate reports with JasperReports
- Where to get support for JasperReports

A brief history of JasperReports

JasperReports was started in 2001 by Teodor Danciu when he was faced with the task of evaluating reporting tools for a project he was working on. The existing solutions, he found, were too expensive for his project's budget; therefore, he decided to write his own reporting engine. The project for which he was evaluating reporting tools got canceled, but nevertheless, he started to work on JasperReports in his spare time. He registered the project on `SourceForge.net` in September 2001. Shortly after, he started getting emails from interested potential users, even though he had not yet released any code. JasperReports version 0.1.5 was released in November 2001. Since then, JasperReports has become immensely popular; it is currently one of the most popular Java reporting tools available.

At first, JasperReports was basically a one-man project, with Teodor working on it in his spare time. Then, in April 2005, a company called *JasperSoft* was formally launched at the MySQL User Conference in California. JasperSoft now sponsors JasperReports' development, allowing Teodor and other JasperSoft developers to work full-time on JasperReports. JasperSoft also provides commercial support and services for JasperReports and related products, including the iReport visual designer for JasperReports. In addition to providing support for JasperReports and iReport, JasperSoft sells commercial applications incorporating JasperReports. JasperSoft has raised over 8 million dollars in venture capital funding, no small feat in these post dot-com days. This investment is a clear indication that venture capitalists have confidence in the success of JasperSoft and, by extension, in the success of JasperReports.

What exactly is JasperReports?

JasperReports is an open source Java library designed to aid developers with the task of adding reporting capabilities to Java applications. It is not a standalone tool and therefore it cannot be installed on its own. Instead, it is embedded into Java applications by including its library in the application's CLASSPATH. Being a Java library, JasperReports is not meant for end users. Rather, it is targeted towards Java developers who need to add reporting capabilities to their applications.

JasperReports is licensed under the **Lesser GNU Public Library** (**LGPL**). This license was chosen for JasperReports because, unlike the GPL, it allows JasperReports to be used in both open source and closed source applications. Applications linking to the JasperReports Java class library do not need to be open source. However, if you are considering making modifications to the existing JasperReports source code, then your modifications will have to be released under the LGPL. Refer to `http://www.gnu.org/copyleft/lesser.html` for the complete license.

Although JasperReports is primarily used to add reporting capabilities to web-based applications using the servlet API, it has absolutely no dependencies on the servlet API or any other Java EE library. It is, therefore, by no means limited to web applications. There is nothing that stops us from creating standalone desktop or command-line Java applications to generate reports with JasperReports. After all, JasperReports is nothing but a Java class library providing an API to facilitate the ability to generate reports from any kind of Java application.

JasperReports requires a **Java Development Kit** (**JDK**) 1.4 or newer in order to successfully compile applications incorporating the JasperReports Java class library and a Java Runtime Environment (JRE) 1.3 or newer to successfully execute these applications. The older versions of JasperReports required a JDK to successfully execute JasperReports applications (strictly speaking, JasperReports requires `tools.jar` to be in the CLASSPATH, and `tools.jar` is included in the JDK, not JRE). As of version 0.6.4, however, JasperReports is bundled with the **Eclipse Java Development Tools** (**JDT**) compiler and no longer needs a JDK to execute deployed applications. Examples in this book were developed using JDK 1.6 but should compile and execute successfully with any JDK or JRE supported by JasperReports.

The features of JasperReports

JasperReports is capable of generating professional reports that include images, charts, and graphs, in addition to textual data. Some of the major JasperReports features include:

- Flexible report layout
- Multiple ways to present data
- Multiple ways to supply data
- Capability of accepting data from multiple datasources
- Capability of generating watermarks
- Capability of generating subreports

It is also capable of exporting reports in a variety of formats. Each of these features is briefly described in the next few sections.

Flexible report layout

JasperReports allows us to separate data into optional report sections. These sections include:

- The report title, which will appear once at the top of the report
- A page header, which will appear at the top of every page
- A detail section, which typically contains the primary report data
- A page footer, which will appear at the bottom of every page
- A summary section, which will appear at the end of the report

All of these and other report sections are discussed in detail in Chapter 6, *Report Layout and Design*.

In addition to allowing us to define report sections, JasperReports allows the creation of elaborate dynamic layouts based on the contents of the report. For example, data can be hidden or displayed in a report, or it can even be grouped into logical sections, depending on the values of the respective report fields. Let's suppose that we are creating a report about cars. JasperReports allows us to group the data by make, model, year, or a combination of these or any other piece of data displayed on the report. Data grouping lets us control the layout of the report better. Data group definitions can also be used to calculate subtotal values based on a subset of the report data. Groups are also used to define datasets for charts and graphs. Data grouping is discussed in detail in Chapter 6, *Report Layout and Design*.

Multiple ways to present data

JasperReports provides the ability to display report data textually or graphically using charts. JasperReports allows us to use report expressions for generating reports that display dynamic data, that is, data that is not directly passed to the report or stored anywhere; instead, it is calculated from the data contained in the datasource and/or report parameters.

Multiple ways to supply data

JasperReports allows developers to pass data to a report through the report parameters. Report parameters can be instances of any Java class.

Data can also be passed to a report by using special classes called **datasources**. Report parameters and datasources can be combined for maximum flexibility.

Multiple datasources

JasperReports can generate reports using any relational database system supported by JDBC, but it is not limited to database reports. It can generate reports from a number of datasources including XML files, **Plain Old Java Objects** (**POJOs**), any class implementing the `java.util.Map` interface, and any class implementing the `javax.swing.table.TableModel` interface.

JasperReports also supports empty datasources, which are used for simple reports that have no dynamic data displayed. If we need to create a report from a datasource that is not directly supported by JasperReports, it also allows us to create our own custom datasources. JDBC datasources are discussed in detail in Chapter 4, *Creating Dynamic Reports from Databases*; other datasource types, including custom datasources, are discussed in detail in Chapter 5, *Working with Other Datasources*.

Watermarks

JasperReports is capable of generating background images or text on the reports it generates. These background images can serve as watermarks for the report. Watermarks can be used for branding reports and for security purposes, as they make it difficult to forge reports. As all report pages have the same watermark, reports can maintain a consistent look and feel.

Subreports

Another feature of JasperReports is its ability to create **subreports**, or reports within reports. Subreports simplify report design significantly by allowing us to extract complex report sections into a separate report and then incorporating that separate report into a master report.

Exporting capabilities

Reports generated with JasperReports can be exported to a number of formats, including PDF, Excel (XLS), and Rich Text Format (RTF). RTF is a format readable and editable by most word processors, such as Microsoft Word, OpenOffice.org Writer, StarOffice Writer, and WordPerfect. Reports created with JasperReports can also be exported to HTML, XML, CSV, plain text, and OpenDocument Format (ODF), the native file format of OpenOffice.org Writer. Exporting reports to these formats is discussed in detail in Chapter 9, *Exporting to Other Formats*.

The following screenshot demonstrates some of JasperReports' features, including data grouping, adding images and watermarks to a report, and exporting to PDF:

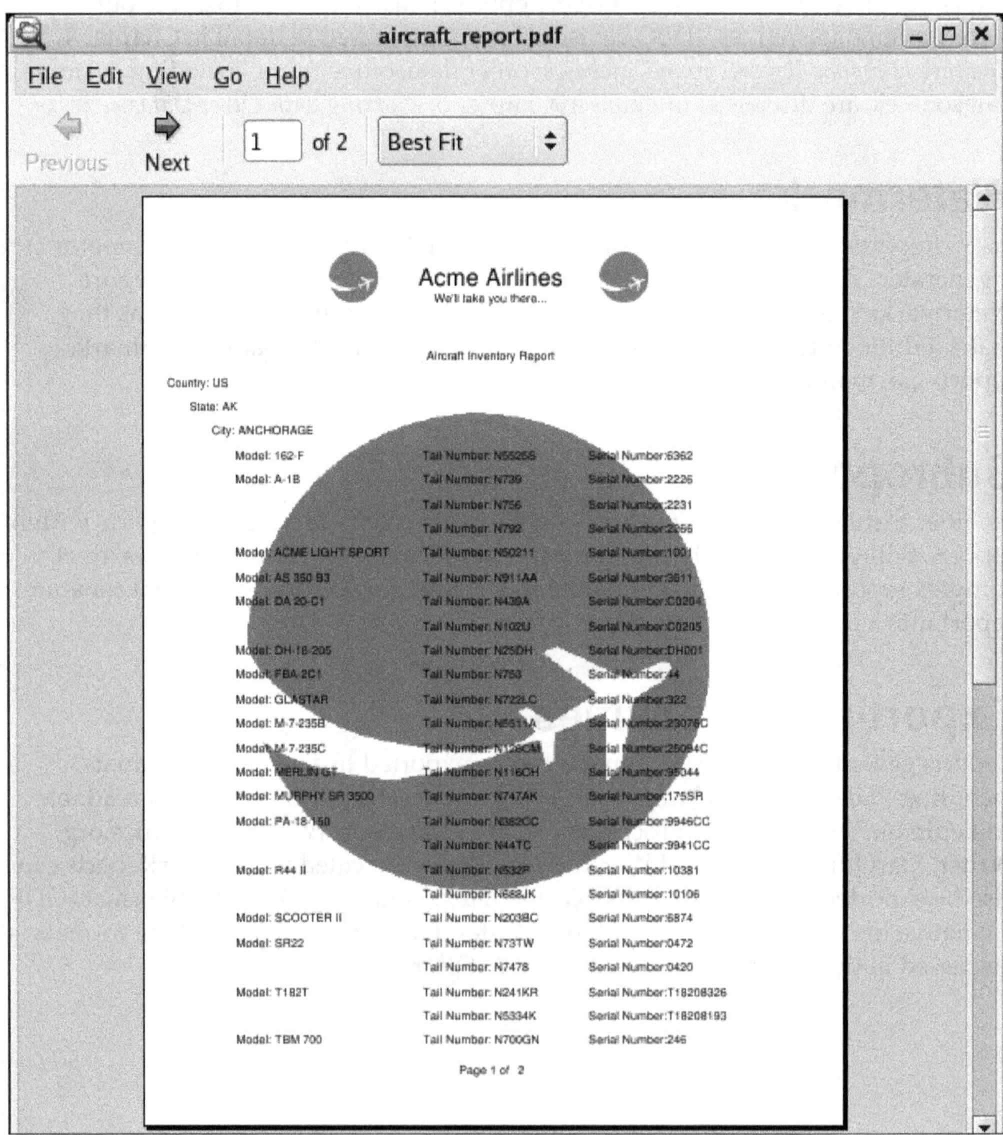

When creating this report, we took advantage of JasperReports' data grouping capabilities to create groups dividing the data by country, state, and city. This grouping allowed us to display the data in a logical, easy-to-follow way. We also took advantage of JasperReports' ability to display images, to add a watermark and a logo in the report heading. The report font in the header section was enlarged and made bold, and the text was laid out in an easy-to-follow format.

In the previous screenshot, the freely available Evince document viewer was used to display the PDF report. Of course, reports exported to PDF can be viewed with any PDF viewer, including Adobe Acrobat, Foxit, and Xpdf.

Class library dependencies

JasperReports leverages other open source Java libraries to implement some of its functionality. Some of the libraries JasperReports builds on include:

- **iText**: A PDF generation and manipulation library. It has the ability of generating and manipulating RTF, XML, and HTML documents. JasperReports takes advantage of iText in order to export reports to PDF and RTF. More information about iText can be found at `http://www.lowagie.com/iText/`.
- **JFreeChart**: A Java library for producing various charts, including pie charts, bar charts, line charts, and area charts. JasperReports takes advantage of JFreeChart to implement its built-in charting functionality. More information about JFreeChart can be found at `http://www.jfree.org/jfreechart`.
- **Apache POI**: A Java class library to create and manipulate various Microsoft Office formats, such as Microsoft's OLE 2 Compound Document format. JasperReports takes advantage of POI to export reports to XLS (Microsoft Excel) format. More information about Apache POI can be found at `http://poi.apache.org/`.
- **JAXP**: Java API for parsing and transforming XML documents. JAXP is used by JasperReports to parse XML files. JAXP is included with Java SE 5.0 and it can be downloaded separately when using earlier versions of Java SE. More information about JAXP can be found at `https://jaxp.dev.java.net/`.
- **Apache Commons**: A collection of Java libraries providing a large number of reusable components. JasperReports takes advantage of the Commons Digester, BeanUtils, and Logging components ofApache Commons to complement JAXP for XML parsing. More information about Apache Commons can be found at `http://commons.apache.org/`.

> URLs provided here are for informational purposes only; the JasperReports class library already includes the required JAR files listed here. There is no need for us to download them to take advantage of their functionality within JasperReports.

Typical workflow

The following flow chart illustrates the typical workflow followed when creating reports with JasperReports.

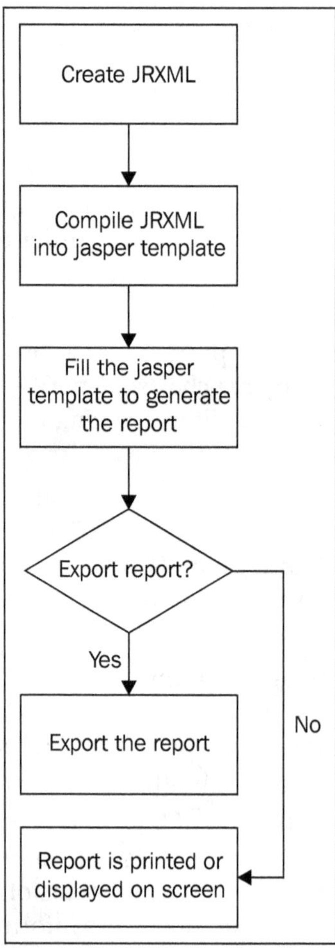

When working with JasperReports, the first step is to create a report template as an XML file. XML report templates can be handcoded or generated by a graphical report designer. Even though JasperReports report templates are XML files, by convention template filenames are given an extension of `.jrxml`. JasperReports XML templates are commonly referred to as JRXML files, which is the term we will use in this book.

Let's take a look at what a typical JRXML file looks like:

```
<?xml version="1.0" encoding="UTF-8" ?>
<!DOCTYPE jasperReport PUBLIC "//JasperReports//DTD Report Design//EN"
"http://jasperreports.sourceforge.net/dtds/jasperreport.dtd">
<jasperReport name="simple_template">
  <title>
    <band height="50">
    </band>
  </title>
  <pageHeader>
    <band height="50">
    </band>
  </pageHeader>
  <columnHeader>
    <band height="30">
    </band>
  </columnHeader>
  <detail>
    <band height="100">
    </band>
  </detail>
  <columnFooter>
    <band height="30">
    </band>
  </columnFooter>
  <pageFooter>
    <band height="50">
    </band>
  </pageFooter>
  <lastPageFooter>
    <band height="50">
    </band>
  </lastPageFooter>
  <summary>
    <band height="50">
    </band>
  </summary>
</jasperReport>
```

This JRXML file illustrates the main elements of a JRXML file. All elements in the JRXML file are optional except for the root `<jasperReport>` element. This JRXML file, when compiled and filled, will generate an empty report, not very practical in its own right, but it can be used as a template for creating more useful templates. As can be seen in the example, each main element of the JRXML file contains a `<band>` element as its only child element. Bands contain the data that is displayed in the report. In the example, all the bands are empty. In real JRXML files, bands contain child elements used to position, format, and display the actual report data, both textual and graphical. There are commercial and open source visual design tools that can aid in the development of JRXML files. One such tool, iReport, the official JasperReports graphical report designer, is covered in detail in Chapter 10, *Graphical Report Design with iReport.*

JRXML files are "compiled" into a JasperReports native binary template either programmatically by calling the appropriate methods on the JasperReports class library, or by using a custom ANT task provided by JasperReports. The resulting compiled template is commonly known as the **jasper** file and is typically saved to disk with a `.jasper` extension. The jasper file is then used to generate the final report by providing it with its required data. This process is known as **filling** the report. A JRXML file has to be compiled only once, while the generated jasper file can be filled as many times as necessary to create and display reports.

The filled reports can be saved to disk in a JasperReports' native format. Reports saved in this format are known as **JasperPrint** files. The JasperPrint file names have a `.jrprint` extension. JasperPrint files can only be viewed with a JasperReports specific viewer. The JasperPrint files can be exported to other formats so that they can be opened with commonly available tools like PDF viewers and word processors. Exporting to other formats is discussed in detail in Chapter 9, *Exporting to Other Formats.*

Where to get help

JasperForge, the official JasperSoft online portal, is the best place to get help with JasperReports and other JasperSoft products. JasperForge can be found at `http://jasperforge.org`.

JasperForge has official online forums where questions about their products, including JasperReports, can be asked. The JasperReports online forums can be found at `http://jasperforge.org/plugins/espforum/browse.php?group_id=102&forumid=103`.

The JasperReports page at JasperForge contains tips, tricks, JavaDoc API documentation, and a quick reference for JRXML elements. We won't repeat that information in this book, as it is readily available online. Commercial support and the training is offered by JasperSoft and other third-party companies.

Summary

In this chapter, we were introduced to JasperReports. We discussed the evolution of JasperReports from a small, one-man project to a project backed and funded by a company that has raised millions of dollars in venture capital. We also had an overview of JasperReports, where we discussed that JasperReports is not a standalone reporting solution. Instead, it is a Java library that allows us to add reporting capabilities to our applications.

Next on the line was JasperReports' open source license (LGPL). The chapter provided us with a brief explanation of the features of JasperReports, including flexibility in report layout, the ability to display report data textually or graphically, and the ability to group report data. The JasperReports' class library dependencies were also discussed along with the typical workflow followed when designing reports. Finally, this chapter provided us with the official online forums where we can seek help.

2

Adding Reporting Capabilities to our Java Applications

We can easily add reporting capabilities to our Java applications by taking advantage of the classes included in the JasperReports class library. JasperReports can be easily embedded into both client and server-side Java applications simply by adding the required libraries to our CLASSPATH and calling the appropriate methods in the JasperReports API.

At the end of this chapter, we will be able to:

- Identify the purpose of the several downloads that can be found at the JasperReports web site
- Set up our development and execution environment to successfully add reporting capabilities to our Java applications
- Identify the required libraries for adding reporting capabilities to Java applications
- Identify the optional libraries that can be used to enhance the reporting capabilities of our Java applications

Downloading JasperReports

JasperReports is distributed as a JAR file that needs to be added to the CLASSPATH of any application we wish to add reporting capabilities to. JasperReports can be downloaded from `http://jasperforge.org/plugins/project/project_home.php?group_id=102`.

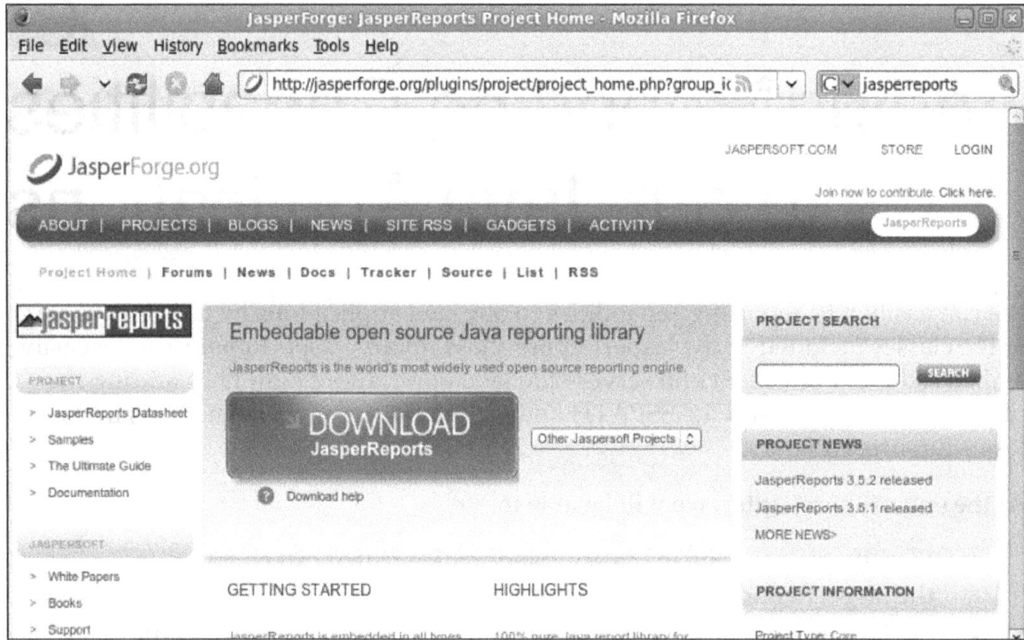

Clicking on the **Download** link around the center of the page will take us to the JasperReports download page on `SourceForge.net`.

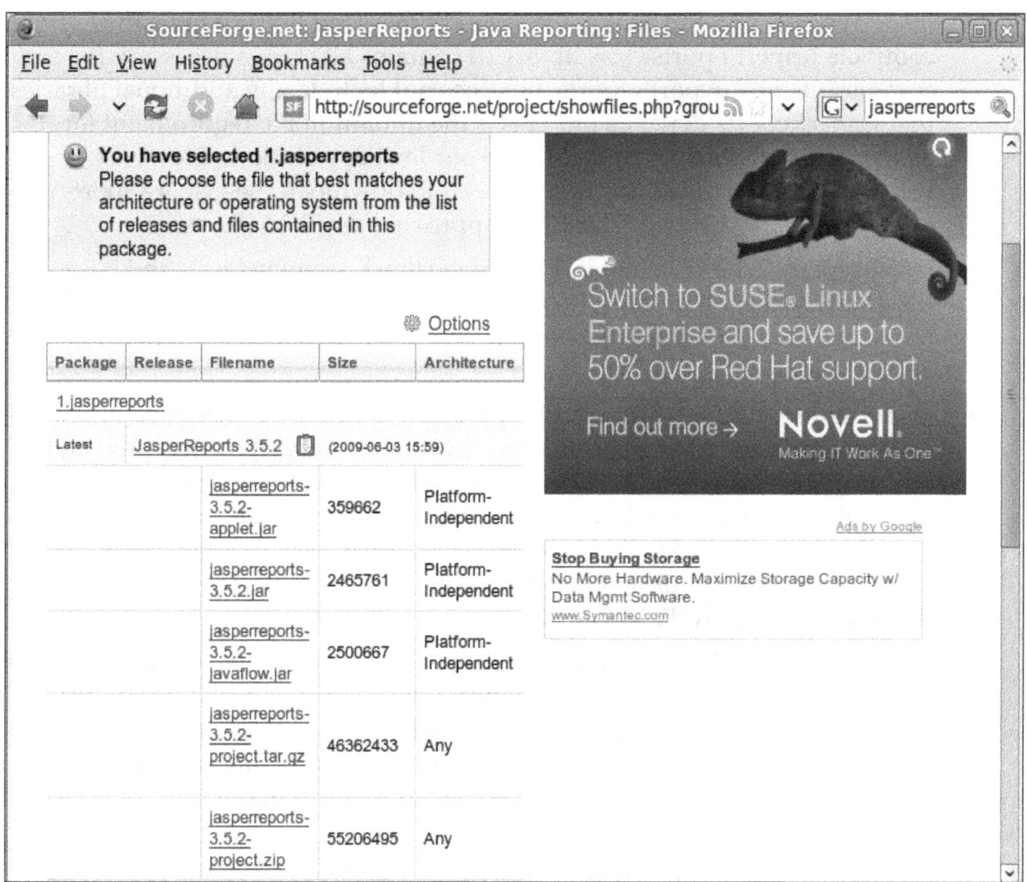

The specific version on your screen might be different; at the time of writing, the latest stable version of JasperReports is 3.5.2.

It is not always clear what exactly is downloaded by clicking on these links; thus, we will provide a brief explanation of what each link is for.

- **jasperreports-3.5.2-applet.jar:** This first download link is for a JAR file containing a subset of the JasperReports functionality. Specifically, it contains classes that can be used to display JasperPrint files, which are reports in JasperReports' native format. This file is offered as a separate download as a convenience for developers; it can be used for applications or applets that don't need full reporting capabilities, yet need to display generated reports. Even though the filename has a suffix of "applet", there is nothing preventing us from using it with standalone applications, without the overhead that the missing JasperReports classes would add to the download. This file is approximately 346 KB in size.

- **jasperreports-3.5.2.jar:** This is the second download link, and it is the complete JasperReports class library. It contains all classes necessary to compile, fill, and export reports, but does not include any additional libraries that JasperReports depends on. This is the minimum file requirement for us to add full reporting capabilities to our Java applications. However, if we choose to download this file, we need to download the JasperReports dependencies separately. This file is approximately 2.2 MB in size.
- **jasperreports-3.5.2-javaflow.jar:** This is the third download link, and it is the javaflow version of JasperReports. This version of JasperReports should be used in environments where multithreading is discouraged. This file is approximately 2.2 MB in size.
- **jasperreports-3.5.2-project.tar.gz:** This is the fourth download link, and it contains the complete JasperReports class library plus all the required and optional libraries. In addition, it contains the entire file as a gzipped TAR file, which is common in Unix and Unix-like systems, such as Linux. This download also includes the JasperReports source code and a lot of source code providing examples of JasperReports' functionality. This gzipped TAR file is approximately 42 MB in size
- **jasperreports-3.5.2-project.zip:** The fifth download link, like the fourth link, contains the complete JasperReports class library plus all the required and optional libraries, along with the JasperReports source code. However, it contains the files in ZIP format, which is more commonly used under Microsoft Windows. This file is approximately 51 MB in size.

Unless Internet connection speed is an issue, we recommend downloading one of the last two mentioned files, as they include everything we need to create reports with JasperReports. Another good reason to download one of these files is that the included examples are a great way to learn how to implement the different JasperReports features. All of the examples in the file come with an ANT build file containing targets to compile and execute them.

We will refer to this file as the *JasperReports project* file, or more succinctly, as the *project* file.

Once we have downloaded the appropriate file for our purposes, we need to set up our environment to be able to start creating reports. In the next section, we discuss how to do this, assuming that the project file was downloaded.

Setting up our environment

To set up our environment to get ready for creating reports, we need to extract the JasperReports project ZIP file to a location of our choice. Once we extract the project ZIP file, we should see a `jasperreports-3.5.2` directory (The actual name of the directory may vary slightly depending on the version of JasperReports.) containing the following files and directories:

- `build`: This directory contains the compiled JasperReports class files.
- `build.xml`: This is an ANT build file, which builds the JasperReports source code. If we don't intend to modify JasperReports, we don't need to use this file as JasperReports is distributed in compiled form.
- `changes.txt`: This file explains the differences between the current and previous versions of the JasperReports' class library.
- `demo`: This directory contains various examples demonstrating several aspects of JasperReports functionality.
- `dist`: This directory contains a JAR file containing the standard, javaflow, and applet versions of the JasperReports library. We should add one of these JAR files to our CLASSPATH to take advantage of JasperReports functionality.
- `docs`: This directory contains a quick reference guide to most XML tags used in JasperReports templates.
- `lib`: This directory contains all the libraries needed to build JasperReports and to use it in our applications.
- `license.txt`: This file contains the full text of the LGPL license.
- `pom.xml`: This is a Maven 2 POM file used to build JasperReports with Maven, just like `build.xml`. We don't need this file because JasperReports is distributed in compiled form.
- `readme.txt`: This file contains instructions on how to build and execute the supplied examples.
- `src`: This directory contains the JasperReports source code.

Getting up and running quickly

To get up and run quickly, the files to add to the CLASSPATH are the JasperReports JAR files, and all the JAR files under the `lib` directory in the project ZIP file. By adding these files to the CLASSPATH, we don't have to worry about the CLASSPATH when implementing additional functionality, for example, when exporting to PDF or producing charts.

JasperReports class library

For all JasperReports-related tasks, we need to add the JasperReports library to our CLASSPATH. The JasperReports library can be found under the `dist` directory in the project file; it is named `jasperreports-3.5.2.jar`. Depending on the version of JasperReports, the filename will vary.

Required libraries for report compilation

The project file described earlier contains all of the required supporting libraries. Once that file is downloaded, all the required libraries can be found under the `lib` subdirectory of the directory created when extracting the ZIP file. JasperReports uses these required files for XML parsing. Therefore, they are needed when compiling JRXML files programmatically, not for filling or displaying reports. JRXML files can be compiled using a custom ANT task provided by JasperReports. If we choose to compile our JRXML files using this custom ANT target, these required libraries need to be added to the CLASSPATH variable of the ANT build file. There are example build files included in the project file and also at `http://www.packtpub.com/files/code/8082_Code.zip`.

Apache Commons

Apache Commons is a collection of Java libraries developed and distributed by the Apache Software Foundation. Apache Commons includes libraries and utility classes providing commonly used functionality, thereby freeing developers from re-implementing it. As we can see from the list of libraries we are about to discuss, JasperReports makes extensive use of Apache Commons, and we should as well. When we are about to implement a piece of functionality that is frequently needed, we should make sure that there isn't a Apache Commons library that implements it for us before digging in. Apache Commons includes libraries for logging, XML parsing, sending and receiving email, I/O, network utility classes, and many others. For more information, visit the Apache Commons at `http://commons.apache.org/`.

The following discussion about libraries highlights the fact that JasperReports makes extensive use of Apache Commons.

Apache Commons Digester

The **Commons Digester** library includes utility classes used to initialize Java objects from XML files. JasperReports takes advantage of the Digester component of the Apache Commons repository to implement its XML parsing functionality. Version 3.5.2 of the JasperReports project ZIP file includes version 1.7 of Commons Digester. The filename is `commons-digester-1.7.jar`, and it must be on your CLASSPATH for your JasperReports application to work correctly.

If you downloaded the bare JasperReports class library, you will need to download Commons Digester separately from `http://commons.apache.org/digester/`.

Apache Commons Collections

Another component of the Apache Commons suite is the **Collections** component. This component provides functionality to complement and augment the Java Collections framework. JasperReports takes advantage of the Collections component of Apache Commons to implement some of its functionality. Like all required libraries included in the project ZIP file, the Commons Collections library can be found under the `lib` subdirectory of the directory created when extracting the project ZIP file. JasperReports project file version 3.5.2 includes version 2.1 of Commons Collections, distributed as a JAR file named `commons-collections-2.1.jar`.

If you have downloaded the bare JasperReports class library, you will need to download Commons Collections separately from `http://commons.apache.org/collections/`.

Apache Commons Logging

Apache Commons Logging is a component of the Apache Commons that provides components to aid developers with sending data to log files. JasperReports takes advantage of this component, which can be found on the `lib` directory of the project ZIP file. The version included with JasperReports 3.5.2 is Commons Logging 1.0.2. The file to be added to your CLASSPATH is `commons-logging-1.0.2.jar`.

If you have downloaded the bare JasperReports class library, you will need to download Commons Logging separately from `http://commons.apache.org/logging/`.

Apache Commons BeanUtils

The last library that JasperReports requires for compiling reports is Apache Commons BeanUtils. BeanUtils is a library that provides easy-to-use wrappers around the Java reflection and introspection APIs. Version 3.5.2 of the JasperReports project ZIP file includes BeanUtils 1.8; the file to add to your CLASSPATH is `commons-beanutils-1.8.jar`.

If you have downloaded the bare JasperReports class library, you will need to download Commons BeanUtils separately from `http://commons.apache.org/beanutils/`.

Optional libraries and tools

There are a number of libraries that are required only if we wish to take advantage of some of JasperReports' features. These optional libraries and their uses are listed next.

Apache ANT

JasperReports comes bundled with some custom ANT targets for previewing report designs and for viewing reports serialized in JasperReports' native format. Although not strictly necessary, it is very helpful to have ANT available to take advantage of these custom targets.

ANT can be downloaded from `http://ant.apache.org/`.

JDT compiler

JDT (Java Development Tools) compiler is the Java compiler included with the Eclipse IDE. The JDT compiler is needed only if the JasperReports application is running under a Java Runtime Environment (JRE) and not under a full JDK.

When creating reports, JasperReports creates temporary Java files and compiles them. When using a JDK, JasperReports takes advantage of `tools.jar` for this functionality. As a JRE does not include `tools.jar`, the JDT compiler is needed. The JasperReports project file version 3.5.2 includes version 3.1.1 of the JDT compiler. It can be found under the `lib` directory of the directory created when extracting the project ZIP file. The file to add to your CLASSPATH is `jdt-compiler-3.1.1.jar`.

This file cannot be downloaded separately; therefore, if we need to execute our code under a JRE. We need to download the JasperReports project ZIP file because it includes this file needed for report compilation.

JDBC driver

When using a JDBC datasource, which is the most common datasource for JasperReports generated reports, the appropriate JDBC driver for our specific RDBMS is needed. The following table lists popular relational database systems and the required JAR files to add to the CLASSPATH. The exact filenames may vary depending on the version, target JDK, and supported JDBC version. The filenames shown here reflect the latest stable versions targeted to the latest available JDK and the latest available version of JDBC at the time of writing.

RDBMS	Driver JAR Files
Firebird	`jaybird-2.1.6.jar`
HSQLDB	`hsqldb.jar`
JavaDB/Derby (included with JDK 1.6+)	`derby.jar` (embedded) `derbyclient.jar` (network)
MySQL	`mysql-connector-java-5.1.7-bin.jar`
Oracle	`ojdbc6.jar`
PostgreSQL	`postgresql-8.3-604.jdbc4.jar`
SQL Server	`sqljdbc_1.2.2828.100_enu.exe` (for Windows systems) `sqljdbc_1.2.2828.100_enu.tar.gz` (for Unix systems)
Sybase	`Jconnect60.zip`

The JasperReports project file includes the JDBC driver for HSQLDB. Consult your RDBMS documentation for information on where to download the appropriate JDBC driver for your RDBMS.

iText

iText is an open source library for creating and manipulating PDF files. It is needed in our CLASSPATH only if we want to export our reports to PDF or RTF format. Version 3.5.2 of the JasperReports project file includes iText version 2.1.0; the file to add to your CLASSPATH is `iText-2.1.0.jar`.

The iText library can be downloaded separately from `http://www.lowagie.com/iText/`.

JFreeChart

JFreeChart is an open source library for creating professional looking charts, including 2D and 3D pie charts, 2D and 3D bar charts, and line charts. It is needed in our CLASSPATH only if we intend to add charts to our reports. JFreeChart 1.0.12 can be found on the `lib` directory inside the JasperReports project file version 3.5.2. The file to add to the CLASSPATH is `jfreechart-1.0.12.jar`.

JFreeChart can be downloaded separately from `http://www.jfree.org/jfreechart/`.

JExcelApi

JExcelApi is a Java library that allows Java applications to read, write, and modify Microsoft Excel files. We need JExcelApi in our CLASSPATH only if we need to export our reports to XLS format. JasperReports 3.5.2 includes JExcelApi version 2.6. To add XLS exporting capabilities to our reports, the file we need to add to our CLASSPATH is `jxl-2.6.jar`.

JExcelApi can be downloaded separately from `http://jexcelapi.sourceforge.net/`.

Summary

This chapter covered the required and optional libraries needed to add reporting capabilities to Java applications. All the libraries covered in this chapter are needed at both compile time and runtime. The chapter provided an explanation of the different files available for downloading on JasperReports' web site and in which conditions it is appropriate to use them. We also saw which libraries are required for report compilation under a JDK and the additional libraries required when compiling JRXML templates under a JRE. Besides, we also learned which libraries are required when using JDBC datasources for our reports, and finally the libraries required when exporting our reports to several formats.

Now that we have a sound understanding of the libraries needed to work with JasperReports, we are ready to create our first report, which is what the next chapter is based on.

3

Creating your First Report

In this chapter, we will create, compile, and preview our first report.

At the end of this chapter, we will be able to:

- Create simple JRXML report templates
- Preview report templates by using JasperReports custom ANT targets
- Generate jasper binary report templates by compiling JRXML files
- Write code that will generate a report from a Jasper report template
- View generated reports in JasperReports' native format, using tools provided by JasperReports
- Generate reports that can be viewed in a web browser
- Identify the JRXML elements corresponding to the different report sections

Creating a JRXML report template

When creating a report, the first step is to create a JRXML template. As we mentioned in Chapter 1, *An Overview of JasperReports*, JasperReports JRXML templates are standard XML files but, by convention, they have an extension of `.jrxml` and are referred to as JRXML files or JRXML templates. JRXML templates can be written by hand, alternatively, a visual report template generator can be used. The most popular JRXML report template generator is iReport. We will cover iReport in Chapter 10, *Grpahical Report Design with iReport*.

All JRXML files contain a root `<jasperReport>` element. The `<jasperReport>` root element can contain many subelements, and all of these subelements are optional. Our goal for this chapter is to get a feel of how to design a report, so we will avert most of the `<jasperReport>` subelements. We will use only one subelement, namely the `<detail>` subelement.

Our first report will display a static string. Its JRXML is as follows:

```
<?xml version="1.0"?>
<jasperReport
    xmlns="http://jasperreports.sourceforge.net/jasperreports"
    xmlns:xsi="http://www.w3.org/2001/XMLSchema-instance"
          xsi:schemaLocation="http://jasperreports.sourceforge.net/
                              jasperreports http://jasperreports.
                              sourceforge.net/xsd/jasperreport.xsd"
    name="FirstReport">
  <detail>
    <band height="20">
      <staticText>
        <reportElement x="20" y="0" width="200" height="20"/>
        <text>
          <![CDATA[If you don't see this, it didn't work]]>
        </text>
      </staticText>
    </band>
  </detail>
</jasperReport>
```

There are some elements in the above JRXML file that we haven't seen before, such as the following:

- `<staticText>` defines static text that does not depend on any datasources, variables, parameters, or report expressions
- `<reportElement>` defines the position and width of the `<staticText>` element
- `<text>` defines the actual static text that is displayed on the report

We have seen the `<band>` element in the previous examples. The `<detail>` element can contain only a single `<band>` element as its only subelement. The `<band>` element can contain many different elements that can be used to display text, charts, images, or geometric figures. The above example contains a single `<staticText>` element.

> `<reportElement>` is a required element of not only the `<staticText>` element, but also of all the subelements of the `<band>` element. The x and y coordinates defined in `<reportElement>` are relative to the band containing its parent element (`<staticText>` in this example).

Previewing the XML report template

JasperReports includes a utility that can be used to preview report designs. This utility makes designing reports much faster. We can immediately preview a report design without having to compile or fill it.

The utility is a standalone Java application included in the JasperReports JAR file. The class that needs to be executed is `net.sf.jasperreports.view.JasperDesignViewer`. The easiest way to execute this class is to use an ANT target to execute it, including all the required libraries in the CLASSPATH. This is the approach that is used in the JasperReports samples included in the project JAR file, and it is the approach we will take. The following ANT build file will launch the **JasperDesignViewer** to preview our report:

```
<project name="FirstReport XML Design Preview" default="viewDesignXML"
         basedir=".">
  <description>
    Previews our First Report XML Design
  </description>
  <property name="file.name" value="FirstReport" />
<!-- Directory where the JasperReports project file was extracted,
     needs to be changed to match the local environment -->
  <property name="jasper.dir"
            value="/opt/jasperreports-3.5.2"/>
  <property name="classes.dir" value="${jasper.dir}/build/classes" />
  <property name="lib.dir" value="${jasper.dir}/lib" />
  <path id="classpath">
  <pathelement location="./"/>
  <pathelement location="${classes.dir}" />
  <fileset dir="${lib.dir}">
    <include name="**/*.jar"/>
  </fileset>
  </path>
  <target name="viewDesignXML"
          description="Launches the design viewer to preview the XML
                       report design.">
    <java classname="net.sf.jasperreports.view.JasperDesignViewer"
          fork="true">
      <arg value="-XML"/>
      <arg value="-F${file.name}.jrxml"/>
      <classpath refid="classpath"/>
    </java>
  </target>
</project>
```

This ANT build file must be saved in the same directory as our JRXML file. It is recommended that the JRXML file be saved with the report name as its filename. The report name is defined in the root `<jasperReport>` element. In this example, we chose to use `FirstReport` as the report name; therefore, the recommended filename for this report template is `FirstReport.jrxml`.

If we save our ANT build file with the standard name of `build.xml`, there is no need to specify the build filename in the command line. The example build file here has one target named `viewDesignXML`. As this target is the default target, there is no need to specify it in the command line. Typing `ant` in the command line will execute the default target, and a preview of our report will be displayed.

```
$ ant
Buildfile: build.xml

viewDesignXML:
```

After executing the `viewDesignXML` target, we should see a window labeled **JasperDesignViewer** displaying our report template preview.

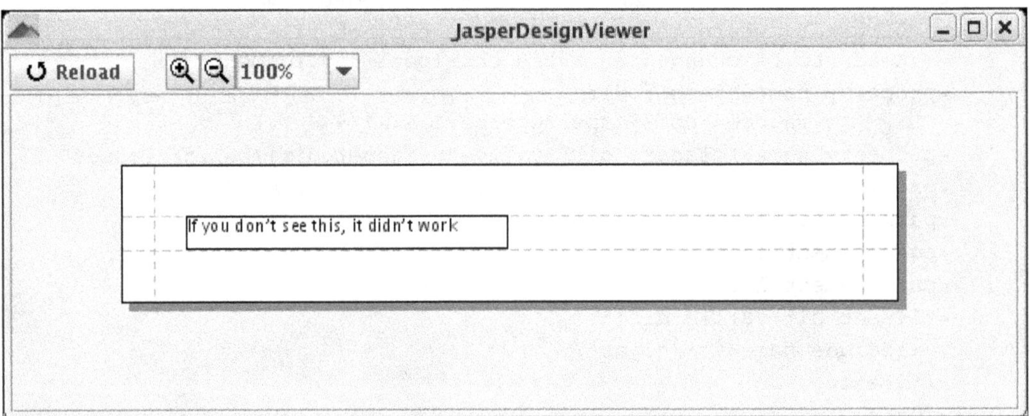

The JasperDesignViewer can be safely terminated by closing the window or by hitting *Ctrl+c* in the command-line window.

In this particular case, we can see all the text in the preview because this report contains only static text. For reports displaying data coming from datasources or report parameters, the actual text won't be displayed in the report. Report expressions for obtaining the data are displayed instead, as JasperDesignViewer does not have access to the actual datasource or report parameters.

Creating a binary report template

The JRXML files cannot be used directly to generate reports. They need to be compiled into JasperReports' native binary format. Compiled report templates are called **jasper files**. There are two ways to compile a JRXML file into a jasper file: We can do it either programmatically or through a custom ANT task provided by JasperReports.

Compiling a JRXML template programmatically

A JRXML template can be compiled into a jasper file and saved to disk by calling the `compileReportToFile()` method on the `net.sf.jasperreports.engine.JasperCompileManager` class. The three overloaded versions of the `JasperCompileManager.compileReportToFile()` method are listed below:

- `JasperCompileManager.compileReportToFile(String sourceFileName)`
- `JasperCompileManager.compileReportToFile(String sourceFileName, String destFileName)`
- `JasperCompileManager.compileReportToFile(JasperDesign jasperDesign, String destFileName)`

The following table illustrates the parameters used in these methods:

Parameter	Description
`String sourceFileName`	This contains the location of the JRXML template used to generate the compiled report template. It can be an absolute or a relative path. The generated compiled report template is saved using the same name and location of the supplied JRXML file, substituting the file extension with jasper.
`String destFileName`	This is used to determine the filename used to save the compiled report template in the filesystem. It can contain an absolute or a relative path.
`JasperDesign jasperDesign`	This contains an in-memory representation of the report design. Instances of `net.sf.jasperreports.engine.design.JaperDesign` can be created by calling one of the several methods in the `net.sf.jasperreports.engine.xml.JRXmlLoader` class.

The following code fragment demonstrates the use of the `JasperCompileManager.compileReportToFile()` method:

```
package net.ensode.jasperbook;

import net.sf.jasperreports.engine.JRException;
import net.sf.jasperreports.engine.JasperCompileManager;

public class FirstReportCompile
{
  public static void main(String[] args)
  {
    try
    {
      System.out.println("Compiling report...");
      JasperCompileManager.compileReportToFile(
                                        "reports/FirstReport.jrxml");
      System.out.println("Done!");
    }
    catch (JRException e)
    {
      e.printStackTrace();
    }
  }
}
```

After compiling and executing this code, we should see a file called `FirstReport.jasper` in the filesystem. This file is the compiled template in JasperReports' native format. For this example, we chose to use the first version of `JasperCompileManager.compileReportToFile()` method we discussed. As by default the root filename is used for the compiled report, and we did not have an in-memory representation of the JRXML template. If we had wished to use a different root filename for the compiled report template, we should have used the second version of `JasperCompileManager.compileReportToFile()` and specified the desired filename as the second parameter.

Previewing the compiled report template

The `net.sf.jasperreports.view.JasperDesignViewer` discussed previously can be used to preview compiled report templates as well as JRXML templates. Again, the easiest way to execute this utility is to wrap a call to it into an ANT target. Let's add a second ANT target to our `build.xml` file. We will call this new target `viewDesign`. It will let us preview the compiled report.

```
<project name="FirstReport XML Design Preview" default="viewDesignXML"
        basedir=".">
  <description>Previews and compiles our First Report</description>
  <property name="file.name" value="FirstReport" />
<!-- Directory where the JasperReports project file was extracted,
     needs to be changed to match the local environment -->
  <property name="jasper.dir"
           value="/opt/jasperreports-3.5.2" />
  <property name="classes.dir" value="${jasper.dir}/build/classes" />
  <property name="lib.dir" value="${jasper.dir}/lib" />
  <path id="classpath">
    <pathelement location="./" />
    <pathelement location="${classes.dir}" />
    <fileset dir="${lib.dir}">
      <include name="**/*.jar" />
    </fileset>
  </path>

  <target name="viewDesignXML"
        description="Launches the design viewer to preview the XML
                     report design.">
    <java classname="net.sf.jasperreports.view.JasperDesignViewer"
        fork="true">
      <arg value="-XML" />
      <arg value="-F${file.name}.jrxml" />
      <classpath refid="classpath" />
    </java>
  </target>

  <target name="viewDesign"
        description="Launches the design viewer to preview the
                     compiled report design.">
    <java classname="net.sf.jasperreports.view.JasperDesignViewer"
        fork="true">
      <arg value="-F${file.name}.jasper" />
      <classpath refid="classpath" />
    </java>
  </target>
  <target name="compile"
        description="Compiles the XML report design and produces the
                     .jasper file.">
  <taskdef name="jrc"
          classname="net.sf.jasperreports.ant.JRAntCompileTask">
    <classpath refid="classpath" />
  </taskdef>
  <jrc destdir=".">
```

```
      <src>
        <fileset dir=".">
          <include name="**/*.jrxml" />
        </fileset>
      </src>
      <classpath refid="classpath" />
    </jrc>
    </target>

    <target name="view"
            description="Launches the report viewer to preview the
                         report stored in the .jrprint file.">
      <java classname="net.sf.jasperreports.view.JasperViewer"
            fork="true">
        <arg value="-F{file.name}.jrprint" />
        <classpath refid="classpath" />
      </java>
    </target>
  </project>
```

We can invoke the new target from the command line as follows:

```
ant viewDesign
```

After invoking the target, we should see a window very similar to the one we saw when previewing the JRXML.

Compiling a JRXML template through ANT

JasperReports includes a custom ANT task that can be used to compile report templates. Compiling reports in this manner is very convenient because we don't have to write code to perform the compilation. For certain applications, however, we need to compile a report programmatically (in situations where the JRXML file is created at runtime, for example). The custom ANT task included by JasperReports is called `jrc`. It is defined in the `net.sf.jasperreports.ant.JRAntCompileTask` class. Let's add a third target to our `build.xml` file to invoke the `jrc` task.

```
<project name="FirstReport XML Design Preview" default="viewDesignXML"
         basedir=".">

  <description>
    Previews and compiles our First Report
  </description>

  <property name="file.name" value="FirstReport" />
  <!-- Directory where the JasperReports project file was extracted,
       needs to be changed to match the local environment -->
```

```
<property name="jasper.dir"
          value="/opt/jasperreports-3.5.2" />
<property name="classes.dir" value="${jasper.dir}/build/classes" />
<property name="lib.dir" value="${jasper.dir}/lib" />

<path id="classpath">
  <pathelement location="./" />
  <pathelement location="${classes.dir}" />
  <fileset dir="${lib.dir}">
    <include name="**/*.jar" />
  </fileset>
</path>

<target name="viewDesignXML"
        description="Launches the design viewer to preview the XML
                     report design.">
  <java classname="net.sf.jasperreports.view.JasperDesignViewer"
        fork="true">
    <arg value="-XML" />
    <arg value="-F${file.name}.jrxml" />
    <classpath refid="classpath" />
  </java>
</target>

<target name="viewDesign"
        description="Launches the design viewer to preview the
                     compiled report design.">
  <java classname="net.sf.jasperreports.view.JasperDesignViewer"
        fork="true">
    <arg value="-F${file.name}.jasper" />
    <classpath refid="classpath" />
  </java>
</target>

<target name="compile"
        description="Compiles the XML report design and produces
                     the .jasper file.">
  <taskdef name="jrc"
           classname="net.sf.jasperreports.ant.JRAntCompileTask">
    <classpath refid="classpath" />
  </taskdef>
  <jrc destdir=".">
    <src>
      <fileset dir=".">
        <include name="**/*.jrxml" />
      </fileset>
    </src>
```

```
        <classpath refid="classpath" />
      </jrc>
    </target>
  </project>
```

The new target can be invoked from the command line:

```
ant compile
```

The compile target produces the following output:

```
Buildfile: build.xml

compile:

       [jrc] Compiling 1 report design files.

       [jrc] File : /home/heffel/NetBeansProjects/Code_8082/jasper_book_
chapter_3/reports/FirstReport.jrxml ... OK.

BUILD SUCCESSFUL

Total time: 3 seconds
```

After successful execution of the `compile` target, we should have a `FirstReport.jasper` file in the filesystem. This file is identical to the one generated programmatically by calling the `net.sf.jasperreports.engine.JasperCompileManager.compileReportToFile()` method.

We can preview the generated jasper file by using the `JasperDesign` utility included by JasperReports, as explained in the previous section. The output will be identical.

Generating the report

In JasperReports lingo, the process of generating a report from a report template or jasper file is known as filling the report. Reports are filled programmatically by calling the `fillReportToFile()` method in the `net.sf.jasperreports.engine.JasperFillManager` class. The `fillReportToFile()` method fills a report and saves it to disk.

There are six overloaded versions of the `fillReportToFile()` method, which are listed below:

1. `JasperFillManager.fillReportToFile( JasperReport jasperReport, String destFileName, Map parameters, Connection connection )`
2. `JasperFillManager.fillReportToFile( JasperReport jasperReport, String destFileName, Map parameters, JRDataSource dataSource )`
3. `JasperFillManager.fillReportToFile( String sourceFileName, Map parameters, Connection connection )`
4. `JasperFillManager.fillReportToFile( String sourceFileName, Map parameters, JRDataSource dataSource )`
5. `JasperFillManager.fillReportToFile( String sourceFileName, String destFileName, Map parameters, JRDataSource dataSource )`
6. `JasperFillManager.fillReportToFile( String sourceFileName, String destFileName, Map parameters, JRDataSource datasource )`

The following table illustrates the parameters used in these methods:

Parameter	Description
`JasperReport jasperReport`	This is used as the report template. Instances of `net.sf.jasperreports.engine.JasperReport` are in-memory representations of compiled report templates.
`String destFileName`	This is used to define the name of the destination file in which to save the report.
`Map parameters`	This is an instance of a class implementing the `java.util.Map` interface. It is used to initialize all the report parameters defined in the report template.
`Connection connection`	This is used to connect to a database in order to execute an SQL query defined in the report template.
`JRDataSource dataSource`	This is an instance of a class implementing the `net.sf.jasperreports.engine.JRDataSource` interface.

As can be seen above, in most cases, we pass data for filling reports using an instance of a class implementing the `net.sf.jasperreports.engine.JRDataSource` interface. The report templates can have embedded SQL queries. These SQL queries are defined inside the `<queryString>` element in the JRXML file. For reports that contain an SQL query, instead of passing a `JRDataSource`, we pass an instance of a class implementing the `java.sql.Connection` interface. JasperReports then uses this connection object to execute the query and obtain the report data from the database.

Although report templates containing an embedded SQL query are easier to develop, passing an instance of `JRDataSource` has an advantage. That is, the same reports can be used with different datasources, such as databases, CSV files, Java objects, and so on. We will cover the database reports in the next chapter. Other datasources supported by JasperReports are covered in detail in Chapter 5, *Working with Other Datasources.*

Our report contains only static text. There is no dynamic data displayed in the report. There is no way to fill a report without passing either a `JRDataSource` or a `Connection`. JasperReports provides an implementation of the `JRDataSource` containing no data. The class is appropriately named `JREmptyDataSource`. As our report does not take any parameters, passing an empty instance of `java.util.HashMap` will be enough for our purposes. We will follow the recommended approach of naming our report using the same name as the one used for the report template (except for the extension). Given all of these facts, the most appropriate version of `fillReportToFile()` for our report is the fourth version. Here is its signature again:

```
JasperFillManager.fillReportToFile(String sourceFileName, Map
parameters, JRDataSource dataSource)
```

The following Java class fills the report and saves it to disk:

```
package net.ensode.jasperbook;
import java.util.HashMap;
import net.sf.jasperreports.engine.JREmptyDataSource;
import net.sf.jasperreports.engine.JRException;
import net.sf.jasperreports.engine.JasperFillManager;
public class FirstReportFill
{
  public static void main(String[] args)
  {
    try
    {
      System.out.println("Filling report...");
      JasperFillManager.fillReportToFile("reports/FirstReport.jasper",
                                          new HashMap(),
                                          new JREmptyDataSource());
      System.out.println("Done!");
    }
    catch (JRException e)
    {
      e.printStackTrace();
    }
  }
}
```

After executing this class, we should have a file named `FirstReport.jrprint` in the same location as our compiled report template, which was named `FirstReport.jasper`.

Viewing the report

JasperReports includes a utility class called `net.sf.jasperreports.view.JasperViewer`, which can be used to view the generated reports. As with the tool to preview designs, the easiest way to use this utility is to wrap it around an ANT target. Again, this is the approach taken by the samples included with JasperReports, and the approach we will use here. Let's add a new target to our ANT build file. Following the conventions established by the JasperReports samples, we will name this target "view".

```
<project name="FirstReport XML Design Preview"
         default="viewDesignXML"
         basedir=".">

  <description>
    Previews and compiles our First Report
  </description>

  <property name="file.name" value="FirstReport" />
<!-- Directory where the JasperReports project file was extracted,
     needs to be changed to match the local environment -->
  <property name="jasper.dir"
            value="/opt/jasperreports-3.5.2" />
  <property name="classes.dir" value="${jasper.dir}/build/classes" />
  <property name="lib.dir" value="${jasper.dir}/lib" />

  <path id="classpath">
    <pathelement location="./" />
    <pathelement location="${classes.dir}" />
    <fileset dir="${lib.dir}">
       <include name="**/*.jar" />
    </fileset>
  </path>

  <target name="viewDesignXML"
          description="Launches the design viewer to preview the XML
                       report design.">
    <java classname="net.sf.jasperreports.view.JasperDesignViewer"
          fork="true">
      <arg value="-XML" />
      <arg value="-F${file.name}.jrxml" />
      <classpath refid="classpath" />
    </java>
```

```
    </target>

    <target name="viewDesign"
            description="Launches the design viewer to preview the
                         compiled report design.">
      <java classname="net.sf.jasperreports.view.JasperDesignViewer"
            fork="true">
        <arg value="-F${file.name}.jasper" />
        <classpath refid="classpath" />
      </java>
    </target>

    <target name="compile"
            description="Compiles the XML report design and produces
                         the .jasper file.">
      <taskdef name="jrc"
               classname="net.sf.jasperreports.ant.JRAntCompileTask">
         <classpath refid="classpath" />
      </taskdef>
      <jrc destdir=".">
        <src>
          <fileset dir=".">
            <include name="**/*.jrxml" />
          </fileset>
        </src>
        <classpath refid="classpath" />
      </jrc>
    </target>

    <target name="view"
            description="Launches the report viewer to preview the
                         report stored in the .jrprint file.">
      <java classname="net.sf.jasperreports.view.JasperViewer"
            fork="true">
        <arg value="-F{file.name}.jrprint" />
        <classpath refid="classpath" />
      </java>
    </target>
  </project>
```

After executing the new ANT target `view`, we should see a window similar to the following:

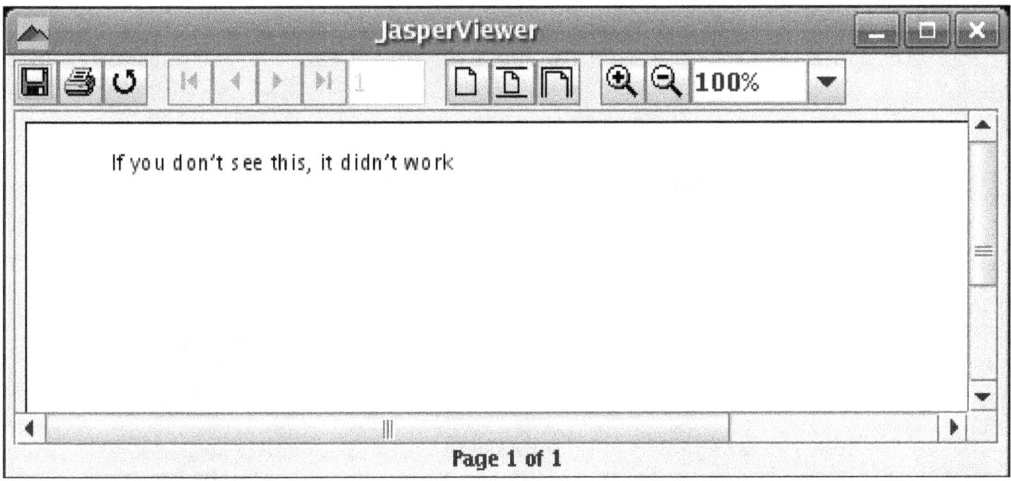

That's it! We have successfully created our first report.

Displaying reports in a web browser

In the previous section, we discussed how to create a report and save it to disk in JasperReports' native format. In this section, we will explain how to display a report in a web browser with the help of the servlet API. The following example demonstrates how to accomplish this:

```
package net.ensode.jasperbook;

import java.io.IOException;
import java.io.InputStream;
import java.io.PrintWriter;
import java.io.StringWriter;
import java.util.HashMap;

import javax.servlet.ServletException;
import javax.servlet.ServletOutputStream;
import javax.servlet.http.HttpServlet;
import javax.servlet.http.HttpServletRequest;
import javax.servlet.http.HttpServletResponse;

import net.sf.jasperreports.engine.JREmptyDataSource;
import net.sf.jasperreports.engine.JRException;
```

```
import net.sf.jasperreports.engine.JasperRunManager;

public class FirstReportSendToBrowserServlet extends HttpServlet
{
  protected void doGet(HttpServletRequest request, HttpServletResponse
                                                            response)
  throws ServletException, IOException
  {
    ServletOutputStream servletOutputStream = response.
                                                  getOutputStream();
    InputStream reportStream =getServletConfig().getServletContext()
                 .getResourceAsStream("/reports/FirstReport.jasper");

    try
    {
      JasperRunManager.runReportToPdfStream(reportStream,
                                        servletOutputStream,
                                        new HashMap(),
                                        new JREmptyDataSource());
      response.setContentType("application/pdf");
      servletOutputStream.flush();
      servletOutputStream.close();
    }
    catch (JRException e)
    {
    // display stack trace in the browser
      StringWriter stringWriter = new StringWriter();
      PrintWriter printWriter = new PrintWriter(stringWriter);
      e.printStackTrace(printWriter);
      response.setContentType("text/plain");
      response.getOutputStream().print(stringWriter.toString());
    }
  }
}
```

Because web browsers are incapable of displaying reports in JasperReports' native format (at least without the help of an applet), we must export the report to a format the browser can understand. JasperReports allows us to export reports to PDF and many other formats. As PDF is one of the most popular formats, we chose it as the export format in this example.

The servlet in the last example calls the static `JasperRunManager.runReportToPdfStream()` method. The signature for this method is as follows:

```
runReportToPdfStream(java.io.InputStream inputStream,
                     java.io.OutputStream outputStream,
                     java.util.Map parameters,
                     JRDataSource jrDataSource)
```

To display the report in the browser, we need to pass the binary report template or jasper file, in the form of a stream, as the first argument to this method. We can accomplish this by calling the `javax.servlet.ServletContext.getResourceAsStream()` method, passing a string containing the location of the jasper file as a parameter. This method will return an instance of `java.io.InputStream`, which can be used as the first argument for the `JasperRunManager.runReportToPdfStream()` method.

The `JasperRunManager.runReportToPdfStream()` method needs an instance of `java.io.OutputStream()` to write the compiled report. We can simply use the default output stream for the servlet, which can be obtained by calling the `javax.servlet.http.HttpServletResponse.getOutputStream()` method.

The next two arguments for the `JasperRunManager.runReportToPdfStream()` method are a `java.util.Map` and a datasource. The former is used to pass any parameters to the report and the latter to pass data in the form of a `net.sf.jasperreports.engine.JRDataSource`. We are not passing any parameters or data to this simple report, hence an empty `HashMap` and `JREmptyDataSource` suffice.

To ensure that the browser displays the report properly, we must set the content type to `application/pdf`. We can accomplish this by calling the `javax.servlet.http.HttpServletResponse.setContentType()` method.

The resulting code for this example needs to be deployed to a servlet container. An ANT script to automate this process can be found as part of the code download for this book, which can be found at `http://www.packtpub.com/files/code/8082_Code.zip`. The following screenshot shows the report being displayed as a PDF in a browser:

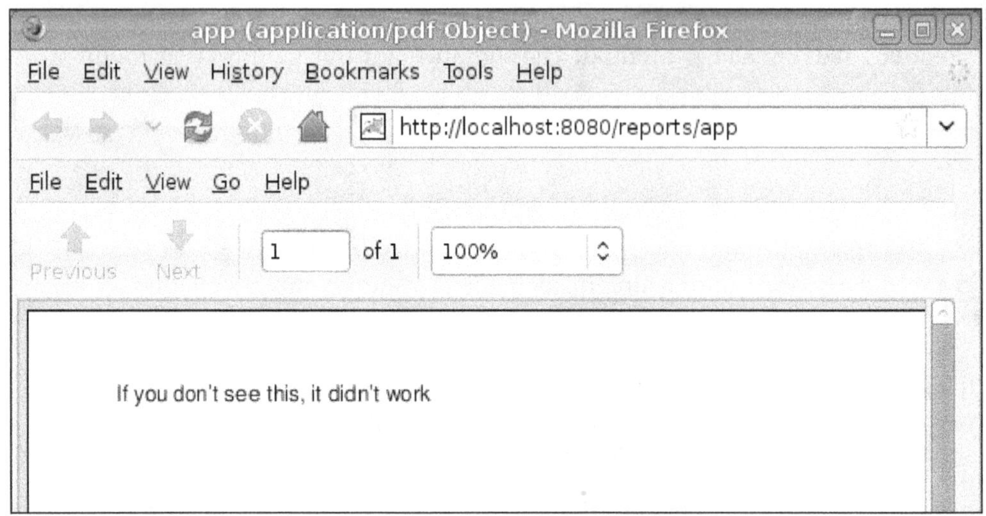

Elements of a JRXML report template

In the previous example, we used the `<detail>` element of the JRXML report template to generate a report displaying some static text. The `<detail>` element is used to display the main section of the report. However, JRXML templates can contain many other sections that allow us to display secondary data on the report or to do some other tasks, such as importing Java packages and controlling how the data is displayed in the report.

The following sections cover all the subelements of the `<jasperReport>` root element. Unless stated otherwise, each element can be used any number of times in the template.

<property>

This element is used for putting arbitrary information in the report template.

```
<property name="someproperty" value="somevalue" />
```

Properties can be retrieved by a Java application that is loading the report by invoking the `JasperReport.getProperty()` method.

<import>

This element is used for importing individual Java classes or complete packages.

```
<import value="java.util.HashMap" />
```

<template>

The report styles can be defined in separate report templates to allow these styles to be reused across the reports. This mechanism is similar to the way cascading stylesheets can be defined in separate CSS files when dealing with HTML. Report style templates can be defined in XML files, which are conventionally saved in JRTX files or, more infrequently, in an instance of a class implementing the `net.sf.jasperreports.engine.JRTemplate` interface.

```
<template>"my_template.jrtx"</template>
```

<style>

This element is used for styling report elements, setting the font style, size, background color, foreground color, and so on. Most other report elements have a `style` attribute that can be used to specify their style. The `<style>` element has an `isDefault` attribute that can be used to specify that the style being defined is the default style, and should be used when other elements don't specify their `style` attribute.

```
<style name="Arial_Normal" isDefault="true"
       fontName="Arial" fontSize="10"
       isBold="false" isItalic="false"
       isUnderline="false" isStrikeThrough="false"/>
```

<subDataset>

The `<subDataset>` element can be used to provide data indirectly in the report to charts and crosstabs in the report template.

```
<subDataset name="Client_Data">
  <parameter name="Client" class="java.lang.String"/>
  <queryString>
    <![CDATA[SELECT foo, bar, temp
             FROM some_table
             WHERE client_code = $P{Client}]]>
  </queryString>
  <field name="foo" class="java.lang.String"/>
```

```
    <field name="bar" class="java.lang.String"/>
    <field name="temp" class="java.lang.String"/>
  </subDataset>
```

Subdatasets need to be referenced by a crosstab or chart.

<parameter>

This element is used to define report parameters. Parameter values are supplied through a `java.util.Map` parameter by calling the appropriate methods in the JasperReports API.

```
<parameter name="SomeParameter"
           class="java.lang.String"/>
```

<queryString>

This element is used to define an SQL query to obtain data from a database.

```
<queryString>
  <![CDATA[SELECT column_name FROM table_name]]>
</queryString>
```

A JRXML template can contain zero or one `<queryString>` element. This element is required if we wish to embed an SQL query in the report template.

<field>

This element is used to map data from datasources or queries to report templates. Fields can be combined in report expressions to obtain the necessary output.

```
<field name="FieldName" class="java.lang.String"/>
```

<sortField>

This element is used to sort the data in the report by the field specified in this element's `name` attribute. Sorting can be ascending or descending, as specified in the `order` attribute. If no order is specified, the default is ascending.

```
<sortField name="BirthDate" order="Descending"/>
```

A JRXML template can have one or more `<sortField>` elements corresponding to fields in the report template.

<variable>

The report expressions used several times in a report can be assigned to the variables to simplify the template.

```
<variable name="VariableName"
          class="java.lang.Double"
          calculation="Sum">
    <variableExpression>
      $F{FieldName}
    </variableExpression>
</variable>
```

<filterExpression>

This element is used to filter out the datasource records from the report.

```
<filterExpression>
  <![CDATA[$F{status}.equals("active") ? Boolean.TRUE :Boolean.FALSE]]>
</filterExpression>
```

If the expression nested inside the `<filterExpression>` element resolves to `Boolean.TRUE`, the current row in the datasource is included in the report. If it resolves to `Boolean.FALSE` or null, the current row is not included in the datasource. Please note that this element is primarily meant to be be used when our datasource type cannot be filtered trivially, such as when we use a CSV file datasource.

A report template can contain zero or one `<filterExpression>` element.

<group>

This element is used to group the consecutive records in a datasource that share some common characteristics.

```
<group name="GroupName">
  <groupExpression>
    <![CDATA[$F{FieldName}]]>
  </groupExpression>
</group>
```

<background>

This element is used to define the page background for all the pages in the report. It can be used to display images or text and is very useful to display watermarks.

```
<background>
  <band height="745">
    <image scaleImage="Clip"
           hAlign="Left" vAlign="Bottom">
       <reportElement x="0" y="0"
        width="160" height="745"/>
       <imageExpression>"image.gif"
       </imageExpression>
      </image>
  </band>
</background>
```

This element cannot be used more than once in a JRXML template.

<title>

This is the report title. It appears only once at the beginning of the report.

```
<title>
  <band height="50">
    <staticText>
      <reportElement x="180" y="0"
                     width="200" height="20"/>
      <text><![CDATA[Title]]></text>
    </staticText>
  </band>
</title>
```

<pageHeader>

This element defines a page header that is printed at the beginning of every page in the report.

```
<pageHeader>
  <band height="20">
    <staticText>
      <reportElement x="180" y="30"
                     width="200" height="20"/>
          <text>
            <![CDATA[Page Header]]>
```

```
        </text>
      </staticText>
    </band>
  </pageHeader>
```

A JRXML template can contain zero or one `<pageHeader>` element.

<columnHeader>

This element defines the contents of column headers. It is ignored if the report has a single column.

```
<columnHeader>
  <band height="20">
    <staticText>
      <reportElement x="180" y="50"
                     width="200" height="20"/>
        <text>
          <![CDATA[Column Header]]>
        </text>
    </staticText>
  </band>
</columnHeader>
```

If present, the number of `<columnHeader>` elements in the template must match the number of columns.

<detail>

This element defines the `detail` section of the report. The content of the `<detail>` section is repeated for each record in the report's datasource.

```
<detail>
  <band height="20">
    <textField>
      <reportElement x="10" y="0"
         width="600" height="20" />
        <textFieldExpression class="java.lang.String">
              <![CDATA[$F{FieldName}]]>
        </textFieldExpression>
    </textField>
  </band>
</detail>
```

A JRXML template can contain zero or one <detail> elements. Most report templates contain a <detail> element; typically, this is where the main data of the report is displayed.

<columnFooter>

This element defines the contents of column footers. It is ignored if the report has a single column.

```
<columnFooter>
  <band height="20">
    <staticText>
      <reportElement x="0" y="0"
                     width="200" height="20"/>
          <text>
            <![CDATA[Column Footer]]>
          </text>
    </staticText>
  </band>
</columnFooter>
```

A JRXML template can contain zero or more <columnFooter> elements. If present, the number of <columnFooter> elements in the template must match the number of columns.

<pageFooter>

This element defines a page footer that is printed at the bottom of every page in the report.

```
<pageFooter>
  <band height="20">
    <staticText>
      <reportElement  x="0" y="5"
                      width="200" height="20"/>
      <text>
        <![CDATA[Page Footer]]>
      </text>
    </staticText>
  </band>
</pageFooter>
```

A JRXML template can contain zero or one <pageFooter> element.

<lastPageFooter>

Data defined in this element is displayed as the page footer of the last page rather than the footer defined in the `<pageFooter>` element.

```
<lastPageFooter>
  <band height="20">
    <staticText>
      <reportElement x="0" y="5"
                     width="200" height="20"/>
      <text>
        <![CDATA[Last Page Footer]]>
      </text>
    </staticText>
  </band>
</lastPageFooter>
```

A JRXML template can contain zero or one `<lastPageFooter>` element.

<summary>

This element is printed once at the end of the report.

```
<summary>
  <band height="20">
    <staticText>
      <reportElement x="0" y="5"
                     width="200" height="20"/>
      <text>
        <![CDATA[Summary]]>
      </text>
    </staticText>
  </band>
</summary>
```

A JRXML template can contain zero or one `<summary>` element.

<noData>

The <noData> element can be used to control what will be generated in the report when the datasource contains no data.

```
<noData>
  <band height="20">
    <staticText>
      <reportElement x="0" y="5"
                     width="200" height="20"/>
      <text>
        <![CDATA[No data found]]>
      </text>
    </staticText>
  </band>
</noData>
```

Just like the <detail> element, most elements discussed in the previous sections contain a single <band> element as its only child element. We will discuss the specific subelements of the <band> element in later chapters.

In the following screenshot, we can see a report that can help us visualize the relative position of the report sections:

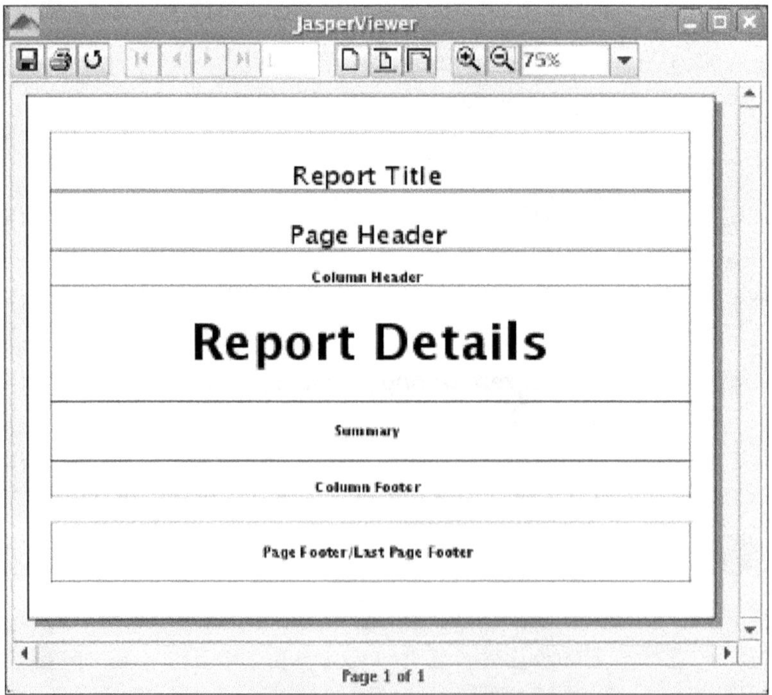

As we can see, the page footer is labeled **Page Footer/Last Page Footer**. If the JRXML template for the report contains a `<lastPageFooter>` element, its contents will be displayed in the last page of the report, instead of the contents of the `<pagefooter>` element. It is worth mentioning that if our report has only one page, and the report template contains both the `<pageFooter>` and the `<lastPageFooter>` elements, then in that case the contents of `<lastPageFooter>` will be displayed as the footer of the first (and only) page; the value of the `<pageFooter>` element will never be displayed.

Before we move on, we should mention that the `<columnHeader>` and `<columnFooter>` elements will be displayed on the report only if it has more than one column. How to add columns to a report is discussed in detail in Chapter 6, *Report Layout and Design*.

Summary

In this chapter, we learned to create a JRXML report template by editing an XML file. We also saw how to preview the template by using the tools supplied by JasperReports. We understood how to compile a JRXML template programmatically and by using a custom ANT task.

After the successful compilation of the report, we filled the report template with data by calling the appropriate methods supplied by the `JasperFillManager` class, and we viewed the generated reports in native JasperReports' format by using the JasperViewer utility. The chapter also guided us through the different report sections in a JRXML template.

Finally, we created web-based reports by displaying generated reports in a web browser. We are now ready to move on to the next chapter.

4
Creating Dynamic Reports from Databases

In the previous chapter, we learned how to create our first report. The simple report in the previous chapter contained no dynamic data. In this chapter, we will explore how to create a report from the data obtained from a database.

In this chapter, we will cover the following topics:

- How to embed SQL queries into a report template
- How to pass rows returned by an SQL query to a report through a datasource
- How to use report fields to display data obtained from a database
- How to display database data in a report by using the `<textField>` element of the JRXML template

Datasource definition

A **datasource** is what JasperReports uses to obtain data for generating a report. Data can be obtained from databases, XML files, arrays of objects, collections of objects, and XML files.

In this chapter, we will focus on using databases as a datasource. The next chapter discusses the other types of datasources.

Database for our reports

We will use a MySQL database to obtain data for our reports. The database is a subset of public domain data that can be downloaded from `http://dl.flightstats.us`. The original download is 1.3 GB, so we deleted most of the tables and a lot of data to trim the download size considerably. MySQL dump of the modified database can be found as part of this book's code download at `http://www.packtpub.com/files/code/8082_Code.zip`.

The `flightstats` database contains the following tables:

- `aircraft`
- `aircraft_models`
- `aircraft_types`
- `aircraft_engines`
- `aircraft_engine_types`

The database structure can be seen in the following diagram:

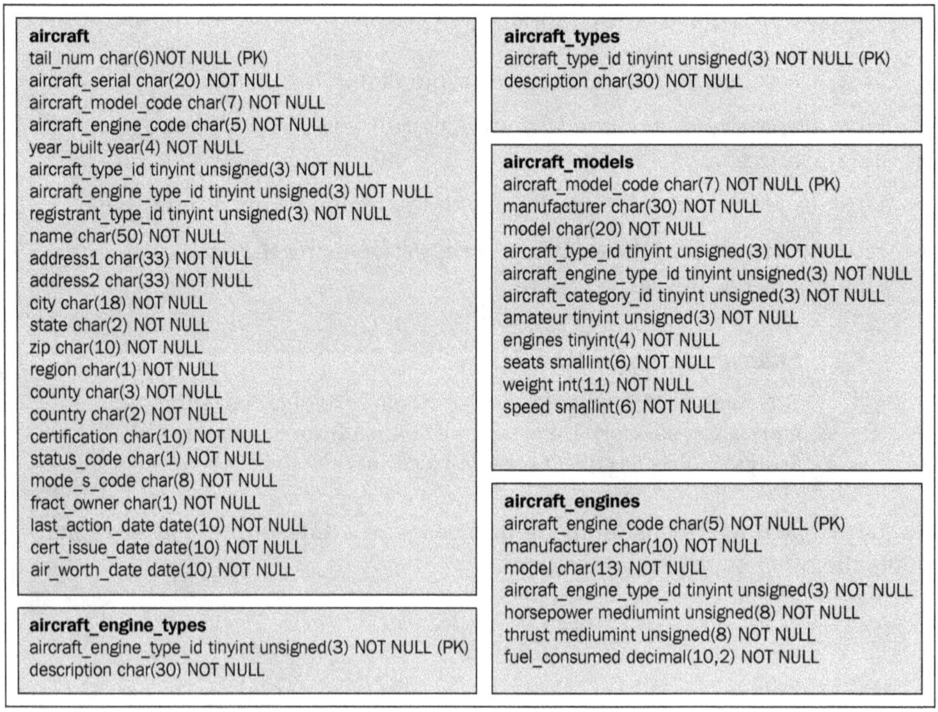

aircraft
tail_num char(6)NOT NULL (PK)
aircraft_serial char(20) NOT NULL
aircraft_model_code char(7) NOT NULL
aircraft_engine_code char(5) NOT NULL
year_built year(4) NOT NULL
aircraft_type_id tinyint unsigned(3) NOT NULL
aircraft_engine_type_id tinyint unsigned(3) NOT NULL
registrant_type_id tinyint unsigned(3) NOT NULL
name char(50) NOT NULL
address1 char(33) NOT NULL
address2 char(33) NOT NULL
city char(18) NOT NULL
state char(2) NOT NULL
zip char(10) NOT NULL
region char(1) NOT NULL
county char(3) NOT NULL
country char(2) NOT NULL
certification char(10) NOT NULL
status_code char(1) NOT NULL
mode_s_code char(8) NOT NULL
fract_owner char(1) NOT NULL
last_action_date date(10) NOT NULL
cert_issue_date date(10) NOT NULL
air_worth_date date(10) NOT NULL

aircraft_engine_types
aircraft_engine_type_id tinyint unsigned(3) NOT NULL (PK)
description char(30) NOT NULL

aircraft_types
aircraft_type_id tinyint unsigned(3) NOT NULL (PK)
description char(30) NOT NULL

aircraft_models
aircraft_model_code char(7) NOT NULL (PK)
manufacturer char(30) NOT NULL
model char(20) NOT NULL
aircraft_type_id tinyint unsigned(3) NOT NULL
aircraft_engine_type_id tinyint unsigned(3) NOT NULL
aircraft_category_id tinyint unsigned(3) NOT NULL
amateur tinyint unsigned(3) NOT NULL
engines tinyint(4) NOT NULL
seats smallint(6) NOT NULL
weight int(11) NOT NULL
speed smallint(6) NOT NULL

aircraft_engines
aircraft_engine_code char(5) NOT NULL (PK)
manufacturer char(10) NOT NULL
model char(13) NOT NULL
aircraft_engine_type_id tinyint unsigned(3) NOT NULL
horsepower mediumint unsigned(8) NOT NULL
thrust mediumint unsigned(8) NOT NULL
fuel_consumed decimal(10,2) NOT NULL

The `flightstats` database uses the default MyISAM storage engine for the MySQL RDBMS, which does not support referential integrity (foreign keys). That is why we don't see any arrows in the diagram indicating dependencies between the tables.

Let's create a report that will show the most powerful aircraft in the database. Let's say, those with horsepower of 1000 or above. The report will show the aircraft tail number and serial number, the aircraft model, and the aircraft's engine model. The following query will give us the required results:

```
SELECT a.tail_num, a.aircraft_serial, am.model as aircraft_model,
       ae.model AS engine_model
FROM aircraft a, aircraft_models am, aircraft_engines ae
WHERE a.aircraft_engine_code in (select aircraft_engine_code
                                 from aircraft_engines
                                 where horsepower >= 1000)
      and am.aircraft_model_code = a.aircraft_model_code
      and ae.aircraft_engine_code = a.aircraft_engine_code
```

The above query retrieves the following data from the database:

tail_num	aircraft_serial	aircraft_model	engine_model
N263Y	T-11	39 ROSCOE TRNR RA	R1830 SERIES
N4087X	BA100-163	BRADLEY AEROBAT	R2800 SERIES
N43JE	HAYABUSA 1	NAKAJIMA KI-43 IIIA	R1830 SERIES
N912S	9973CC	PA18-150	R-1820 SER

Generating database reports

There are two ways to generate database reports—either by embedding SQL queries into the JRXML report template or by passing data from the database to the compiled report through a datasource. We will discuss both of these techniques.

We will first create the report by embedding the query into the JRXML template. Then, we will generate the same report by passing it through a datasource containing the database data.

Embedding SQL queries into a report template

JasperReports allows us to embed database queries into a report template. This can be achieved by using the `<queryString>` element of the JRXML file. The following example demonstrates this technique:

```
<?xml version="1.0" encoding="UTF-8" ?>
<jasperReport
    xmlns="http://jasperreports.sourceforge.net/jasperreports"
    xmlns:xsi="http://www.w3.org/2001/XMLSchema-instance"
          xsi:schemaLocation="http://jasperreports.sourceforge.net
              /jasperreports http://jasperreports.sourceforge.net/
              xsd/jasperreport.xsd"
    name="DbReport">
  <queryString>
    <![CDATA[SELECT a.tail_num, a.aircraft_serial,
                    am.model as aircraft_model,
                    ae.model as engine_model
             FROM aircraft a, aircraft_models am, aircraft_engines ae
             WHERE a.aircraft_engine_code in (
                     select aircraft_engine_code
                     from aircraft_engines
                     where horsepower >= 1000)
             AND am.aircraft_model_code = a.aircraft_model_code
             AND ae.aircraft_engine_code = a.aircraft_engine_code]]>
  </queryString>
  <field name="tail_num" class="java.lang.String" />
  <field name="aircraft_serial" class="java.lang.String" />
  <field name="aircraft_model" class="java.lang.String" />
  <field name="engine_model" class="java.lang.String" />
  <pageHeader>
    <band height="30">
      <staticText>
        <reportElement x="0" y="0" width="69" height="24" />
        <textElement verticalAlignment="Bottom" />
        <text>
          <![CDATA[Tail Number: ]]>
        </text>
      </staticText>
      <staticText>
        <reportElement x="140" y="0" width="79" height="24" />
        <text>
          <![CDATA[Serial Number: ]]>
        </text>
```

```
        </staticText>
        <staticText>
          <reportElement x="280" y="0" width="69" height="24" />
          <text>
            <![CDATA[Model: ]]>
          </text>
        </staticText>
        <staticText>
          <reportElement x="420" y="0" width="69" height="24" />
          <text>
            <![CDATA[Engine: ]]>
          </text>
        </staticText>
      </band>
    </pageHeader>
    <detail>
      <band height="30">
        <textField>
          <reportElement x="0" y="0" width="69" height="24" />
          <textFieldExpression class="java.lang.String">
            <![CDATA[$F{tail_num}]]>
          </textFieldExpression>
        </textField>
        <textField>
            <reportElement x="140" y="0" width="69" height="24" />
          <textFieldExpression class="java.lang.String">
            <![CDATA[$F{aircraft_serial}]]>
          </textFieldExpression>
        </textField>
        <textField>
          <reportElement x="280" y="0" width="69" height="24" />
          <textFieldExpression class="java.lang.String">
            <![CDATA[$F{aircraft_model}]]>
          </textFieldExpression>
        </textField>
        <textField>
          <reportElement x="420" y="0" width="69" height="24" />
          <textFieldExpression class="java.lang.String">
            <![CDATA[$F{engine_model}]]>
          </textFieldExpression>
        </textField>
      </band>
    </detail>
  </jasperReport>
```

There are a few JRXML elements in this example that we haven't seen before.

As stated before, the `<queryString>` element is used to embed a database query into the report template. In the given code example, the `<queryString>` element contains the query wrapped in a `CDATA` block for execution. The `<queryString>` element has no attributes or subelements other than the `CDATA` block containing the query.

> Text wrapped inside an XML `CDATA` block is ignored by the XML parser. As seen in the given example, our query contains the > character, which would invalidate the XML block if it wasn't inside a `CDATA` block. A `CDATA` block is optional if the data inside it does not break the XML structure. However, for consistency and maintainability, we chose to use it wherever it is allowed in the example.

The `<field>` element defines fields that are populated at runtime when the report is filled. Field names must match the column names or alias of the corresponding columns in the SQL query. The `class` attribute of the `<field>` element is optional; its default value is `java.lang.String`. Even though all of our fields are strings, we still added the `class` attribute for clarity. In the last example, the syntax to obtain the value of a report field is `$F{field_name}`, where `field_name` is the name of the field as defined.

The next element that we haven't seen before is the `<textField>` element. Text fields are used to display dynamic textual data in reports. In this case, we are using them to display the value of the fields. Like all the subelements of `<band>`, text fields must contain a `<reportElement>` subelement indicating the text field's height, width, and x, y coordinates within the band. The data that is displayed in text fields is defined by the `<textFieldExpression>` subelement of `<textField>`. The `<textFieldExpresson>` element has a single subelement, which is the report expression that will be displayed by the text field and wrapped in an XML `CDATA` block. In this example, each text field is displaying the value of a field. Therefore, the expression inside the `<textFieldExpression>` element uses the field syntax `$F{field_name}`, as explained before.

Compiling a report containing a query is no different from compiling a report without a query. It can be done programmatically or by using the custom JasperReports `jrc` ANT task. We covered compiling reports in the previous chapter.

Generating the report

As we have mentioned previously, in JasperReports terminology, the action of generating a report from a binary report template is called **filling** the report. To fill a report containing an embedded database query, we must pass a database connection object to the report. The following example illustrates this process:

```
package net.ensode.jasperbook;

import java.sql.Connection;
import java.sql.DriverManager;
import java.sql.SQLException;
import java.util.HashMap;

import net.sf.jasperreports.engine.JRException;
import net.sf.jasperreports.engine.JasperFillManager;

public class DbReportFill
{
  Connection connection;

  public void generateReport()
  {
    try
    {
      Class.forName("com.mysql.jdbc.Driver");

      connection = DriverManager.getConnection("jdbc:mysql://
               localhost:3306/flightstats?user=user&password=secret");

      System.out.println("Filling report...");
      JasperFillManager.fillReportToFile("reports/DbReport.jasper",
                                         new HashMap(), connection);
      System.out.println("Done!");

      connection.close();
    }
    catch (JRException e)
    {
      e.printStackTrace();
    }
    catch (ClassNotFoundException e)
    {
      e.printStackTrace();
    }
    catch (SQLException e)
    {
      e.printStackTrace();
    }
  }
```

```
    public static void main(String[] args)
    {
      new DbReportFill().generateReport();
    }
  }
```

As seen in this example, a database connection is passed to the report in the form of a `java.sql.Connection` object as the last parameter of the static `JasperFillManager.fillReportToFile()` method. The first two parameters are as follows: a string (used to indicate the location of the binary report template or jasper file) and an instance of a class implementing the `java.util.Map` interface (used for passing additional parameters to the report). As we don't need to pass any additional parameters for this report, we used an empty `HashMap`.

There are six overloaded versions of the `JasperFillManager.fillReportToFile()` method, three of which take a connection object as a parameter. Refer to the previous chapter for a description of the other versions of this method that take a connection object as a parameter.

For simplicity, our examples open and close database connections every time they are executed. It is usually a better idea to use a connection pool, as connection pools increase the performance considerably. Most Java EE application servers come with connection pooling functionality, and the **commons-dbcp** component of Apache Commons includes utility classes for adding connection pooling capabilities to the applications that do not make use of an application server.

After executing the above example, a new report, or JRPRINT file is saved to disk. We can view it by using the JasperViewer utility included with JasperReports.

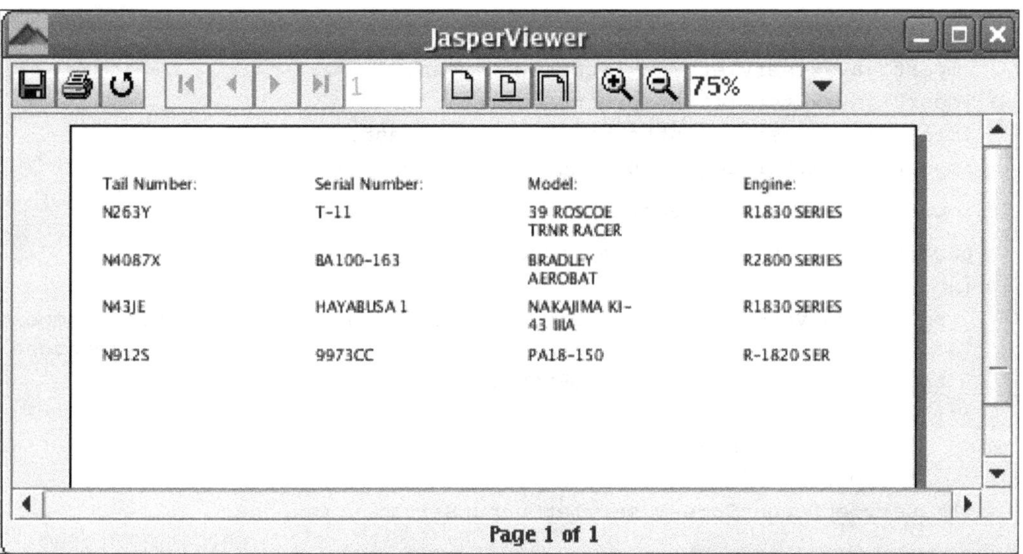

In this example, we created the report and immediately saved it to disk. The `JasperFillManager` class also contains methods to send a report to an output stream or to store it in memory in the form of a JasperPrint object. Storing the compiled report in a JasperPrint object allows us to manipulate the report in our code further. We could, for example, export it to PDF or another format.

The method used to store a report into a JasperPrint object is `JasperFillManager.fillReport()`. The method used for sending the report to an output stream is `JasperFillManager.fillReportToStream()`. These two methods accept the same parameters as `JasperFillManager.fillReportToFile()` and are trivial to use once we are familiar with this method. Refer to the JasperReports API for details.

In the next example, we will fill our report and immediately export it to PDF by taking advantage of the `net.sf.jasperreports.engine.JasperRunManager.runReportToPdfStream()` method.

```
package net.ensode.jasperbook;

import java.io.IOException;
import java.io.InputStream;
import java.io.PrintWriter;
import java.io.StringWriter;
import java.sql.Connection;
import java.sql.DriverManager;
import java.util.HashMap;
```

```
import javax.servlet.ServletException;
import javax.servlet.ServletOutputStream;
import javax.servlet.http.HttpServlet;
import javax.servlet.http.HttpServletRequest;
import javax.servlet.http.HttpServletResponse;

import net.sf.jasperreports.engine.JasperRunManager;

public class DbReportServlet extends HttpServlet
{
  protected void doGet(HttpServletRequest request, HttpServletResponse
                                                              response)
  throws ServletException, IOException
  {
    Connection connection;
    response.setContentType("application/pdf");
    ServletOutputStream servletOutputStream = response
                                                 .getOutputStream();
    InputStream reportStream = getServletConfig().getServletContext()
                   .getResourceAsStream("/reports/DbReport.jasper");
    try
    {
      Class.forName("com.mysql.jdbc.Driver");
      connection = DriverManager.getConnection("jdbc:mysql:
           //localhost:3306/flightstats?user=dbUser&password=secret");
      JasperRunManager.runReportToPdfStream(reportStream,
                  servletOutputStream, new HashMap(), connection);
      connection.close();

      servletOutputStream.flush();
      servletOutputStream.close();
    }
    catch (Exception e)
    {
      // display stack trace in the browser
      StringWriter stringWriter = new StringWriter();
      PrintWriter printWriter = new PrintWriter(stringWriter);
      e.printStackTrace(printWriter);
      response.setContentType("text/plain");
      response.getOutputStream().print(stringWriter.toString());
    }
  }
}
```

We have already discussed this technique in the previous chapter. The only difference here is that we are passing a connection to the report for generating a database report. After deploying this servlet and pointing the browser to its URL, we should see a screen similar to the following screenshot:

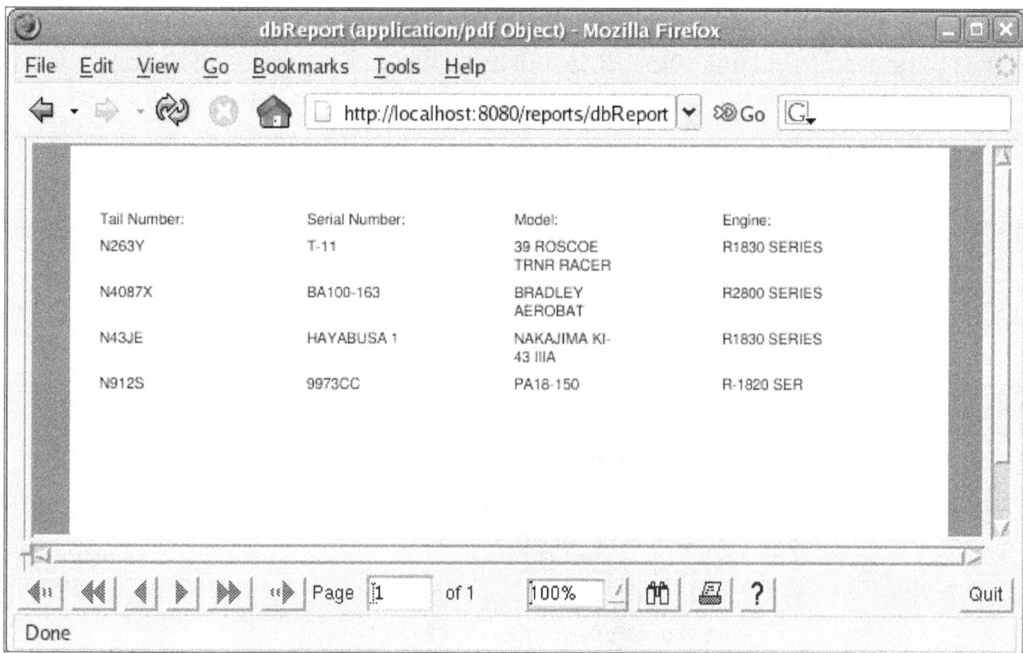

Although not directly related to database reporting, one more thing worth mentioning is that we used the `<pageHeader>` element of the JRXML template to lay out the report labels. If our report had more than one page, these labels would appear at the top of every page.

Modifying a report query through report parameters

Although embedding a database query into a report template is the simplest way to generate a database report, this approach is not very flexible. As in order to modify the report query, it is also necessary to modify the report's JRXML template.

The example JRXML template that we discussed in the previous section generates a report that displays all the aircraft in the database with a horsepower equal to or greater than 1000. If we wanted to generate a report to display all the aircraft with a horsepower greater than or equal to 750, then we would have to modify the JRXML and recompile it. Too much of work for such a small change! Fortunately, JasperReports allows us to modify an embedded database query easily by using the report parameters. The following JRXML template is a new version of the one we saw in the previous section but modified to take advantage of report parameters:

```
<?xml version="1.0" encoding="UTF-8" ?>
<jasperReport xmlns="http://jasperreports.sourceforge.net
                       /jasperreports"
  xmlns:xsi="http://www.w3.org/2001/XMLSchema-instance"
        xsi:schemaLocation="http://jasperreports
            .sourceforge.net/jasperreports http://jasperreports
            .sourceforge.net/xsd/jasperreport.xsd"
        name="DbReportParam">
  <parameter name="hp" class="java.lang.Integer" />
  <queryString>
    <![CDATA[SELECT a.tail_num, a.aircraft_serial, am.model as
                     aircraft_model, ae.model as engine_model
            FROM aircraft a, aircraft_models am, aircraft_engines ae
            WHERE a.aircraft_engine_code in (
                  select aircraft_engine_code
                  from aircraft_engines
                  where horsepower >= $P{hp})
           AND am.aircraft_model_code = a.aircraft_model_code
           AND ae.aircraft_engine_code = a.aircraft_engine_code]]>
  </queryString>
  <field name="tail_num" class="java.lang.String" />
  <field name="aircraft_serial" class="java.lang.String" />
  <field name="aircraft_model" class="java.lang.String" />
  <field name="engine_model" class="java.lang.String" />
  <pageHeader>
    <band height="30">
      <staticText>
        <reportElement x="0" y="0" width="69" height="24" />
        <textElement verticalAlignment="Bottom" />
        <text>
          <![CDATA[Tail Number: ]]>
        </text>
      </staticText>
      <staticText>
        <reportElement x="140" y="0" width="79" height="24" />
        <text>
          <![CDATA[Serial Number: ]]>
        </text>
```

```
        </staticText>
        <staticText>
          <reportElement x="280" y="0" width="69" height="24" />
          <text>
            <![CDATA[Model: ]]>
          </text>
        </staticText>
        <staticText>
          <reportElement x="420" y="0" width="69" height="24" />
          <text>
            <![CDATA[Engine: ]]>
          </text>
        </staticText>
      </band>
    </pageHeader>
    <detail>
      <band height="30">
        <textField>
          <reportElement x="0" y="0" width="69" height="24" />
          <textFieldExpression class="java.lang.String">
            <![CDATA[$F{tail_num}]]>
          </textFieldExpression>
        </textField>
        <textField>
          <reportElement x="140" y="0" width="69" height="24" />
          <textFieldExpression class="java.lang.String">
            <![CDATA[$F{aircraft_serial}]]>
          </textFieldExpression>
        </textField>
        <textField>
          <reportElement x="280" y="0" width="69" height="24" />
          <textFieldExpression class="java.lang.String">
            <![CDATA[$F{aircraft_model}]]>
          </textFieldExpression>
        </textField>
        <textField>
          <reportElement x="420" y="0" width="69" height="24" />
          <textFieldExpression class="java.lang.String">
            <![CDATA[$F{engine_model}]]>
          </textFieldExpression>
        </textField>
      </band>
    </detail>
  </jasperReport>
```

The only difference between this JRXML template and the previous one is that we declared a report parameter in the following line:

```
<parameter name="hp" class="java.lang.Integer" />
```

We then used the declared parameter to retrieve the horsepower dynamically in the `where` clause of the report query. As can be seen in this example, the value of a report parameter can be retrieved by using the syntax `$P{paramName}`, where `paramName` is the parameter name as defined in its declaration (`hp` in this example).

Passing a parameter to a report from Java code is very simple. In most of the examples we have seen so far, we have been passing an empty `HashMap` to report templates when we fill them. The purpose of that `HashMap` is to pass parameters to the report template. The following servlet is a new version of the one we saw in the previous section but modified to send a report parameter to the report template:

```
package net.ensode.jasperbook;

import java.io.IOException;
import java.io.InputStream;
import java.io.PrintWriter;
import java.io.StringWriter;
import java.sql.Connection;
import java.sql.DriverManager;
import java.util.HashMap;

import javax.servlet.ServletException;
import javax.servlet.ServletOutputStream;
import javax.servlet.http.HttpServlet;
import javax.servlet.http.HttpServletRequest;
import javax.servlet.http.HttpServletResponse;

import net.sf.jasperreports.engine.JasperRunManager;

public class DbReportParamServlet extends HttpServlet
{
  protected void doGet(HttpServletRequest request, HttpServletResponse
                                                              response)
  throws ServletException, IOException
  {
    Connection connection;
    response.setContentType("application/pdf");
    ServletOutputStream servletOutputStream = response
                                              .getOutputStream();
```

```
        InputStream reportStream = getServletConfig().getServletContext()
                    .getResourceAsStream("/reports/DbReportParam.jasper");

        HashMap parameterMap = new HashMap();
        parameterMap.put("hp", new Integer(750));

        try
        {
          Class.forName("com.mysql.jdbc.Driver");
          connection = DriverManager.getConnection("jdbc:mysql://
                 localhost:3306/flightstats?user=dbuser&password=secret");

          JasperRunManager.runReportToPdfStream(reportStream,
                         servletOutputStream, parameterMap, connection);

          connection.close();

          servletOutputStream.flush();
          servletOutputStream.close();
        }
        catch (Exception e)
        {
          // display stack trace in the browser
          StringWriter stringWriter = new StringWriter();
          PrintWriter printWriter = new PrintWriter(stringWriter);
          e.printStackTrace(printWriter);
          response.setContentType("text/plain");
          response.getOutputStream().print(stringWriter.toString());
        }
      }
    }
```

The only difference between this servlet and the one in the previous section is that here we declare a `HashMap` and populate it with the report parameters. Notice how the `HashMap` key must match the report parameter name.

After deploying the servlet and directing the browser to its URL, we should see a report as seen in the following screenshot:

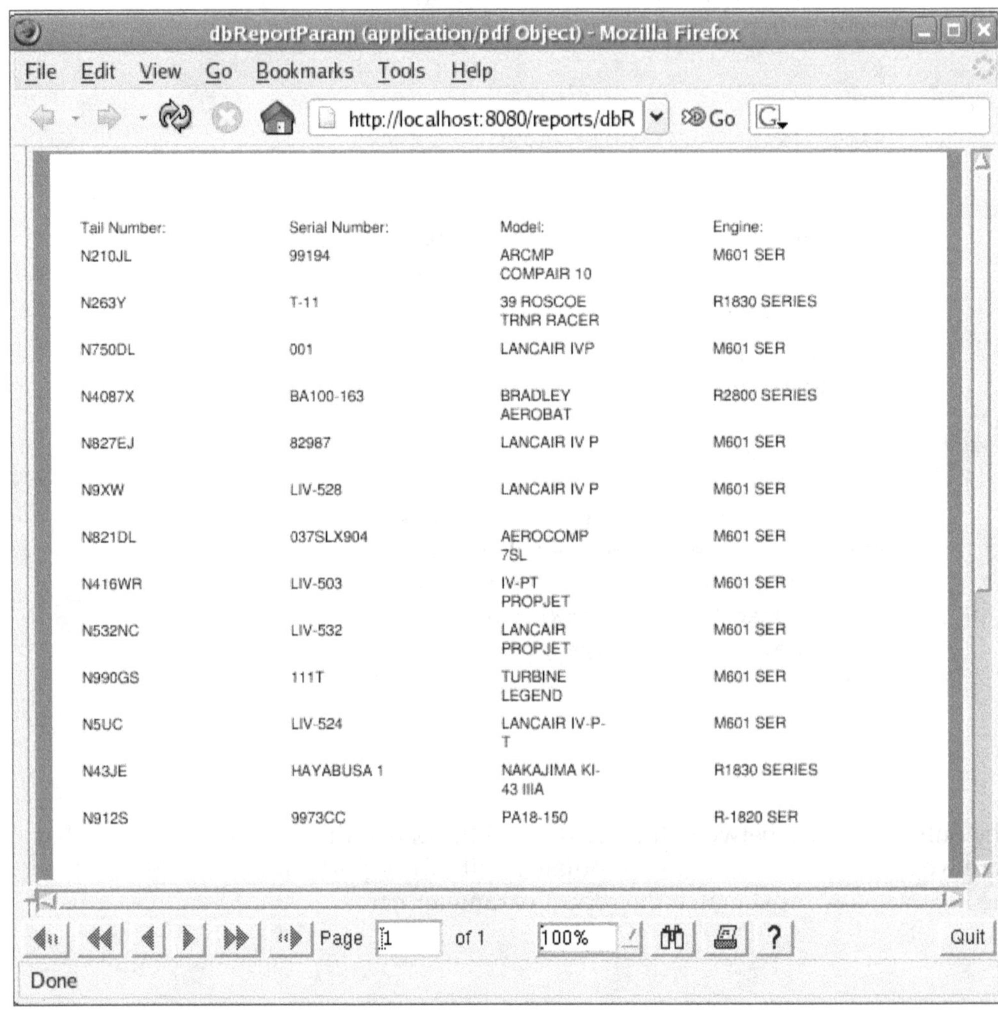

Tail Number:	Serial Number:	Model:	Engine:
N210JL	99194	ARCMP COMPAIR 10	M601 SER
N263Y	T-11	39 ROSCOE TRNR RACER	R1830 SERIES
N750DL	001	LANCAIR IVP	M601 SER
N4087X	BA100-163	BRADLEY AEROBAT	R2800 SERIES
N827EJ	82987	LANCAIR IV P	M601 SER
N9XW	LIV-528	LANCAIR IV P	M601 SER
N821DL	037SLX904	AEROCOMP 7SL	M601 SER
N416WR	LIV-503	IV-PT PROPJET	M601 SER
N532NC	LIV-532	LANCAIR PROPJET	M601 SER
N990GS	111T	TURBINE LEGEND	M601 SER
N5UC	LIV-524	LANCAIR IV-P-T	M601 SER
N43JE	HAYABUSA 1	NAKAJIMA KI-43 IIIA	R1830 SERIES
N912S	9973CC	PA18-150	R-1820 SER

Dynamically modifying the report queries is only one of many possible uses of report parameters. Report parameters are discussed in detail in the next chapter.

Database reporting through a datasource

Another way we can generate reports based on database data is by using a datasource. In JasperReports terminology, a datasource is a class implementing the `net.sf.jasperreports.engine.JRDataSource` interface.

To use a database as a datasource, the JasperReports API provides the `net.sf.jasperreports.engine.JRResultSetDataSource` class. This class implements the `JRDataSource` interface. It has a single `public` constructor that takes a `java.sql.ResultSet` as its only parameter. The `JRResultSetDataSource` class provides no `public` methods or variables. To use it, all we need to do is provide a result set to its constructor and pass it to the report through the `JasperFillManager` class.

Let's modify the last JRXML template so that it uses a `JRResultSetDataSource` class to obtain database data.

The only change we need to make in the JRXML template is to remove the `<queryString>` element.

```
<?xml version="1.0" encoding="UTF-8" ?>
<!DOCTYPE jasperReport PUBLIC "//JasperReports//DTD Report Design//EN"
        "http://jasperreports.sourceforge.net/dtds/jasperreport.dtd">
<jasperReport name="DbReportDS">
  <field name="tail_num" class="java.lang.String" />
  <field name="aircraft_serial" class="java.lang.String" />
  <field name="aircraft_model" class="java.lang.String" />
  <field name="engine_model" class="java.lang.String" />
  <pageHeader>
    <band height="30">
      <staticText>
        <reportElement x="0" y="0" width="69" height="24" />
        <textElement verticalAlignment="Bottom" />
        <text>
          <![CDATA[Tail Number: ]]>
        </text>
      </staticText>
      <staticText>
        <reportElement x="140" y="0" width="69" height="24" />
        <text>
          <![CDATA[Serial Number: ]]>
        </text>
      </staticText>
      <staticText>
        <reportElement x="280" y="0" width="69" height="24" />
        <text>
          <![CDATA[Model: ]]>
        </text>
      </staticText>
      <staticText>
        <reportElement x="420" y="0" width="69" height="24" />
        <text>
```

```
            <![CDATA[Engine: ]]>
          </text>
        </staticText>
      </band>
    </pageHeader>
    <detail>
      <band height="30">
        <textField>
          <reportElement x="0" y="0" width="69" height="24" />
          <textFieldExpression class="java.lang.String">
            <![CDATA[$F{tail_num}]]>
          </textFieldExpression>
        </textField>
        <textField>
          <reportElement x="140" y="0" width="69" height="24" />
          <textFieldExpression class="java.lang.String">
            <![CDATA[$F{aircraft_serial}]]>
          </textFieldExpression>
        </textField>
        <textField>
          <reportElement x="280" y="0" width="69" height="24" />
          <textFieldExpression class="java.lang.String">
            <![CDATA[$F{aircraft_model}]]>
          </textFieldExpression>
        </textField>
        <textField>
          <reportElement x="420" y="0" width="69" height="24" />
          <textFieldExpression class="java.lang.String">
            <![CDATA[$F{engine_model}]]>
          </textFieldExpression>
        </textField>
      </band>
    </detail>
  </jasperReport>
```

The procedure for compiling a database report by using `JRResultSetDataSource` is no different from what we have already seen. To fill the report, we need to execute a database query in our Java code and pass the query results to the report in a datasource, as seen in the following example:

```
package net.ensode.jasperbook;

import java.sql.Connection;
import java.sql.DriverManager;
import java.sql.ResultSet;
```

```
import java.sql.SQLException;
import java.sql.Statement;
import java.util.HashMap;

import net.sf.jasperreports.engine.JRException;
import net.sf.jasperreports.engine.JRResultSetDataSource;
import net.sf.jasperreports.engine.JasperFillManager;

public class DbReportDSFill
{
  Connection connection;
  Statement statement;
  ResultSet resultSet;

  public void generateReport()
  {
    try
    {
      String query = "SELECT a.tail_num, a.aircraft_serial, "
                            + "am.model as aircraft_model,
                            ae.model as engine_model
                      FROM aircraft a, " + "aircraft_models am,
                           aircraft_engines ae
                      WHERE a.aircraft_engine_code in (" + "select
                                                  aircraft_engine_code
                                             from aircraft_engines " +
                                            "where horsepower >= 1000)
                  AND am.aircraft_model_code = a.aircraft_model_code "
            + "and ae.aircraft_engine_code = a.aircraft_engine_code";
      Class.forName("com.mysql.jdbc.Driver");

      connection = DriverManager.getConnection("jdbc:mysql:
             //localhost:3306/flightstats?user=user&password=secret");
      statement = connection.createStatement();
      resultSet = statement.executeQuery(query);

      JRResultSetDataSource resultSetDataSource = new
                                JRResultSetDataSource(resultSet);

      System.out.println("Filling report...");
      JasperFillManager.fillReportToFile("reports/DbReportDS.jasper",
                             new HashMap(), resultSetDataSource);
      System.out.println("Done!");

      resultSet.close();
      statement.close();
      connection.close();
    }
    catch (JRException e)
    {
```

```
        e.printStackTrace();
      }
      catch (ClassNotFoundException e)
      {
        e.printStackTrace();
      }
      catch (SQLException e)
      {
        e.printStackTrace();
      }
    }
    public static void main(String[] args)
    {
      new DbReportDSFill().generateReport();
    }
  }
```

As seen in this example, to provide a report with database data by using `JRResultSetDataSource`, we must execute the database query from the Java code and wrap the resulting `resultSet` object into an instance of `JRResultSetDataSource` by passing it to its constructor. The instance of `JRResultSetDataSource` must then be passed to the `JasperFillManager.fillReportToFile()` method. Strictly speaking, any method that takes an instance of a class implementing `JRDataSource` can be called. In this example, we wished to save the report to a file, so we chose to use `fillReportToFile()`. This method fills the report with data from the datasource and saves it to a file in the filesystem. It has the potential of throwing a `JRException` if there is something wrong. Consequently, this exception must either be caught or declared in the `throws` clause.

After executing this code, a report identical to the first one we saw in the previous section is generated. The following example demonstrates how a web-based report can be created by using a database datasource:

```
package net.ensode.jasperbook;

import java.io.IOException;
import java.io.InputStream;
import java.io.PrintWriter;
import java.io.StringWriter;
import java.sql.Connection;
import java.sql.DriverManager;
import java.sql.ResultSet;
import java.sql.Statement;
import java.util.HashMap;

import javax.servlet.ServletException;
```

```
import javax.servlet.ServletOutputStream;
import javax.servlet.http.HttpServlet;
import javax.servlet.http.HttpServletRequest;
import javax.servlet.http.HttpServletResponse;

import net.sf.jasperreports.engine.JRResultSetDataSource;
import net.sf.jasperreports.engine.JasperRunManager;

public class DbDSReportServlet extends HttpServlet
{
  protected void doGet(HttpServletRequest request, HttpServletResponse
                                                             response)
  throws ServletException, IOException
  {
    Connection connection;
    Statement statement;
    ResultSet resultSet;

    response.setContentType("application/pdf");
    ServletOutputStream servletOutputStream = response
                                               .getOutputStream();
    InputStream reportStream = getServletConfig().getServletContext()
                .getResourceAsStream("/reports/DbReportDS.jasper");

    try
    {
      String query = "select a.tail_num, a.aircraft_serial, "
                   + "am.model as aircraft_model, ae.model as
                      engine_model from aircraft a, "
                   + "aircraft_models am, aircraft_engines ae
                      where a.aircraft_engine_code in ("
                   + "select aircraft_engine_code from
                      aircraft_engines "
                   + "where horsepower >= 1000) and
                   am.aircraft_model_code = a.aircraft_model_code "
                   + "and ae.aircraft_engine_code =
                      a.aircraft_engine_code";

      Class.forName("com.mysql.jdbc.Driver");

      connection = DriverManager.getConnection("jdbc:mysql:
           //localhost:3306/flightstats?user=dbuser&password=secret");
      statement = connection.createStatement();
      resultSet = statement.executeQuery(query);

      JRResultSetDataSource resultSetDataSource = new
                                  JRResultSetDataSource(resultSet);

      JasperRunManager.runReportToPdfStream(reportStream,
             servletOutputStream, new HashMap(), resultSetDataSource);

      resultSet.close();
```

```
            statement.close();
            connection.close();

            servletOutputStream.flush();
            servletOutputStream.close();
        }
        catch (Exception e)
        {
            // display stack trace in the browser
            StringWriter stringWriter = new StringWriter();
            PrintWriter printWriter = new PrintWriter(stringWriter);
            e.printStackTrace(printWriter);
            response.setContentType("text/plain");
            response.getOutputStream().print(stringWriter.toString());
        }
    }
}
```

This code is very similar to the previous examples. It executes an SQL query through JDBC and wraps the resulting resultSet in an instance of `JRResultSetDataSource`. This instance of `JRResultSetDataSource` is then passed to the `JasperRunManager.runReportToPdfStream()` method to export the report to PDF format and stream it to the browser window.

All the examples in this chapter use simple SQL `select` queries to obtain report data. It is also possible to obtain report data from the database by calling stored procedures or functions (if supported by the RDBMS and JDBC driver we are using).

A comparison of database report methods

Although embedding a database query into a report template is the simpler way that JasperReports allows us to create database reports, it is also the least flexible one. Using a `JRResultSetDataSource` involves writing some more code but results in more flexible reports, as the same report template can be used for different datasources.

Which method to use depends on our needs. If we are sure that we will always be using a database as a datasource for our report, and the database query is unlikely to change much, then embedding the database query into the JRXML template at design time is the most straightforward solution. If the query is likely to change, or if we need to use datasources other than a database for our reports, then using a datasource provides the most flexibility.

Some report design tools will only generate database reports by embedding a database query into the report template. If we are using one of these tools, then we have little choice but to use this method. We are free to remove the `<queryString>` element from the JRXML after we are done designing the report and passing the `JRResultSetDataSource` at runtime. However, if we do this, we lose the ability to modify the report template from the report designer.

Summary

In this chapter, we learned the different ways we can create database reports and how to use the `<queryString>` JRXML element to embed SQL queries in a report template.

Additionally, we saw how to populate an instance of `JRResultSetDataSource` with data from a result set and use it to fill a report. We also covered how to declare report fields to access data from individual columns in the result set of the query used to fill the report. Finally, we learned how to generate reports that are displayed both in the user's web browser and in PDF format.

5
Working with Other Datasources

As we mentioned previously, JasperReports allows us to use not only databases, but also many other sources of data to generate reports. In this chapter, we will learn how to use datasources other than databases to create our reports. As creating web-based reports is by far the most common use of JasperReports, most examples in this chapter will use the technique described in Chapter 3, *Creating your First Report*, to stream a PDF report to a web browser through the `JasperRunManager.runReportToPdfStream()` method.

By the end of the chapter, we will be able to:

- Use empty datasources for reports that don't require an external datasource
- Use any implementation of `java.util.Map` as a datasource
- Use arrays or collections of Java objects as datasources
- Use TableModels as datasources
- Use XML files as datasources
- Use CSV files as datasources
- Create our own custom datasources

All the JasperReports datasources implement the `net.sf.jasperreports.engine.JRDataSource` interface. Reports are generated, or *filled*, by calling one of several static methods in the `net.sf.jasperreports.JasperFillManager` class. The `JasperFillManager` class contains several overloaded versions of the following three methods:

- `JasperFillManager.fillReport()`: This method creates a report and stores it in a `net.sf.jasperreports.engine.JasperPrint()` object.
- `JasperFillManager.fillReportToFile()`: This method creates a report and stores it in the filesystem as a JRPRINT file, JasperReports' native report format.
- `JasperFillmanager.fillReportToStream()`: This method generates a report and streams it through a `java.io.OutputStream` object.

Each of these methods takes an instance of a `net.sf.jasperreports.engine.JRDataSource` object as one of its arguments or an instance of `java.sql.Connection` to connect directly to the database. In the previous chapter, we saw how we can pass either a connection object or an instance of `JRResultSetDataSource` to a report template to generate a report from database data. Report templates don't need to change at all if we decide to change the type of datasource we will use to populate them. For most examples in this chapter, we will use a slightly modified version of the report template we used in the previous chapter, populating it with different types of datasources. As a matter of fact, the only example that will not use the template from the previous chapter is the one illustrating empty datasources, which we'll discuss next.

Empty datasources

The first type of datasources that we will discuss in this chapter are empty datasources. There is no way to create a report without using either a database connection or a datasource. If we need to create simple reports that require no external datasources, we can use an empty datasource to accomplish this. JasperReports provides the `net.sf.jasperreports.engine.JREmptyDataSource` that we can use for these situations. Let's create a simple report template containing only static data to illustrate this process.

```
<?xml version="1.0"?>
<jasperReport
  xmlns="http://jasperreports.sourceforge.net/jasperreports"
  xmlns:xsi="http://www.w3.org/2001/XMLSchema-instance"
        xsi:schemaLocation="http://jasperreports.sourceforge.net
                            /jasperreports http://jasperreports
                            .sourceforge.net/xsd/jasperreport.xsd"
        name="EmptyDataSourceReport">
```

```
    <detail>
      <band height="20">
        <staticText>
          <reportElement x="20" y="0" width="300" height="20"/>
            <text>
              <![CDATA[This simple report contains only static data.]]>
            </text>
        </staticText>
      </band>
    </detail>
  </jasperReport>
```

As we can see, the above JRXML template contains no fields or any kind of dynamic data. It simply generates some static text in the final report.

In the above JRXML template, we chose to add an XML `CDATA` section between the `<text>` and `</text>` tags. Although not strictly necessary in this case, doing so allows us to easily modify the text between these tags to include text that would prevent the XML from parsing successfully.

After compiling this report, the binary template `EmptyDataSource.jasper` is created in the filesystem. We can use the following servlet code to fill the report and stream it as a PDF to the web browser:

```
package net.ensode.jasperbook;

import java.io.IOException;
import java.io.InputStream;
import java.io.PrintWriter;
import java.io.StringWriter;
import java.util.HashMap;

import javax.servlet.ServletException;
import javax.servlet.ServletOutputStream;
import javax.servlet.http.HttpServlet;
import javax.servlet.http.HttpServletRequest;
import javax.servlet.http.HttpServletResponse;

import net.sf.jasperreports.engine.JREmptyDataSource;
import net.sf.jasperreports.engine.JRException;
import net.sf.jasperreports.engine.JasperRunManager;

public class EmptyDSReportServlet extends HttpServlet
{
  protected void doGet(HttpServletRequest request, HttpServletResponse
                                                             response)
  throws ServletException, IOException
  {
```

```
        ServletOutputStream servletOutputStream = response
                                                    .getOutputStream();
        InputStream reportStream = getServletConfig().getServletContext()
            .getResourceAsStream("/reports/EmptyDataSourceReport.jasper");
        try
        {
          JasperRunManager.runReportToPdfStream(reportStream,
             servletOutputStream, new HashMap(), new JREmptyDataSource());
          response.setContentType("application/pdf");
          servletOutputStream.flush();
          servletOutputStream.close();
        }
        catch (JRException e)
        {
          // display stack trace in the browser
          StringWriter stringWriter = new StringWriter();
          PrintWriter printWriter = new PrintWriter(stringWriter);
          e.printStackTrace(printWriter);
          response.setContentType("text/plain");
          response.getOutputStream().print(stringWriter.toString());
        }
      }
    }
```

After deploying this servlet and directing the browser to its URL, our browser will display the report as a PDF, as seen in the following screenshot:

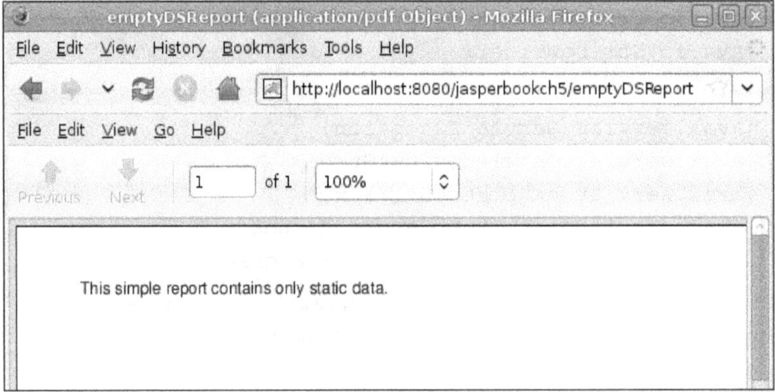

If empty datasources could be used only to generate reports with static data, they wouldn't be very useful; we might as well type the report with our favorite word processor. JasperReports allows us to pass parameters to a report. We can send some dynamic data to the report by sending it some parameters.

The following JRXML file demonstrates how parameters are retrieved in a report:

```
<?xml version="1.0"?>
<jasperReport xmlns="http://jasperreports.sourceforge.net
                                                    /jasperreports"
  xmlns:xsi="http://www.w3.org/2001/XMLSchema-instance"
        xsi:schemaLocation="http://jasperreports.sourceforge.net
            /jasperreports http://jasperreports.sourceforge.net/xsd
            /jasperreport.xsd"
            name="ParameterReport">
  <parameter name="paramName" class="java.lang.String"/>
  <detail>
    <band height="35">
      <staticText>
        <reportElement x="20" y="0" width="115" height="30"/>
          <text>
            <![CDATA[Parameter Value:]]>
          </text>
      </staticText>
      <textField>
        <reportElement x="135" y="11" width="100" height="19"/>
        <textFieldExpression>
          <![CDATA[$P{paramName}]]>
        </textFieldExpression>
      </textField>
    </band>
  </detail>
</jasperReport>
```

As can be seen in the above example, just like report fields, report parameters need to be declared at the beginning of the JRXML template. The `class` attribute defaults to `java.lang.String`. Even though our report parameter is a string, we included it in the JRXML template for clarity. The value of the parameter can be retrieved by using the syntax `$P{name}`, where `name` is the name of the parameter as declared in the JRXML template.

Every method in the `net.sf.jasperreports.engine.JasperFillManager` class contains a `java.util.Map` as one of its arguments. The purpose of this argument is to allow us to send some parameters to the report. So far we have been using empty `HashMap` classes for the reports we have been creating because none of them required any parameters. In the following example, we will send a parameter to the report template created by the previous JRXML file:

```
package net.ensode.jasperbook;

import java.io.IOException;
import java.io.InputStream;
import java.io.PrintWriter;
import java.io.StringWriter;
import java.util.HashMap;

import javax.servlet.ServletException;
import javax.servlet.ServletOutputStream;
import javax.servlet.http.HttpServlet;
import javax.servlet.http.HttpServletRequest;
import javax.servlet.http.HttpServletResponse;

import net.sf.jasperreports.engine.JREmptyDataSource;
import net.sf.jasperreports.engine.JRException;
import net.sf.jasperreports.engine.JasperRunManager;

public class ParameterReportServlet extends HttpServlet
{
  protected void doGet(HttpServletRequest request, HttpServletResponse
                                                             response)
  throws ServletException, IOException
  {
    ServletOutputStream servletOutputStream = response
                                                  .getOutputStream();
    InputStream reportStream = getServletConfig().getServletContext()
             .getResourceAsStream("/reports/ParameterReport.jasper");
    HashMap parameterMap = new HashMap();

    parameterMap.put("paramName", "paramValue");

    try
    {
      JasperRunManager.runReportToPdfStream(reportStream,
          servletOutputStream, parameterMap, new JREmptyDataSource());

      response.setContentType("application/pdf");
      servletOutputStream.flush();
      servletOutputStream.close();
    }
    catch (JRException e)
    {
```

```
        // display stack trace in the browser
         StringWriter stringWriter = new StringWriter();
         PrintWriter printWriter = new PrintWriter(stringWriter);
         e.printStackTrace(printWriter);
         response.setContentType("text/plain");
         response.getOutputStream().print(stringWriter.toString());
       }
     }
   }
```

In this servlet, we populate a key/value pair in an instance of `java.util.HashMap` and pass that `HashMap` to the report template through the `JasperRunManager.runReportToPdfStream()` method. As can be seen in the code, the key of the `Map` must match the parameter name in the JRXML template. After deploying the servlet and browsing the appropriate URL, we should see a PDF report being rendered in the browser, as demonstrated in the following screenshot:

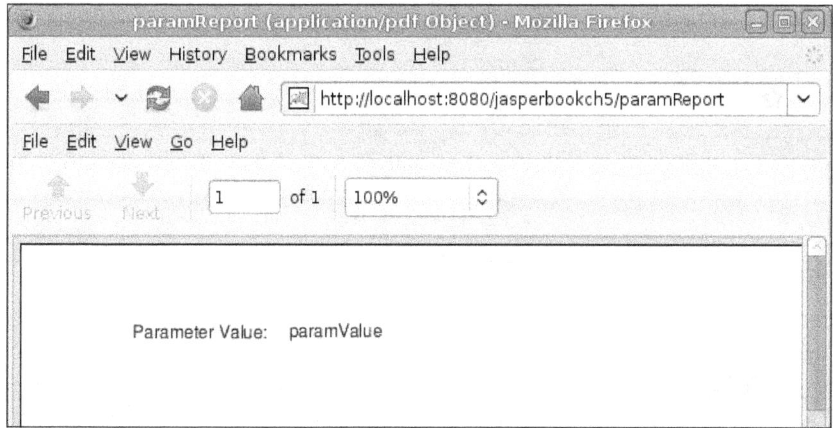

As we can see, the value we used for the `paramName` parameter in the servlet is displayed in the report.

Report parameters can be assigned values in the report template. That way, we can assign a default value to any parameter that contains a `null` value. The syntax to assign a default value to a report parameter is demonstrated in the following JRXML snippet:

```
<parameter name="someParam" class="java.lang.String">
    <defaultValueExpression>
       new java.lang.String("default parameter value");
    </defaultValueExpression>
</parameter>
```

Of course, if a parameter value is sent for a parameter that has a default value defined in the JRXML template, the value passed as a parameter takes precedence over the default value.

In addition to allowing us to send report parameters, all JasperReports reports have a number of built-in parameters that are always present, without us having to pass them explicitly. The following table lists all of the built-in report parameters:

Built-in Parameter	**Description**
`REPORT_PARAMETERS_MAP`	Can be used to obtain a reference to the instance of `java.util.Map` containing the parameters for the report.
`REPORT_DATA_SOURCE`	Can be used to obtain a reference to the instance of `net.sf.jasperreports.engine.JRDataSource` containing the fields for the report.
`REPORT_CONNECTION`	Can be used to obtain a reference to the `java.sql.Connection` passed to the report to connect to the database. If no database connection was passed to the report, it returns `null`.
`IS_IGNORE_PAGINATION`	JasperReports allows reports to be exported to several formats. Some of these formats are not page-oriented (for example, HTML). Setting the value of `IS_IGNORE_PAGINATION` to `Boolean.TRUE` makes JasperReports ignore all the page breaking settings in the report and generates a report containing a single (and in cases of reports with a lot of data, a very long) page.
`REPORT_LOCALE`	Determines the language to be used to generate reports when the report is localized. Localized reports are translated "on the fly" to the language corresponding to the value of this parameter.
`REPORT_RESOURCE_BUNDLE`	Indicates the `java.util.ResourceBundle` instance used to localize the report.
`REPORT_MAX_COUNT`	Indicates the maximum number of records that will be processed by the report.
`REPORT_SCRIPTLET`	When a report uses a scriptlet, this parameter returns a reference to it. If the report does not use a scriptlet, this parameter returns an instance of `net.sf.jasperreports.engine.JRDefaultScriptlet`.

Built-in Parameter	Description
REPORT_VIRTUALIZER	Sometimes reports are too large to be handled by the available memory. Setting this parameter to an instance of a class implementing net.sf.jasperreports.engine.JRVirtualizer will allow JasperReports to store temporary data in serialized form in order to reduce the amount of memory required to fill the report.

Some of the built-in parameters might not make sense yet, however, they will make more sense as we discuss some more JasperReports features in future chapters. The primary use of the REPORT_CONNECTION and REPORT_DATA_SOURCE built-in parameters is for passing them to subreports, which are discussed in detail in the next chapter. Report localization and report scriptlets will be covered in Chapter 8, *Other JasperReports Features*.

Map datasources

JasperReports allows us to use instances of any class implementing the java.util.Map interface as a datasource. We can use either an array or a collection of Map objects to generate a report. Each Map in the collection or array is a record that will be used to generate the data for each row in the detail area of the report. The JasperReports API provides an implementation of net.sf.jasperreports.engine.JRDataSource called net.sf.jasperreports.engine.data.JRMapArrayDataSource that we can use for using an array of Map objects as a datasource. The following example demonstrates this class in action:

```
package net.ensode.jasperbook;

import java.io.IOException;
import java.io.InputStream;
import java.io.PrintWriter;
import java.io.StringWriter;
import java.util.HashMap;
import java.util.Map;
```

```
import javax.servlet.ServletException;
import javax.servlet.ServletOutputStream;
import javax.servlet.http.HttpServlet;
import javax.servlet.http.HttpServletRequest;
import javax.servlet.http.HttpServletResponse;

import net.sf.jasperreports.engine.JRDataSource;
import net.sf.jasperreports.engine.JasperRunManager;
import net.sf.jasperreports.engine.data.JRMapArrayDataSource;

public class MapArrayDSReportServlet extends HttpServlet
{
  private JRDataSource createReportDataSource()
  {
    JRMapArrayDataSource dataSource;
    Map[] reportRows = initializeMapArray();

    dataSource = new JRMapArrayDataSource(reportRows);

    return dataSource;
  }

    private Map[] initializeMapArray()
    {
      HashMap[] reportRows = new HashMap[4];
      HashMap row1Map = new HashMap();
      HashMap row2Map = new HashMap();
      HashMap row3Map = new HashMap();
      HashMap row4Map = new HashMap();
      row1Map.put("tail_num", "N263Y");
      row1Map.put("aircraft_serial", "T-11");
      row1Map.put("aircraft_model", "39 ROSCOE TRNR RACER");
      row1Map.put("engine_model", "R1830 SERIES");

      row2Map.put("tail_num", "N4087X");
      row2Map.put("aircraft_serial", "BA100-163");
      row2Map.put("aircraft_model", "BRADLEY AEROBAT");
      row2Map.put("engine_model", "R2800 SERIES");

      row3Map.put("tail_num", "N43JE");
      row3Map.put("aircraft_serial", "HAYABUSA 1");
      row3Map.put("aircraft_model", "NAKAJIMA KI-43 IIIA");
      row3Map.put("engine_model", "R1830 SERIES");

      row4Map.put("tail_num", "N912S");
      row4Map.put("aircraft_serial", "9973CC");
      row4Map.put("aircraft_model", "PA18-150");
      row4Map.put("engine_model", "R-1820 SER");

      reportRows[0] = row1Map;
```

```
        reportRows[1] = row2Map;
        reportRows[2] = row3Map;
        reportRows[3] = row4Map;

        return reportRows;
      }

      protected void doGet(HttpServletRequest request,
                                         HttpServletResponse response)
      throws ServletException, IOException
      {
        ServletOutputStream servletOutputStream = response
                                                   .getOutputStream();
        InputStream reportStream = getServletConfig()
                               .getServletContext().getResourceAsStream
                                   ("/reports/AircraftReport.jasper");

      try
      {
        JRDataSource dataSource = createReportDataSource();

        JasperRunManager.runReportToPdfStream(reportStream,
                      servletOutputStream, new HashMap(), dataSource);

        esponse.setContentType("application/pdf");
        servletOutputStream.flush();
        servletOutputStream.close();
      }
      catch (Exception e)
      {
        // display stack trace in the browser
        StringWriter stringWriter = new StringWriter();
        PrintWriter printWriter = new PrintWriter(stringWriter);
        e.printStackTrace(printWriter);
        response.setContentType("text/plain");
        response.getOutputStream().print(stringWriter.toString());
      }
    }
  }
```

The `JRMapArrayDataSource` class has a single public constructor. This constructor takes an array of `Map` objects as its only argument. The array must already contain the maps to be used to populate the report before we pass it to `JRMapArrayDataSource`. `Map` keys must map field names in the report template so that the JasperReports engine knows what values to use to populate the report template's fields.

In addition to allowing us to use arrays of maps as datasources, JasperReports also allows us to use a collection of `Map` objects as a datasource. JasperReports provides an implementation of `JRDataSource` that we can use for this purpose; it is called `net.sf.jasperreports.engine.data.JRMapCollectionDataSource`. Using this class is very similar to using `JRMapArrayDataSource`. The only difference is that we pass a collection of `Map` objects to its constructor instead of an array. The following example illustrates this:

```
package net.ensode.jasperbook;

import java.io.IOException;
import java.io.InputStream;
import java.io.PrintWriter;
import java.io.StringWriter;
import java.util.ArrayList;
import java.util.Collection;
import java.util.HashMap;

import javax.servlet.ServletException;
import javax.servlet.ServletOutputStream;
import javax.servlet.http.HttpServlet;
import javax.servlet.http.HttpServletRequest;
import javax.servlet.http.HttpServletResponse;

import net.sf.jasperreports.engine.JRDataSource;
import net.sf.jasperreports.engine.JasperRunManager;
import net.sf.jasperreports.engine.data.JRMapCollectionDataSource;

public class MapCollectionDSReportServlet extends HttpServlet
{
  private JRDataSource createReportDataSource()
  {
    JRMapCollectionDataSource dataSource;
    Collection reportRows = initializeMapCollection();
    dataSource = new JRMapCollectionDataSource(reportRows);
    return dataSource;
  }

  private Collection initializeMapCollection()
  {
    ArrayList reportRows = new ArrayList();
    HashMap row1Map = new HashMap();
    HashMap row2Map = new HashMap();
    HashMap row3Map = new HashMap();
    HashMap row4Map = new HashMap();

    row1Map.put("tail_num", "N263Y");
    row1Map.put("aircraft_serial", "T-11");
```

```
    row1Map.put("aircraft_model", "39 ROSCOE TRNR RACER");
    row1Map.put("engine_model", "R1830 SERIES");

    row2Map.put("tail_num", "N4087X");
    row2Map.put("aircraft_serial", "BA100-163");
    row2Map.put("aircraft_model", "BRADLEY AEROBAT");
    row2Map.put("engine_model", "R2800 SERIES");

    row3Map.put("tail_num", "N43JE");
    row3Map.put("aircraft_serial", "HAYABUSA 1");
    row3Map.put("aircraft_model", "NAKAJIMA KI-43 IIIA");
    row3Map.put("engine_model", "R1830 SERIES");

    row4Map.put("tail_num", "N912S");
    row4Map.put("aircraft_serial", "9973CC");
    row4Map.put("aircraft_model", "PA18-150");
    row4Map.put("engine_model", "R-1820 SER");

    reportRows.add(row1Map);
    reportRows.add(row2Map);
    reportRows.add(row3Map);
    reportRows.add(row4Map);

    return reportRows;
  }

  protected void doGet(HttpServletRequest request,HttpServletResponse
                                                            response)
  throws ServletException, IOException
  {
    ServletOutputStream servletOutputStream = response
                                                .getOutputStream();
    InputStream reportStream = getServletConfig().getServletContext()
               .getResourceAsStream("/reports/AircraftReport.jasper");

    try
    {
      JRDataSource dataSource = createReportDataSource();

      JasperRunManager.runReportToPdfStream(reportStream,
                     servletOutputStream, new HashMap(), dataSource);

      response.setContentType("application/pdf");
      servletOutputStream.flush();
      servletOutputStream.close();
    }
    catch (Exception e)
    {
      // display stack trace in the browser
      StringWriter stringWriter = new StringWriter();
      PrintWriter printWriter = new PrintWriter(stringWriter);
```

```
        e.printStackTrace(printWriter);
        response.setContentType("text/plain");
        response.getOutputStream().print(stringWriter.toString());
      }
    }
  }
```

This example is very similar to the previous example. The only difference is that here we use a collection of `Map` objects instead of an array, and pass that to the constructor of `JRMapCollectionDataSource` so that the `Map` objects can be used to populate the report. It is worth noting that, even though we use `java.util.ArrayList` to group the `Map` objects, this does not have to be the case; any class implementing the `java.util.Collection` interface will work just as well.

Java objects as datasources

In addition to databases and maps, JasperReports allows us to use **Plain Old Java Objects (POJOs)** as datasources. We can use any Java object that adheres to the JavaBeans specification as a datasource. The only requirement for an object to adhere to the JavaBeans specification is that it must have no public properties, it must have a no-argument constructor, and it must provide getter and setter methods to access its private and protected properties. Let's create a Java object to be used as a datasource for our next example:

```
package net.ensode.jasperbook;
public class AircraftData
{
  public AircraftData(String tail, String serial, String model,
                                                 String engine)
  {
    setTailNum(tail);
    setAircraftSerial(serial);
    setAircraftModel(model);
    setEngineModel(engine);
  }
  public AircraftData()
  {
  }
  private String tailNum;
  private String aircraftSerial;
  private String aircraftModel;
  private String engineModel;
  public String getAircraftModel()
```

```
    {
      return aircraftModel;
    }
    public void setAircraftModel(String aircraftModel)
    {
      this.aircraftModel = aircraftModel;
    }
    public String getAircraftSerial()
    {
      return aircraftSerial;
    }
    public void setAircraftSerial(String aircraftSerial)
    {
      this.aircraftSerial = aircraftSerial;
    }
    public String getEngineModel()
    {
      return engineModel;
    }
    public void setEngineModel(String engineModel)
    {
      this.engineModel = engineModel;
    }
    public String getTailNum()
    {
      return tailNum;
    }
    public void setTailNum(String tailNum)
    {
      this.tailNum = tailNum;
    }
  }
```

This type of object is called a **data object** or a **data transfer object (DTO)** or a **value object (VO)**. As one of the requirements of the JavaBeans specification is to have a no-argument constructor, we included one in our Bean. We also included another convenience constructor that initializes all the properties in it. It is always a good idea to follow standard naming conventions, a practice we followed in the above code. Because this object's properties don't match the report template's field names, we need to modify the report template. The modified JRXML template looks like the following:

```
<?xml version="1.0" encoding="UTF-8" ?>
<jasperReport
  xmlns="http://jasperreports.sourceforge.net/jasperreports"
  xmlns:xsi="http://www.w3.org/2001/XMLSchema-instance"
        xsi:schemaLocation="http://jasperreports.sourceforge.net
                            /jasperreports http://jasperreports
                            .sourceforge.net/xsd/jasperreport.xsd"
```

```
name="AircraftReport">
<field name="tailNum" class="java.lang.String" />
<field name="aircraftSerial" class="java.lang.String" />
<field name="aircraftModel" class="java.lang.String" />
<field name="engineModel" class="java.lang.String" />
<pageHeader>
  <band height="30">
    <staticText>
      <reportElement x="0" y="0" width="69" height="24" />
      <textElement verticalAlignment="Bottom" />
      <text>
        <![CDATA[Tail Number: ]]>
      </text>
    </staticText>
    <staticText>
      <reportElement x="140" y="0" width="69" height="24" />
      <text>
        <![CDATA[Serial Number: ]]>
      </text>
    </staticText>
    <staticText>
      <reportElement x="280" y="0" width="69" height="24" />
        <text>
          <![CDATA[Model: ]]>
        </text>
    </staticText>
    <staticText>
      <reportElement x="420" y="0" width="69" height="24" />
      <text>
        <![CDATA[Engine: ]]>
      </text>
    </staticText>
  </band>
</pageHeader>
<detail>
  <band height="30">
    <textField>
      <reportElement x="0" y="0" width="69" height="24" />
      <textFieldExpression class="java.lang.String">
        <![CDATA[$F{tailNum}]]>
      </textFieldExpression>
    </textField>
    <textField>
      <reportElement x="140" y="0" width="69" height="24" />
      <textFieldExpression class="java.lang.String">
        <![CDATA[$F{aircraftSerial}]]>
      </textFieldExpression>
```

```
        </textField>
        <textField>
          <reportElement x="280" y="0" width="69" height="24" />
          <textFieldExpression class="java.lang.String">
            <![CDATA[$F{aircraftModel}]]>
          </textFieldExpression>
        </textField>
        <textField>
          <reportElement x="420" y="0" width="69" height="24" />
          <textFieldExpression class="java.lang.String">
            <![CDATA[$F{engineModel}]]>
          </textFieldExpression>
        </textField>
      </band>
    </detail>
  </jasperReport>
```

The only difference between this JRXML template and the one we've been using so far is in the field names. Initially, they were mapping to database columns, but now because we are using a JavaBean to populate the report, they map to the corresponding fields in the Bean.

As with `Map` objects, JasperReports allows us to group JavaBeans in either a collection or an array. The `JRDataSource` implementation used to pass an array of JavaBeans to a report template is called `net.sf.jasperreports.engine.JRBeanArrayDataSource`. The following example demonstrates how to use it:

```
package net.ensode.jasperbook;

import java.io.IOException;
import java.io.InputStream;
import java.io.PrintWriter;
import java.io.StringWriter;
import java.util.HashMap;

import javax.servlet.ServletException;
import javax.servlet.ServletOutputStream;
import javax.servlet.http.HttpServlet;
import javax.servlet.http.HttpServletRequest;
import javax.servlet.http.HttpServletResponse;

import net.sf.jasperreports.engine.JRDataSource;
import net.sf.jasperreports.engine.JasperRunManager;
import net.sf.jasperreports.engine.data.JRBeanArrayDataSource;

public class BeanArrayDSReportServlet extends HttpServlet
{
  private JRDataSource createReportDataSource()
```

```
{
  JRBeanArrayDataSource dataSource;
  AircraftData[] reportRows = initializeBeanArray();
  dataSource = new JRBeanArrayDataSource(reportRows);
  return dataSource;
}
private AircraftData[] initializeBeanArray()
{
  AircraftData[] reportRows = new AircraftData[4];
  reportRows[0] = new AircraftData("N263Y", "T-11",
                  "39 ROSCOE TRNR RACER", "R1830 SERIES");
  reportRows[1] = new AircraftData("N4087X", "BA100-163",
                  "BRADLEY AEROBAT", "R2800 SERIES");
  reportRows[2] = new AircraftData("N43JE", "HAYABUSA 1",
                  "NAKAJIMA KI-43 IIIA", "R1830 SERIES");
  reportRows[3] = new AircraftData("N912S", "9973CC", "PA18-150",
                  "R-1820 SER");
  return reportRows;
}
protected void doGet(HttpServletRequest request,HttpServletResponse
                                                        response)
throws ServletException, IOException
{
  ServletOutputStream servletOutputStream = response
                                         .getOutputStream();
  InputStream reportStream = getServletConfig().getServletContext()
              .getResourceAsStream("/reports/BeanDSReport.jasper");
  try
  {
    JRDataSource dataSource = createReportDataSource();
    JasperRunManager.runReportToPdfStream(reportStream,
                servletOutputStream, new HashMap(), dataSource);
    response.setContentType("application/pdf");
    servletOutputStream.flush();
    servletOutputStream.close();
  }
  catch (Exception e)
  {
  // display stack trace in the browser
    StringWriter stringWriter = new StringWriter();
    PrintWriter printWriter = new PrintWriter(stringWriter);
    e.printStackTrace(printWriter);
```

```
            response.setContentType("text/plain");
            response.getOutputStream().print(stringWriter.toString());
        }
    }
}
```

In this example, we populate an array with `AircraftData` objects, which contain the data to be displayed in the report. We then pass this array to the constructor of `JRBeanArrayDataSource`, then pass the new instance of `JRBeanArrayDataSource` to the `JasperRunManager.runReportToPdfStream()` method, which generates the report and exports it to PDF on the fly. The generated report is then displayed in the browser.

If we need to group our Beans in a collection instead of an array, JasperReports provides the `net.sf.jasperreports.engine.data.JRBeanCollectionDataSource()` class. This class has only one public constructor. It takes a `java.util.Collection` as its only parameter. It expects this collection to be populated with JavaBeans used to populate the report. The following example demonstrates how to use `JRBeanCollectionDataSource` to populate our reports:

```
package net.ensode.jasperbook;
import java.io.IOException;
import java.io.InputStream;
import java.io.PrintWriter;
import java.io.StringWriter;
import java.util.ArrayList;
import java.util.Collection;
import java.util.HashMap;
import javax.servlet.ServletException;
import javax.servlet.ServletOutputStream;
import javax.servlet.http.HttpServlet;
import javax.servlet.http.HttpServletRequest;
import javax.servlet.http.HttpServletResponse;
import net.sf.jasperreports.engine.JRDataSource;
import net.sf.jasperreports.engine.JasperRunManager;
import net.sf.jasperreports.engine.data.JRBeanCollectionDataSource;
public class BeanCollectionDSReportServlet extends HttpServlet
{
  private JRDataSource createReportDataSource()
  {
    JRBeanCollectionDataSource dataSource;
    Collection reportRows = initializeBeanCollection();
    dataSource = new JRBeanCollectionDataSource(reportRows);
    return dataSource;
```

```
    }
    private Collection initializeBeanCollection()
    {
      ArrayList reportRows = new ArrayList();
      reportRows.add(new AircraftData("N263Y", "T-11",
                            "39 ROSCOE TRNR RACER", "R1830 SERIES"));
      reportRows.add(new AircraftData("N4087X", "BA100-163",
                                 "BRADLEY AEROBAT", "R2800 SERIES"));
      reportRows.add(new AircraftData("N43JE", "HAYABUSA 1",
                             "NAKAJIMA KI-43 IIIA", "R1830 SERIES"));
      reportRows.add(new AircraftData("N912S", "9973CC", "PA18-150",
                                                      "R-1820 SER"));

      return reportRows;
    }
      protected void doGet(HttpServletRequest request,
                                      HttpServletResponse response)
      throws ServletException, IOException
      {
        ServletOutputStream servletOutputStream = response
                                               .getOutputStream();
        InputStream reportStream = getServletConfig().getServletContext()
                   .getResourceAsStream("/reports/BeanDSReport.jasper");
      try
      {
        JRDataSource dataSource = createReportDataSource();
        JasperRunManager.runReportToPdfStream(reportStream,
                    servletOutputStream, new HashMap(), dataSource);
        response.setContentType("application/pdf");
        servletOutputStream.flush();
        servletOutputStream.close();
      }
      catch (Exception e)
      {
      // display stack trace in the browser
        StringWriter stringWriter = new StringWriter();
        PrintWriter printWriter = new PrintWriter(stringWriter);
        e.printStackTrace(printWriter);
        response.setContentType("text/plain");
        response.getOutputStream().print(stringWriter.toString());
      }
    }
  }
```

The main difference between this example and the previous one is that here we are grouping our data objects in a `java.util.ArrayList` instead of an array. When using `JRBeanCollectionDataSource` to populate our reports, we do not necessarily need to use an `ArrayList` to populate our Beans. Any class implementing `java.util.Collection` will work just as well. `JRBeanCollectionDataSource` works the same as the previous `JRDataSource` implementations we have seen before; that is, it has a single public constructor that takes a collection of objects as its only argument. We can then use the initialized `JRBeanCollectionDataSource` to fill the report. This is accomplished by calling the `JasperRunManager.runReportToPdfStream()` method in the `doGet()` method in the last example.

TableModels as datasources

In many client-side applications, data is displayed in tabular format. A common requirement in many applications is to allow the user to print this tabular format as a report.

JasperReports provides an implementation of the `JRDataSource` interface that makes the task of generating reports from tabular format trivial for Swing applications. The class in question is `net.sf.jasperreports.engine.data.JRTableModelDataSource`. This class takes a `javax.swing.table.TableModel` as its only parameter. Because tables in Swing are populated through TableModels, all we need to do for generating a report from a table is to pass the appropriate table's `TableModel` as a parameter. The following example is a simple but complete Swing application demonstrating this process:

```
package net.ensode.jasperbook;

import java.awt.BorderLayout;
import java.awt.event.ActionEvent;
import java.awt.event.ActionListener;
import java.util.HashMap;

import javax.swing.JButton;
import javax.swing.JFrame;
import javax.swing.JLabel;
import javax.swing.JTable;
import javax.swing.table.DefaultTableModel;

import net.sf.jasperreports.engine.JRException;
import net.sf.jasperreports.engine.JasperFillManager;
import net.sf.jasperreports.engine.JasperPrint;
import net.sf.jasperreports.engine.data.JRTableModelDataSource;
import net.sf.jasperreports.view.JasperViewer;

public class TableModelReport
```

```
{
  JFrame mainFrame;
  BorderLayout borderLayout;
  DefaultTableModel tableModel;
  JTable table = new JTable();
  JButton generateReportButton = new JButton("Generate Report");

  public TableModelReport()
  {
    mainFrame = new JFrame("Aircraft Data");
    borderLayout = new BorderLayout();
    generateReportButton.addActionListener(new ReportGenerator());

    populateTableModel();

    mainFrame.setSize(640, 150);
    mainFrame.setVisible(true);
    mainFrame.getContentPane().setLayout(borderLayout);
    mainFrame.add(new JLabel("Aircraft Data"), BorderLayout.NORTH);
    table.setModel(tableModel);
    mainFrame.getContentPane().add(table, BorderLayout.CENTER);
    mainFrame.getContentPane().add(generateReportButton,
                                   BorderLayout.SOUTH);

    mainFrame.setVisible(true);
  }

  private void populateTableModel()
  {
    String[] columnNames = {"tail_num", "aircraft_serial",
                            "aircraft_model", "engine_model"};
    String[][] data = {
       {"N263Y", "T-11", " 39 ROSCOE TRNR RACER", "R1830 SERIES"},
       {"N4087X", "BA100-163", "BRADLEY AEROBAT", "R2800 SERIES"},
       {"N43JE", "HAYABUSA 1", "NAKAJIMA KI-43 IIIA", "R1830 SERIES"},
       {"N912S", "9973CC", "PA18-150", "R-1820 SER"}};

    tableModel = new DefaultTableModel(data, columnNames);
  }

  private void displayReport()
  {
    JasperPrint jasperPrint = generateReport();
    JasperViewer jasperViewer = new JasperViewer(jasperPrint);
    jasperViewer.setVisible(true);
  }

  private JasperPrint generateReport()
  {
    JasperPrint jasperPrint = null;
```

```
        try
        {
          jasperPrint = JasperFillManager.fillReport(
                        "reports/AircraftReportColumnIndex.jasper",
                         new HashMap(),
                         new JRTableModelDataSource(tableModel));
        }
        catch (JRException e)
        {
          e.printStackTrace();
        }
        return jasperPrint;
      }
      private class ReportGenerator implements ActionListener
      {
        public void actionPerformed(ActionEvent e)
        {
          displayReport();
        }
      }
        public static void main(String[] args)
        {
          new TableModelReport();
        }
    }
```

This example, when executed, will display a window on the screen with a table containing the **Aircraft Data** we have been using for most of the examples in this chapter, along with a **Generate Report** button at the bottom, as can be seen in the following screenshot:

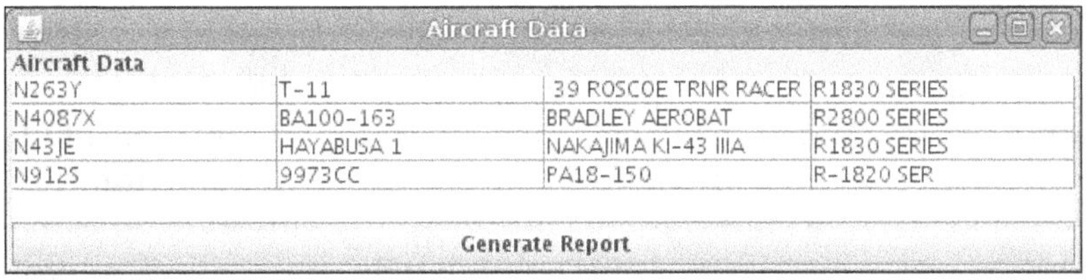

Aircraft Data

Aircraft Data

N263Y	T-11	39 ROSCOE TRNR RACER	R1830 SERIES
N4087X	BA100-163	BRADLEY AEROBAT	R2800 SERIES
N43JE	HAYABUSA 1	NAKAJIMA KI-43 IIIA	R1830 SERIES
N912S	9973CC	PA18-150	R-1820 SER

Generate Report

Clicking on the **Generate Report** button will generate the report in JasperReports' native format, and display it on the screen, which is ready for printing.

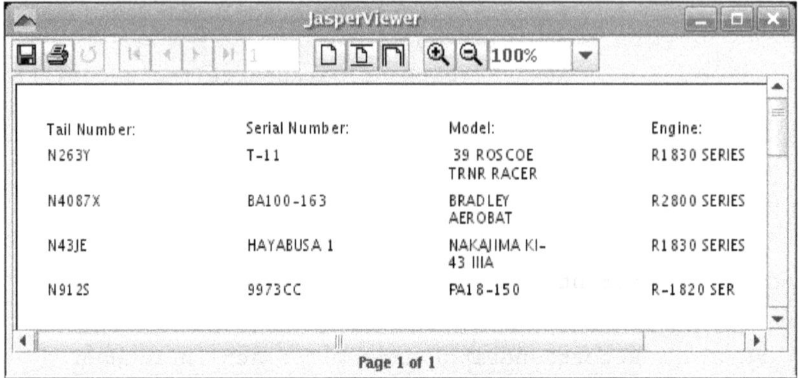

This window should look familiar. What we are seeing here is the same application we used before to view reports in JasperReports' native format. The only difference is that, instead of invoking the application from an ANT script, we invoked it programmatically from our code. The class in question is `net.sf.jasperreports.view.JasperViewer`; its constructor takes a `JasperPrint` object as its only parameter. A `JasperPrint` object is an in-memory representation of a report in JasperReports' native format. `JasperViewer` extends `javax.swing.JFrame`. Therefore, to make it visible, all we need to do is call its `setVisible()` method, passing the Boolean value `true` as a parameter. The `displayReport()` method in the last example illustrates this procedure.

Of course, before we can display the report, we need to generate it by filling the report template. Like we mentioned earlier, reports are generated from a `TableModel` by passing the `TableModel` as a parameter to the constructor of `JRTableModelDataSource`, as seen in the `generateReport()` method in the last example.

Normally, when generating reports from a `TableModel`, report fields must match the column names of `TableModel`. Sometimes it is impractical to use the column names as report fields. JasperReports provides a way to generate reports from TableModels without having to map the table columns to the report fields. We can name our report fields COLUMN_X, where x is the column index, starting with zero. The following JRXML template illustrates this. It will generate a report identical to the one in the previous screenshot.

```
<?xml version="1.0" encoding="UTF-8" ?>
<jasperReport
  xmlns="http://jasperreports.sourceforge.net/jasperreports"
  xmlns:xsi="http://www.w3.org/2001/XMLSchema-instance"
```

```
        xsi:schemaLocation="http://jasperreports.sourceforge
            .net/jasperreports http://jasperreports.sourceforge
            .net/xsd/jasperreport.xsd"
  name="AircraftReport">
  <field name="COLUMN_0" class="java.lang.String" />
  <field name="COLUMN_1" class="java.lang.String" />
  <field name="COLUMN_2" class="java.lang.String" />
  <field name="COLUMN_3" class="java.lang.String" />
  <pageHeader>
    <band height="30">
      <staticText>
        <reportElement x="0" y="0" width="69" height="24" />
        <textElement verticalAlignment="Bottom" />
        <text>
          <![CDATA[Tail Number: ]]>
        </text>
      </staticText>
      <staticText>
        <reportElement x="140" y="0" width="69" height="24" />
        <text>
          <![CDATA[Serial Number: ]]>
        </text>
      </staticText>
      <staticText>
        <reportElement x="280" y="0" width="69" height="24" />
        <text>
          <![CDATA[Model: ]]>
        </text>
      </staticText>
      <staticText>
        <reportElement x="420" y="0" width="69" height="24" />
        <text>
          <![CDATA[Engine: ]]>
        </text>
      </staticText>
    </band>
  </pageHeader>
  <detail>
    <band height="30">
      <textField>
        <reportElement x="0" y="0" width="69" height="24" />
        <textFieldExpression class="java.lang.String">
          <![CDATA[$F{COLUMN_0}]]>
        </textFieldExpression>
      </textField>
      <textField>
        <reportElement x="140" y="0" width="69" height="24" />
```

```
        <textFieldExpression class="java.lang.String">
          <![CDATA[$F{COLUMN_1}]]>
        </textFieldExpression>
      </textField>
      <textField>
        <reportElement x="280" y="0" width="69" height="24" />
        <textFieldExpression class="java.lang.String">
          <![CDATA[$F{COLUMN_2}]]>
        </textFieldExpression>
      </textField>
      <textField>
        <reportElement x="420" y="0" width="69" height="24" />
        <textFieldExpression class="java.lang.String">
          <![CDATA[$F{COLUMN_3}]]>
        </textFieldExpression>
      </textField>
    </band>
  </detail>
</jasperReport>
```

Because we changed the report name, we need to change a single line in the above example to make it work with this report template.

```
jasperPrint = JasperFillManager.fillReport("reports/AircraftReport
   .jasper", new HashMap(), new JRTableModelDataSource(tableModel));
```

Needs to be changed to:

```
jasperPrint = JasperFillManager.fillReport("reports/
              AircraftReportColumnIndex.jasper", new HashMap(),
              new JRTableModelDataSource(tableModel));
```

Had we not changed the report name, the code in the example would have worked without any modification with the new report template.

XML datasources

JasperReports allows us to use any well formatted XML document as a datasource. JasperReports uses XPath expressions to traverse the XML documents and extract the data for the report.

XPath is a language used to navigate through an XML document's attributes and elements. More information about XPath can be found at `http://www.w3.org/TR/xpath`.

For our next example, we'll need an XML file from which we'll read the data. The following XML document will serve this purpose:

```
<?xml version="1.0" encoding="UTF-8"?>
<AircraftData>
  <aircraft>
    <tail_num>N263Y</tail_num>
    <aircraft_serial>T-11</aircraft_serial>
    <aircraft_model>39 ROSCOE TRNR RACER</aircraft_model>
    <engine_model>R1830 SERIES</engine_model>
  </aircraft>
  <aircraft>
    <tail_num>N4087X</tail_num>
    <aircraft_serial>BA100-163</aircraft_serial>
    <aircraft_model>BRADLEY AEROBAT</aircraft_model>
    <engine_model>R2800 SERIES</engine_model>
  </aircraft>
  <aircraft>
    <tail_num>N43JE</tail_num>
    <aircraft_serial>HAYABUSA 1</aircraft_serial>
    <aircraft_model>NAKAJIMA KI-43 IIIA</aircraft_model>
    <engine_model>R1830 SERIES</engine_model>
  </aircraft>
  <aircraft>
    <tail_num>N912S</tail_num>
    <aircraft_serial>9973CC</aircraft_serial>
    <aircraft_model>PA18-150</aircraft_model>
    <engine_model>R-1820 SER</engine_model>
  </aircraft>
</AircraftData>
```

We need to make a slight modification to the JRXML template to be able to create a report from an XML datasource successfully. We need to add a `<fieldDescription>` element inside each `<field>` element. The following JRXML template illustrates this modification:

```
<?xml version="1.0" encoding="UTF-8" ?>
<jasperReport
  xmlns="http://jasperreports.sourceforge.net/jasperreports"
  xmlns:xsi="http://www.w3.org/2001/XMLSchema-instance"
        xsi:schemaLocation="http://jasperreports.sourceforge.net
            /jasperreports http://jasperreports.sourceforge.net
            /xsd/jasperreport.xsd"
  name="AircraftReportWithDescription">
  <field name="tail_num" class="java.lang.String">
    <fieldDescription>
      <![CDATA[tail_num]]>
```

```
    </fieldDescription>
  </field>
  <field name="aircraft_serial" class="java.lang.String">
    <fieldDescription>
      <![CDATA[aircraft_serial]]>
    </fieldDescription>
  </field>
  <field name="aircraft_model" class="java.lang.String">
    <fieldDescription>
      <![CDATA[aircraft_model]]>
    </fieldDescription>
  </field>
  <field name="engine_model" class="java.lang.String">
    <fieldDescription>
      <![CDATA[engine_model]]>
    </fieldDescription>
  </field>
  <pageHeader>
    <band height="30">
      <staticText>
        <reportElement x="0" y="0" width="69" height="24" />
        <textElement verticalAlignment="Bottom" />
        <text>
          <![CDATA[Tail Number: ]]>
        </text>
      </staticText>
      <staticText>
        <reportElement x="140" y="0" width="79" height="24" />
        <text>
          <![CDATA[Serial Number: ]]>
        </text>
      </staticText>
      <staticText>
        <reportElement x="280" y="0" width="69" height="24" />
        <text>
          <![CDATA[Model: ]]>
        </text>
      </staticText>
      <staticText>
        <reportElement x="420" y="0" width="69" height="24" />
        <text>
          <![CDATA[Engine: ]]>
```

```
        </text>
      </staticText>
    </band>
  </pageHeader>
  <detail>
    <band height="30">
      <textField>
        <reportElement x="0" y="0" width="69" height="24" />
        <textFieldExpression class="java.lang.String">
          <![CDATA[$F{tail_num}]]>
        </textFieldExpression>
      </textField>
      <textField>
        <reportElement x="140" y="0" width="69" height="24" />
        <textFieldExpression class="java.lang.String">
          <![CDATA[$F{aircraft_serial}]]>
        </textFieldExpression>
      </textField>
      <textField>
        <reportElement x="280" y="0" width="69" height="24" />
        <textFieldExpression class="java.lang.String">
          <![CDATA[$F{aircraft_model}]]>
        </textFieldExpression>
      </textField>

      <textField>
        <reportElement x="420" y="0" width="69" height="24" />
        <textFieldExpression class="java.lang.String">
          <![CDATA[$F{engine_model}]]>
        </textFieldExpression>
      </textField>
    </band>
  </detail>
</jasperReport>
```

The main difference between the above JRXML template and the one we've been using for most of our examples is the addition of the `<fieldDescription>` element for each field. The purpose of the `<fieldDescription>` element is to map the field name with the appropriate element in the XML file. In this particular example, field names match the corresponding XML elements, but this is not always the case; this is why `<fieldDescription>` elements are required for XML datasources.

The `JRDataSource` implementation we need to use to create reports from XML files is called `net.sf.jasperreports.engine.data.JRXmlDataSource`. The following example demonstrates how to use it:

```
package net.ensode.jasperbook;

import java.io.BufferedInputStream;
import java.io.IOException;
import java.io.InputStream;
import java.io.PrintWriter;
import java.io.StringWriter;
import java.util.HashMap;

import javax.servlet.ServletException;
import javax.servlet.ServletOutputStream;
import javax.servlet.http.HttpServlet;
import javax.servlet.http.HttpServletRequest;
import javax.servlet.http.HttpServletResponse;

import net.sf.jasperreports.engine.JasperRunManager;
import net.sf.jasperreports.engine.data.JRXmlDataSource;

public class XmlDSReportServlet extends HttpServlet
{
  protected void doGet(HttpServletRequest request, HttpServletResponse
                                                              response)
  throws ServletException, IOException
  {
    ServletOutputStream servletOutputStream = response
                                                .getOutputStream();
    InputStream reportStream = getServletConfig().getServletContext()
                            .getResourceAsStream("/reports
                            /AircraftReportWithDescription.jasper");

    try
    {
      JRXmlDataSource xmlDataSource = new JRXmlDataSource(
                      new BufferedInputStream(getServletConfig()
                      .getServletContext().getResourceAsStream(
                       "/reports/AircraftData.xml")),
                       "/AircraftData/aircraft");

      JasperRunManager.runReportToPdfStream(reportStream,
                servletOutputStream, new HashMap(), xmlDataSource);

      response.setContentType("application/pdf");
      servletOutputStream.flush();
      servletOutputStream.close();
    }
    catch (Exception e)
    {
    // display stack trace in the browser
      StringWriter stringWriter = new StringWriter();
      PrintWriter printWriter = new PrintWriter(stringWriter);
```

```
            e.printStackTrace(printWriter);
            response.setContentType("text/plain");
            response.getOutputStream().print(stringWriter.toString());
        }
    }
}
```

As can be seen in this example, we need to pass the XML document and an XPath expression to the constructor of `JRXmlDataSource`. The example assumes we saved the XML file shown at the beginning of this section as `AircraftData.xml`. In this particular case, we chose to pass the XML document as an input stream. `JRXmlDataSource` contains other constructors that allow us to send the XML document as an `org.w3c.dom.Document`, a `java.io.File`, or a string containing a **Uniform Resource Identifier (URI)**. Passing an XPath expression is optional. If we don't pass one, then the datasource will be created from all the subelements of the root element in the XML file. If we do pass one, then the datasource will be created from all the elements inside the XPath expression.

CSV datasources

JasperReports allows us to use **Comma Separated Value (CSV)** files as sources of data for our reports.

We will use the following CSV file to provide data for our report:

```
tail_num,aircraft_serial,aircraft_model,engine_model

N263Y,T-11,39 ROSCOE TRNR RACER,R1830 SERIES

N4087X,BA100-163,BRADLEY AEROBAT,R2800 SERIES

N43JE,HAYABUSA 1,NAKAJIMA KI-43 IIIA,R1830 SERIES

N912S,9973CC,PA18-150,R-1820 SER
```

The `JRDataSource` implementation we need to use to create reports from CSV files is called `net.sf.jasperreports.engine.data.JRCsvDataSource`. The following example demonstrates how to use it:

```
package net.ensode.jasperbook;

import java.io.IOException;
import java.io.InputStream;
import java.io.InputStreamReader;
import java.io.PrintWriter;
import java.io.StringWriter;
import java.util.HashMap;
```

```
import javax.servlet.ServletException;
import javax.servlet.ServletOutputStream;
import javax.servlet.http.HttpServlet;
import javax.servlet.http.HttpServletRequest;
import javax.servlet.http.HttpServletResponse;

import net.sf.jasperreports.engine.JasperRunManager;
import net.sf.jasperreports.engine.data.JRCsvDataSource;

public class CsvDSReportServlet extends HttpServlet
{
  protected void doGet(HttpServletRequest request, HttpServletResponse
                                                              response)
  throws ServletException, IOException
  {
    ServletOutputStream servletOutputStream = response
                                            .getOutputStream();
    InputStream reportStream = getServletConfig().getServletContext()
           .getResourceAsStream("/reports/AircraftReport.jasper");

    try
    {
      JRCsvDataSource jRCsvDataSource = new JRCsvDataSource(new
      InputStreamReader(getServletConfig().getServletContext()
                 .getResourceAsStream("/reports/AircraftData.csv")));

      jRCsvDataSource.setUseFirstRowAsHeader(true);

      JasperRunManager.runReportToPdfStream(reportStream,
                servletOutputStream, new HashMap(), jRCsvDataSource);

      response.setContentType("application/pdf");
      servletOutputStream.flush();
      servletOutputStream.close();
    }
    catch (Exception e)
    {
    // display stack trace in the browser
      StringWriter stringWriter = new StringWriter();
      PrintWriter printWriter = new PrintWriter(stringWriter);
      e.printStackTrace(printWriter);
      response.setContentType("text/plain");
      response.getOutputStream().print(stringWriter.toString());
    }
  }
}
```

Here, we need to pass the CSV filename to the constructor of the `JRCsvDataSource` class. The example assumes we saved the CSV file shown at the beginning of this section as `AircraftData.csv`. In this particular case, we chose to pass the CSV file as an input stream. The `JRCsvDataSource` class contains other constructors that allow us to send the CSV file as an instance of `java.io.File` or as an instance of `java.io.Reader`.

The `setUseFirstRowAsHeader()` method defined in `JRCsvDataSource` allows us to specify if we would like the first row in our CSV file to define the headers in our report. In our case, the CSV file we are using defines headers this way; therefore, we set this value to `true`. If our CSV file had not had header definitions on the first column, we would have had to set this value to `false` and invoke the `setColumnNames()` method of `JRCsvDataSource`to pass an array of string objects containing the header names to be used in our report.

Custom datasources

So far we've seen all of the `JRDataSource` implementations provided by JasperReports. If we need to extract data from a type of datasource not directly supported by JasperReports, we can create a class implementing `JRDataSource` to meet our needs. In this section, we will create a custom datasource allowing us to generate reports from an instance of `java.util.List` containing arrays of strings as its elements.

Writing a custom JRDataSource implementation

In our previous examples, all JasperReports datasources implement the `JRDataSource` interface. JasperReports also includes the `net.sf.jasperreports.engine.JRRewindableDataSource` interface. This interface extends `JRDatasource`, adding a single method called `moveFirst()`. The `moveFirst()` method is intended to move the cursor to the first element in the datasource. Our custom datasource will implement `JRRewindableDataSource`.
Let's take a look at the source of the custom datasource class.

```
package net.ensode.jasperbook;

import java.util.List;
import net.sf.jasperreports.engine.JRException;
import net.sf.jasperreports.engine.JRField;
import net.sf.jasperreports.engine.JRRewindableDataSource;
import org.apache.commons.lang.ArrayUtils;
```

```
public class ListOfArraysDataSource implements JRRewindableDataSource
{
  private List<String[]> listOfArrays;
  private String[] fieldNames;
  private int index = -1;
  public ListOfArraysDataSource(List<String[]> listOfArrays)
  {
    this.listOfArrays = listOfArrays;
  }
  public void moveFirst() throws JRException
  {
    index = 0;
  }
  public boolean next() throws JRException
  {
    index++;
    boolean returnVal = true;
    if (index >= listOfArrays.size())
    {
      returnVal = false;
    }
        return returnVal;
    }
    public Object getFieldValue(JRField jrField) throws JRException
{
    int fieldIndex = ArrayUtils.indexOf(fieldNames, jrField.getName());
    if (fieldIndex == ArrayUtils.INDEX_NOT_FOUND)
    {
      throw new JRException("Invalid field: " + jrField.getName());
    }
    return listOfArrays.get(index)[fieldIndex];
  }
  public void setListOfArrays(List<String[]> listOfArrays)
  {
    this.listOfArrays = listOfArrays;
  }
  public void setFieldNames(String[] fieldNames)
  {
    this.fieldNames = fieldNames;
  }
}
```

JasperReports datasources contain **elements** and **fields**. When using a database as a datasource, a database row is considered an element and the columns are considered fields. When using Java objects as datasources, each object is an element, and each attribute of the object is a field. For our custom datasource, each string array is considered an element, and each element in each array is considered a field.

The `next()` method defined in `JRDataSource` moves the cursor to the next element in the datasource. It returns a Boolean indicating if the move was successful or not. In our implementation, we have an `index` variable indicating the current element in the `List`. In our `next()` method, we increase `index` by one and return `false` if its value is greater than or equal to the size of the list; otherwise, we return `true`.

The `getFieldValue()` method retrieves the value for the current field in the datasource. It takes a `net.sf.jasperreports.engine.JRField` as its only argument. The `JRField` interface contains a `getName()` method that is used to retrieve the value of the field from its name. The way this is done depends on the type of datasource. For example, `JRBeanCollectionDataSource` uses utility classes from Apache Commons-BeanUtils to retrieve the Bean's property value from its name. `JRXmlDataSource` uses a combination of Xalan, an XML transformation library, and Apache Commons for its implementation.

For our `getFieldValue()` implementation, we followed one of the conventions established by the standard JasperReports `JRCsvDataSource`: The field names can be passed to the datasource itself. The `setFieldNames()` method in our custom datasource takes an array of strings specifying the field names for each of our elements. In our `getFieldValue()` implementation, with the help of the `ArrayUtils` class from the Apache Commons **lang** library, we obtain the index of the corresponding field in the `fieldNames` array and obtain the value of the corresponding element in the current array of strings.

For our `moveFirst()` implementation, we simply reset the values of the `index` variable to zero.

Using the custom JRDataSource implementation

Writing code to take advantage of a custom `JRDataSource` implementation is not much different from writing code that uses standard JasperReports datasources. After all, both custom and standard datasources implement the `JRDataSource` interface. The following example illustrates how to take advantage of our custom datasource implementation:

```
package net.ensode.jasperbook;

import java.io.IOException;
import java.io.InputStream;
import java.io.PrintWriter;
import java.io.StringWriter;
import java.util.ArrayList;
import java.util.HashMap;
import java.util.List;
import javax.servlet.ServletException;
import javax.servlet.ServletOutputStream;
import javax.servlet.http.HttpServlet;
import javax.servlet.http.HttpServletRequest;
import javax.servlet.http.HttpServletResponse;

import net.sf.jasperreports.engine.JRDataSource;
import net.sf.jasperreports.engine.JasperRunManager;

public class CustomDataSourceReportServlet extends HttpServlet
{
  private JRDataSource createReportDataSource()
  {
    String[] headers = {"tail_num", "aircraft_serial",
                        "aircraft_model", "engine_model"};
    ListOfArraysDataSource dataSource;
    List<String[]> reportRows = initializeListOfArrays();
    dataSource = new ListOfArraysDataSource(reportRows);
    dataSource.setFieldNames(headers);
    return dataSource;
  }
  private List<String[]> initializeListOfArrays()
  {
    List<String[]> reportRows = new ArrayList<String[]>();
    String[] row1 = {"N263Y", "T-11", "39 ROSCOE TRNR RACER",
                     "R1830 SERIES"};
    String[] row2 = {"N4087X", "BA100-163", "BRADLEY AEROBAT",
                     "R2800 SERIES"};
    String[] row3 = {"N43JE", "HAYABUSA 1", "NAKAJIMA KI-43 IIIA",
                     "R1830 SERIES"};
    String[] row4 = {"N912S", "9973CC", "PA18-150", "R-1820 SER"};
    reportRows.add(row1);
    reportRows.add(row2);
    reportRows.add(row3);
    reportRows.add(row4);
```

```
      return reportRows;
    }
    protected void doGet(HttpServletRequest request, HttpServletResponse
                                                                 response)
    throws ServletException, IOException
    {
      ServletOutputStream servletOutputStream = response
                                                   .getOutputStream();
      InputStream reportStream = getServletConfig().getServletContext()
               .getResourceAsStream("/reports/AircraftReport.jasper");
      try
      {
        JRDataSource dataSource = createReportDataSource();
        JasperRunManager.runReportToPdfStream(reportStream,
                      servletOutputStream, new HashMap(), dataSource);
        response.setContentType("application/pdf");
        servletOutputStream.flush();
        servletOutputStream.close();
      }
      catch (Exception e)
      {
       // display stack trace in the browser
        StringWriter stringWriter = new StringWriter();
        PrintWriter printWriter = new PrintWriter(stringWriter);
        e.printStackTrace(printWriter);
        response.setContentType("text/plain");
        response.getOutputStream().print(stringWriter.toString());
      }
    }
  }
```

In this example, we simply create an instance of our custom datasource, passing a list of arrays to the constructor. Once we have a reference to an instance of our datasource, we treat it just like any other JasperReports datasource. In this particular example, like in most examples of this chapter, we simply fill the report and display it in the browser as a PDF. We do this by invoking the static method `runReportToPdfStream()`, which is defined in the `net.sf.jasperreports.engine.JasperRunManager` class. The fact that we are using a custom datasource in this case does not make any difference.

One more way JasperReports can obtain data to be displayed in reports is by writing queries in the MDX query language. **MDX** stands for **Multi Dimensional Expressions** and is frequently used when working with **Online Analytical Processing (OLAP)** databases. MDX and OLAP are complex subjects with whole books dedicated to them; we couldn't do them justice in a short section of this book. To find out more about how to write MDX queries to populate reports, please refer to the `mondrian` sample included with the JasperReports project file.

Summary

This chapter has given us a quick run through all the non-database datasources supported by JasperReports, including how to create our own.

We have created reports that use no external datasources by using an empty datasource. We also used instances of a class implementing `java.util.Map` as a datasource by taking advantage of the `net.sf.jasperreports.engine.data.JRMapArrayDataSource` class. We learned to use plain Java objects as datasources by employing the `net.sf.jasperreports.engine.JRBeanArrayDataSource` and `net.sf.jasperreports.engine.JRBeanCollectionDataSource` classes. Besides, we also saw the use of a Swing `TableModel` and an XML document as a datasource by implementing the `net.sf.jasperreports.engine.data.JRTableModelDataSource` and `net.sf.jasperreports.engine.data.JRXmlDataSource` classes respectively. We also saw how **CSV** files can be used as datasources for our reports by taking advantage of the `net.sf.jasperreports.engine.data.JRCsvDataSource` class.

We have covered not only the datasources supported by JasperReports, but also created custom datasources by creating our own JRDataSource implementation. In addition to datasources, we also discussed how to pass data in the form of report parameters.

6

Report Layout and Design

All reports we have created so far contain simple layouts. In this chapter, we will cover how to create elaborate layouts, including, among other JasperReports features, adding background images or text to a report, logically grouping report data, conditionally printing report data, and creating subreports.

In this chapter, we will cover the following topics:

- How to control report-wide layout properties
- How to use styles to control the look of report elements
- How to add multiple columns to a report
- How to divide report data into logical groups
- How to allow report text fields to stretch for displaying large amounts of data
- How to control the layout of the report elements, including how to control their position, width, and height, among other layout properties
- How to use the `<frame>` element to visually group report elements
- How to add background text to a report
- How to add dynamic data to a report through report expressions and variables
- How to conditionally print data based on a report expression
- How to create subreports

Most of the techniques described in this chapter are encapsulated in the JRXML template. For this reason, we will not be showing Java code for most examples as it would illustrate nothing we haven't seen before. The code to generate all the reports in this chapter can be downloaded as part of this book's code, available at `http://www.packtpub.com/files/code/8082_Code.zip`.

Controlling report-wide layout properties

The `<jasperReport>` root element of the JRXML template contains a number of attributes that allow us to control report layout. The following table summarizes these attributes:

Attribute	Description	Valid values	Default values
`pageWidth`	Determines the width of the page in pixels.	Any non-negative integer.	`595`
`pageHeight`	Determines the height of the page in pixels.	Any non-negative integer.	`842`
`leftMargin`	Determines the left margin of the page in pixels.	Any non-negative integer.	`20`
`rightMargin`	Determines the right margin of the page in pixels.	Any non-negative integer.	`20`
`topMargin`	Determines the top margin of the page in pixels.	Any non-negative integer.	`30`
`bottomMargin`	Determines the bottom margin of the page in pixels.	Any non-negative integer.	`30`
`orientation`	Determines the orientation of the page.	`Portrait, Landscape`	`Portrait`
`whenNoDataType`	Determines how to create reports with no data in its datasource.	`NoPages, BlankPage, AllSectionsNoDetail`	`NoPages`
`isTitleNewPage`	Determines if the title section of the report will be printed on a separate page.	`true, false`	`false`
`isSummaryNewPage`	Determines if the summary section of the report will be printed on a separate page.	`true, false`	`false`

Most of the attributes in the table are self-explanatory, and their use should be intuitive. However, the `whenNoDataType` attribute deserves more explanation.

When there is no data in the report's datasource, by default JasperReports will not generate a report. This happens because the default value of `whenNoDataType` is `BlankPage`. Setting `whenNoDataType` to `BlankPage` will result in a single blank page report. If we would like a report displaying all sections except the detail section, we can accomplish this by setting `whenNoDataType` to `AllSectionsNoDetail`.

Setting text properties

JasperReports provides several ways to control text properties in the report. We can control the font, whether the text is bold, italic, underlined, its background and foreground colors, and so on.

Styles

One way JasperReports allows us to control text properties is by using the `<style>` element. This element allows us to control the foreground and background colors, the style of font (bold, italic, or normal), the font size, a border for the font, and many other attributes. Styles can extend other styles and add to or override properties of the parent style.

The following JRXML template illustrates the use of styles:

```
<?xml version="1.0" encoding="UTF-8"  ?>
<jasperReport name="ReportStylesDemo"
              xmlns="http://jasperreports.sourceforge.net/
                                                 jasperreports"
              xmlns:xsi="http://www.w3.org/2001/XMLSchema-instance"
                   xsi:schemaLocation="http://jasperreports
                      .sourceforge.net/jasperreports http://
                      jasperreports.sourceforge.net/xsd/
                      jasperreport.xsd">
  <style name="parentStyle" isDefault="true" fontName="Times"
         isBold="true" fontSize="13" pdfFontName="Helvetica-Bold"/>
  <style name="childStyle" fontSize="9"/>
  <detail>
    <band height="60">
      <staticText>
        <reportElement x="0" y="0" width="555" height="35" />
        <text>
          <![CDATA[This text uses the default report style,
                in this report it is called "parentStyle".]]>
```

```
            </text>
          </staticText>
          <staticText>
            <reportElement x="0" y="35" width="555" height="25"
                           style="childStyle"/>
            <text>
              <![CDATA[This text uses the style called "childStyle", this
                       style inherits all the properties of it's parents,
                       and overrides only the size.]]>
            </text>
          </staticText>
        </band>
      </detail>
    </jasperReport>
```

There are a few things to note about this example. First, notice the `isDefault="true"` attribute of the parent style. It makes all the report elements use this style by default without having to explicitly declare it. Because the first `<staticText>` element does not indicate what style to use, it will use the style named `parentStyle` by default. The style report used by the elements is defined by the `style` attribute of the `<reportElement>` style, as can be seen in the second `<staticText>` element in this template.

After compiling, filling, and exporting this JRXML template, we should have a report like the following:

This text uses the default report style, in this report it is called "parentStyle".

This text uses the style called "childStyle", this style inherits all the properties of it's parents, and overrides only the size.

The `<style>` element contains numerous attributes. The complete list of attributes can be found at `http://jasperforge.org/uploads/publish/jasperreportswebsite/JR%20Website/jasperreports_quickref.html#style`. Some of the most commonly used style attributes are outlined in the following table:

Attribute	Description	Valid values
forecolor	Indicates the text color.	Either a hexadecimal RGB value preceded by the # character or one of the following predefined values: black, blue, cyan, darkGray, gray, green, lightGray, magenta, orange, pink, red, yellow, white
backcolor	Indicates the text background color.	Refer to the valid values of forecolor above.
hAlign	Indicates the horizontal alignment of the element.	Center, Justified, Left, Right
vAlign	Indicates the vertical alignment of the element.	Bottom, Middle, Top
fontName	Indicates what font to use for the element.	A string indicating the font to be used.
fontSize	Indicates the size of the font.	An integer indicating the text size to be used.
isBold	Indicates whether the font is bold.	true, false
IsItalic	Indicates whether the font is italic.	true, false
IsUnderline	Indicates whether the font is underlined.	true, false
isStrikeThrough	Indicates whether the font is strikethrough.	true, false
lineSpacing	Determines the spacing between lines of text. A value of 1_1_2 indicates a line and a half of space between lines of text.	1_1_2, Double, Single
markup	Allows the element to be styled using HTML snippets, RTF snippets or the JasperReports specific "styled" markup.	none, html, rtf, styled

All the attributes that are not specific to textual information (`forecolor`, `backcolor`, `hAlign`, and so on) can be used for any kind of element, not just textual elements. The `markup` attribute is used to allow segments of the text to be styled using HTML markup, RTF snippets, or using the JasperReports specific `<style>` XML element. This is covered in detail later in this chapter.

Reusing styles through style templates

Although adding styles directly to a report template is fairly straightforward, it does have one disadvantage: if we need to add the same style to several reports, then we need to add the style individually to each report. Furthermore, if we need to change a style, then we need to go and modify the style definition in each report template.

To avoid the situation described in the previous paragraph, JasperReports allows us to define styles in a **style template**. When using a style template, styles can be defined separately from the report template and reused across several reports. Additionally, if we need to modify a style, all we need to do is modify the template, as opposed to having to update each report template individually.

The following JRXML template takes advantage of a style template that defines the text styles used in the report:

```
<?xml version="1.0" encoding="UTF-8"  ?>
<jasperReport name="ReportStylesDemo"
              xmlns="http://jasperreports.sourceforge.net
                     /jasperreports"
              xmlns:xsi="http://www.w3.org/2001/XMLSchema-instance"
                   xsi:schemaLocation="http://jasperreports
                       .sourceforge.net/jasperreports http://
                       jasperreports.sourceforge.net/xsd
                       /jasperreport.xsd">
  <template>
    "http://localhost:8080/jasperbookch6/reports/styles.jrtx"
  </template>
  <detail>
    <band height="60">
      <staticText>
        <reportElement x="0" y="0" width="555" height="35" />
        <text>
          <![CDATA[This text uses the default report style, in this
                   report it is called "parentStyle".]]>
        </text>
      </staticText>
      <staticText>
```

```
        <reportElement x="0" y="35" width="555" height="25"
                       style="childStyle"/>
        <text>
          <![CDATA[This text uses the style called "childStyle", this
                   style inherits all the properties of its parents,
                   and overrides only the size.]]>
        </text>
      </staticText>
    </band>
  </detail>
</jasperReport>
```

This JRXML template is a slightly modified version of the report template we saw in the previous report. The only difference is that, instead of defining styles in the JRXML template, they are defined in an external report style template. As we can see, we can import an external template by using the `<template>` tag. The body of this tag must be the URL or the full/relative path to the report template.

Notice how the URL for the style template is absolute, it includes the protocol, host, port, and path. This allows us to "publish" our template in a web server or servlet container and easily reuse it in the future.

The actual style template is shown below:

```
<?xml version="1.0"?>
<!DOCTYPE jasperTemplate
  PUBLIC "-//JasperReports//DTD Template//EN"
  "http://jasperreports.sourceforge.net/dtds/jaspertemplate.dtd">
<jasperTemplate>
  <style name="parentStyle" isDefault="true" fontName="Times"
         isBold="true" fontSize="13" pdfFontName="Helvetica-Bold"/>
  <style name="childStyle" style="parentStyle" fontSize="9"/>
</jasperTemplate>
```

Notice how a style template simply contains style definitions just like the ones we used inside a JRXML template. These definitions must be nested inside a `<jaspertemplate>` tag.

Setting text style for individual report elements

Report styles can be shared among several report elements. JasperReports allows us to set some properties for individual report elements. This can be accomplished by setting attributes in the `<textElement>` subelement of `<staticText>` and `<textField>`. These attributes are outlined in the following table:

Attribute	Description	Valid values
`lineSpacing`	Determines the spacing between lines of text. A value of `1_1_2` indicates a line and a half of space between lines of text.	`1_1_2`, `Double`, `Single`
`rotation`	Indicates the text direction by rotating it 90 degrees in the specified direction.	`Left`, `None`, `Right`
`textAlignment`	Indicates the horizontal alignment of the text.	`Center`, `Justified`, `Left`, `Right`
`markup`	Allows the text to be styled using a markup language such as HTML or RTF.	`none`, `html`, `rtf`, `styled`

The following snippet of a JRXML template illustrates how to use these attributes:

```
<staticText>
  <reportElement x="0" y="0" width="555" height="60"/>
  <textElement lineSpacing="Double" textAlignment="Center"
               verticalAlignment="Middle"/>
  <text>
    <![CDATA[This text is not really important.Its only purpose is
             to illustrate text style.]]>
  </text>
</staticText>
```

This snippet would generate text both horizontally and vertically centered using double-spacing.

This text is not really important.

Its only purpose is to illustrate text style.

Notice how the text is double-spaced and vertically and horizontally centered, like we specified in the attributes of the `<textElement>` JRXML element.

It is worth noting that because `<textElement>` is a subelement of both `<staticText>` and `<textField>`, the technique described here can be applied to static text as well as to dynamic text coming from a report expression.

Use styles to create more maintainable reports

In the short run, it is usually faster to set the text properties using the `<textElement>` element. However, doing it this way prevents us from reusing the styles across several elements. Report styles allow us to do this, and they provide much more control than the attributes in `<textElement>`, saving us time in the long run.

Using markup to style text

Like we briefly mentioned in past sections, JasperReports allows us to use markup languages such as HTML and RTF to style report text. The JasperReports specific XML `<style>` element can also be used to style report text.

The techniques illustrated in the following sections can be used for JRXML `<staticText>` and `<textField>` elements. For simplicity, all the examples use static text, but the techniques can be used just as easily for dynamically generated text rendered inside a `<textField>` element.

Styled text

The text property modification techniques described so far apply the text properties to a complete text element. Sometimes we want certain segments of a text element to have a different style. For example, we might want to emphasize a word by making it bold or italic. JasperReports allows us to do this by using styled text.

As we have seen in previous sections, both the `<textElement>` and `<style>` elements contain a `markup` attribute, and we need to set this attribute to `styled` to use styled text. When this attribute is set to `styled`, the text inside a `<textField>` or `<staticText>` element is not interpreted as regular text, but as XML instead. The text to be styled needs to be nested between `<style>` elements to obtain a different style from the rest of the text. This `<style>` element contains attributes similar to the JRXML `<style>` element discussed previously.

The following table lists all the attributes available to this `<style>` element:

Attribute	Description	Valid values
`fontName`	Indicates the font to be used for the element.	A string indicating the font to be used.
`size`	Indicates the size of the font.	An integer indicating the text size to be used.
`isBold`	Indicates whether the font is bold.	`true, false`
`IsItalic`	Indicates whether the font is italic.	`true, false`
`IsUnderline`	Indicates whether the font is underlined.	`true, false`
`isStrikeThrough`	Indicates whether the font is strikethrough.	`true, false`
`pdfFontName`	Indicates the name of the font to be used if the report is exported to PDF.	`Courier, Courier-Bold, Courier-BoldOblique, Courier-Oblique, Helvetica, Helvetica Bold, Helvetica BoldOblique, Helvetica Oblique, Symbol, Times-Roman, Times-Bold, Times-BoldItalic, Times-Italic, ZapfDingbats`
`pdfEncoding`	Indicates the encoding to be used if the report is exported to PDF.	A string indicating the encoding to be used when the report is exported to PDF.
`isPdfEmbedded`	Indicates whether the PDF font should be embedded in the document.	`true, false`
`forecolor`	Indicates the color of the text.	See valid values for `forecolor` in the *Styles* section of this chapter.
`backcolor`	Indicates the background color of the text.	See valid values for `backcolor` in the *Styles* section of this chapter.

The following example illustrates how to use the `styled` value for the `markup` attribute to style text in a report:

```
<?xml version="1.0" encoding="UTF-8"?>
<jasperReport
  xmlns="http://jasperreports.sourceforge.net/jasperreports"
  xmlns:xsi="http://www.w3.org/2001/XMLSchema-instance"
        xsi:schemaLocation="http://jasperreports.sourceforge.net
            /jasperreports http://jasperreports.sourceforge.net/xsd
            /jasperreport.xsd"
            name="StyledTextMarkupDemoReport" pageWidth="595"
            pageHeight="842" columnWidth="555" leftMargin="20"
            rightMargin="20" topMargin="30" bottomMargin="30">
  <detail>
    <band height="50">
      <staticText>
        <reportElement x="0" y="0" width="500" height="48"/>
        <textElement markup="styled">
          <font size="10" fontName="Courier"/>
        </textElement>
        <text>
          <![CDATA[This text is <style isBold="true">styled</style>
                   using the value of
                   <style isItalic="true">styled</style>
                   for the <style forecolor="blue">markup</style>
                   attribute.]]>
        </text>
      </staticText>
    </band>
  </detail>
</jasperReport>
```

As we can see in the above example, all we need to do is wrap the sections of text we want to style in `<style>` tags, and then use the appropriate attributes (`isBold`, `isItalic`, and so on) to style the text.

This JRXML template will generate a report containing text using the expected font styles.

This text is **styled** using the value of *styled* forthe markup attribute.

HTML

In addition to using styled text to set text style, we can use HTML markup for the same purpose. It allows us to use familiar HTML tags, such as `<b>`, `<font>`, and `<i>` to style our text. The following example illustrates how to do this:

```
<?xml version="1.0" encoding="UTF-8"?>
<jasperReport xmlns="http://jasperreports.sourceforge.net
                    /jasperreports"
  xmlns:xsi="http://www.w3.org/2001/XMLSchema-instance"
        xsi:schemaLocation="http://jasperreports.sourceforge.net
            /jasperreports http://jasperreports.sourceforge.net/xsd
            /jasperreport.xsd"
        name="HtmlMarkupDemoReport" pageWidth="595"
        pageHeight="842" columnWidth="555"
        leftMargin="20" rightMargin="20" topMargin="30"
        bottomMargin="30">
  <detail>
    <band height="50">
      <staticText>
        <reportElement x="0" y="0" width="500" height="48"/>
        <textElement markup="html">
          <font size="10" fontName="Courier"/>
        </textElement>
        <text>
          <![CDATA[This text is <b>styled</b> using the value of
                   <i>html</i> for the <font color="blue">
                   markup</font> attribute.]]>
        </text>
      </staticText>
    </band>
  </detail>
</jasperReport>
```

As we can see, all we need to do is set the value of the `markup` attribute of the `<textElement>` element to `"html"`. After that, we can use HTML markup in the body of the `<text>` element, which then will be rendered as expected in the report.

This JRXML template will generate a report containing text using the expected font styles.

This text is **styled** using the value of *html* for the markup attribute.

Rich Text Format

The third markup style supported "out of the box" by JasperReports is Rich Text Format, or RTF. RTF is a format that is supported by almost all existing word processors. RTF markup is human readable; JasperReports is able to interpret RTF markup and render text as expected.

The following example illustrates how to format text using RTF:

```
<?xml version="1.0" encoding="UTF-8"?>
<jasperReport
  xmlns="http://jasperreports.sourceforge.net/jasperreports"
  xmlns:xsi="http://www.w3.org/2001/XMLSchema-instance"
        xsi:schemaLocation="http://jasperreports.sourceforge
                            .net/jasperreports http://jasperreports
                            .sourceforge.net/xsd/jasperreport.xsd"
            name="RtfMarkupDemoReport" pageWidth="595"
                  pageHeight="842" columnWidth="555" leftMargin="20"
                  rightMargin="20" topMargin="30" bottomMargin="30">
  <detail>
    <band height="50">
      <staticText>
        <reportElement x="0" y="0" width="500" height="48"/>
        <textElement markup="rtf">
          <font size="10" fontName="Courier"/>
        </textElement>
        <text>
          {\rtf1\ansi\deff0\adeflang1025
            {\fonttbl
              {\f0\froman\fprq2\fcharset0 Times New Roman;}
              {\f1\froman\fprq2\fcharset0 Times New Roman;}
              {\f2\fswiss\fprq2\fcharset0 Arial;}
              {\f3\fnil\fprq2\fcharset128 AlMothnna;}
              {\f4\fnil\fprq1\fcharset128 Courier 10 Pitch;}
              {\f5\fmodern\fprq1\fcharset128 Courier New;}
              {\f6\fmodern\fprq1\fcharset128 Courier
                {\*\falt Courier New};
              }
              {\f7\fnil\fprq2\fcharset0 DejaVu Sans;}
            }
            {\colortbl;\red0\green0\blue0;\red35\green0\blue220;
             \red128\green128\blue128;
            }
            {\stylesheet
              {\s1\cf0
                {\*\hyphen2\hyphlead2\hyphtrail2\hyphmax0}
               \rtlch\af7\afs24\lang255\ltrch\dbch\af7
```

```
    \langfe255\hich\f0\fs24\lang1033\loch\f0\fs24
    \lang1033\snext1 Normal;
   }
   {\s2\sb240\sa120\keepn\cf0
     {\*\hyphen2\hyphlead2\hyphtrail2\hyphmax0}
    \rtlch\afs28\lang255\ltrch\dbch\langfe255\hich
    \f2\fs28\lang1033\loch\f2\fs28\lang1033
    \sbasedon1\snext3 Heading;
   }
   {\s3\sa120\cf0
     {\*\hyphen2\hyphlead2\hyphtrail2\hyphmax0}
    \rtlch\af7\afs24\lang255\ltrch\dbch\af7
    \langfe255\hich\f0\fs24\lang1033\loch\f0\fs24
    \lang1033\sbasedon1\snext3 Body Text;
   }
   {\s4\sa120\cf0
     {\*\hyphen2\hyphlead2\hyphtrail2\hyphmax0}
    \rtlch\af7\afs24\lang255\ltrch\dbch\af7
    \langfe255\hich\f0\fs24\lang1033\loch\f0\fs24
    \lang1033\sbasedon3\snext4 List;
   }
   {\s5\sb120\sa120\cf0
     {\*\hyphen2\hyphlead2\hyphtrail2\hyphmax0}
    \rtlch\af7\afs24\lang255\ai\ltrch\dbch\af7
    \langfe255\hich\f0\fs24\lang1033\i\loch\f0\fs24
    \lang1033\i\sbasedon1\snext5 caption;
   }
   {\s6\cf0
     {\*\hyphen2\hyphlead2\hyphtrail2\hyphmax0}
     \rtlch\af7\afs24\lang255\ltrch\dbch\af7
     \langfe255\hich\f0\fs24\lang1033\loch\f0\fs24
     \lang1033\sbasedon1\snext6 Index;
   }
 }
 {\info
   {\creatim\yr2009\mo3\dy29\hr17\min23}
   {\revtim\yr0\mo0\dy0\hr0\min0}
   {\printim\yr0\mo0\dy0\hr0\min0}
   {\comment StarWriter}
   {\vern3000}
 }
 \deftab709
 {\*\pgdsctbl
   {\pgdsc0\pgdscuse195\pgwsxn12240\pghsxn15840
    \marglsxn1134\margrsxn1134\margtsxn1134
    \margbsxn1134\pgdscnxt0 Standard;
   }
```

```
                }
              \paperh15840\paperw12240\margl1134\margr1134
              \margt1134\margb1134\sectd\sbknone\pgwsxn12240
              \pghsxn15840\marglsxn1134\margrsxn1134
              \margtsxn1134\margbsxn1134\ftnbj\ftnstart1
              \ftnrstcont\ftnnar\aenddoc\aftnrstcont\aftnstart1
              \aftnnrlc\pard\plain\ltrpar\s1\cf0
                {\*\hyphen2\hyphlead2\hyphtrail2\hyphmax0}
              \rtlch\af7\afs22\lang255\ltrch\dbch\af7\langfe255
              \hich\f6\fs22\lang1033\loch\f6\fs22\lang1033
                {\rtlch \ltrch\loch\f6\fs22\lang1033\i0\b0
                 This text is
                  {\rtlch\ltrch\dbch\hich\b\loch\b styled}
                 using the value of
                  {\rtlch\ltrch\dbch\hich\i\loch\i rtf}
                 for the {\cf2 markup} attribute.
                }
             \par
             }
           </text>
         </staticText>
       </band>
     </detail>
   </jasperReport>
```

The highlighted code is the RTF markup. When the report is rendered, the text inside the `<textElement>` and `<text>` elements will be rendered using the correct style.

> Don't worry too much if you don't understand RTF markup. Very few people create RTF by hand these days. As a matter of fact, we admit we cheated to create this example! We simply wrote the text in a word processor, applied the desired styles, and saved in RTF format. Then, we opened the RTF file in a text editor and pasted the markup into the JRXML file.

This text is **styled** using the value of *rtf* for the markup attribute.

Setting a report's background

Reports can have elements that appear in the report background, behind all other report elements. We can add any report element to the background by using the JRXML `<background>` element. The following JRXML template demonstrates how to do this:

```
<?xml version="1.0" encoding="UTF-8"  ?>
<jasperReport
  xmlns="http://jasperreports.sourceforge.net/jasperreports"
  xmlns:xsi="http://www.w3.org/2001/XMLSchema-instance"
        xsi:schemaLocation="http://jasperreports.sourceforge
            .net/jasperreports http://jasperreports.sourceforge
            .net/xsd/jasperreport.xsd"
            name="BackgroundDemoReport" >
  <style name="centeredText" hAlign="Center" vAlign="Middle" />
  <style name="boldCentered" style="centeredText" isBold="true" />
  <style name="backgroundStyle" style="boldCentered"
         fontName="Helvetica" pdfFontName="Helvetica-Bold"
         forecolor="lightGray" fontSize="90"/>
  <background>
    <band height="782">
      <staticText>
        <reportElement x="0" y="0" width="555" height="782"
                       style="backgroundStyle" mode="Transparent" />
        <textElement rotation="None"/>
        <text>
          <![CDATA[SAMPLE]]>
        </text>
      </staticText>
    </band>
  </background>
  <title>
    <band height="60">
      <staticText>
        <reportElement x="0" y="0" width="555" height="60"
                       style="boldCentered" />
        <text>
          <![CDATA[Report Background Demo]]>
        </text>
      </staticText>
    </band>
  </title>
  <detail>
```

```
        <band height="600">
          <staticText>
            <reportElement x="0" y="300" width="555" height="60"
                           mode="Transparent" style="centeredText" />
            <text>
              <![CDATA[This report demonstrates how to set the report
                       background.]]>
            </text>
          </staticText>
        </band>
      </detail>
    </jasperReport>
```

The JRXML `<background>` element (highlighted in this JRXML template), just like all other JRXML elements that create a report section, contains a single `<band>` element as its only subelement. The `<background>` element is different from other section elements because it is designed to span a complete page, with its contents shown behind all other report elements. It is worth noting that, in order to allow report backgrounds to display correctly, the `mode` attribute of other report sections must be set to `Transparent`.

After compiling the last JRXML template and filling the resulting Jasper template, we should obtain a report like the following:

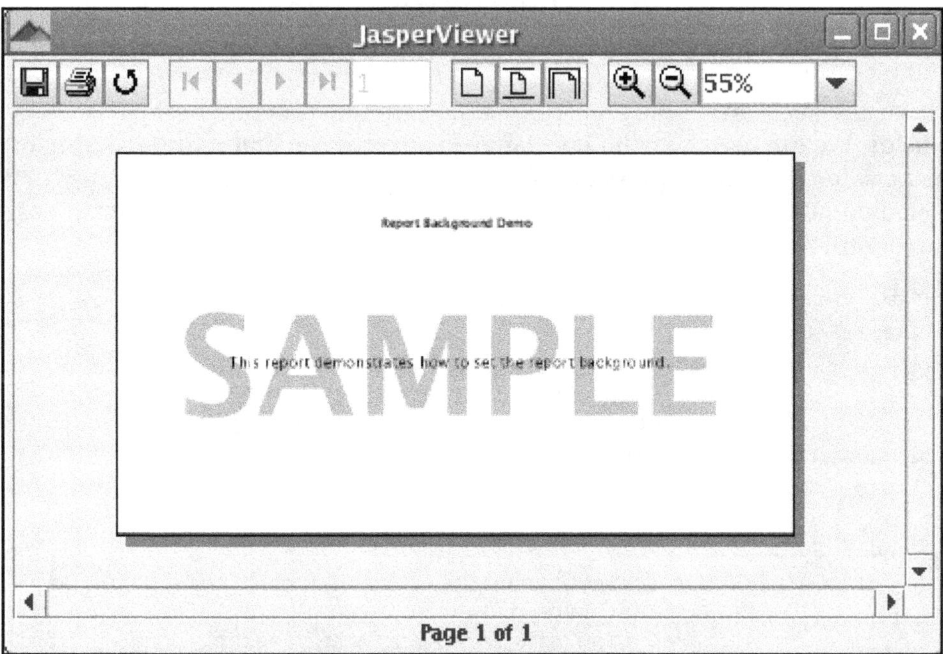

Notice how the background text appears to be behind the text in the `<band>` element.

It is common to set an image, usually a company logo, as a watermark like a report background. In the next chapter we will learn how to add images to a report. The techniques explained there can be used to add an image as a report background.

Report expressions

Using report expressions, another feature of JasperReports, we can display calculated data on a report. Calculated data is the data that is not static and not specifically passed as a report parameter or a datasource field.

Report expressions are built from combining report parameters, fields, and static data. By default, report expressions can be built using the Java language, but JasperReports can support any other language supported by the JVM. The JasperReports project file includes examples of using BeanShell and Groovy to build report expressions.

By far the most commonly used report expressions are Java expressions, so we will cover only those. Refer to the examples distributed with the JasperReports project ZIP file if you need to create expressions in BeanShell or Groovy.

We have already seen simple report expressions in the form of report parameters and fields. We can use any valid Java language expression that returns a string or a numeric value as report expressions. For example, we can concatenate strings or call any method in a report expression. The following JRXML template demonstrates these concepts:

```
<?xml version="1.0" encoding="UTF-8"  ?>
<jasperReport
  xmlns="http://jasperreports.sourceforge.net/jasperreports"
         xmlns:xsi="http://www.w3.org/2001/XMLSchema-instance"
               xsi:schemaLocation="http://jasperreports.sourceforge
                    .net/jasperreports http://jasperreports
                    .sourceforge.net/xsd/jasperreport.xsd"
               name="ReportExpressionsDemo">
  <queryString>
    <![CDATA[SELECT (select count(*) from aircraft_models am where
             am.aircraft_type_id = 4)
             AS fixed_wing_single_engine_cnt, (select count(*) from
             aircraft_models am where am.aircraft_type_id = 5)
```

```
            AS fixed_wing_multiple_engine_cnt,(select count(*) from
                    aircraft_models am where am.aircraft_type_id = 6)
            AS rotorcraft_cnt]]>
</queryString>
<field name="fixed_wing_single_engine_cnt"
       class="java.lang.Integer" />
<field name="fixed_wing_multiple_engine_cnt"
       class="java.lang.Integer" />
<field name="rotorcraft_cnt" class="java.lang.Integer" />
<detail>
  <band height="100">
    <textField>
      <reportElement x="20" y="0" height="20" width="500" />
      <textFieldExpression>
        <![CDATA["Total Fixed Wing Single Engine Aircraft Models: "
                  + $F{fixed_wing_single_engine_cnt}]]>
        </textFieldExpression>
    </textField>
    <textField>
      <reportElement x="20" y="20" height="20" width="500" />
      <textFieldExpression>
        <![CDATA["Total Fixed Wing Multiple Engine Aircraft " +
                  "Models:" + $F{fixed_wing_multiple_engine_cnt}]]>
      </textFieldExpression>
    </textField>
    <textField>
      <reportElement x="20" y="40" height="20" width="500" />
      <textFieldExpression>
        <![CDATA["Total Fixed Wing Aircraft Models: " +
                 ($F{fixed_wing_single_engine_cnt}.intValue() +
                  $F{fixed_wing_multiple_engine_cnt}.intValue())]]>
      </textFieldExpression>
    </textField>
    <textField>
      <reportElement x="20" y="60" height="20" width="500" />
      <textFieldExpression>
        <![CDATA["Total Rotorcraft Aircraft Models: " +
                  $F{rotorcraft_cnt}]]>
      </textFieldExpression>
    </textField>
    <textField>
      <reportElement x="20" y="80" height="20" width="500" />
      <textFieldExpression>
        <![CDATA["Total Aircraft Models Reported: " +
```

```
                         ($F{fixed_wing_single_engine_cnt}.intValue() +
                           $F{fixed_wing_multiple_engine_cnt}.intValue() +
                           $F{rotorcraft_cnt}.intValue())]]>
          </textFieldExpression>
        </textField>
      </band>
    </detail>
  </jasperReport>
```

This JRXML generates a report on the total number of fixed-wing single engine, fixed-wing multiple engine, and rotorcraft aircraft in the `flightstats` database. It then calculates the total number of fixed-wing aircraft in the database by adding the first two fields. Lastly, it calculates the total number of aircraft reported by adding all three fields.

The following servlet generates a PDF report from the jasper file generated by the previous JRXML template and directs it to the browser:

```
package net.ensode.jasperbook;

import java.io.IOException;
import java.io.InputStream;
import java.io.PrintWriter;
import java.io.StringWriter;
import java.sql.Connection;
import java.sql.DriverManager;
import java.util.HashMap;

import javax.servlet.ServletException;
import javax.servlet.ServletOutputStream;
import javax.servlet.http.HttpServlet;
import javax.servlet.http.HttpServletRequest;
import javax.servlet.http.HttpServletResponse;

import net.sf.jasperreports.engine.JasperRunManager;

public class ReportExpressionsDemoServlet extends HttpServlet
{
  protected void doGet(HttpServletRequest request,HttpServletResponse
                                                              response)
  throws ServletException, IOException
  {
    Connection connection;
    ServletOutputStream servletOutputStream = response
                                                   .getOutputStream();
    InputStream reportStream = getServletConfig().getServletContext()
                               .getResourceAsStream("/reports
                               /ReportExpressionsDemo.jasper");
```

```
        try
        {
          Class.forName("com.mysql.jdbc.Driver");
          connection = DriverManager.getConnection("jdbc:mysql:
                       //localhost:3306/flightstats?
                       user=dbuser&password=secret");
          JasperRunManager.runReportToPdfStream(reportStream,
                          servletOutputStream, new HashMap(), connection);
          connection.close();
          response.setContentType("application/pdf");
          servletOutputStream.flush();
          servletOutputStream.close();
        }
        catch (Exception e)
        {
          // display stack trace in the browser
          StringWriter stringWriter = new StringWriter();
          PrintWriter printWriter = new PrintWriter(stringWriter);
          e.printStackTrace(printWriter);
          response.setContentType("text/plain");
          response.getOutputStream().print(stringWriter.toString());
        }
      }
    }
```

In the above code, there is nothing that we haven't seen before. The logic to add report expressions is encapsulated in the JRXML template.

After deploying this servlet and directing the browser to its URL, we should see a report similar to the following:

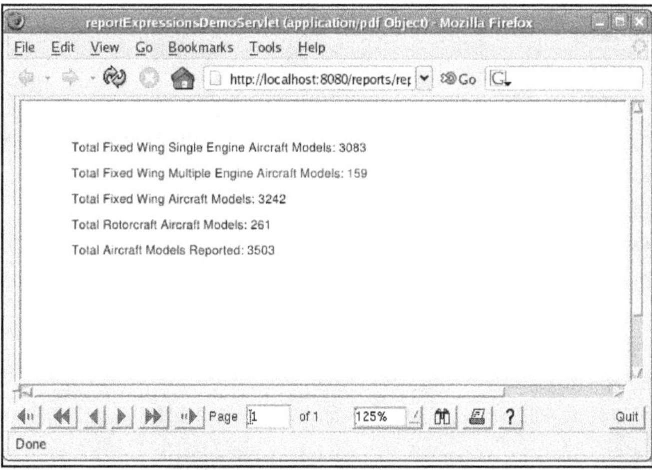

Adding multiple columns to a report

JasperReports allows us to generate reports with multiple columns. Reports we have seen so far seem to have multiple columns. For example, the report we created in the previous section has a column for model, another column for tail number, and one more for serial number. However, all three of these fields are laid out in a single `<band>` element.

When we add multiple columns to a report, we should think of the data inside a band as a cell, regardless of how the data is laid out inside that band.

The `flightstats` database we used for the examples in Chapter 4, *Creating Dynamic Reports from Databases*, contains the country, state, and city where an aircraft is registered. Let's create a report displaying the tail number of all aircraft registered in the state of New York in the United States. Our report will display the data in three columns. The following JRXML template will generate a report with the desired layout:

```
<?xml version="1.0" encoding="UTF-8"  ?>

<jasperReport
  xmlns="http://jasperreports.sourceforge.net/jasperreports"
  xmlns:xsi="http://www.w3.org/2001/XMLSchema-instance"
        xsi:schemaLocation="http://jasperreports.sourceforge.net
            /jasperreports http://jasperreports.sourceforge.net/xsd
            /jasperreport.xsd"
        name="MultipleColumnDemo"
        columnCount="3"
        columnWidth="180">
  <queryString>
    <![CDATA[select a.tail_num from aircraft a where a.country = 'US'
       and a.state = 'NY' order by a.tail_num]]>
  </queryString>
  <field name="tail_num" class="java.lang.String" />
  <columnHeader>
    <band height="20">
      <staticText>
        <reportElement x="0" y="0" height="20" width="84" />
        <text>Tail Number</text>
      </staticText>
      </band>
  </columnHeader>
  <detail>
    <band height="20">
      <textField>
        <reportElement x="0" y="0" height="20" width="84" />
```

```
            <textFieldExpression>
              <![CDATA[$F{tail_num}]]>
            </textFieldExpression>
          </textField>
        </band>
      </detail>
    </jasperReport>
```

As we can see in this JRXML template, the number of columns and the column width are specified by the `columnCount` and `columnWidth` attributes of the `<jasperReport>` root element.

> The column width defaults to 555 pixels, which is also the default width of a report page, excluding its margins. If we want to create a report with multiple columns, we must specify a smaller `columnWidth` attribute than the default; otherwise, our JRXML template will fail to compile.

As can be seen in the last example, we can define a column header to be displayed at the top of every column. This can be accomplished by the `<columnHeader>` JRXML element. We can also choose to display a column footer at the bottom of every column by adding a `<columnFooter>` element to our JRXML template (not shown in the example). Just like all the other JRXML templates defining report sections, `<columnHeader>` and `<columnFooter>` contain a single `<band>` element as their only child element. This `<band>` element can contain report fields, static text, images, graphs, or anything else we can display in any of the other report sections.

The following servlet will generate a PDF report from the jasper file generated from the last JRXML template and direct it to the browser:

```
package net.ensode.jasperbook;

import java.io.IOException;
import java.io.InputStream;
import java.io.PrintWriter;
import java.io.StringWriter;
import java.sql.Connection;
import java.sql.DriverManager;
import java.util.HashMap;

import javax.servlet.ServletException;
import javax.servlet.ServletOutputStream;
import javax.servlet.http.HttpServlet;
import javax.servlet.http.HttpServletRequest;
import javax.servlet.http.HttpServletResponse;

import net.sf.jasperreports.engine.JasperRunManager;
```

```
public class MultipleColumnDemoServlet extends HttpServlet
{
  protected void doGet(HttpServletRequest request,HttpServletResponse
                                                              response)
  throws ServletException, IOException
  {
    Connection connection;
    ServletOutputStream servletOutputStream = response
                                              .getOutputStream();
    InputStream reportStream = getServletConfig().getServletContext()
          .getResourceAsStream("/reports/MultipleColumnDemo.jasper");
    try
    {
      Class.forName("com.mysql.jdbc.Driver");
      connection = DriverManager.getConnection("jdbc:mysql:
                  //localhost:3306/flightstats" +
                  "?user=dbuser&password=secret");
      JasperRunManager.runReportToPdfStream(reportStream,
                     servletOutputStream, new HashMap(), connection);
      connection.close();
      response.setContentType("application/pdf");
      servletOutputStream.flush();
      servletOutputStream.close();
    }
    catch (Exception e)
    {
      // display stack trace in the browser
      StringWriter stringWriter = new StringWriter();
      PrintWriter printWriter = new PrintWriter(stringWriter);
      e.printStackTrace(printWriter);
      response.setContentType("text/plain");
      response.getOutputStream().print(stringWriter.toString());
    }
  }
}
```

There is nothing we haven't seen before in this servlet. The logic for multiple-column data is encapsulated in the JRXML. After deploying this servlet and directing the browser to its URL, we should see a report like the following:

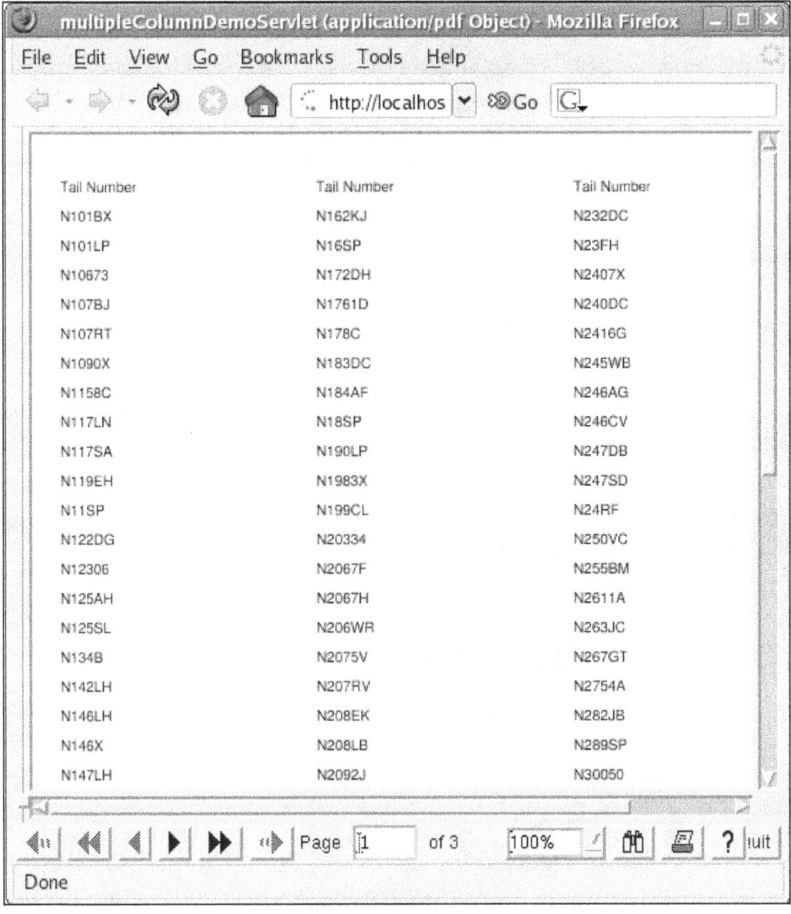

As we can see, the data is displayed in three columns. This way, we can create the whole report using about one-third of the pages we would have had to use with one column. Please note that each column would show all the report elements defined inside the `<band>` element in the `<detail>` section of the report template. In this particular example, we have a single text field corresponding to each aircraft's tail number. If we would have defined additional report elements (for example, two more text fields for the aircraft model and serial number), each of these fields would be displayed in a single column. Adjusting the width of the column would be necessary to accommodate the additional data.

Final notes about report columns

There are a few more things we should know about report columns before we move on. Because these features are fairly straightforward, we decided not to show any examples. However, we should be aware of them.

Report columns by default have no space between them. (In the last report, the columns are wider than the displayed tail number. There is a lot of whitespace inside the columns.) We can change this default behavior by using the `columnSpacing` attribute of the root `<jasperReport>` element of the JRXML template.

By default, report columns are filled vertically, which means the first column is filled to completion first, then the second, then the third, and so on. If we want to fill the columns by row, that is, fill the first row first , then the second row, and so on, we can achieve this by setting the `printOrder` attribute of the root `<jasperReport>` element to `Horizontal`.

Column footers by default are printed at the bottom of the page. If a report column does not have enough data to fill a page, there will be some blank space between the end of the column and the column footer. If we want the column footer to be printed right after the end of the column, we can do it by setting the `isFloatColumnFooter` attribute of the `<jasperReport>` element to `true`.

Grouping report data

JasperReports allows us to group report data in a logical manner. For example, if we were creating a report about cars, we could group the data by car make and/or model. If we were creating a report about sales figures, we could group the report data by geographical area.

The `flightstats` database we used for the examples in Chapter 4, *Creating Dynamic Reports from Databases*, contains the country, state, and city where an aircraft is registered. Let's create a report displaying aircraft data registered in any state starting with the letter "A" in the United States. We will group the report data by state abbreviation. The JRXML template for the report is as follows:

```
<?xml version="1.0" encoding="UTF-8"  ?>
<jasperReport
  xmlns="http://jasperreports.sourceforge.net/jasperreports"
        xmlns:xsi="http://www.w3.org/2001/XMLSchema-instance"
              xsi:schemaLocation="http://jasperreports.sourceforge
                  .net/jasperreports http://jasperreports
                  .sourceforge.net/xsd/jasperreport.xsd"
              name="DataGroupingDemo">
  <queryString>
```

```
    <![CDATA[select a.tail_num, a.aircraft_serial, am.model, a.state
             from aircraft a, aircraft_models am where
             a.aircraft_model_code = am.aircraft_model_code and
             a.country = 'US' and state like 'A%' order by state,
             model]]>
  </queryString>
  <field name="tail_num" class="java.lang.String" />
  <field name="aircraft_serial" class="java.lang.String" />
  <field name="model" class="java.lang.String" />
  <field name="state" class="java.lang.String" />
  <group name="StateGroup">
    <groupExpression>
      <![CDATA[$F{state}]]>
    </groupExpression>
    <groupHeader>
      <band height="40">
        <staticText>
          <reportElement x="0" y="10" width="115" height="20" />
          <textElement>
            <font isBold="true" />
          </textElement>
          <text>Aircraft Registered In:</text>
        </staticText>
        <textField>
          <reportElement x="116" y="10" width="20" height="20" />
          <textFieldExpression>$F{state}</textFieldExpression>
        </textField>
      </band>
    </groupHeader>
    <groupFooter>
      <band height="40">
        <staticText>
          <reportElement x="0" y="10" width="140" height="20" />
          <textElement>
            <font isBold="true" />
          </textElement>
          <text>End Aircraft Registered In:</text>
        </staticText>
        <textField>
          <reportElement x="141" y="10" width="20" height="20" />
          <textFieldExpression>$F{state}</textFieldExpression>
        </textField>
```

```
        </band>
      </groupFooter>
    </group>
    <detail>
      <band height="20">
        <staticText>
          <reportElement x="20" y="0" height="20" width="35" />
          <text>Model:</text>
        </staticText>
        <textField>
          <reportElement x="56" y="0" height="20" width="164" />
          <textFieldExpression>
            <![CDATA[$F{model}]]>
          </textFieldExpression>
        </textField>
        <staticText>
          <reportElement x="220" y="0" height="20" width="65" />
          <text>Tail Number:</text>
        </staticText>
        <textField>
          <reportElement x="286" y="0" height="20" width="84" />
          <textFieldExpression>
            <![CDATA[$F{tail_num}]]>
          </textFieldExpression>
        </textField>
        <staticText>
          <reportElement x="380" y="0" height="20" width="75" />
          <text>Serial Number:</text>
        </staticText>
        <textField>
          <reportElement x="456" y="0" height="20" width="94" />
          <textFieldExpression>
            <![CDATA[$F{aircraft_serial}]]>
          </textFieldExpression>
        </textField>
      </band>
    </detail>
  </jasperReport>
```

As can be seen in this example, a group is defined by the `<group>` element. The `<group>` element must contain a `name` attribute defining the group's name. A group must also contain a `<groupExpression>` subelement. This subelement indicates the data that must change to start a new data group. In this example, every time the state changes, we begin a new data grouping.

A group can optionally contain either a group header or a group footer. They are useful to place labels at the beginning and end of the grouped data. The group header and footer contain a single `<band>` element as their only child element. This is a regular `<band>` element. We can place any report element in it according to our wish, just as if it were inside any of the other report sections (title, page header, column header, detail, and so on). In the example just discussed, we chose to place some static text and report fields identifying the state to which the aircraft in the group are registered.

The servlet to generate a PDF report is virtually identical to the one we saw in the previous section, the only difference being the location of the jasper template. After deploying this servlet and directing the browser to its URL, we should see a report like the following:

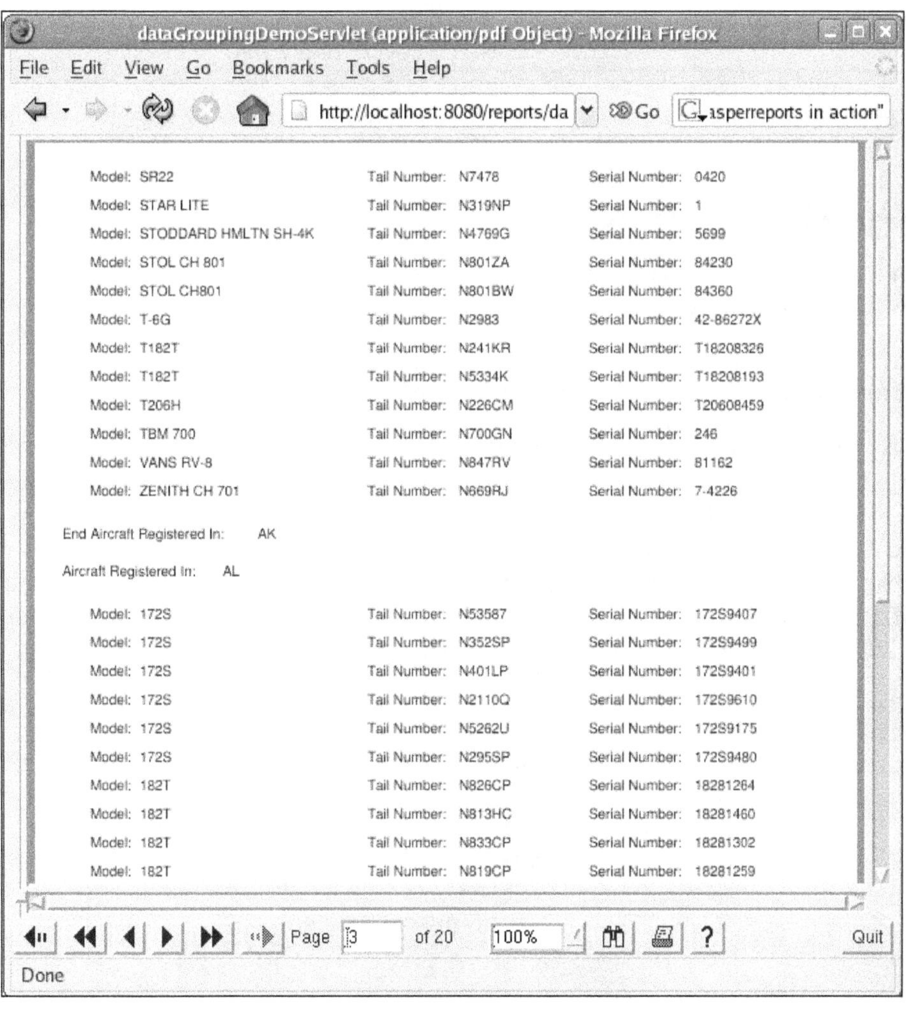

Model: SR22	Tail Number: N7478	Serial Number: 0420
Model: STAR LITE	Tail Number: N319NP	Serial Number: 1
Model: STODDARD HMLTN SH-4K	Tail Number: N4769G	Serial Number: 5699
Model: STOL CH 801	Tail Number: N801ZA	Serial Number: 84230
Model: STOL CH801	Tail Number: N801BW	Serial Number: 84360
Model: T-6G	Tail Number: N2983	Serial Number: 42-86272X
Model: T182T	Tail Number: N241KR	Serial Number: T18208326
Model: T182T	Tail Number: N5334K	Serial Number: T18208193
Model: T206H	Tail Number: N226CM	Serial Number: T20608459
Model: TBM 700	Tail Number: N700GN	Serial Number: 246
Model: VANS RV-8	Tail Number: N847RV	Serial Number: 81162
Model: ZENITH CH 701	Tail Number: N669RJ	Serial Number: 7-4226
End Aircraft Registered In: AK		
Aircraft Registered In: AL		
Model: 172S	Tail Number: N53587	Serial Number: 172S9407
Model: 172S	Tail Number: N352SP	Serial Number: 172S9499
Model: 172S	Tail Number: N401LP	Serial Number: 172S9401
Model: 172S	Tail Number: N2110Q	Serial Number: 172S9610
Model: 172S	Tail Number: N5262U	Serial Number: 172S9175
Model: 172S	Tail Number: N295SP	Serial Number: 172S9480
Model: 182T	Tail Number: N826CP	Serial Number: 18281264
Model: 182T	Tail Number: N813HC	Serial Number: 18281460
Model: 182T	Tail Number: N833CP	Serial Number: 18281302
Model: 182T	Tail Number: N819CP	Serial Number: 18281259

We chose to display the third page on the screenshot to illustrate the group header and footer.

The `<group>` element contains attributes that allow us to control the layout of the group data. The following table summarizes these attributes:

Attribute	Description
`isStartNewPage`	When set to `true`, each data group will begin on a new page.
`isStartNewColumn`	When set to `true`, each data group will begin in a new column.
`isReprintHeaderOnEachPage`	When set to `true`, the group header will be reprinted on every page.
`isResetPageNumber`	When set to `true`, the report page number will be reset every time a new group starts.

Each of the attributes described in the table above default to `false`.

Report variables

When we wrote the report in the *Report Expressions* section, we had to type the following expression twice:

```
$F{fixed_wing_single_engine_cnt}.intValue() +
$F{fixed_wing_multiple_engine_cnt}.intValue())
```

This expression was typed once to calculate the number of fixed-wing aircraft reported, and again to calculate the total number of aircraft reported. This duplication is not a good thing because, if we need to change the expression for any reason, we would have to do it twice. JasperReports allows us to assign report expressions to a variable, eliminating the need to type the expression multiple times. The following JRXML template is a modified version of the one we wrote in that section, this version takes advantage of report variables to eliminate the duplicate expression.

```
<?xml version="1.0" encoding="UTF-8"  ?>
<jasperReport
  xmlns="http://jasperreports.sourceforge.net/jasperreports"
        xmlns:xsi="http://www.w3.org/2001/XMLSchema-instance"
              xsi:schemaLocation= "http://jasperreports
                  .sourceforge.net/jasperreports http://jasperreports
                  .sourceforge.net/xsd/jasperreport.xsd"
              name="ReportVariablesDemo">
  <queryString>
```

```
<![CDATA[SELECT
               (select count(*) from aircraft_models am
                where am.aircraft_type_id = 4)
        AS fixed_wing_single_engine_cnt,
               (select count(*) from aircraft_models am
                where am.aircraft_type_id = 5)
        AS fixed_wing_multiple_engine_cnt,
               (select count(*) from aircraft_models am where
                am.aircraft_type_id = 6)
        AS rotorcraft_cnt]]>
</queryString>
<field name="fixed_wing_single_engine_cnt"
       class="java.lang.Integer" />
<field name="fixed_wing_multiple_engine_cnt"
       class="java.lang.Integer" />
<field name="rotorcraft_cnt" class="java.lang.Integer" />
<variable name="fixed_wing_engine_cnt" class="java.lang.Integer">
  <variableExpression>
    <![CDATA[new Integer
            ($F{fixed_wing_single_engine_cnt}.intValue() +
             $F{fixed_wing_multiple_engine_cnt}.intValue())]]>
  </variableExpression>
</variable>
<detail>
  <band height="100">
    <textField>
      <reportElement x="20" y="0" height="20" width="500" />
      <textFieldExpression>
        <![CDATA["Total Fixed Wing Single Engine Aircraft Models: "
                + $F{fixed_wing_single_engine_cnt}]]>
      </textFieldExpression>
    </textField>
    <textField>
      <reportElement x="20" y="20" height="20" width="500" />
      <textFieldExpression>
        <![CDATA["Total Fixed Wing Multiple Engine Aircraft " +
                "Models: " + $F{fixed_wing_multiple_engine_cnt}]]>
      </textFieldExpression>
    </textField>
    <textField>
      <reportElement x="20" y="40" height="20" width="500" />
      <textFieldExpression>
        <![CDATA["Total Fixed Wing Aircraft Models: " +
                $V{fixed_wing_engine_cnt}]]>
      </textFieldExpression>
```

```
        </textField>
        <textField>
          <reportElement x="20" y="60" height="20" width="500" />
          <textFieldExpression>
            <![CDATA["Total Rotorcraft Aircraft Models: " +
                     $F{rotorcraft_cnt}]]>
          </textFieldExpression>
        </textField>
        <textField>
          <reportElement x="20" y="80" height="20" width="500" />
          <textFieldExpression>
            <![CDATA["Total Aircraft Models Reported: " +
                     ($V{fixed_wing_engine_cnt}.intValue() +
                      $F{rotorcraft_cnt}.intValue())]]>
          </textFieldExpression>
        </textField>
      </band>
    </detail>
  </jasperReport>
```

As can be seen in the above example, report expressions can be assigned to a variable by using the `<variable>` element in a JRXML file. We give the variable a name by using the name attribute of the `<variable>` field. The actual expression we want to assign to a variable must be enclosed inside a `<variableExpression>` element. Variable values can be accessed in other report expressions by using the `$V{variable_name}` notation, where `variable_name` is the name we gave the variable by using the `name` attribute within the `<variable>` element.

Output for the above example is identical to the output of the example given in the *Report Expressions* section.

The JRXML `<variable>` element contains a number of attributes, which are summarized in the following table:

Attribute	Description	Valid values	Default value
`Name`	Sets the `variable` name.	Any valid XML attribute value.	N/A
`Class`	Sets the `variable` class.	Any Java class available in the CLASSPATH.	`java.lang.String`

Attribute	Description	Valid values	Default value
`calculation`	Determines what calculation to perform on the variable when filling the report.	`Average`—variable value is the average of every non-null value of the variable expression. Valid for numeric variables only. `Count`—variable value is the count of non-null instances of the variable expression. `First`—variable value is the value of the first instance of the variable expression. Subsequent values are ignored. `Highest`—variable value is the highest value for the variable expression. `Lowest`—variable value is the lowest value in the report for the variable expression. `Nothing`—no calculations are performed on the variable. `StandardDeviation`—variable value is the standard deviation of all non-null values matching the report expression. Valid for numeric variables only. `Sum`—variable value is the sum of all non-null values matching the report expression. `System`—variable value is a custom calculation. `Variance`—variable value is the variance of all non-null values matching the report expression.	`Nothing`

Attribute	Description	Valid values	Default value
`incrementGroup`	Determines the name of the group at which the variable value is recalculated, when `incrementType` is `Group`.	The name of any group declared in the JRXML report template.	N/A
`resetType`	Determines when the value of a variable is reset.	`Column` – the variable value is reset at the beginning of each column. `Group` – the variable value is reset when the group specified by `incrementGroup` changes. `None` – the variable value is never reset. `Page` – the variable value is recalculated at the beginning of every page. `Report` – the variable value is recalculated once at the beginning of the report.	`Report`
`resetGroup`	Determines the name of the group where the variable value is reset, when `resetType` is `Group`.	The name of any group declared in the JRXML report template.	N/A

As can be inferred from the table, JasperReports variables can be used not only to simplify report expressions, but also to perform calculations and display the result of those calculations on the report.

Let's modify the report that we developed in the previous section so that it displays the total number of aircraft in each state. To accomplish this, we need to create a report variable and set its `calculation` attribute to `Count`. The following JRXML template illustrates this concept:

```
<?xml version="1.0" encoding="UTF-8"  ?>
<jasperReport
  xmlns="http://jasperreports.sourceforge.net/jasperreports"
        xmlns:xsi="http://www.w3.org/2001/XMLSchema-instance"
              xsi:schemaLocation="http://jasperreports.sourceforge
                  .net/jasperreports http://jasperreports.sourceforge
```

```
                .net/xsd/jasperreport.xsd"
            name="VariableCalculationDemo">
<queryString>
  <![CDATA[select a.tail_num, a.aircraft_serial, am.model, a.state
          from aircraft a, aircraft_models am
          where a.aircraft_model_code = am.aircraft_model_code
          and a.country = 'US' and state like 'A%'
          order by state, model]]>
</queryString>
<field name="tail_num" class="java.lang.String" />
<field name="aircraft_serial" class="java.lang.String" />
<field name="model" class="java.lang.String" />
<field name="state" class="java.lang.String" />
<variable name="aircraft_count" class="java.lang.Integer"
          calculation="Count" resetType="Group"
          resetGroup="StateGroup">
  <variableExpression>
    <![CDATA[$F{aircraft_serial}]]>
  </variableExpression>
  <initialValueExpression>
    <![CDATA[new java.lang.Integer(0)]]>
  </initialValueExpression>
</variable>

<group name="StateGroup">
  <groupExpression>
    <![CDATA[$F{state}]]>
  </groupExpression>
  <groupHeader>
    <band height="40">
      <staticText>
        <reportElement x="0" y="10" width="115" height="20" />
        <textElement>
          <font isBold="true" />
        </textElement>
        <text>Aircraft Registered In:</text>
      </staticText>
      <textField>
        <reportElement x="116" y="10" width="20" height="20" />
        <textFieldExpression>$F{state}</textFieldExpression>
      </textField>
    </band>
  </groupHeader>
  <groupFooter>
    <band height="40">
```

```
          <textField>
            <reportElement x="0" y="10" width="325" height="20" />
            <textFieldExpression>
              <![CDATA["Total Number Of Aircraft Registered In " +
                      $F{state} + ": " + $V{aircraft_count}]]>
            </textFieldExpression>
          </textField>
        </band>
      </groupFooter>
    </group>
    <detail>
      <band height="20">
        <staticText>
          <reportElement x="20" y="0" height="20" width="35" />
          <text>Model:</text>
        </staticText>
        <textField>
          <reportElement x="56" y="0" height="20" width="164" />
          <textFieldExpression>
            <![CDATA[$F{model}]]>
          </textFieldExpression>
        </textField>
        <staticText>
        <reportElement x="220" y="0" height="20" width="65" />
          <text>Tail Number:</text>
        </staticText>
        <textField>
          <reportElement x="286" y="0" height="20" width="84" />
          <textFieldExpression>
            <![CDATA[$F{tail_num}]]>
          </textFieldExpression>
        </textField>
        <staticText>
          <reportElement x="380" y="0" height="20" width="75" />
          <text>Serial Number:</text>
        </staticText>
        <textField>
          <reportElement x="456" y="0" height="20" width="94" />
          <textFieldExpression>
            <![CDATA[$F{aircraft_serial}]]>
          </textFieldExpression>
        </textField>
      </band>
    </detail>
  </jasperReport>
```

In this report template, setting the calculation attribute of the <variable> field to Count allowed us to obtain the number of aircraft in each state. By setting the report expression to $F{aircraft_serial}, each time a serial number is displayed in the report, the variable value is increased by one. Setting the resetType attribute to Group allows us to reset the variable value to its initial value, which in turn is set by the <initialValueExpression> field.

The code for the servlet that fills and exports the jasper file generated by this JRXML has nothing we haven't seen before and, therefore, it is not shown. After directing the browser to its URL, we should see a report similar to the following:

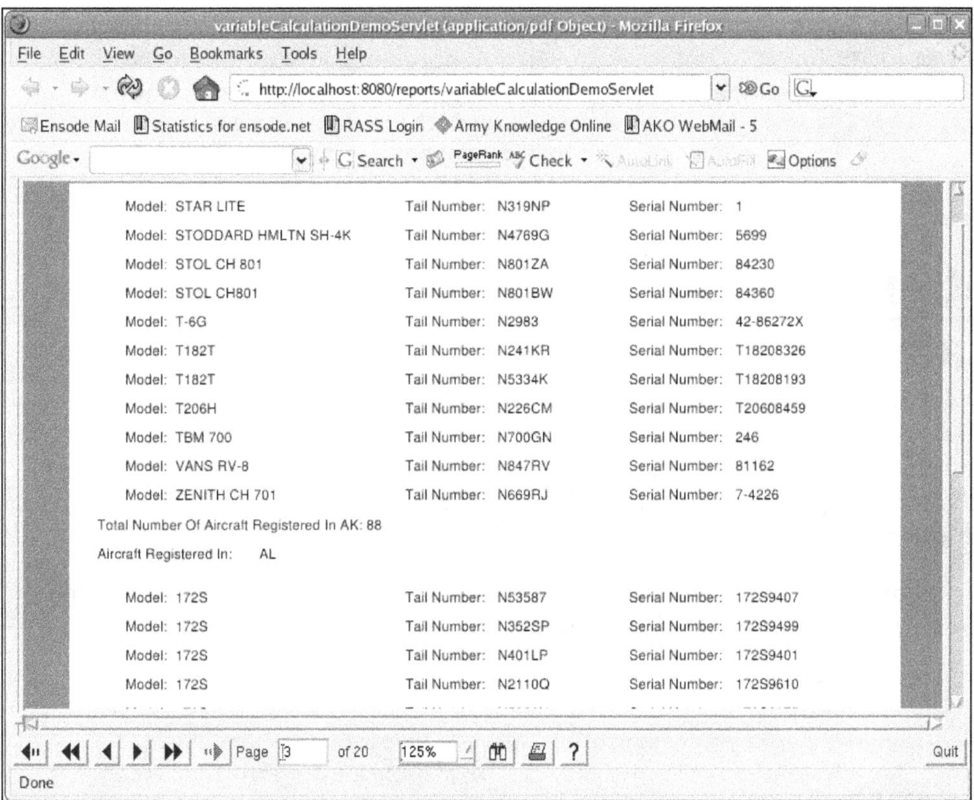

The same concepts we saw here can be applied to the other calculation values and reset types.

Built-in report variables

JasperReports has a number of built-in report variables that we can use in our reports without having to declare them. They are listed and described in the following table:

Built-In Variable	Description
PAGE_COUNT	Contains the total number of pages in the report.
PAGE_NUMBER	Contains the current page number.
COLUMN_COUNT	Contains the total number of columns in the report.
COLUMN_NUMBER	Contains the current column number.
REPORT_COUNT	Contains the total number of records in the report.
NameOfGroup_COUNT	Contains the total number of records in the group named NameOfGroup. The exact report variable name will match the group name in the report; for example, for a group named MyGroup, the variable name will be MyGroup_COUNT.

Stretching text fields to accommodate data

By default, `<textField>` elements have a fixed size. If the data they need to display does not fit in their defined size, it is simply not displayed in the report. This is rarely the behavior we would want. Luckily, JasperReports allows us to alter this default behavior. This is accomplished by setting the `isStretchWithOverflow` attribute of the `<textField>` element to `true`.

The following JRXML template demonstrates how to allow text fields to stretch so that they can accommodate large amounts of data:

```
<?xml version="1.0" encoding="UTF-8" ?>
<jasperReport
  xmlns="http://jasperreports.sourceforge.net/jasperreports"
        xmlns:xsi="http://www.w3.org/2001/XMLSchema-instance"
              xsi:schemaLocation="http://jasperreports.sourceforge
                  .net/jasperreports http://jasperreports.sourceforge
                  .net/xsd/jasperreport.xsd"
              name="TextFieldStretchDemo">
  <field name="lots_of_data" class="java.lang.String" />
  <detail>
    <band height="30">
      <textField isStretchWithOverflow="true">
        <reportElement x="0" y="0" width="100" height="24" />
```

```
        <textFieldExpression class="java.lang.String">
          <![CDATA[$F{lots_of_data}]]>
        </textFieldExpression>
      </textField>
    </band>
  </detail>
</jasperReport>
```

The following servlet fills the jasper template generated from the above JRXML and directs the generated report to the browser window in PDF format:

```
package net.ensode.jasperbook;
import java.io.IOException;
import java.io.InputStream;
import java.io.PrintWriter;
import java.io.StringWriter;
import java.util.ArrayList;
import java.util.Collection;
import java.util.HashMap;
import javax.servlet.ServletException;
import javax.servlet.ServletOutputStream;
import javax.servlet.http.HttpServlet;
import javax.servlet.http.HttpServletRequest;
import javax.servlet.http.HttpServletResponse;
import net.sf.jasperreports.engine.JRDataSource;
import net.sf.jasperreports.engine.JasperRunManager;
import net.sf.jasperreports.engine.data.JRMapCollectionDataSource;
public class TextFieldStretchDemoServlet extends HttpServlet
{
  private JRDataSource createReportDataSource()
  {
    JRMapCollectionDataSource dataSource;
    Collection reportRows = initializeMapCollection();
    dataSource = new JRMapCollectionDataSource(reportRows);
    return dataSource;
  }
  private Collection initializeMapCollection()
  {
    ArrayList reportRows = new ArrayList();
    HashMap datasourceMap = new HashMap();
    datasourceMap.put("lots_of_data", "This element contains so much
                      data, " + "there is no way it will ever fit in
                      the text field without it stretching.");
    reportRows.add(datasourceMap);
    return reportRows;
  }
  protected void doGet(HttpServletRequest request, HttpServletResponse
                                                           response)
  throws ServletException, IOException
```

```
  {
    ServletOutputStream servletOutputStream =
                                     response.getOutputStream();
    InputStream reportStream = getServletConfig().getServletContext()
        .getResourceAsStream("/reports/TextFieldStretchDemo.jasper");
    try
    {
      JRDataSource dataSource = createReportDataSource();
      JasperRunManager.runReportToPdfStream(reportStream,
                      servletOutputStream, new HashMap(), dataSource);
      response.setContentType("application/pdf");
      servletOutputStream.flush();
      servletOutputStream.close();
    }
    catch (Exception e)
    {
      // display stack trace in the browser
      StringWriter stringWriter = new StringWriter();
      PrintWriter printWriter = new PrintWriter(stringWriter);
      e.printStackTrace(printWriter);
      response.setContentType("text/plain");
      response.getOutputStream().print(stringWriter.toString());
    }
  }
}
```

We should see a report like the following after directing the browser to this servlet's URL:

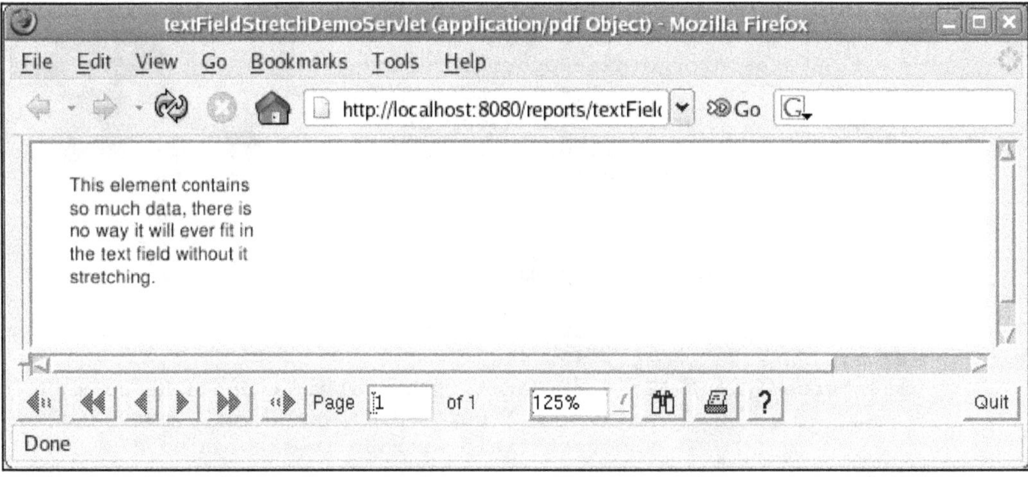

When a <textField> element stretches to accommodate its data, its parent <band> element stretches accordingly. When a <band> element stretches due to one of its child <textField> elements stretching, JasperReports allows us to control how other child elements of the <band> element will be positioned when the band stretches. This will be discussed in detail in the next section.

Laying out report elements

As we saw in Chapter 3, *Creating your First Report*, a report can contain the following sections: a report title, a page header, a page footer, a column header, a column footer, a detail section, a report summary, and a last page footer. These sections are defined by the `<title>`, `<pageHeader>`, `<pageFooter>`, `<columnHeader>`, `<columnFooter>`, `<detail>`, `<summary>`, and `<lastPageFooter>` JRXML elements, respectively.

Each of these elements contains a single `<band>` element as its only subelement. The `<band>` element can contain zero or more `<line>`, `<rectangle>`, `<ellipse>`, `<image>`, `<staticText>`, `<textField>`, `<subReport>`, or `<elementGroup>` subelements. Except for `<elementGroup>`, each of these elements must contain a single `<reportElement>` as its first element. The `<reportElement>` subelement determines how data is laid out for that particular element. In this section, we will see how the different attributes of `<reportElement>` affect the way data is laid out in its parent element.

The following table summarizes all the attributes of `<reportElement>`:

Attribute	Description	Valid values
`x`	Specifies the x coordinate of the element within the band.	An integer value indicating the x coordinate of the element in pixels. This attribute is required.
`y`	Specifies the y coordinate of the element within the band.	An integer value indicating the y coordinate of the element in pixels. This attribute is required.
`width`	Specifies the width of the element.	An integer value indicating the element width in pixels. This attribute is required.
`height`	Specifies the height of the element.	An integer value indicating the element height in pixels. This attribute is required.

Attribute	Description	Valid values
`key`	Uniquely identifies the element within the band and does not affect layout.	A unique string used to identify the containing element.
`stretchType`	Specifies how the element stretches when the containing band stretches.	`NoStretch` (default)—the element will not stretch. `RelativeToTallestObject`—the element will stretch to accommodate the tallest object in its group. `RelativeToBand`—the element will stretch to fit the band's height.
`positionType`	Specifies the element's position when the band stretches.	`Float`—the element will move depending on the size of the surrounding elements. `FixRelativeToTop` (default)—the element will maintain a fixed position relative to the band's top. `FixRelativeToBottom`—the element will maintain a fixed position relative to the band's bottom.
`isPrintRepeatedValues`	Specifies if repeated values are printed.	`true` (default)—repeated values will be printed. `false`—repeated values will not be printed.
`mode`	Specifies the background mode of the element.	`Opaque, Transparent`
`isRemoveLineWhenBlank`	Specifies whether the element should be removed when it is blank and there are no other elements in the same horizontal space.	`true, false`

Attribute	Description	Valid values
`isPrintInFirstWholeBand`	Specifies whether the element must be printed in a whole band, which is aband that is not divided between report pages or columns.	`true, false`
`isPrintWhenDetailOverFlows`	Specifies whether the element will be printed when the band overflows to a new page or column.	`true, false`
`printWhenGroupChanges`	Specifies that the element will be printed when the specified group changes.	A string corresponding to the group that must change for the element to be printed.
`forecolor`	Specifies the foreground color of the element.	Either a hexadecimal RGB value preceded by the # character or one of the following predefined values: `black`, `blue`, `cyan`, `darkGray`, `gray`, `green`, `lightGray`, `magenta`, `orange`, `pink`, `red`, `yellow`, `white`
`backcolor`	Specifies the background color of the element.	Refer to the valid values of `forecolor` above.

Most of the `<reportElement>` attributes described in the table are self-explanatory. We will discuss some of them in the next few sections.

Setting the size and position of a report element

The x and y attributes of `<reportElement>` specify the x and y coordinates (in pixels) of the element within the band. A common mistake in the beginning is to assume that the x and y coordinates defined here are absolute for the page. Again, the x and y coordinates defined by the x and y attributes are relative to the `<band>` where the element is contained. Coordinates (0, 0) are at the top left of the band. The x and y attributes of `<reportElement>` are required.

The width and height elements of `<reportElement>`, unsurprisingly, define the width and height (in pixels) of the element, respectively. The `width` and `height` attributes of `<reportElement>` are required. We have already seen several examples demonstrating the use of the x, y, width, and height elements of `<reportElement>`. Here is the JRXML template for the report we created in Chapter 3, *Creating your First Report*:

```
<?xml version="1.0"?>
<jasperReport
  xmlns="http://jasperreports.sourceforge.net/jasperreports"
         xmlns:xsi="http://www.w3.org/2001/XMLSchema-instance"
               xsi:schemaLocation="http://jasperreports.sourceforge
                               .net/jasperreports http://jasperreports
                               .sourceforge.net/xsd/jasperreport.xsd"
               name="FirstReport">
  <detail>
    <band height="20">
      <staticText>
        <reportElement x="20" y="0" width="200" height="20"/>
        <text>
          <![CDATA[If you don't see this, it didn't work]]>
        </text>
      </staticText>
    </band>
  </detail>
</jasperReport>
```

In this example, the static text will appear 20 pixels from the left margin, aligned with the top of the band. Refer to Chapter 3 to see a rendered report based on this template.

The `positionType` attribute defines the element's position when the band is stretched. As can be seen in the previous table, there are three legal values for this attribute: `Float`, `FixRelativeToTop`, and `FixRelativeToBottom`. Let's modify the example we discussed in the *Stretching text fields to accommodate data* section by adding some static text right under the existing text field. We will see the effect of the different `positionType` values on its positioning.

```
<?xml version="1.0" encoding="UTF-8" ?>
<jasperReport
  xmlns="http://jasperreports.sourceforge.net/jasperreports"
        xmlns:xsi="http://www.w3.org/2001/XMLSchema-instance"
              xsi:schemaLocation="http://jasperreports.sourceforge
              .net/jasperreports http://jasperreports.sourceforge
              .net/xsd/jasperreport.xsd"
        name="TextFieldStretchDemo">
  <field name="lots_of_data" class="java.lang.String" />
  <detail>
    <band height="55">
      <textField isStretchWithOverflow="true">
        <reportElement x="0" y="0" width="100" height="24" />
        <textFieldExpression class="java.lang.String">
          <![CDATA[$F{lots_of_data}]]>
        </textFieldExpression>
      </textField>
      <staticText>
        <reportElement width="500" y="25" x="0" height="30"
                         positionType="FixRelativeToTop" />
        <box>
          <pen lineWidth="1"/>
        </box>
        <text>
          <![CDATA[This staticText element has a default positionType
                  of "FixRelativeToTop"]]>
        </text>
      </staticText>
    </band>
  </detail>
</jasperReport>
```

The `<textField>` element in the JRXML template has a `y` position of zero and a height of 24 pixels. We positioned the new `<staticText>` element to have a `y` position of 25, just below the text field.

> For clarity, we explicitly set the `positionType` attribute of `<reportElement>` to `FixRelativeToTop`. It wasn't really necessary to do it, as `FixRelativeToTop` is its default value.

Notice the <box> element we added to the <textField> and <staticText> elements. This <box> field allows us to display a border around the elements, making very clear where the element starts and ends. We chose to do this to be able to easily see the position of the elements within the report.

Again, the code to fill and export the report shows nothing we haven't seen before; therefore, we chose not to display it. The generated report should look like the following:

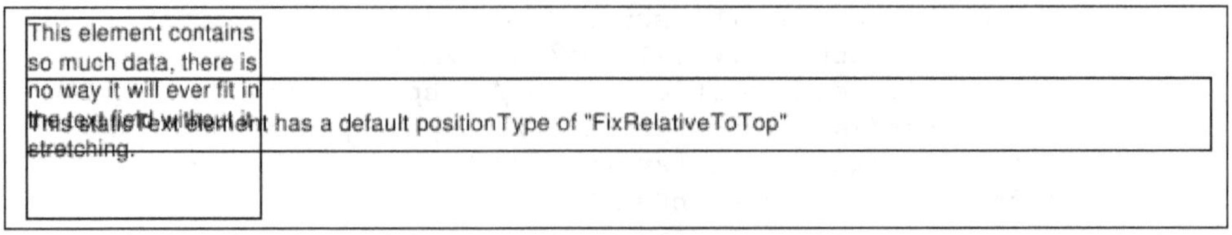

This element contains so much data, there is no way it will ever fit in the text field without it stretching.

This staticText element has a default positionType of "FixRelativeToTop"

As the FixRelativeToTop value of the positionType attribute of <reportElement> forces the element to stay in the same position whether or not any other element stretches. We ended up with the two elements overlapping each other, that is probably not what we want.

It would be nice if the <staticText> element could be pushed down in case the <textField> element stretches. We can accomplish this by setting positionType to Float.

```
<?xml version="1.0" encoding="UTF-8" ?>
<jasperReport
  xmlns="http://jasperreports.sourceforge.net/jasperreports"
        xmlns:xsi="http://www.w3.org/2001/XMLSchema-instance"
              xsi:schemaLocation="http://jasperreports.sourceforge
                  .net/jasperreports http://jasperreports.sourceforge
                  .net/xsd/jasperreport.xsd"
              name="TextFieldStretchDemo">
  <field name="lots_of_data" class="java.lang.String" />
  <detail>
    <band height="55">
      <textField isStretchWithOverflow="true">
        <reportElement x="0" y="0" width="100" height="24" />
        <textFieldExpression class="java.lang.String">
          <![CDATA[$F{lots_of_data}]]>
        </textFieldExpression>
      </textField>
      <staticText>
        <reportElement width="500" y="25" x="0" height="30"
                       positionType="Float" />
        <box>
```

```
            <pen lineWidth="1"/>
          </box>
          <text>
            <![CDATA[This staticText element has a default positionType
                    of "Float"]]>
          </text>
        </staticText>
      </band>
    </detail>
  </jasperReport>
```

After compiling, filling, and exporting this JRXML template, we should get a report that looks like this:

This element contains so much data, there is no way it will ever fit in the text field without it stretching.

This staticText element has a positionType of "Float"

As we can see, setting the `positionType` attribute of `<reportElement>` to `Float` made JasperReports ignore the y position of the `<staticText>` element, which was "pushed" down by the stretched `<textField>` element.

The third possible value for `positionType` is `FixRelativeToBottom`. This value is similar to `FixRelativeToTop`, with the only difference being that the element keeps its position relative to the bottom of the band as opposed to its top.

When an element of a band stretches, it is possible to control not only the position but also the size of the elements inside the band. This is accomplished by the `stretchType` attribute of `<reportElement>` element. The following example demonstrates how we can set a report element to stretch in order to match the tallest element in its group:

```
<?xml version="1.0" encoding="UTF-8" ?>
<jasperReport xmlns="http://jasperreports.sourceforge.net
                    /jasperreports"
  xmlns:xsi="http://www.w3.org/2001/XMLSchema-instance"
        xsi:schemaLocation="http://jasperreports.sourceforge.net
            /jasperreports http://jasperreports.sourceforge.net/xsd
            /jasperreport.xsd"
            name="RelativeToTallestObjectDemo">
```

```
<field name="lots_of_data" class="java.lang.String" />
<detail>
  <band height="50">
    <elementGroup>
      <textField isStretchWithOverflow="true">
        <reportElement x="0" y="0" width="100" height="24" />
        <box>
          <pen lineWidth="1"/>
        </box>
        <textFieldExpression class="java.lang.String">
          <![CDATA[$F{lots_of_data}]]>
        </textFieldExpression>
      </textField>
      <textField isStretchWithOverflow="true">
        <reportElement x="101" y="0" width="150" height="24" />
        <box>
          <pen lineWidth="1"/>
        </box>
        <textFieldExpression class="java.lang.String">
          <![CDATA[$F{lots_of_data}]]>
        </textFieldExpression>
      </textField>
      <staticText>
        <reportElement width="300" y="0" x="252" height="24"
                       stretchType="RelativeToTallestObject" />
        <box>
          <pen lineWidth="1"/>
        </box>
        <text>
          <![CDATA[staticText element stretchType is
                   "RelativeToTallestObject"]]>
        </text>
      </staticText>
      <staticText>
        <reportElement width="250" y="25" x="0" height="24"
                       positionType="Float" />
        <box>
          <pen lineWidth="1"/>
        </box>
        <text>
          <![CDATA[This text is here to stretch the band a bit
                   more.]]>
```

```
            </text>
          </staticText>
        </elementGroup>
      </band>
    </detail>
  </jasperReport>
```

After compiling the above JRXML template and filling the resulting jasper template, we should see a report like the following:

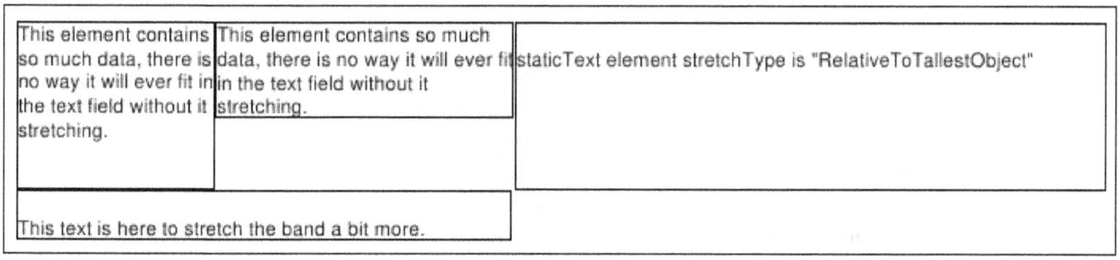

This element contains so much data, there is no way it will ever fit in the text field without it stretching.
This element contains so much data, there is no way it will ever fit in the text field without it stretching.
staticText element stretchType is "RelativeToTallestObject"
This text is here to stretch the band a bit more.

Once again, we decided to display borders around every element to demarcate the boundaries of an element. As we can see in the screenshot, the static text stretched to match the height of the tallest object. This is because we set the value of the `stretchType` property of `<reportElement>` to be `RelativeToTallestObject`.

Notice the `<elementGroup>` element in this JRXML template. The purpose of this element is to group elements together so that we can control the behavior of report elements better when one of them stretches. The `stretchType` property `RelativeToTallestObject` will stretch the appropriate element to match the height of the tallest object in the element's group. All elements between `<elementGroup>` and `</elementGroup>` are in the same group. The `<elementGroup>` element can have other nested `<elementGroup>` elements. If no `<elementGroup>` element is defined inside a `<band>`, then all elements inside the band are considered to be in the same group.

Setting common element properties

JasperReports 1.1 introduced a new report element, the `<frame>` element, allowing us to group elements together and give them a common look. For example, we can set the background color of the frame, and it will be inherited across all the elements contained within the frame. Frames also provide a straightforward way of placing a border around multiple report elements. The following JRXML template is a new version of the example in the previous section. It has been modified to illustrate the use of frames.

```
<?xml version="1.0" encoding="UTF-8" ?>
<jasperReport
  xmlns="http://jasperreports.sourceforge.net/jasperreports"
        xmlns:xsi="http://www.w3.org/2001/XMLSchema-instance"
              xsi:schemaLocation= "http://jasperreports.sourceforge
                  .net/jasperreports http://jasperreports.sourceforge
                  .net/xsd/jasperreport.xsd"
              name="FrameDemo">
  <field name="lots_of_data" class="java.lang.String" />
  <detail>
    <band height="60">
      <frame>
        <reportElement x="0" y="0" width="555" height="60"
                      mode="Opaque" backcolor="lightGray" />
        <box padding="1">
          <pen lineStyle="Dotted" lineWidth="1"/>
        </box>
        <textField isStretchWithOverflow="true">
          <reportElement x="0" y="0" width="100" height="24" />
          <box>
            <pen lineWidth="1"/>
          </box>
          <textFieldExpression class="java.lang.String">
            <![CDATA[$F{lots_of_data}]]>
          </textFieldExpression>
        </textField>
        <textField isStretchWithOverflow="true">
          <reportElement x="101" y="0" width="150" height="24" />
          <box>
            <pen lineWidth="1"/>
          </box>
          <textFieldExpression class="java.lang.String">
            <![CDATA[$F{lots_of_data}]]>
          </textFieldExpression>
        </textField>
        <staticText>
          <reportElement width="290" y="0" x="252" height="24"
                      stretchType="RelativeToTallestObject" />
          <box>
            <pen lineWidth="1"/>
          </box>
          <text>
            <![CDATA[staticText element stretchType is
                  "RelativeToTallestObject"]]>
          </text>
        </staticText>
        <staticText>
          <reportElement width="250" y="25" x="0" height="24"
                      positionType="Float" />
```

```
            <box>
              <pen lineWidth="1"/>
            </box>
            <text>
              <![CDATA[This text is here to stretch the band a bit
                      more.]]>
            </text>
          </staticText>
        </frame>
      </band>
    </detail>
  </jasperReport>
```

In this JRXML template, we replaced the `<elementGroup>` element of the previous example with a `<frame>` element, and slightly modified some of the elements' sizes. We added a `<reportElement>` subelement to the `<frame>` element to set the frame to a light gray background. We then added a `<box>` element to set the frame's element. Because the `<reportElement>` and box apply to the whole frame, they are applied to all the elements inside the frame. After compiling and filling this JRXML template, it should generate a report as the following:

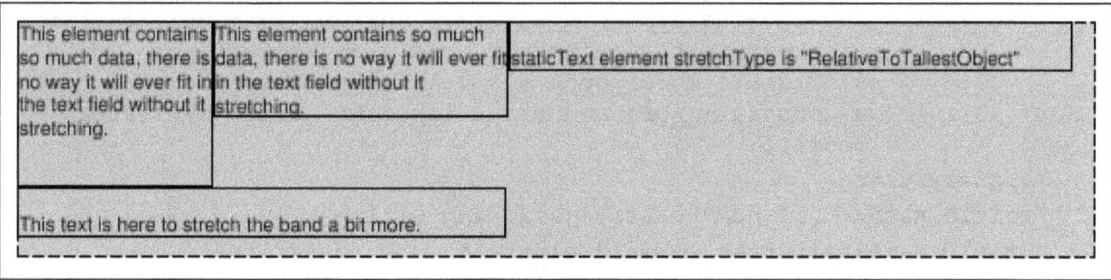

The code to generate the report has nothing we haven't seen before. Therefore, we are not showing it here.

Hiding repeated values

Sometimes report elements can have the same value over and over. For example, the report we created in the *Grouping report data* section is sorted by model number. For airplanes that are the same model, we see the model number repeated over and over again. Perhaps the report would be easier to read if we printed the model number only when it is different from the previous one. This will add to report readability, as the person reading the report would not have to look at the model number unless it is different from the previous one. In the following example, we will modify the JRXML template discussed in that section to accomplish this:

```
<?xml version="1.0" encoding="UTF-8"  ?>
   <jasperReport xmlns="http://jasperreports.sourceforge.net/
   jasperreports"
         xmlns:xsi="http://www.w3.org/2001/XMLSchema-instance"
               xsi:schemaLocation="http://jasperreports.sourceforge
                             .net/jasperreports http://jasperreports
                             .sourceforge.net/xsd/jasperreport.xsd"
               name="IsPrintRepeatedValuesDemo">
     <queryString>
       <![CDATA[select a.tail_num, a.aircraft_serial, am.model, a.state
                from aircraft a, aircraft_models am where
                a.aircraft_model_code = am.aircraft_model_code and
                a.country = 'US' and state like 'A%' order by state,
                model]]>
     </queryString>
     <field name="tail_num" class="java.lang.String" />
     <field name="aircraft_serial" class="java.lang.String" />
     <field name="model" class="java.lang.String" />
     <field name="state" class="java.lang.String" />
     <group name="StateGroup">
       <groupExpression>
         <![CDATA[$F{state}]]>
       </groupExpression>
       <groupHeader>
         <band height="40">
           <staticText>
             <reportElement x="0" y="10" width="115" height="20" />
             <textElement>
               <font isBold="true" />
             </textElement>
             <text>Aircraft Registered In:</text>
           </staticText>
           <textField>
             <reportElement x="116" y="10" width="20" height="20" />
```

```
          <textFieldExpression>$F{state}</textFieldExpression>
        </textField>
      </band>
    </groupHeader>
    <groupFooter>
      <band height="40">
        <staticText>
          <reportElement x="0" y="10" width="140" height="20" />
          <textElement>
            <font isBold="true" />
          </textElement>
          <text>End Aircraft Registered In:</text>
        </staticText>
        <textField>
          <reportElement x="141" y="10" width="20" height="20" />
          <textFieldExpression>$F{state}</textFieldExpression>
        </textField>
      </band>
    </groupFooter>
  </group>
  <detail>
    <band height="20">
      <textField>
        <reportElement x="56" y="0" height="20" width="164"
                       isPrintRepeatedValues="false" />
        <textFieldExpression>
          <![CDATA["Model: " + $F{model}]]>
        </textFieldExpression>
      </textField>
      <staticText>
        <reportElement x="220" y="0" height="20" width="65" />
        <text>Tail Number:</text>
      </staticText>
      <textField>
        <reportElement x="286" y="0" height="20" width="84" />
        <textFieldExpression>
          <![CDATA[$F{tail_num}]]>
        </textFieldExpression>
      </textField>
    <staticText>
      <reportElement x="380" y="0" height="20" width="75" />
      <text>Serial Number:</text>
    </staticText>
    <textField>
```

```
          <reportElement x="456" y="0" height="20" width="94" />
          <textFieldExpression>
            <![CDATA[$F{aircraft_serial}]]>
          </textFieldExpression>
        </textField>
        </band>
      </detail>
    </jasperReport>
```

There are two main differences between the above JRXML template and the one discussed in the *Grouping report data* section. The first difference is that we consolidated the `<staticText>` element rendering the string `Model:` and the `<textField>` element rendering the model field into a single `<textField>` element. The other, more significant difference is that we set the `isPrintRepeatedValues` element in the corresponding `<reportElement>` element to `false`. After compiling the above JRXML template, filling the resulting jasper template, and exporting the resulting report, we should see a report like the following:

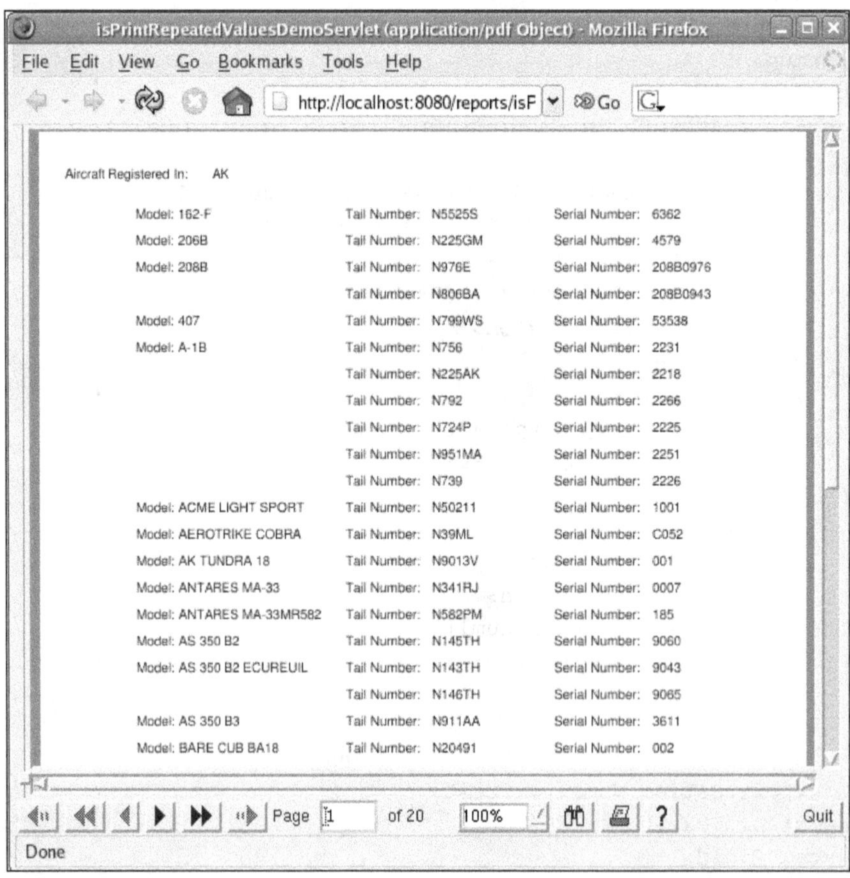

As we can see from the screenshot, the aircraft model is displayed only when it changes. This layout makes it a lot easier to see aircraft of the same model.

When `isPrintRepeatedValues` is set to `"false"` in a `<reportElement>` element inside an `<image>` element, the image will not be displayed repeatedly only if its `isUsingCache` attribute is set to `"true"`, and its corresponding image expression is the same for each row. Adding images to a report is discussed in detail in the next chapter.

Subreports

One nice feature of JasperReports is that it allows incorporating a report within another report. That is, one report can be a subreport of another. Subreports allow us to keep report designs simple, as we can create many simple reports and encapsulate them into a master report.

Let's create a more detailed version of the report discussed in the previous section. This new version divides the reported aircraft into the city to which they are registered. We will create one report that displays the aircraft registered in each city for a particular state. Then, we'll use that report as a subreport for a master report that divides the aircraft by state. The JRXML template for the subreport is as follows:

```
<?xml version="1.0" encoding="UTF-8"  ?>
<jasperReport
  xmlns="http://jasperreports.sourceforge.net/jasperreports"
        xmlns:xsi="http://www.w3.org/2001/XMLSchema-instance"
             xsi:schemaLocation="http://jasperreports.sourceforge
                 .net/jasperreports http://jasperreports.sourceforge
                 .net/xsd/jasperreport.xsd"
             name="AircraftCityReport">
  <parameter name="state" class="java.lang.String" />
  <parameter name="city" class="java.lang.String" />
  <queryString>
    <![CDATA[select a.tail_num, a.aircraft_serial, am.model, a.state
            from aircraft a, aircraft_models am
            where a.aircraft_model_code = am.aircraft_model_code
            and a.country = 'US' and a.state = $P{state}
            and a.city = $P{city}
            order by model]]>
  </queryString>
  <field name="tail_num" class="java.lang.String" />
  <field name="aircraft_serial" class="java.lang.String" />
  <field name="model" class="java.lang.String" />
  <title>
```

```
    <band height="30">
      <textField>
        <reportElement x="0" y="0" width="300" height="24" />
        <textElement markup="styled" />
        <textFieldExpression>
          <![CDATA["<style isBold=\"true\" pdfFontName=\
                  "Helvetica-Bold\"> Aircraft Registered in " +
                   $P{city} + ", " + $P{state} + "</style>"]]>
        </textFieldExpression>
      </textField>
    </band>
  </title>
  <pageHeader>
    <band height="30">
      <staticText>
        <reportElement width="100" x="0" y="0" height="30" />
          <textElement markup="styled" verticalAlignment="Middle" />
          <text>
            <![CDATA[<style isBold="true"
                         pdfFontName="Helvetica-Bold">Model</style>]]>
          </text>
        </staticText>
        <staticText>
          <reportElement width="100" x="110" y="0" height="30" />
          <textElement markup="styled" verticalAlignment="Middle" />
          <text>
            <![CDATA[<style isBold="true"
                       pdfFontName="Helvetica-Bold">
                       Tail Number</style>]]>
          </text>
        </staticText>
      <staticText>
        <reportElement width="105" x="220" y="0" height="30" />
        <textElement markup="styled" verticalAlignment="Middle" />
        <text>
          <![CDATA[<style isBold="true" pdfFontName="Helvetica-Bold">
                  Serial Number</style>]]>
        </text>
      </staticText>
    </band>
  </pageHeader>
  <detail>
    <band height="24">
      <textField>
        <reportElement x="0" y="0" width="100" height="24" />
        <textElement verticalAlignment="Middle" />
        <textFieldExpression>
          <![CDATA[$F{model}]]>
        </textFieldExpression>
      </textField>
```

```
        <textField>
          <reportElement x="110" y="0" width="100" height="24" />
          <textElement verticalAlignment="Middle" />
          <textFieldExpression>
            <![CDATA[$F{tail_num}]]>
          </textFieldExpression>
        </textField>
        <textField>
          <reportElement x="220" y="0" width="100" height="24" />
          <textElement verticalAlignment="Middle" />
          <textFieldExpression>
            <![CDATA[$F{aircraft_serial}]]>
          </textFieldExpression>
        </textField>
      </band>
    </detail>
  </jasperReport>
```

As we can see, we didn't have to do anything special to make this report a subreport. This is because any report can be used as a subreport. Let's see what the parent report's JRXML looks like.

```
<?xml version="1.0" encoding="UTF-8"  ?>
<jasperReport
  xmlns="http://jasperreports.sourceforge.net/jasperreports"
         xmlns:xsi="http://www.w3.org/2001/XMLSchema-instance"
               xsi:schemaLocation="http://jasperreports.sourceforge
                  .net/jasperreports http://jasperreports.sourceforge
                  .net/xsd/jasperreport.xsd"
         name="AircraftStateReport">
  <parameter name="state" class="java.lang.String" />
  <queryString>
    <![CDATA[select city from aircraft where state = $P{state}]]>
  </queryString>
  <field name="city" class="java.lang.String" />
  <title>
    <band height="30">
      <textField>
        <reportElement x="0" y="0" width="300" height="24" />
        <textElement markup="styled" />
          <textFieldExpression>
            <![CDATA["<style isBold=\"true\"
                     pdfFontName=\"Helvetica-Bold\"> Aircraft
                     Registered in " + $P{state} + "</style>"]]>
        </textFieldExpression>
      </textField>
    </band>
  </title>
  <detail>
    <band height="10">
```

```
        <subreport>
          <reportElement x="0" y="0" height="10" width="500"
                         isPrintWhenDetailOverflows="true" />
          <subreportParameter name="state">
            <subreportParameterExpression>
              <![CDATA[$P{state}]]>
            </subreportParameterExpression>
          </subreportParameter>
          <subreportParameter name="city">
            <subreportParameterExpression>
              <![CDATA[$F{city}]]>
            </subreportParameterExpression>
          </subreportParameter>
          <connectionExpression>
            <![CDATA[$P{REPORT_CONNECTION}]]>
          </connectionExpression>
          <subreportExpression class="java.lang.String">
              <![CDATA["http://localhost:8080/reports/reports/
                       AircraftCityReport.jasper"]]>
          </subreportExpression>
        </subreport>
      </band>
    </detail>
  </jasperReport>
```

As can be seen in the above JRXML, we place a subreport into a master report by using the `<subreport>` element. The `<subReportParameter>` element is used to pass parameters to the subreport. The `<connectionExpression>` element is used to pass a `java.sql.Connection` to the subreport. It needs to be used only if the subreport template requires a database connection (as opposed to a datasource) to be filled. Recall from Chapter 5, *Working with Other Datasources*, that the built-in report parameter `REPORT_CONNECTION` resolves into a reference to the instance of `java.util.Connection` passed to the report. If the parent report uses a datasource instead of a connection and the subreport needs a connection, the easiest way to pass the connection to a subreport is to pass it as a parameter to the parent report, which can then pass it to the subreport by using the corresponding parameter name in `<connectionExpression>`. The `<subReportExpression>` element indicates where to find the compiled report template for the subreport.

When the `class` attribute of `<subreportExpression>` is a string, JasperReports attempts to resolve a URL for the string contents. If that fails, it then assumes that the string contents represent the template's location in the filesystem and tries to load the report template from disk. If that also fails, it assumes that the string represents a CLASSPATH location and attempts to load the report template from the CLASSPATH. If all of these fail, JasperReports will throw an exception because, in that case, it will not be able to find the template for the subreport.

Other valid values for the class attribute of report expressions include net.sf.jasperreports.engine.JasperReport, java.io.File, java.io.InputStream, and java.net.URL. The most common way to obtain these values is to have the Java code filling the report pass them as a parameter and resolve them inside the <subreportExpression> tags using the $P{paramName} syntax we have seen before.

After compiling, filling, and exporting the last JRXML template, the following report will be generated:

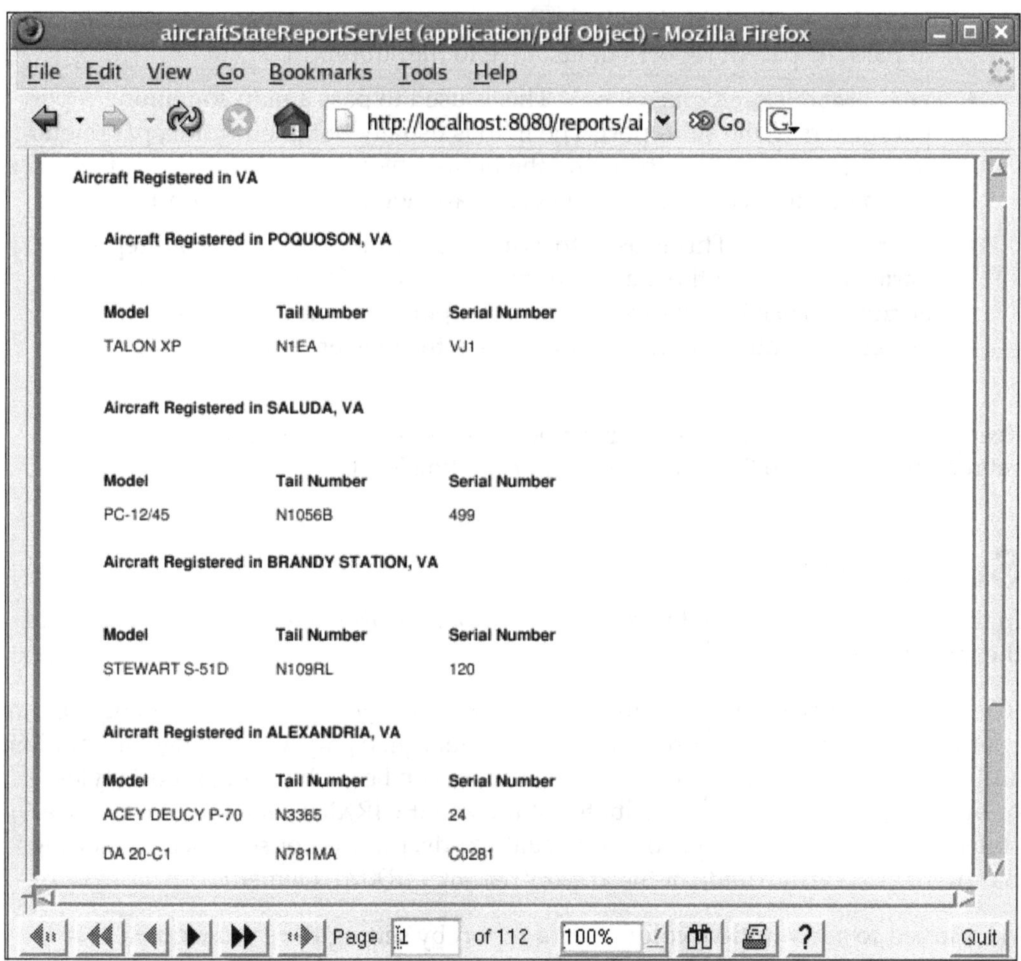

The **Model**, **Tail Number**, and **Serial Number** section of the above report is an embedded report within the main report. In JasperReports jargon, we call it a subreport. Each time we passed a different city as a parameter, it generated a report for the appropriate city.

The `<subreport>` JRXML element can contain a number of subelements that were not used in the above example. These subelements include:

- `<dataSourceExpression>`: This is used to pass a datasource to the subreport. This datasource is usually obtained from a parameter in the master report or by using the built-in `REPORT_DATA_SOURCE` parameter to pass the parent report's datasource to the subreport.
- `<parametersMapExpression>`: This is used to pass a map containing report parameters to the subreport. The map is usually obtained from a parameter in the master report or by using the built-in `REPORTS_PARAMETERS_MAP` parameter to pass the parent report's parameters to the subreport.
- `<returnValue>`: This is used to assign the value of one of the subreport's variables to one of the master report's variables. The `subreportVariable` attribute is used for indicating the subreport variable to be used, and the `toVariable` attribute is used to indicate the master report variable to be used.

Keep in mind that subreports can have other subreports, which in turn can have more subreports. There is no limit for the subreport nesting level.

Summary

In this chapter, we discussed several JasperReports features that allow us to control the layout of a report.

By setting the appropriate attributes of the `<jasperReport>` JRXML element, we can control report-wide layout properties, such as margins, page width, page orientation, and others. Text properties such as size and font can be set by using report styles or by setting the appropriate attributes of the `<text>` JRXML element. We can use styled text to modify the style of individual words, phrases, or sentences by setting the `isStyledText` attribute of the `<textElement>` JRXML element.

We learned to add multiple columns to a report by setting the `columnCount` attribute of the `<jasperReport>` JRXML element. We also learned to divide the report data into logical groups by using the `<group>` JRXML element. The chapter also dealt with displaying dynamic data in a report by using report expressions, encapsulating report expressions using report variables, and performing automated report calculations.

This chapter explained how to stretch text fields to accommodate large amounts of data by setting the `isStretchWithOverflow` attribute of the `<textField>` JRXML element to `true`. We went about setting the appropriate attributes of the `<reportElement>` JRXML element to control the layout of individual report elements, including their size, width, height, and how they react to having another element stretch beyond its declared size. We also learned to set properties that affect a group of elements by grouping them in a frame through the `<frame>` JRXML element. We also saw how to set the `isPrintRepeatedValues` attribute of the `<reportElement>` JRXML element to `false` to avoid printing repeated values between datasource records. Lastly, we created subreports by taking advantage of the `<subReport>` JRXML element.

7

Adding Charts and Graphics to Reports

All of the reports we have seen so far contain only textual data. JasperReports has the capability to create reports with graphical data in them, including simple geometric shapes, images, and charts. Adding graphical representation of the data makes it easier to visualize. Adding images and other graphical elements allows us to create more appealing reports. In this chapter, we will learn how to take advantage of JasperReports' graphical features.

We are going to cover the following topics in this chapter:

- Adding simple geometrical shapes to a report
- Adding images to a report
- Adding different types of 2D and 3D charts to a report

Adding geometrical shapes to a report

JasperReports supports adding lines, rectangles, and ellipses to a report. This capability allows us to display simple graphics in a report. The following sections will discuss each one of these elements in detail:

Adding lines to a report

Lines can be added to a report by using the JRXML element `<line>`. A line is drawn as a diagonal from one corner of the area defined by its `<reportElement>` subelement to the other. The JRXML `<line>` element has a single attribute `direction`; this attribute has two valid values: `BottomUp`, which indicates that the line will go from the bottom corner to the top one, and `TopDown`, which indicates that the line will go from the top corner to the bottom one. The default value for the `direction` attribute is `TopDown`.

The following example demonstrates the use of the `<line>` element:

```
<?xml version="1.0" encoding="UTF-8"  ?>
<jasperReport
  xmlns="http://jasperreports.sourceforge.net/jasperreports"
        xmlns:xsi="http://www.w3.org/2001/XMLSchema-instance"
        xsi:schemaLocation="http://jasperreports.sourceforge.net
            /jasperreports http://jasperreports.sourceforge.net/xsd
            /jasperreport.xsd"
        name="LineDemoReport">
  <detail>
    <band height="100">
      <line>
        <reportElement x="0" y="0" width="555" height="25" />
      </line>
      <line direction="BottomUp">
        <reportElement x="0" y="26" width="555" height="25"/>
      </line>
      <line>
        <reportElement x="0" y="50" width="1" height="25" />
      </line>
      <line>
        <reportElement x="0" y="75" width="555" height="0" />
      </line>
    </band>
  </detail>
</jasperReport>
```

After compiling this JRXML template and filling the resulting binary jasper template, we should get a report that looks like the following:

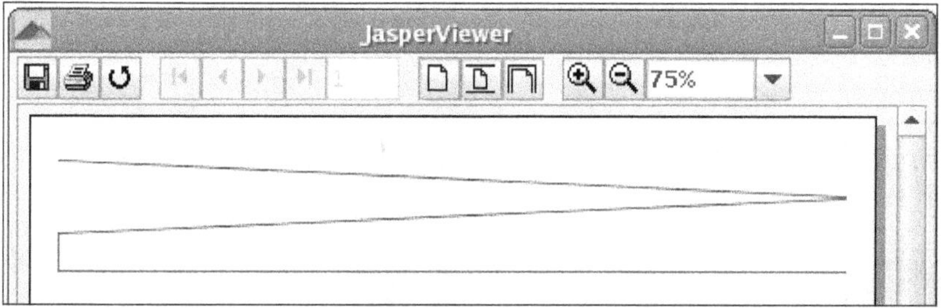

As can be seen in this example, the default value for direction is `TopDown`. Also, as there is no way to directly create a vertical or horizontal line, the way we can achieve this is by setting either the width (for vertical lines) or height (for horizontal lines) of the `<reportElement>` subelement of `<line>` to zero. Notice how the lines go from one corner of the area defined by `<reportElement>` to the other. Altering the value of the `direction` attribute allows us to define which way the line will slope.

Adding rectangles to a report

Adding a rectangle to a report can be achieved by using the JRXML element `<rectangle>`. A rectangle simply outlines the area defined by its `<reportElement>` subelement. We can create rectangles with round corners by setting the `radius` property of the `<rectangle>` element. The following JRXML template illustrates how to create rectangles in a report:

```
<?xml version="1.0" encoding="UTF-8"?>
<jasperReport
  xmlns="http://jasperreports.sourceforge.net/jasperreports"
         xmlns:xsi="http://www.w3.org/2001/XMLSchema-instance"
         xsi:schemaLocation="http://jasperreports.sourceforge.net
             /jasperreports http://jasperreports.sourceforge.net/xsd
             /jasperreport.xsd"
               name="RectangleDemoReport">
  <detail>
    <band height="100">
      <rectangle>
        <reportElement x="0" y="0" width="555" height="30" />
      </rectangle>
      <rectangle radius="5">
        <reportElement x="0" y="70" width="555" height="30"
                       forecolor="lightGray"/>
        <graphicElement>
```

```
          <pen lineWidth="4"/>
        </graphicElement>
      </rectangle>
    </band>
  </detail>
</jasperReport>
```

After compiling this JRXML template and filling the resulting binary jasper template, we should see a report like the following:

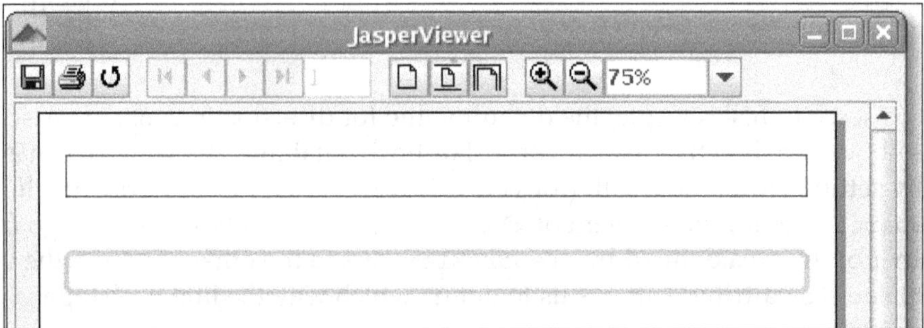

Notice how the line outlining the second rectangle is thicker than the first one. This is because we used the `<graphicElement>` subelement of the `<rectangle>` element. Like every text element can contain a subelement called `<textElement>`, every graphic element can also contain a subelement called `<graphicElement>`.

The `<graphicElement>` subelement has only one non-deprecated attribute, `fill`. The `fill` attribute controls the pattern to use for painting the inside area of the element. Currently, JasperReports supports only one value for this element—`Solid`. This value fills the inside of the element with solid color. The `<graphicElement>` JRXML element should have a `<pen>` subelement. This element has a `lineWidth` attribute that determines the width of the line used to draw the parent element of `<graphicElement>` (`<rectangle>`, in our example). It also has a `lineStyle` attribute that determines the style of the line (solid, dashed, dotted, or double) and a `lineColor` attribute that determines the color of the line used to draw said parent element.

Adding ellipses to a report

Ellipses are added to a report by using the JRXML element `<ellipse>`. The `<ellipse>` element contains no attributes. Its shape is determined by its `<reportElement>` attributes `width` and `height`.

The following JRXML template illustrates how to add ellipses to a report:

```
<?xml version="1.0" encoding="UTF-8"?>
<jasperReport
  xmlns="http://jasperreports.sourceforge.net/jasperreports"
         xmlns:xsi="http://www.w3.org/2001/XMLSchema-instance"
         xsi:schemaLocation= "http://jasperreports.sourceforge.net
             /jasperreports http://jasperreports.sourceforge.net/xsd
             /jasperreport.xsd"
             name="EllipseDemoReport">
  <detail>
    <band height="100">
      <ellipse>
        <reportElement x="280" y="0" height="20" width="20"/>
      </ellipse>
      <ellipse>
        <reportElement x="280" y="20" height="50" width="20" />
      </ellipse>
      <ellipse>
        <reportElement x="275" y="60" height="40" width="10" />
      </ellipse>
      <ellipse>
        <reportElement x="295" y="60" height="40" width="10" />
      </ellipse>
      <ellipse>
        <reportElement x="297" y="25" height="10" width="30" />
      </ellipse>
      <ellipse>
        <reportElement x="253" y="25" height="10" width="30" />
      </ellipse>
    </band>
  </detail>
</jasperReport>
```

After compiling this JRXML template and filling the resulting binary jasper template, we should see a report like the following:

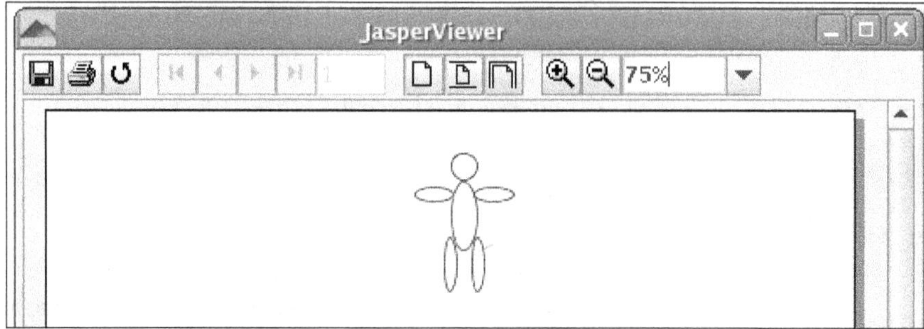

As we can see from the last example, we can create a circle by using the same value for the `width` and `height` attributes of the `<reportElement>` element inside the `<ellipse>` element.

Adding images to a report

Images can be added to a report by using the JRXML element `<image>`. The report images can be loaded from memory, disk, or a URL. Where to obtain the image is determined by the `<imageExpression>` subelement of the `<image>` element.

The following example illustrates how to add an image to a report:

```
<?xml version="1.0" encoding="UTF-8"?>
<jasperReport
  xmlns="http://jasperreports.sourceforge.net/jasperreports"
         xmlns:xsi="http://www.w3.org/2001/XMLSchema-instance"
         xsi:schemaLocation="http://jasperreports.sourceforge.net
             /jasperreports http://jasperreports.sourceforge.net/xsd
             /jasperreport.xsd"
  name="ImageDemoReport">
  <background>
    <band height="391">
      <image>
         <reportElement x="65" y="0" width="391" height="391"/>
         <imageExpression class="java.lang.String">
           <![CDATA["reports/company_logo.gif"]]>
         </imageExpression>
      </image>
    </band>
  </background>
</jasperReport>
```

After compiling this JRXML template and filling the resulting binary jasper template, we should have a report that looks like the following:

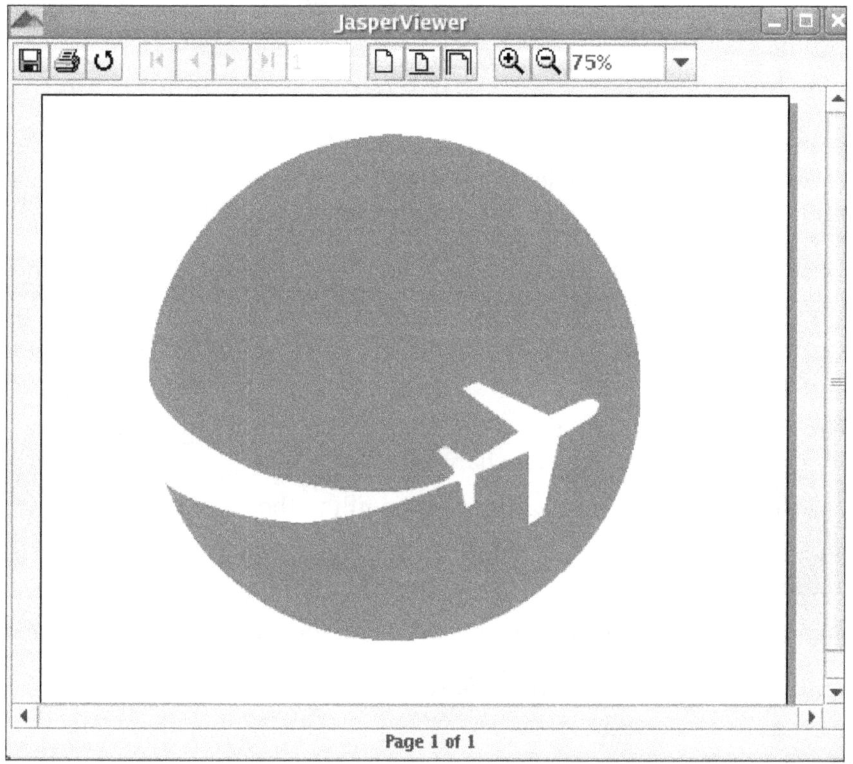

In this example, we set the width and height of the band to match the image size. Sometimes, the image is not available at the time of designing the report; therefore, we might not know the exact image dimensions. We can control how the image will look if its dimensions do not match the area defined by the `<reportElement>` subelement of the `<image>` element. This can be accomplished by using the `scaleImage` attribute of the `<image>` element. Following are the valid values for the `scaleImage` attribute:

- `Clip`: The report will display only that portion of the image that fits into the area defined by `<reportElement>`.
- `FillFrame`: The image will stretch vertically and/or horizontally to fit in the area defined by `<reportElement>`.
- `RetainShape`: The image will resize itself to fit in the area defined by `<reportElement>`. If the image width changes to fit in this area, the height will be proportionally changed so that the image retains its shape, and vice versa.

Attributes of the <image> element

The `<image>` element contains other attributes that allow us to control how the image will be displayed in the report. The following sections summarize most of these attributes.

evaluationTime

The `evaluationTime` attribute determines when the associated `<imageExpression>` will be evaluated. The valid values for this attribute are as follows:

- `Band`: The expression is evaluated when the containing band has rendered all other components.
- `Column`: The expression is evaluated when the end of the current column is reached.
- `Group`: The expression is evaluated when the group indicated by the `evaluationGroup` attribute changes.
- `Now`: The expression is evaluated when filling the containing band.
- `Page`: The expression is evaluated when the end of the current page is reached.
- `Report`: The expression is evaluated when the end of the report is reached.

The default value of `evaluationTime` is `Now`.

evaluationGroup

When `evaluationTime` is `Group`, the `evaluationGroup` attribute determines the group name to use in order to evaluate the associated `<imageExpression>`. The value for this attribute must match the group name we would like to use as the evaluation group.

hAlign

The `hAlign` attribute indicates the horizontal alignment of the image. The valid values for this attribute are as follows:

- `Center`: The image will be centered.
- `Left`: The image will be left-aligned.
- `Right`: The image will be right-aligned.

The default value of `hAlign` is `Left`.

vAlign

This attribute indicates the vertical alignment of the image. The valid values for this attribute are as follows:

- `Bottom`: The image will be placed at the bottom of the area defined by its `<reportElement>`.
- `Middle`: The image will be vertically centered between the top and bottom boundaries defined by `<reportElement>`.
- `Top`: The image will be placed at the top of the area defined by `<reportElement>`.

The default value of `vAlign` is `Top`.

IsLazy

This attribute determines whether the image is loaded when the report is filled or when the report is viewed or exported. The valid values for this attribute are as follows:

- `true`: The image will be loaded when the report is viewed or exported.
- `false`: The image will be loaded when the report is filled.

The default value of `IsLazy` is `false`.

isUsingCache

The `isUsingCache` attribute indicates whether images loaded from the same `<imageExpression>` will be cached. The valid values for this attribute are as follows:

- `true`: The image will be cached.
- `false`: The image will not be cached.

The default value of `isUsingCache` is `true`.

onErrorType

The `onErrorType` attribute determines the report's behavior when there is a problem loading the image. The valid values for this attribute are as follows:

- `Blank`: Only blank space will be displayed instead of the image.
- `Error`: An exception will be thrown, and the report will not be filled or viewed.
- `Icon`: An icon indicating a missing image will be displayed.

The default value of `onErrorType` is `Error`.

The `<image>` element contains other attributes to support hyperlinks and bookmarks, which are discussed in detail in Chapter 8, *Other JasperReports Features*.

Adding charts to a report

JasperReports supports several kinds of charts, such as pie charts, bar charts, XY bar charts, stacked bar charts, line charts, XY line charts, area charts, XY area charts, scatter plot charts, bubble charts, time series charts, high low charts, and candlestick charts. We will discuss each one of these in detail, but before we do so, let's discuss common properties among all charts.

There is a JRXML element used to create each type of chart; all of these elements will be discussed in subsequent sections. Each of these elements must contain a `<chart>` element as one of its subelements. The `<chart>` element must contain a `<reportElement>` element to define the chart's dimensions and position as one of its subelements. It may also contain a `<box>` element to draw a border around the chart, a `<chartTitle>` subelement to define and format the chart's title, and a `<chartSubtitle>` subelement to define and format the chart's subtitle.

Attributes of the <chart> element

The JRXML `<chart>` element contains a number of attributes that allow us to control the way a chart looks and behaves. The most commonly used attributes are listed in the following sections.

customizerClass

This attribute defines the name of a class that can be used to customize the chart. The value for this element must be a string containing the name of a customizer class.

evaluationGroup

When `evaluationTime` is `Group`, the `evaluationGroup` attribute determines the name of the group to use for evaluating the chart's expressions. The value for this attribute must match the group name we would like to use as the chart's evaluation group.

evaluationTime

The `evaluationTime` attribute determines when the chart's expression will be evaluated. The valid values for this attribute are as follows:

- `Band`: The chart is rendered when the containing band has finished rendering all other elements.
- `Column`: The chart is rendered when finished rendering all other elements in the current column.
- `Group`: The chart is rendered when the group specified by `evaluationGroup` changes.
- `Now`: The chart is rendered when its containing band is filled.
- `Page`: The chart is rendered when finished rendering all the other elements in the same page.
- `Report`: The chart is rendered when finished rendering all the other elements in the report.

The default value of `evaluationTime` is `Now`.

isShowLegend

The `isShowLegend` attribute is used to determine whether a chart legend will be displayed on the report. The valid values for this attribute are as follows:

- `true`: A legend will be displayed on the report.
- `false`: A legend will not be displayed on the report.

The default value of `isShowLegend` is `true`.

Chart customization

JasperReports uses `JFreeChart` as the underlying charting library; `JFreeChart` contains features that are not directly supported by JasperReports. We can take advantage of these features by supplying a `customizer` class through the `customizerClass` attribute.

All the customizer classes must implement the `net.sf.jasperreports.engine.JRChartCustomizer` interface, which contains a single method. The signature for that method is:

```
customize(org.jfree.chart.JFreeChart chart, JRChart jasperChart)
```

`org.jfree.chart.JFreeChart` is the `JFreeChart` library's representation of a chart, whereas `JRChart` is JasperReports' representation of a chart. Because the `customize()` method is automatically called by JasperReports when filling a report, we don't need to worry about instantiating and initializing instances of these classes.

Chart customization is more of a `JFreeChart` feature rather than a JasperReports feature. Therefore, we will refrain from showing an example.

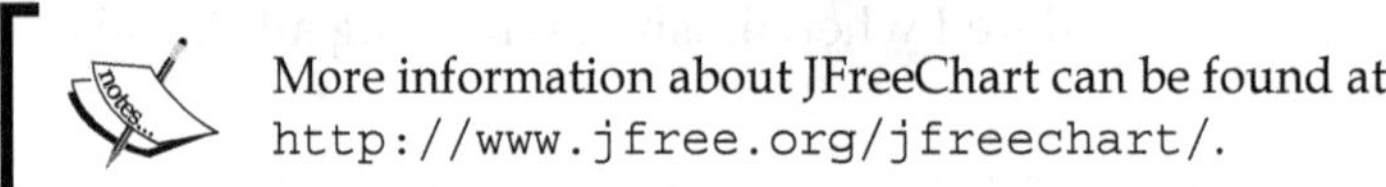

More information about JFreeChart can be found at `http://www.jfree.org/jfreechart/`.

The JRXML `<chart>` element contains some attributes used to support bookmarks and hyperlinks. These attributes are discussed in detail in the next chapter.

Chart datasets

Another common property across all the chart types is a dataset. Although each chart type contains different subelements to define a chart's expressions defining the data used to generate the chart, all of these subelements contain a `<dataset>` element that defines when the chart's expressions are evaluated and reset.

Attributes of the <dataset> element

The following sections describe all of the attributes for the JRXML `<dataset>` element.

incrementType

The `incrementType` attribute determines when to recalculate the value of the chart expression. The valid values for this attribute are as follows:

- `Column`: The chart expression is recalculated at the end of each column.
- `Group`: The chart expression is recalculated when the group specified by `incrementGroup` changes.
- `None`: The chart expression is recalculated with every record.
- `Page`: The chart expression is recalculated at the end of every page.
- `Report`: The chart expression is recalculated once at the end of the report.

The default value of `incrementType` is `None`.

incrementGroup

The `incrementGroup` attribute determines the name of the group at which the chart expression is recalculated when `incrementType` is `Group`. The value for this attribute must match the name of a group declared in the JRXML report template.

resetType

The `resetType` attribute determines when the value of the chart expression is reset. The valid values for this attribute are as follows:

- `Column`: The chart expression is reset at the beginning of each column.
- `Group`: The chart expression is reset when the group specified by `incrementGroup` changes.
- `None`: The chart expression is never reset.
- `Page`: The chart expression is recalculated at the beginning of every page.
- `Report`: The chart expression is recalculated once at the beginning of the report.

The default value of `resetType` is `Report`.

resetGroup

The `resetGroup` determines the name of the group at which the chart expression value is reset, when `resetType` is `Group`. The value for this attribute must match the name of any group declared in the JRXML report template.

Plotting charts

Another JRXML element that is common to all the chart types is the `<plot>` element. The JRXML `<plot>` element allows us to define several of the chart's characteristics, such as orientation and background color.

Attributes of the <plot> element

All attributes for the JRXML `<plot>` element are described in the next sections.

backcolor

The `backcolor` attribute defines the chart's background color. Any six-digit hexadecimal value is a valid value for this attribute, and it represents the RGB value of the chart's background color. The hexadecimal value must be preceded by a `#` character.

backgroundAlpha

The `backgroundAlpha` attribute defines the transparency of the chart's background color. The valid values for this attribute include any decimal number between `0` and `1`, both inclusive. The higher the number, the less transparent the background will be.

The default value of `backgroundAlpha` is `1`.

foregroundAlpha

The `foregroundAlpha` attribute defines the transparency of the chart's foreground colors. The valid values for this attribute include any decimal number between `0` and `1`, both inclusive. The higher the number, the less transparent the foreground will be.

The default value of `foregroundAlpha` is `1`.

orientation

The `orientation` attribute defines the chart's orientation (vertical or horizontal). The valid values for this attribute are as follows:

- `Horizontal`
- `Vertical`

The default value of `orientation` is `Vertical`.

Now that we have seen the attributes that are common to all the chart types, let's take a look at the chart types that are supported by JasperReports.

Pie charts

JasperReports allows us to create pie charts both in 2D and 3D. The procedure to create the 2D and 3D pie charts is almost identical; so, we will discuss them together.

Suppose we are asked to create a report indicating the most popular aircraft models registered in a particular city, as they appear in the `flightstats` database (refer to Chapter 4, *Creating Dynamic Reports from Databases*). This information can be nicely summarized in a pie chart. The following screenshot shows a report displaying this information for Washington, DC:

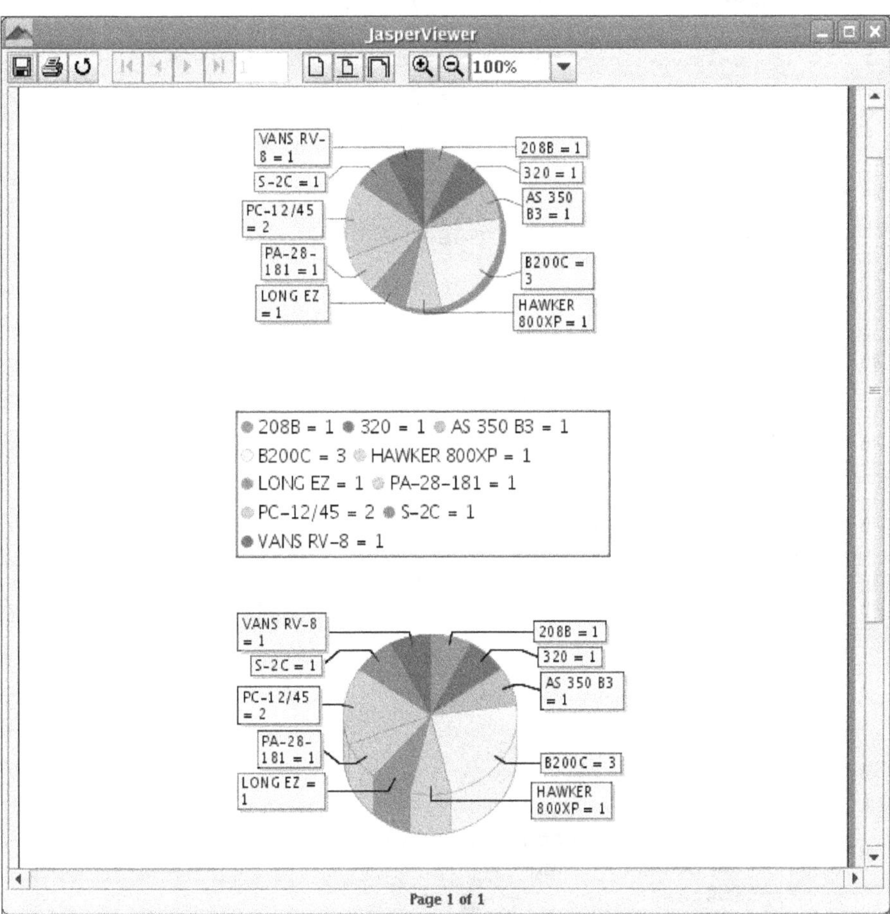

The JRXML template to create the report is as follows:

```
<?xml version="1.0" encoding="UTF-8"  ?>
<jasperReport
  xmlns="http://jasperreports.sourceforge.net/jasperreports"
```

```
        xmlns:xsi="http://www.w3.org/2001/XMLSchema-instance"
              xsi:schemaLocation="http://jasperreports.sourceforge
                  .net/jasperreports http://jasperreports
                  .sourceforge.net/xsd/jasperreport.xsd"
name="PieChartDemoReport">
<queryString>
  <![CDATA[select am.model from aircraft a, aircraft_models am
          where city='WASHINGTON' and state='DC'
          and a.aircraft_model_code = am.aircraft_model_code
          order by model]]>
</queryString>
<field name="model" class="java.lang.String" />
<variable name="totalAircraft" class="java.lang.Integer"
          calculation="Count" resetType="Group"
          resetGroup="modelGroup">
  <variableExpression>
    <![CDATA[$F{model}]]>
  </variableExpression>
  <initialValueExpression>
    <![CDATA[new java.lang.Integer(0)]]>
  </initialValueExpression>
</variable>
<group name="modelGroup">
  <groupExpression>
    <![CDATA[$F{model}]]>
  </groupExpression>
</group>
<summary>
  <band height="750">
  <!-- Start 2D Pie Chart -->
    <pieChart>
      <chart evaluationTime="Report">
        <reportElement x="135" y="0" width="270" height="350" />
      </chart>
      <pieDataset>
        <dataset incrementType="None" />
        <keyExpression>
          <![CDATA[$F{model}]]>
        </keyExpression>
        <valueExpression>
          <![CDATA[$V{totalAircraft}]]>
        </valueExpression>
      </pieDataset>
      <piePlot>
        <plot/>
      </piePlot>
    </pieChart>
<!-- End 2D Pie Chart -->

<!-- Start 3D Pie Chart -->
```

```
        <pie3DChart>
          <chart evaluationTime="Report" isShowLegend="false">
            <reportElement x="125" y="375" width="300" height="200" />
          </chart>
          <pieDataset>
            <dataset incrementType="None" />
            <keyExpression>
              <![CDATA[$F{model}]]>
            </keyExpression>
            <valueExpression>
              <![CDATA[$V{totalAircraft}]]>
            </valueExpression>
          </pieDataset>
          <pie3DPlot>
            <plot/>
          </pie3DPlot>
        </pie3DChart>
    <!-- End 3D Pie Chart -->
      </band>
    </summary>
  </jasperReport>
```

We can see from this example that the JRXML element to create a 2D pie chart is `<pieChart>`, and the JRXML element to create a 3D pie chart is `<pie3DChart>`. Just like all the other JRXML chart elements, these elements also contain a `<chart>` subelement. They contain a `<pieDataSet>` subelement too, which in turn contains the `<dataset>` element (for the chart), a `<keyExpression>` and `<valueExpression>` subelements. `<keyExpression>` contains a report expression indicating what to use as a key in the chart. The `<valueExpression>` element contains an expression used to calculate the value for the key. The values we see to the left of the equals sign in the chart labels correspond to the key expression (aircraft model, in this case). The values we see to the right of the equals sign in the labels correspond to the value expression (number of aircraft of a particular model, in this case).

In this example, the aircraft model is used as the key and is represented by the report field called `model`. The value to be used in the chart is the total number of aircraft of a particular model, represented by the `totalAircraft` report variable.

Element `<pieChart>` must contain a `<piePlot>` subelement containing the chart's `<plot>` element. Also, element `<pie3DChart>` must contain an analogous `<pie3DPlot>` element. The `<piePlot>` element has no attributes, whereas the `<pie3DPlot>` element has a single optional attribute called `depthFactor`. This attribute indicates the depth (how tall or short the pie chart is) of the 3D pie chart; its default value is 0.2.

Bar charts

Bar charts, just like pie charts, can be used to illustrate quantitative differences between chart elements. They can be used to display the same data a pie chart displays, but in a different way. One advantage that bar charts have over pie charts is that the same data for more than one category can be displayed.

Suppose we are asked to produce a report comparing the number of aircraft registered in Washington, DC, with the number of aircraft registered in New York city. The report must also illustrate the most popular aircraft models in each city. If we wanted to display this data graphically using a pie chart, we would have to create a pie chart for each city. With a bar chart, however, we can display the whole picture using a single chart, as can be seen in the following screenshot:

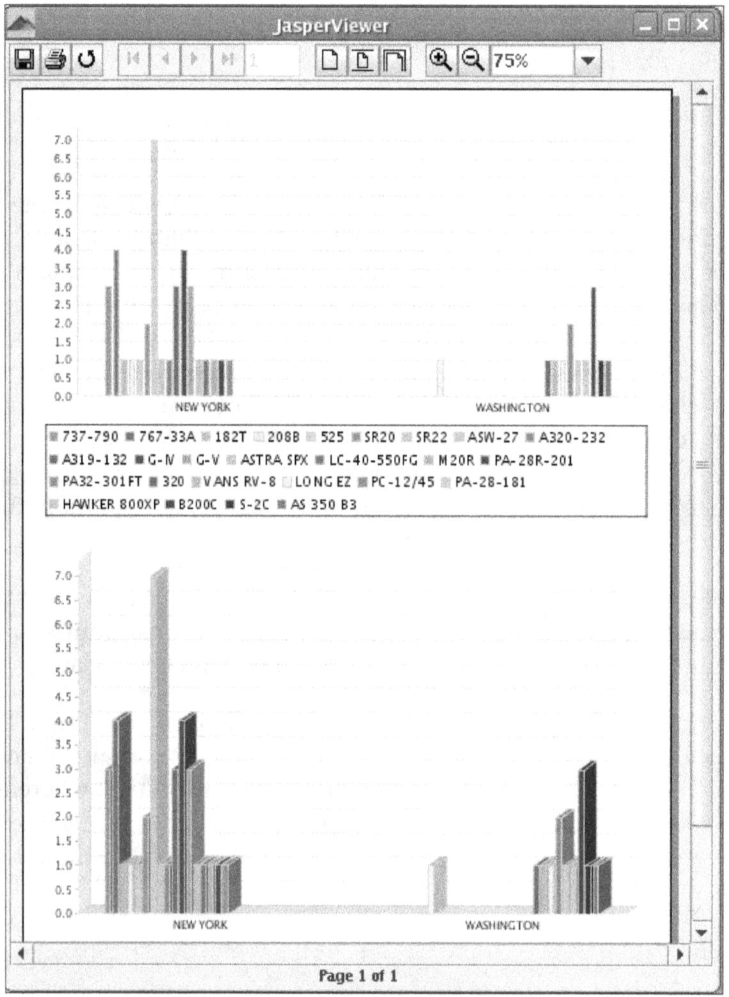

The JRXML template used to generate this report is as follows:

```
<?xml version="1.0" encoding="UTF-8"  ?>
<jasperReport
  xmlns="http://jasperreports.sourceforge.net/jasperreports"
         xmlns:xsi="http://www.w3.org/2001/XMLSchema-instance"
         xsi:schemaLocation="http://jasperreports.sourceforge.net
          /jasperreports http://jasperreports.sourceforge.net
          /xsd/jasperreport.xsd" name="BarChartDemoReport">
  <queryString>
    <![CDATA[(select a.city, am.model
              from aircraft a, aircraft_models am
              where city='NEW YORK' and state='NY'
              and a.aircraft_model_code = am.aircraft_model_code
              order by model)
                 UNION ALL
             (select a.city, am.model
              from aircraft a, aircraft_models am
              where city='WASHINGTON' and state='DC'
              and a.aircraft_model_code = am.aircraft_model_code
              order by model)]]>
  </queryString>
  <field name="city" class="java.lang.String" />
  <field name="model" class="java.lang.String" />
  <variable name="totalAircraft" class="java.lang.Integer"
            calculation="Count" resetType="Group"
            resetGroup="modelGroup">
    <variableExpression>
      <![CDATA[$F{model}]]>
    </variableExpression>
    <initialValueExpression>
      <![CDATA[new java.lang.Integer(0)]]>
    </initialValueExpression>
  </variable>
  <group name="modelGroup">
    <groupExpression>
      <![CDATA[$F{model}]]>
    </groupExpression>
  </group>
  <summary>
    <band height="750">
  <!-- Start 2D Bar Chart -->
      <barChart>
        <chart evaluationTime="Report">
          <reportElement x="0" y="0" width="555" height="350" />
        </chart>
```

```
          <categoryDataset>
            <dataset incrementType="None" />
            <categorySeries>
              <seriesExpression>
                <![CDATA[$F{model}]]>
              </seriesExpression>
              <categoryExpression>
                <![CDATA[$F{city}]]>
              </categoryExpression>
              <valueExpression>
                <![CDATA[$V{totalAircraft}]]>
              </valueExpression>
            </categorySeries>
          </categoryDataset>
          <barPlot isShowTickMarks="false">
            <plot />
          </barPlot>
        </barChart>
    <!-- End 2D Bar Chart -->
    <!-- Start 3D Bar Chart -->
        <bar3DChart>
          <chart evaluationTime="Report" isShowLegend="false">
            <reportElement x="0" y="375" width="555" height="350" />
          </chart>
          <categoryDataset>
            <dataset incrementType="None" />
            <categorySeries>
              <seriesExpression>
                <![CDATA[$F{model}]]>
              </seriesExpression>
              <categoryExpression>
                <![CDATA[$F{city}]]>
              </categoryExpression>
              <valueExpression>
                <![CDATA[$V{totalAircraft}]]>
              </valueExpression>
            </categorySeries>
          </categoryDataset>
          <bar3DPlot>
            <plot />
          </bar3DPlot>
        </bar3DChart>
    <!-- End 3D Bar Chart -->
      </band>
    </summary>
  </jasperReport>
```

As we can see in this example, the process used to create bar charts is very similar to the one for creating pie charts. This example creates two bar charts, a 2D and a 3D. Let's discuss the 2D bar chart first.

The JRXML element used to create a 2D bar chart is `<barChart>`. Just like all the other charts in JasperReports, it must contain a `<chart>` subelement, which contains a `<reportElement>` subelement defining the chart's dimensions and position.

The `<dataset>` element in a bar chart must be enclosed between the `<categoryDataSet>` and `</categoryDataset>` JRXML elements. The `<categoryDataSet>` element must contain a `<categorySeries>` element. This element defines what data element the bars will represent (aircraft models, in this example). The `<categoryDataSet>` element must also contain a `<categoryExpression>` element, which defines how the data will be separated into categories for comparison. In this example, data is separated by cities. The `<valueExpression>` element defines what expression to use for determining the value of each bar in the chart.

If we want to create 3D bar charts, the JRXML element to use is `<bar3DChart>`, which works almost exactly the same as `<barChart>`, the only difference being that the `<plot/>` element must be a subelement of `<bar3DPlot>`. The `<bar3DPlot>` element contains three attributes:

- `isShowLabels`: It determines whether labels will be shown in the chart.
- `xOffset`: Its valid value is any numeric value indicating the number of pixels to use for the 3D effect on the x axis.
- `yOffset`: Its valid value is any numeric value indicating the number of pixels to use for the 3D effect on the y axis.

XY line charts

XY line charts allow us to view the relationship between two numerical values. For our next example, let's suppose that we need to generate a report for a flight school to illustrate the operating cost for flying a particular model of their aircraft. Let's assume the flight school has an inventory of 43 of these aircraft, and the operating cost of each aircraft is $45 per day. The JRXML to generate a report with a chart illustrating the operating cost would look like the following:

```
<?xml version="1.0" encoding="UTF-8"  ?>
<jasperReport
  xmlns="http://jasperreports.sourceforge.net/jasperreports"
         xmlns:xsi="http://www.w3.org/2001/XMLSchema-instance"
         xsi:schemaLocation="http://jasperreports.sourceforge.net
         /jasperreports http://jasperreports.sourceforge.net/xsd
```

```
        /jasperreport.xsd"
  name="XYLineChartReportDemo">
  <queryString>
    <![CDATA[select tail_num from aircraft
       where aircraft_model_code = 0033001]]>
  </queryString>
  <field name="tail_num" class="java.lang.String" />
  <variable name="grandTotalAircraft" class="java.lang.Integer"
            calculation="Count" resetType="Report">
    <variableExpression>
      <![CDATA[$F{tail_num}]]>
    </variableExpression>
    <initialValueExpression>
      <![CDATA[new java.lang.Integer(0)]]>
    </initialValueExpression>
  </variable>
  <summary>
    <band height="750">
  <!-- Start X Y Line Chart -->
      <xyLineChart>
        <chart evaluationTime="Report">
          <reportElement x="0" y="0" width="555" height="350" />
        </chart>
        <xyDataset>
          <dataset incrementType="None" />
          <xySeries>
            <seriesExpression>
              <![CDATA["CH 2000"]]>
            </seriesExpression>
            <xValueExpression>
              <![CDATA[$V{grandTotalAircraft}]]>
            </xValueExpression>
            <yValueExpression>
              <![CDATA[new Long($V{grandTotalAircraft}.longValue()
                *45L)]]>
            </yValueExpression>
          </xySeries>
        </xyDataset>
        <linePlot>
          <plot />
        </linePlot>
      </xyLineChart>
  <!-- End X Y Line Chart -->
    </band>
  </summary>
</jasperReport>
```

The generated report would look like this:

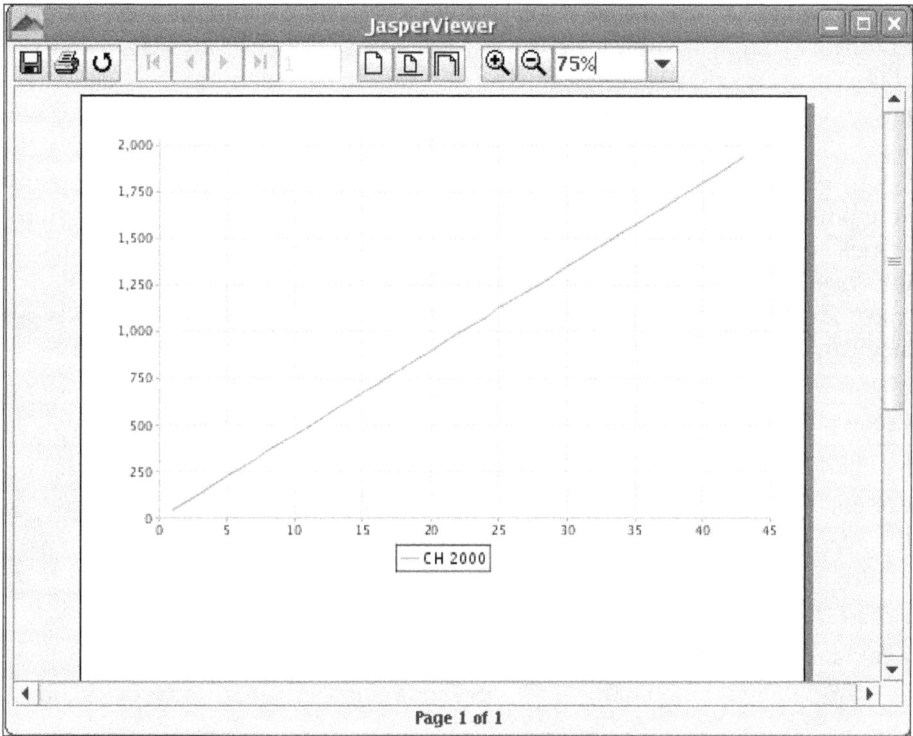

As we can see in the example, for XY line charts, the `<dataset>` element must be inside an `<xyDataset>` element and this element has no attributes. In addition to the `<dataset>` element, `<xyDataset>` may contain one or more `<xySeries>` element.

`<xySeries>` may contain a `<seriesExpression>` element, which is used to generate the label at the bottom of the chart in the example. The `<xySeries>` element may also contain an `<xValueExpression>` element and a `<yValueExpression>` element. These last two elements contain report expressions for the `X` and `Y` values in the chart, respectively.

Other types of charts

As we have seen in the previous examples, all the JRXML elements used to display a chart follow a pattern. First, we have the element that determines what chart to plot (`<pieChart>`, `<barChart>`, and so on). Inside that element is a `<chart>` element followed by an element enclosing the `<dataset>` element (`<pieDataset>`, `<categoryDataset>`, and so on), which, in turn, is followed by an element enclosing the `<plot>` element (`<piePlot>`, `<barPlot>`, and so on). As all of the charts follow the same pattern, we thought it would be redundant to show examples for all the chart types supported by JasperReports. In the following sections, we will discuss the elements used to create all other supported chart types, without explicitly showing examples. The JasperReports project files include examples for all the chart types, and they can be found in the `demo/samples/charts` directory:

Chart type	Chart element	Dataset element	Plot element
XY bar chart	`<xyBarChart>`	`<xyDataset>`	`<barPlot>`
Stacked bar chart	`<stackedBarChart>`	`<categoryDataset>`	`<barPlot>`
Line chart	`<lineChart>`	`<categoryDataset>`	`<linePlot>`
Area chart	`<areaChart>`	`<categoryDataset>`	`<areaPlot>`
XY area chart	`<xyAreaChart>`	`<xyDataset>`	`<areaPlot>`
Scatter plot chart	`<scatterChart>`	`<xyDataset>`	`<scatterPlot>`
Bubble chart	`<bubbleChart>`	`<xyDataset>`	`<bubblePlot>`
Time series chart	`<timeSeriesChart>`	`<timeSeriesDataset>`	`<timeSeriesPlot>`
High low chart	`<highLowChart>`	`<highLowDataset>`	`<highLowPlot>`
Candlestick chart	`<candlestickChart>`	`<highLowDataset>`	`<candlestickPlot>`
Gantt chart	`<ganttChart>`	`<ganttDataset>`	`<barPlot>`
Meter chart	`<meterChart>`	`<valueDataset>`	`<meterPlot>`
Multiple axis chart	`<multiAxisChart>`	`<categoryDataset>`	`<multiAxisPlot>`
Stacked area chart	`<stackedAreaChart>`	`<categoryDataset>`	`<areaPlot>`
Thermometer chart	`<thermometerChart>`	`<valueDataset>`	`<thermometerPlot>`
XY line chart	`<xyLineChart>`	`<xyDataset>`	`<linePlot>`

You can find details of the attributes for each of these at http://jasperforge.org/uploads/publish/jasperreportswebsite/JR%20Website/jasperreports_quickref.html.

Summary

In this chapter, we learned how to add graphical elements to our reports. We also understood how to add geometric figures and lines to our reports by using the <line>, <rectangle>, and <ellipse> JRXML elements.

We also discussed how to add images to our reports by using the <image> JRXML element. Adding several types of charts to our reports by using the appropriate JRXML elements, such as <pieChart>, <barChart>, and <xyLineChart> was also covered.

8
Other JasperReports Features

JasperReports has several features that allow us to create elaborate reports. In this chapter, we will discuss some of these features.

Some of the features we will cover in this chapter include:

- How to display report text in different languages by using report localization/internationalization
- How to execute snippets of Java code by using scriptlets
- How to create crosstab (cross-tabulation) reports
- How to use subdatasets to run a query with the results of a different query
- How to add anchors, hyperlinks, and bookmarks to the reports in order to ease navigation between report sections

Report localization

JasperReports takes advantage of the Java language's internationalization features to be able to generate reports in different languages. The following JRXML template will generate a report displaying a line of text that will be different depending on the locale used:

```
<?xml version="1.0" encoding="UTF-8"  ?>
<jasperReport xmlns="http://jasperreports.sourceforge.net
                     /jasperreports"
  xmlns:xsi="http://www.w3.org/2001/XMLSchema-instance"
       xsi:schemaLocation="http://jasperreports.sourceforge.net
           /jasperreports http://jasperreports.sourceforge.net/xsd
           /jasperreport.xsd"
```

```
                name="LocalizationDemoReport"
                resourceBundle="localizationdemo">
  <summary>
    <band height="60">
      <textField>
        <reportElement x="0" y="0" width="200" height="30" />
        <textFieldExpression>
          <![CDATA[$R{localization.text1}]]>
        </textFieldExpression>
      </textField>
    </band>
  </summary>
</jasperReport>
```

The `resourceBundle` attribute of the `<jasperReport>` element tells JasperReports where to get the localized strings to use for the report. For this attribute to work correctly, a property file with a root name matching the value of the attribute must exist anywhere in the CLASSPATH when filling the report. In the example, a property file with the name `localizationdemo.properties` must exist in the CLASSPATH when using the default locale. To use a different locale, the name of the file must be `localizationdemo_[locale].properties`. For example, to use a Spanish locale, the name would be `localizationdemo_es.properties`.

The following property file can be used with this template to generate the report using the default locale:

```
localization.text1=This is English text.
```

This, of course, assumes that the default locale uses the English language. In order to enable the JasperReports to pick it up as the resource bundle for the default locale, the file must be saved as `localizationdemo.properties`.

To generate a report from this template in Spanish, `localization_es.properties` must look like this:

```
localization.text1=Este texto es en Español.
```

Notice how in both the property files the key (text before the equals sign) is the same. This must be the case for each locale property file that we wish to use because JasperReports uses this key to obtain the localized text to display in the report. As can be seen in the example, the syntax to obtain the value for resource bundle properties is `$R{key}`.

To let JasperReports know what locale we wish to use, we need to assign a value to a built-in parameter. This parameter's name is defined as a constant called `REPORT_LOCALE`. This constant is defined in the `net.sf.jasperreports.engine.JRParameter` class, and its value must be an instance of `java.util.Locale`. The following example demonstrates this procedure:

```
package net.ensode.jasperbook;

import java.util.HashMap;
import java.util.Locale;

import net.sf.jasperreports.engine.JREmptyDataSource;
import net.sf.jasperreports.engine.JRException;
import net.sf.jasperreports.engine.JRParameter;
import net.sf.jasperreports.engine.JasperFillManager;

public class LocalizationDemoReportFill
{
  public static void main(String[] args)
  {
    try
    {
      HashMap parameterMap = new HashMap();

      if (args.length > 0)
      {
        parameterMap.put(JRParameter.REPORT_LOCALE,
                         new Locale(args[0]));
      }

      System.out.println("Filling report...");
      JasperFillManager.fillReportToFile(
                           "reports/LocalizationDemoReport.jasper",
                            parameterMap, new JREmptyDataSource());
      System.out.println("Done!");
    }
    catch (JRException e)
    {
      e.printStackTrace();
    }
  }
}
```

This example assumes that we have already created a jasper template from the JRXML template. If no command-line parameters are sent to this code, it will use the default locale; otherwise, it will use the first command-line parameter as the locale. Passing the string `es` as the first command-line parameter will result in the report being generated in Spanish. This happens because the highlighted code in the example puts the string we get as a command-line parameter into a `HashMap` containing report parameters that we pass to our report in the `JasperFillManager.fillReportToFile()` call. The generated report will look like the following:

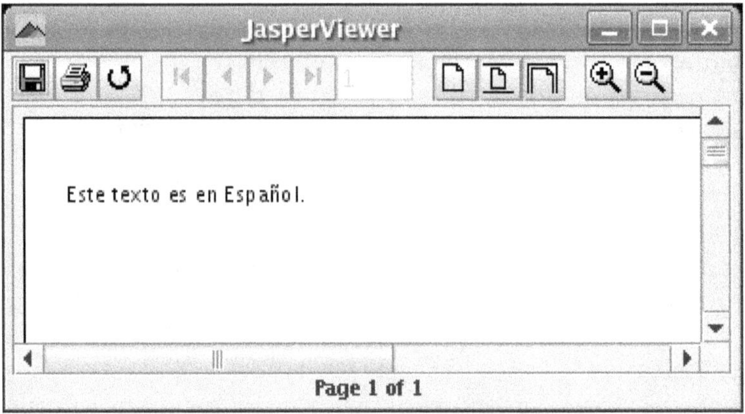

Passing no parameters to the code will result in a report using the default locale.

Scriptlets

JasperReports allows us to execute snippets of Java code at certain points during the report filling process. We can accomplish this by writing **scriptlets**. All the scriptlets must extend either `net.sf.jasperreports.engine.JRAbstractScriptlet` or `net.sf.jasperreports.engine.JRDefaultScriptlet`. Following is a brief explanation on these classes:

- `JRAbstractScriptlet`: This contains a number of abstract methods that must be overridden in every implementation. These methods are called automatically by JasperReports at the appropriate moment.
- `JRDefaultScriptlet`: This is a convenience class containing default empty implementations of every method in `JRAbstractScriptlet`. It can be used whenever we wish to override only a few of the methods in `JRAbstractScriptlet`.

The following table summarizes these methods:

Method	Description
`public void beforeReportInit()`	Called before report initialization.
`public void afterReportInit()`	Called after report initialization.
`public void beforePageInit()`	Called before each page is initialized.
`public void afterPageInit()`	Called after each page is initialized.
`public void beforeColumnInit()`	Called before each column is initialized.
`public void afterColumnInit()`	Called after each column is initialized.
`public void beforeGroupInit(String groupName)`	Called before the group specified in the parameter is initialized.
`public void afterGroupInit(String groupName)`	Called after the group specified in the parameter is initialized.
`public void beforeDetailEval()`	Called before each record in the detail section of the report is evaluated.
`public void afterDetailEval()`	Called after each record in the detail section of the report is evaluated.

Scriptlets allow us to add complex functionality to our reports, not easily achievable by report expressions or variables. We indicate that we want to use a scriptlet by setting the `scriptletClass` attribute of the `<jasperReport>` element in the JRXML template to the fully qualified name of the scriptlet (including the entire package name).

Suppose we have a report that is taking a long time to fill. The following scriptlet could help us find out which specific part of the report was taking a long time to fill so that we would know what to optimize:

```
package net.ensode.jasperbook;

import net.sf.jasperreports.engine.JRAbstractScriptlet;
import net.sf.jasperreports.engine.JRScriptletException;

public class PerformanceScriptlet extends JRAbstractScriptlet
{
  private long reportInitStartTime;
  private long reportInitEndTime;
  private long pageInitStartTime;
  private long pageInitEndTime;
  private long columnInitStartTime;
  private long columnInitEndTime;
  private long groupInitStartTime;
  private long groupInitEndTime;
  private long detailEvalStartTime;
  private long detailEvalEndTime;
```

```
public void beforeReportInit() throws JRScriptletException
{
  reportInitStartTime = System.currentTimeMillis();
}
public void afterReportInit() throws JRScriptletException
{
  reportInitEndTime = System.currentTimeMillis();
  System.out.println("Report initialization took " +
                     (reportInitEndTime - reportInitStartTime) +
                     " milliseconds.");
}
public void beforePageInit() throws JRScriptletException
{
  pageInitStartTime = System.currentTimeMillis();
}
public void afterPageInit() throws JRScriptletException
{
  pageInitEndTime = System.currentTimeMillis();
  Integer pageNum = (Integer) getVariableValue("PAGE_NUMBER");
  System.out.println("Page " + pageNum + " initialization took " +
                     (pageInitEndTime - pageInitStartTime) +
                     " milliseconds.");
}
public void beforeColumnInit() throws JRScriptletException
{
  columnInitStartTime = System.currentTimeMillis();
}
public void afterColumnInit() throws JRScriptletException
{
  columnInitEndTime = System.currentTimeMillis();
  Integer columnNum = (Integer) getVariableValue("COLUMN_NUMBER");
 System.out.println("Column " + columnNum + " initialization took "
                     + (columnInitEndTime - columnInitStartTime) +
                    " milliseconds.");
}

public void beforeGroupInit(String groupName)
throws JRScriptletException
{
  groupInitStartTime = System.currentTimeMillis();
}
public void afterGroupInit(String groupName)
throws JRScriptletException
{
  groupInitEndTime = System.currentTimeMillis();
```

```
        System.out.println("Group " + groupName + " initialization took "
                          + (groupInitEndTime - groupInitStartTime) +
                          " milliseconds.");
    }
    public void beforeDetailEval() throws JRScriptletException
    {
        detailEvalStartTime = System.currentTimeMillis();
    }
    public void afterDetailEval() throws JRScriptletException
    {
        detailEvalEndTime = System.currentTimeMillis();
        System.out.println("Detail evaluation took "
                          + (detailEvalEndTime - detailEvalStartTime) +
                          " milliseconds.");
    }
}
```

Each of the methods in this scriptlet would be run at the appropriate time, giving us an idea of the area(s) that are suffering from performance problems. Like we mentioned before, all that's needed to use a scriptlet in a report is to provide its fully qualified name to the `scriptletClass` attribute of the root `<jasperreport>` element in the JRXML template. The following example illustrates this concept:

```
<?xml version="1.0" encoding="UTF-8"  ?>
<jasperReport
    xmlns="http://jasperreports.sourceforge.net/jasperreports"
           xmlns:xsi="http://www.w3.org/2001/XMLSchema-instance"
           xsi:schemaLocation= "http://jasperreports.sourceforge.net
           /jasperreports http://jasperreports.sourceforge.net/xsd
           /jasperreport.xsd"
    name="ScriptletDemoReport" resourceBundle="localizationdemo"
    scriptletClass="net.ensode.jasperbook.PerformanceScriptlet">
  <summary>
    <band height="60">
      <textField>
        <reportElement x="0" y="0" width="200" height="30" />
        <textFieldExpression>
          <![CDATA[$R{localization.text1}]]>
        </textFieldExpression>
      </textField>
    </band>
  </summary>
</jasperReport>
```

This JRXML template is a slightly modified version of the template we saw in the previous section. The only difference is that we assigned a value to the scriptlet attribute of `<jasperReport>`. When filling the jasper template generated by the this JRXML template, we should see some console output similar to the following:

```
Column 1 initialization took 0 milliseconds.
Page 1 initialization took 0 milliseconds.
Report initialization took 0 milliseconds.
Detail evaluation took 31 milliseconds.
```

As can be seen in the Java source, scriptlets have access to the report variables. Their value can be obtained by calling the `getVariableValue()` method. In this example, we access only built-in variables, but there is nothing preventing scriptlets from accessing normal variables. Similarly, scriptlets can access report fields and parameters, both built-in and custom, by calling the `getFieldValue()` and `getParameterValue()` methods, respectively. Just like the `getVariableValue()` method, both of these methods take a single string parameter indicating the name of the field or parameter to obtain. Scriptlets can only access, not modify, report fields and parameters; however, scriptlets can modify report variable values. This can be accomplished by calling the `setVariableValue()` method. This method is defined in the `JRAbstractScriptlet` class, which is always the parent class of any scriptlet. The following example illustrates how to modify a report variable from a scriptlet:

```
package net.ensode.jasperbook;
import net.sf.jasperreports.engine.JRDefaultScriptlet;
import net.sf.jasperreports.engine.JRScriptletException;
public class ReportVariableModificationScriptlet extends
JRDefaultScriptlet
{
  public void afterReportInit() throws JRScriptletException
  {
    setVariableValue("someVar", new String(
                          "This value was modified by the scriptlet."));
  }
}
```

This class will modify a variable `someVar` to have the value modified by the scriptlet.

Notice how this scriptlet extends `JRDefaultScriptlet` instead of `JRAbstractScriptlet`. The `JRDefaultScriptlet` class is a convenience class included with JasperReports. It includes empty implementations of all the abstract methods in `JRAbstractScriptlet`, allowing us to override only those methods that concern our particular case.

The following JRXML template uses this scriptlet to modify the value of its `someVar` variable:

```
<?xml version="1.0" encoding="UTF-8"?>
<jasperReport xmlns="http://jasperreports.sourceforge.net
                     /jasperreports"
  xmlns:xsi="http://www.w3.org/2001/XMLSchema-instance"
        xsi:schemaLocation= "http://jasperreports.sourceforge.net
            /jasperreports http://jasperreports.sourceforge.net/xsd
            /jasperreport.xsd"
  name="ScriptletVariableModificationReport"
  scriptletClass= "net.ensode.jasperbook
                  .ReportVariableModificationScriptlet">
  <variable name="someVar" class="java.lang.String">
    <initialValueExpression>
      <![CDATA["This is the initial variable value."]]>
    </initialValueExpression>
  </variable>
  <title>
    <band height="30">
      <textField>
        <reportElement width="555" height="30" x="0" y="0" />
        <textFieldExpression>
          <![CDATA[$V{someVar}]]>
        </textFieldExpression>
      </textField>
    </band>
  </title>
</jasperReport>
```

Compiling and filling this JRXML template results in the following report:

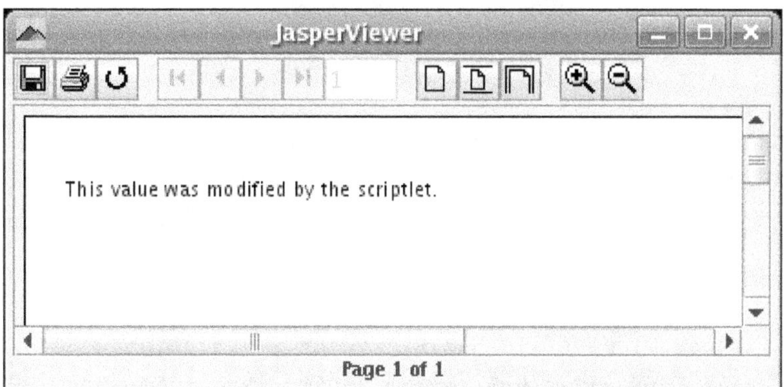

Notice how the report displays the variable value set in the scriptlet.

Before moving on, it is worth mentioning that we can add any additional methods we need to our scriptlets. Reports can call these methods by using the built-in parameter `REPORT_SCRIPTLET`. For example, if our scriptlet has a method called `foo()`, a report could access it by using the syntax `$P{REPORT_SCRIPTLET}.foo()`.

Crosstabs

Crosstabs (cross-tabulation) reports are the reports containing tables that tabulate the data across rows and columns. This feature was introduced in JasperReports 1.1. The following example illustrates the use of crosstabs in a report. The JRXML template will generate a report displaying a table containing the number of aircraft in each city of the state of New York. The last column of the table will display the total number of aircraft for all models in each city. The last row will display the total number of aircraft of each model in the table. To avoid having an unmanageable number of columns in the table, we will limit the report to aircraft models that start with the letter "C".

```
<?xml version="1.0" encoding="UTF-8"  ?>
<jasperReport xmlns="http://jasperreports.sourceforge.net
                    /jasperreports"
  xmlns:xsi="http://www.w3.org/2001/XMLSchema-instance"
  xsi:schemaLocation="http://jasperreports.sourceforge.net
      /jasperreports http://jasperreports.sourceforge.net/xsd
      /jasperreport.xsd"
        name="CrossTabDemoReport" leftMargin="5" rightMargin="5">
  <queryString>
    <![CDATA[select a.city, am.model, a.tail_num
             from aircraft a, aircraft_models am
             where a.state='NY' and am.model like 'C%'
             and a.aircraft_model_code = am.aircraft_model_code
             order by city, model]]>
  </queryString>
  <field name="tail_num" class="java.lang.String" />
  <field name="model" class="java.lang.String" />
  <field name="city" class="java.lang.String" />
  <summary>
    <band height="60">
      <crosstab>
        <reportElement width="782" y="0" x="0" height="60" />
        <rowGroup name="cityGroup" width="100" totalPosition="End">
          <bucket>
            <bucketExpression class="java.lang.String">
```

```
          <![CDATA[$F{city}]]>
        </bucketExpression>
      </bucket>
      <crosstabRowHeader>
        <cellContents>
          <box>
            <pen lineColor="black" lineWidth="1"/>
          </box>
          <textField>
            <reportElement width="100" y="0" x="0" height="20" />
            <textElement textAlignment="Right"
                         verticalAlignment="Middle" />
            <textFieldExpression>
              <![CDATA[$V{cityGroup}]]>
            </textFieldExpression>
          </textField>
        </cellContents>
      </crosstabRowHeader>
      <crosstabTotalRowHeader>
        <cellContents>
          <box>
            <pen lineColor="black" lineWidth="1"/>
          </box>
          <staticText>
            <reportElement x="0" y="0" width="60" height="20" />
            <textElement verticalAlignment="Middle" />
            <text>TOTAL</text>
          </staticText>
        </cellContents>
      </crosstabTotalRowHeader>
    </rowGroup>
    <columnGroup name="modelGroup" height="20"
                 totalPosition="End">
      <bucket>
        <bucketExpression class="java.lang.String">
          $F{model}
        </bucketExpression>
      </bucket>
      <crosstabColumnHeader>
        <cellContents>
          <box>
            <pen lineColor="black" lineWidth="1"/>
          </box>
          <textField isStretchWithOverflow="true">
```

```
              <reportElement width="60" y="0" x="0" height="20" />
              <textElement verticalAlignment="Bottom" />
              <textFieldExpression>
                <![CDATA[$V{modelGroup}]]>
              </textFieldExpression>
            </textField>
          </cellContents>
        </crosstabColumnHeader>
        <crosstabTotalColumnHeader>
          <cellContents>
            <box>
              <pen lineColor="black" lineWidth="1"/>
            </box>
            <staticText>
              <reportElement width="60" y="0" x="0" height="20" />
              <textElement verticalAlignment="Bottom" />
              <text>TOTAL</text>
            </staticText>
          </cellContents>
        </crosstabTotalColumnHeader>
      </columnGroup>
      <measure name="tailNumCount" class="java.lang.Integer"
               calculation="Count">
        <measureExpression>$F{tail_num}</measureExpression>
      </measure>
      <crosstabCell height="20" width="60">
        <cellContents backcolor="#FFFFFF">
          <box>
            <pen lineColor="black" lineWidth="1"/>
          </box>
          <textField>
            <reportElement x="5" y="0" width="55" height="20" />
            <textElement textAlignment="Left"
                         verticalAlignment="Bottom" />
            <textFieldExpression class="java.lang.Integer">
              $V{tailNumCount}
            </textFieldExpression>
          </textField>
        </cellContents>
      </crosstabCell>
    </crosstab>
  </band>
</summary>
</jasperReport>
```

Compiling and filling this JRXML template results in the following report:

JasperViewer

75%

	C90A	CGS HAWK	CH 2000	CHALLENGER II	CL-600-2B16	COZY MARK IV	CW-3	TOTAL
BROOKLYN	0	0	0	0	0	1	0	1
HOLLEY	0	0	0	1	0	0	0	1
MAYVILLE	0	0	0	0	0	0	1	1
MECHANICVILLE	0	0	0	1	0	0	0	1
SAINT JAMES	1	0	0	0	0	0	0	1
SAYVILLE	0	0	2	0	0	0	0	2
WATERTOWN	0	1	0	0	0	0	0	1
WEST HENRIETTE	0	0	0	1	0	0	0	1
WHITE PLAINS	0	0	0	0	1	0	0	1
TOTAL	1	1	2	3	1	1	1	10

Page 1 of 1

To keep the example as simple as possible, we refrained from adding any styles to the text in the crosstab. There is nothing preventing us from altering the text to have different fonts, alignments, and so on, as discussed in Chapter 6, *Report Layout and Design*.

In this example, the crosstab is defined by the `<crosstab>` element. The `<rowGroup>` element defines a group to split the data into rows. In the example, each row displays data for a different city. The `<bucket>` and `<bucketExpression>` elements define what report expression to use as a group delimiter for `<rowGroup>`. We have used the `city` field as a delimiter in order to achieve the splitting of the data into rows by city. The `<crosstabRowHeader>` element defines the expression to use as a row header. It contains a single subelement, namely `<cellContents>`, which acts as a sort of inner band inside crosstabs.

Notice that the variable name for the text field inside `<crosstabRowHeader>` is not declared in the JRXML template. This is because the name assigned to `<rowGroup>` (through its `name` attribute) creates an implicit variable. The `<crosstabTotalRowHeader>` element defines the contents of the header cell for the **TOTAL** row; it takes a single `<cellContents>` as its only subelement.

The `<columnGroup>` element, along with its subelements, is analogous to the `<rowGroup>` element, except that it affects columns instead of rows. `<columnGroup>` has the same subelements as `<rowGroup>`. The use of the `<columnGroup>` element is illustrated in the above example.

The <measure> element defines the calculation to be performed across the rows and columns. Possible values for its calculation attribute includes Average, Count, First, Highest, Lowest, Nothing, StandardDeviation, Sum, and Variance. These values work just like the analogous values for the calculation attribute for report variables. For a brief explanation refer to Chapter 6, *Report Layout and Design*.

The <crosstabCell> element defines how data in the non-header cells will be laid out. This element also contains a single <cellContents> element as its only subelement. If we wish to format cells displaying totals differently from other cells, we can accomplish this by adding additional <crosstabCell> elements and setting their rowTotalGroup and/or columnTotalGroup attributes to match the names defined in <rowGroup> and <columnGroup>.

Crosstab subelements

The <crosstab> element contains a number of subelements not shown in the example. The following sections describe all of the subelements of <crosstab>. Most of the elements shown in the following sections contain additional subelements. For more details visit the **JRXML Schema Reference** at http://jasperforge.org/uploads/publish/jasperreportswebsite/trunk/schema.reference.html.

<columnGroup>

The <columnGroup> subelement defines a group used to split the data into columns. Attributes for this element include:

- height: This defines the height of the column group header.
- name: This defines the name of the column group.
- headerPosition: This defines the position of the header contents (Right, Left, Center, Stretch).
- totalPosition: This defines the position of the **TOTAL** column (Start, End, None).

<crosstabCell>

The <crosstabCell> subelement defines how data in the non-header cells will be laid out. Attributes for this element include:

- columnTotalGroup: This indicates the group to use to calculate the column total.
- height: This defines the height of the cell.

- `rowTotalGroup`: This indicates the group to use in order to calculate the row total.
- `width`: This defines the width of the cell.

<crosstabDataset>

The `<crosstabDataset>` subelement defines the dataset to be used in order to populate the crosstab. (See the next section for a detailed explanation.) The only attribute for this element is:

- `isDataPreSorted`: This indicates whether the data in the dataset is pre-sorted.

<crosstabParameter>

The `<crosstabParameter>` subelement is used to access report variables and parameters from within the crosstab. Attributes for this element include:

- `name`: This defines the parameter name.
- `class`: This indicates the parameter class.

<measure>

The `<measure>` subelement defines the calculation to be performed across the rows and columns. Attributes for this element include:

- `name`: This defines the measure name.
- `class`: This indicates the measure class.
- `calculation`: This indicates the calculation to be performed between crosstab cell values.

<parametersMapExpression>

The `<parametersMapExpression>` subelement is used to pass a report variable or parameter containing an instance of `java.util.Map` as a set of parameters for the crosstab. This element contains no attributes.

<reportElement>

The `<reportElement>` subelement defines the position, width, and height of the crosstab within its enclosing band. Attributes for this element include all standard `<reportElement>` attributes.

<rowGroup>

The `<rowGroup>` subelement defines a group used to split the data into rows. Attributes for this element include:

- `name`: This defines the name of the row group.
- `width`: This defines the width of the row group.
- `headerPosition`: This defines the position of the header contents (`Top`, `Middle`, `Bottom`, `Stretch`).
- `totalPosition`: This defines the position of the **TOTAL** column (`Start`, `End`, `None`).

<whenNoDataCell>

The `<whenNoDataCell>` subelement defines what to display on an empty crosstab cell. This element contains no attributes.

Subdatasets

Sometimes we would like to display related charts or crosstabs for similar data grouped differently. For example, in the previous section, we generated a crosstab displaying the total number of aircraft of a particular set of models in the state of New York. We can display the same set of data for different states by using subdatasets. The following example illustrates how to do this:

```
<?xml version="1.0" encoding="UTF-8"  ?>
<jasperReport
  xmlns="http://jasperreports.sourceforge.net/jasperreports"
         xmlns:xsi="http://www.w3.org/2001/XMLSchema-instance"
         xsi:schemaLocation= "http://jasperreports.sourceforge.net
             /jasperreports http://jasperreports.sourceforge.net/xsd
             /jasperreport.xsd"
  name="DatasetDemoReport" leftMargin="5" rightMargin="5">
  <subDataset name="Aircraft_Models">
    <parameter name="StateParam" class="java.lang.String" />
    <queryString>
      <![CDATA[select a.city, am.model, a.tail_num
```

```
            from aircraft a, aircraft_models am
            where a.state=$P{StateParam} and am.model like 'C%'
            and a.aircraft_model_code = am.aircraft_model_code
            order by city, model]]>
  </queryString>
  <field name="tail_num" class="java.lang.String" />
  <field name="model" class="java.lang.String" />
  <field name="city" class="java.lang.String" />
</subDataset>
<queryString>
  <![CDATA[select distinct state from aircraft where state
          in ('MD', 'NY', 'VA') order by state]]>
</queryString>
<field name="state" class="java.lang.String" />
<detail>
  <band height="100">
    <textField>
      <reportElement x="0" y="10" width="500" height="20" />
      <textFieldExpression>
        <![CDATA["Aircraft registered in " + $F{state}]]>
      </textFieldExpression>
    </textField>
    <crosstab>
      <reportElement width="782" y="30" x="0" height="60" />
      <crosstabDataset>
        <dataset>
          <datasetRun subDataset="Aircraft_Models">
            <datasetParameter name="StateParam">
              <datasetParameterExpression>
                <![CDATA[$F{state}]]>
              </datasetParameterExpression>
            </datasetParameter>
          </datasetRun>
        </dataset>
      </crosstabDataset>
      <rowGroup name="cityGroup" width="100" totalPosition="End">
        <bucket>
          <bucketExpression class="java.lang.String">
            <![CDATA[$F{city}]]>
          </bucketExpression>
        </bucket>
      <crosstabRowHeader>
        <cellContents>
          <box>
```

```
          <pen lineColor="black" lineWidth="1"/>
        </box>
        <textField>
          <reportElement width="100" y="0" x="0" height="20" />
            <textElement textAlignment="Right"
                         verticalAlignment="Middle" />
            <textFieldExpression>
              <![CDATA[$V{cityGroup}]]>
            </textFieldExpression>
          </textField>
        </cellContents>
      </crosstabRowHeader>
      <crosstabTotalRowHeader>
        <cellContents>
          <box>
            <pen lineColor="black" lineWidth="1"/>
          </box>
          <staticText>
            <reportElement x="0" y="0" width="60" height="20" />
            <textElement verticalAlignment="Middle" />
            <text>TOTAL</text>
          </staticText>
        </cellContents>
      </crosstabTotalRowHeader>
    </rowGroup>
    <columnGroup name="modelGroup" height="20"
                 totalPosition="End">
      <bucket>
        <bucketExpression class="java.lang.String">
          $F{model}
        </bucketExpression>
      </bucket>
      <crosstabColumnHeader>
        <cellContents>
          <box>
            <pen lineColor="black" lineWidth="1"/>
          </box>
          <textField isStretchWithOverflow="true">
            <reportElement width="100" y="0" x="0" height="20" />
            <textElement verticalAlignment="Bottom" />
            <textFieldExpression>
              <![CDATA[$V{modelGroup}]]>
            </textFieldExpression>
          </textField>
```

```
          </cellContents>
        </crosstabColumnHeader>
        <crosstabTotalColumnHeader>
          <cellContents>
            <box>
              <pen lineColor="black" lineWidth="1"/>
            </box>
            <staticText>
              <reportElement width="60" y="0" x="0" height="20" />
              <textElement verticalAlignment="Bottom" />
              <text>TOTAL</text>
            </staticText>
          </cellContents>
        </crosstabTotalColumnHeader>
      </columnGroup>
      <measure name="tailNumCount" class="java.lang.Integer"
               calculation="Count">
        <measureExpression>
          $F{tail_num}
        </measureExpression>
      </measure>
      <crosstabCell height="20" width="100">
        <cellContents backcolor="#FFFFFF">
          <box>
            <pen lineColor="black" lineWidth="1"/>
          </box>
          <textField>
            <reportElement x="5" y="0" width="55" height="20" />
            <textElement textAlignment="Left"
                         verticalAlignment="Bottom" />
            <textFieldExpression class="java.lang.Integer">
              $V{tailNumCount}
            </textFieldExpression>
          </textField>
        </cellContents>
      </crosstabCell>
    </crosstab>
  </band>
</detail>
</jasperReport>
```

After compiling this template and filling the resulting jasper file, we should get a report that looks like the following:

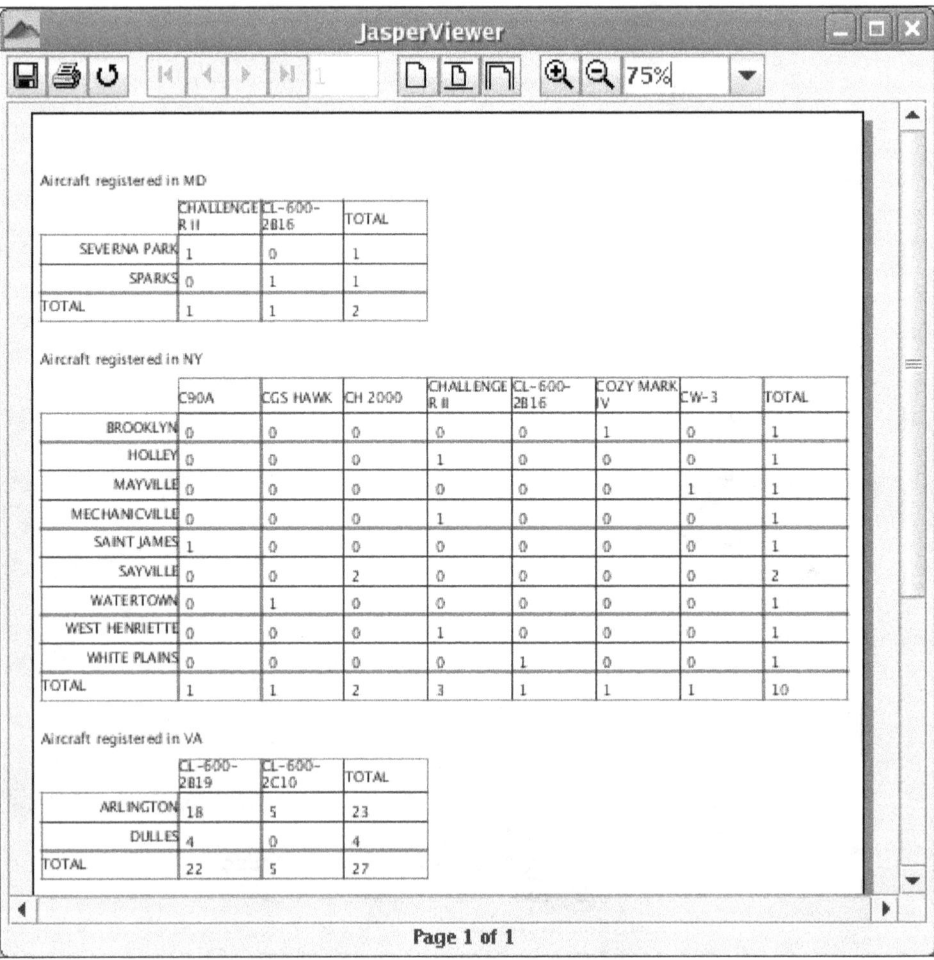

Aircraft registered in MD

	CHALLENGER II	CL-600-2B16	TOTAL
SEVERNA PARK	1	0	1
SPARKS	0	1	1
TOTAL	1	1	2

Aircraft registered in NY

	C90A	CGS HAWK	CH 2000	CHALLENGER II	CL-600-2B16	COZY MARK IV	CW-3	TOTAL
BROOKLYN	0	0	0	0	0	1	0	1
HOLLEY	0	0	0	1	0	0	0	1
MAYVILLE	0	0	0	0	0	0	1	1
MECHANICVILLE	0	0	0	1	0	0	0	1
SAINT JAMES	1	0	0	0	0	0	0	1
SAYVILLE	0	0	2	0	0	0	0	2
WATERTOWN	0	1	0	0	0	0	0	1
WEST HENRIETTE	0	0	0	1	0	0	0	1
WHITE PLAINS	0	0	0	0	1	0	0	1
TOTAL	1	1	2	3	1	1	1	10

Aircraft registered in VA

	CL-600-2B19	CL-600-2C10	TOTAL
ARLINGTON	18	5	23
DULLES	4	0	4
TOTAL	22	5	27

As we can see, the report template generates a different crosstab for each record in the `<detail>` section of the report. To accomplish this, we need to create a query inside `<subdataSet>` elements. The query must have one or more parameters, also defined inside `<subdataSet>`. This parameter needs to be populated with a report expression. In the example, we use the `city` field for this purpose.

To populate the dataset parameters with the desired report expression, we need to use the `<crosstabDataset>` element inside the crosstab. This element must contain a single `<dataset>` element, which in turn contains a `<datasetRun>` element. This element contains a `name` attribute indicating the subdataset to use in order to populate the crosstab. It also contains a `<datasetParameterExpression>` subelement indicating the report element to use to populate the dataset parameter.

Subdatasets can also be used in a similar manner to create related charts in each report record. To accomplish this, the `<dataset>` element must be placed inside the appropriate dataset element for the chart (`<categoryDataset>`, `<pieDataset>`, and so on). The following example demonstrates this for a bar chart. The report generated by the JRXML template will display a bar chart illustrating the number of aircraft registered in the states of Maryland, New York, and Virginia.

```
<?xml version="1.0" encoding="UTF-8"  ?>
<jasperReport
  xmlns="http://jasperreports.sourceforge.net/jasperreports"
         xmlns:xsi="http://www.w3.org/2001/XMLSchema-instance"
         xsi:schemaLocation= "http://jasperreports.sourceforge.net
             /jasperreports http://jasperreports.sourceforge.net/xsd
             /jasperreport.xsd"
  name="ChartDatasetDemoReport" leftMargin="5" rightMargin="5">
  <subDataset name="Aircraft_Registrations">
    <parameter name="StateParam" class="java.lang.String" />
    <queryString>
      <![CDATA[select a.city, count(*) as aircraft_count
               from aircraft a
               where a.state=$P{StateParam}
               and a.city like 'A%'
               group by city]]>
    </queryString>
    <field name="aircraft_count" class="java.lang.Integer" />
    <field name="city" class="java.lang.String" />
  </subDataset>
  <queryString>
    <![CDATA[select distinct state from aircraft
            where state in ('MD', 'NY', 'VA') order by state]]>
  </queryString>
  <field name="state" class="java.lang.String" />
  <detail>
  <band height="200">
    <textField>
      <reportElement x="0" y="10" width="500" height="20" />
      <textFieldExpression>
        <![CDATA["Aircraft registered in " + $F{state}]]>
```

```
        </textFieldExpression>
      </textField>
      <barChart>
        <chart>
          <reportElement width="500" y="30" x="0" height="170" />
        </chart>
        <categoryDataset>
          <dataset>
            <datasetRun subDataset="Aircraft_Registrations">
              <datasetParameter name="StateParam">
                <datasetParameterExpression>
                  <![CDATA[$F{state}]]>
                </datasetParameterExpression>
              </datasetParameter>
            </datasetRun>
          </dataset>
          <categorySeries>
            <seriesExpression>"City"</seriesExpression>
            <categoryExpression>
              <![CDATA[$F{city}]]>
            </categoryExpression>
            <valueExpression>
              <![CDATA[$F{aircraft_count}]]>
            </valueExpression>
          </categorySeries>
        </categoryDataset>
        <barPlot isShowTickMarks="true" isShowTickLabels="true">
          <plot orientation="Horizontal"/>
        </barPlot>
      </barChart>
    </band>
      </detail>
  </jasperReport>
```

Notice how the `<dataset>` element inside `<categoryDataset>` contains a `<datasetRun>` element with its `subdataset` attribute set to the subdataset declared at the beginning of the report. After compiling this JRXML template and filling the resulting jasper template, we should get a report like the following:

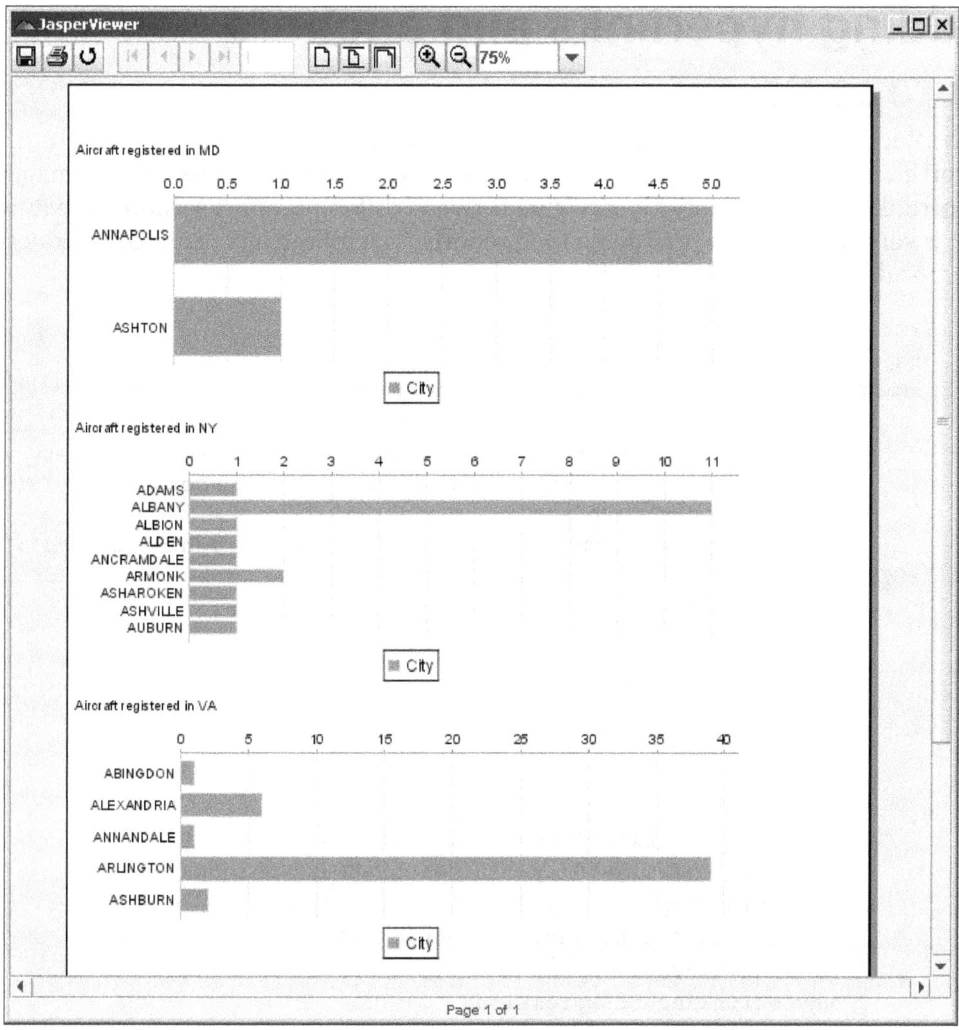

Each chart corresponds to a different state in the main report query. Data in each chart corresponds to cities for the corresponding state.

Adding hyperlinks and anchors to reports

JasperReports allows us to add hyperlinks and anchors to our reports. The only report elements that can be hyperlinks or anchors are text fields, charts, and images. Hyperlinks allow us to quickly navigate between different report sections, a feature that is very useful when producing long reports. The following example illustrates how to add hyperlinks to our reports:

```
<?xml version="1.0" encoding="UTF-8"  ?>
<jasperReport
  xmlns="http://jasperreports.sourceforge.net/jasperreports"
         xmlns:xsi="http://www.w3.org/2001/XMLSchema-instance"
         xsi:schemaLocation="http://jasperreports.sourceforge.net
             /jasperreports http://jasperreports.sourceforge.net/xsd
             /jasperreport.xsd"
         name="HyperLinkDemoReport" leftMargin="5" rightMargin="5">
  <title>
    <band height="60">
      <staticText>
        <reportElement x="0" y="0" width="555" height="30" />
          <text>
            <![CDATA[In a rush?]]>
          </text>
      </staticText>
      <textField hyperlinkType="LocalAnchor">
        <reportElement x="0" y="30" width="555" height="30" />
        <textFieldExpression>
          <![CDATA["Go to summary section."]]>
        </textFieldExpression>
        <hyperlinkAnchorExpression>
          <![CDATA["summary_section"]]>
        </hyperlinkAnchorExpression>
      </textField>
    </band>
  </title>
  <detail>
    <band height="60">
      <textField isStretchWithOverflow="true">
        <reportElement x="0" y="0" width="555" height="30" />
        <textFieldExpression>
          <![CDATA["This is the main report area, if this area had "
             + "a lot of text and the person reading " + "the report
             did not have time to read it all, " + "we can direct
```

```
                them to the summary section " + "by using a hyperlink.
                Let's add some more text " + "to make this area look
                more realistic. Boy, " + "if I was reading this report I
                would be bored " + "by now. Perhaps reading only the
                summary would " + "be a good idea? Why don't we do just
                that?"]]>
          </textFieldExpression>
        </textField>
      </band>
    </detail>
    <summary>
      <band height="60">
        <textField isStretchWithOverflow="true">
          <reportElement x="0" y="0" width="555" height="30" />
          <textFieldExpression>
            <![CDATA["This is the summary section. It contains less
                text so that the person reading the report can get the
                gist of the report data."]]>
          </textFieldExpression>
        <anchorNameExpression>
          <![CDATA["summary_section"]]>
        </anchorNameExpression>
      </textField>
    </band>
    </summary>
  </jasperReport>
```

As we can see from the example, we can turn a text field into a hyperlink by using the `hyperlinkType` attribute. In this example, we set `hyperlinkType` to be `LocalAnchor`, which means that the hyperlink target is another area of the report specified by an anchor expression. The `<hyperlinkAnchorExpression>` element indicates what the target for the hyperlink will be. To create the target for the anchor, we need to use the `<anchorNameExpression>` JRXML element. Notice how the contents of the `<anchorNameExpression>` match the contents of `<hyperlinkAnchorExpression>` in the example. This is how we link hyperlinks with the corresponding anchor.

In addition to pointing to specific anchors, hyperlinks can point to external resources or specific pages in the report. When a hyperlink points to an external resource, the enclosing element (text field, image, or chart) must contain a `<hyperlinkReferenceExpression>` element containing a report expression indicating the name of the external resource (usually a URL).

The following table summarizes the different types of hyperlinks supported by JasperReports:

Hyperlink type	Description	Elements defining hyperlink target
`LocalAnchor`	Hyperlink points to an anchor in the report, defined by the `<anchorNameExpression>` element.	`<hyperlinkAnchorExpression>`
`LocalPage`	Hyperlink points to a page in the current report.	`<hyperlinkPageExpression>`
`None`	Used to indicate that the element containing the `hyperlinkType` attribute is not an anchor. (This is the default.)	N/A
`Reference`	Hyperlink points to an external resource.	`<hyperlinkReferenceExpression>`
`RemoteAnchor`	Hyperlink points to an anchor in an external resource.	`<hyperlinkAnchorExpression>` `<hyperlinkReferenceExpression>`
`RemotePage`	Hyperlink points to a page in an external resource.	`<hyperlinkPageExpression>` `<hyperlinkReferenceExpression>`

The text field, chart, or image containing the `hyperlinkType` attribute must contain the corresponding element defining the hyperlink target as shown in the table. Of all these elements, the only element we haven't discussed is `<hyperlinkPageExpression>`. This element must contain a report expression resolving into a numeric value corresponding to the page number where the hyperlink will take us.

Turning chart items into hyperlinks

Another interesting JasperReports feature is that it allows us to turn chart items into hyperlinks; that is, it lets us click on them to quickly navigate to another report section or to an external resource. The following example, which is a slightly modified version of the chart example in the *Subdatasets* section, illustrates how to do this:

```
<?xml version="1.0" encoding="UTF-8"  ?>
<jasperReport
  xmlns="http://jasperreports.sourceforge.net/jasperreports"
         xmlns:xsi="http://www.w3.org/2001/XMLSchema-instance"
         xsi:schemaLocation= "http://jasperreports.sourceforge.net
             /jasperreports http://jasperreports.sourceforge.net/xsd
             /jasperreport.xsd"
  name="ChartHyperlinkDemoReport" leftMargin="5" rightMargin="5">
  <subDataset name="Aircraft_Registrations">
    <parameter name="StateParam" class="java.lang.String" />
    <queryString>
      <![CDATA[select a.city, count(*) as aircraft_count
               from aircraft a
               where a.state=$P{StateParam} and a.city like 'A%'
               group by city]]>
    </queryString>
    <field name="aircraft_count" class="java.lang.Integer" />
    <field name="city" class="java.lang.String" />
  </subDataset>
  <queryString>
    <![CDATA[select distinct state from aircraft where state in
      ('MD', 'NY', 'VA') order by state]]>
  </queryString>
  <field name="state" class="java.lang.String" />
  <detail>
    <band height="200">
      <textField>
        <reportElement x="0" y="10" width="500" height="20" />
        <textFieldExpression>
          <![CDATA["Aircraft registered in " + $F{state}]]>
        </textFieldExpression>
      </textField>
      <barChart>
        <chart>
          <reportElement width="500" y="30" x="0" height="170" />
        </chart>
        <categoryDataset>
          <dataset>
            <datasetRun subDataset="Aircraft_Registrations">
              <datasetParameter name="StateParam">
                <datasetParameterExpression>
                  <![CDATA[$F{state}]]>
                </datasetParameterExpression>
              </datasetParameter>
            </datasetRun>
```

```
          </dataset>
          <categorySeries>
            <seriesExpression>"City"</seriesExpression>
            <categoryExpression>
              <![CDATA[$F{city}]]>
            </categoryExpression>
            <valueExpression>
              <![CDATA[$F{aircraft_count}]]>
            </valueExpression>
            <itemHyperlink hyperlinkType="Reference"
                           hyperlinkTarget="Blank">
              <hyperlinkReferenceExpression>
                <![CDATA["http://maps.google.com?q=" + $F{city} + ","
                   + $P{StateParam}]]>
              </hyperlinkReferenceExpression>
              <hyperlinkTooltipExpression>
                <![CDATA["Map of " + $F{city} + ", "
                   + $P{StateParam}]]>
              </hyperlinkTooltipExpression>
            </itemHyperlink>
          </categorySeries>
        </categoryDataset>
        <barPlot isShowTickMarks="true" isShowTickLabels="true">
          <plot orientation="Horizontal"/>
        </barPlot>
      </barChart>
    </band>
  </detail>
</jasperReport>
```

As we can see, all we need to do to turn a chart item into a hyperlink is add an `<itemHyperlink>` subelement to the chart's `<categorySeries>` element. The `<itemHyperlink>` element has a `hyperlinkType` attribute that is equivalent to the same attribute in the `<textField>`, `<chart>`, or `<image>` elements. Refer to the table in the previous section to see all the valid values for this attribute. In this example, we created a reference hyperlink, which means that clicking on a chart element will take us to an external resource (a map of the selected city, in our example).

The `<itemHyperlink>` element also has a `hyperlinkTarget` attribute, which determines the target window for the hyperlink target when the report is exported to HTML. The valid values for `hyperlinkTarget` include:

Hyperlink target	**Description**
`Blank`	The hyperlink target will open in a new window.
`Parent`	The hyperlink target will open in the parent frame.
`Self`	The hyperlink target will open in the window and frame containing the hyperlink.
`Top`	The hyperlink target will open in the top browser window, replacing all the frames in the browser.

We should note that the `<textField>`, `<image>`, and `<chart>` elements also have a `hyperlinkTarget` attribute that works as described in the above table.

When the value of the `hyperlinkType` attribute is either `Reference`, `RemoteAnchor`, or `RemotePage`, a `<hyperlinkReferenceExpression>` element must be used to indicate the URL of the remote resource that the hyperlink points to. In our example, we simply direct the user to Google Maps, passing the state and city the user clicked on as URL parameters.

If the value of `hyperlinkType` is `RemoteAnchor`, then a `<remoteAnchorExpression>` subelement must be added to the parent element (`<chart>`, `<image>`, `<textField>`, or `<itemHyperlink>`). The body of this element must be a string expression resolving to an anchor target in the remote URL pointed to by the `<hyperlinkReferenceExpression>` element. Similarly, if the value of `hyperlinkType` is `RemotePage`, then a `<hyperlinkPageExpression>` element must be specified. The value of this element must resolve to an integer indicating the page of the remote resource specified by `<hyperlinkReferenceExpression>`.

Any element that can be turned into a hyperlink (`<chart>`, `<image>`, `<textField>`, or `<itemHyperlink>`) has an optional `<hyperlinkTooltipExpression>` element that can be used to generate a `tooltip` when the user hovers the mouse pointer over the element. In our example, we follow the most common and logical approach, which is to create a `tooltip` displaying some descriptive text that explains what will happen when the user clicks on the hyperlink.

After compiling, filling, exporting our example to HTML, and then opening the exported result in a browser, we can see our hyperlinks in action.

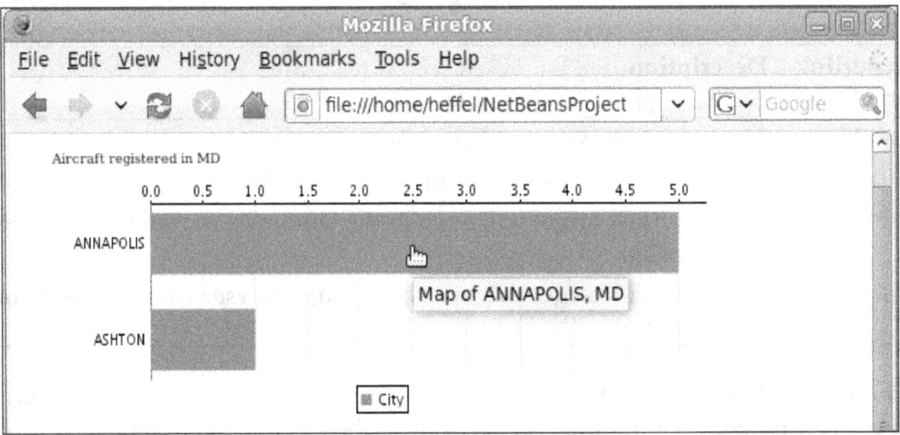

Clicking on any of the bars in any of the bar charts will take us to the map of the city corresponding to the bar.

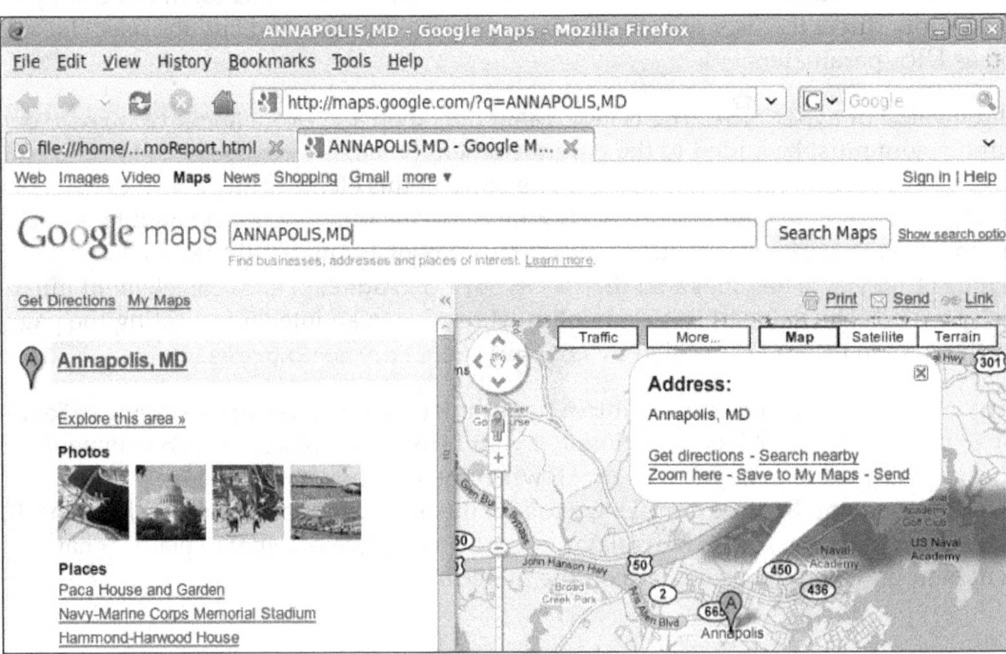

Bookmarks

The PDF documents can have a tree-like "table of contents" that allows easy navigation between the document sections. This table of contents is labeled **bookmarks** in most PDF viewers. JasperReports can generate bookmarks in reports exported to PDF by setting the `bookmarkLevel` attribute of any image, chart, or text field containing an `<anchorExpression>` subelement. The following JRXML template illustrates the use of the `bookmarkLevel` attribute to create bookmarks. It is a slightly modified version of the second subdataset example from the previous section.

```
<?xml version="1.0" encoding="UTF-8"?>
<!DOCTYPE jasperReport PUBLIC "-//JasperReports//DTD Report Design
  //EN" "http://jasperreports.sourceforge.net/dtds/jasperreport.dtd">
<jasperReport name="BookmarkDemoReport" leftMargin="5"
              rightMargin="5">
  <subDataset name="Aircraft_Registrations">
    <parameter name="StateParam" class="java.lang.String" />
    <queryString>
      <![CDATA[select a.city, count(*) as aircraft_count
               from aircraft a
               where a.state=$P{StateParam} and a.city like 'A%'
               group by city]]>
    </queryString>
    <field name="aircraft_count" class="java.lang.Integer" />
    <field name="city" class="java.lang.String" />
  </subDataset>
  <queryString>
    <![CDATA[select distinct state from aircraft where state in
            ('MD', 'NY', 'VA') order by state]]>
  </queryString>
  <field name="state" class="java.lang.String" />
  <detail>
    <band height="200">
      <textField bookmarkLevel="1">
        <reportElement x="0" y="10" width="500" height="20" />
        <textFieldExpression>
          <![CDATA["Aircraft registered in " + $F{state}]]>
        </textFieldExpression>
        <anchorNameExpression>
          <![CDATA["Aircraft registered in " + $F{state}]]>
        </anchorNameExpression>
      </textField>
      <barChart>
        <chart bookmarkLevel="2">
          <reportElement width="500" y="30" x="0" height="170" />
```

```
              <anchorNameExpression>
                <![CDATA["Chart"]]>
              </anchorNameExpression>
            </chart>
            <categoryDataset>
              <dataset>
                <datasetRun subDataset="Aircraft_Registrations">
                  <datasetParameter name="StateParam">
                    <datasetParameterExpression>
                      <![CDATA[$F{state}]]>
                    </datasetParameterExpression>
                  </datasetParameter>
                </datasetRun>
              </dataset>
              <categorySeries>
                <seriesExpression>"City"</seriesExpression>
                <categoryExpression>
                  <![CDATA[$F{city}]]>
                </categoryExpression>
                <valueExpression>
                  <![CDATA[$F{aircraft_count}]]>
                </valueExpression>
              </categorySeries>
            </categoryDataset>
            <barPlot isShowTickMarks="true" isShowTickLabels="true">
              <plot orientation="Horizontal" />
            </barPlot>
          </barChart>
        </band>
      </detail>
    </jasperReport>
```

The value for the `bookmarkLevel` attribute must be a positive integer indicating the relative position of the item in the bookmark tree structure. A value of `1` indicates a root node in the tree. After compiling, filling, and exporting this JRXML template, we should get a PDF containing bookmarks, with the chart titles as root nodes and the charts themselves as child nodes.

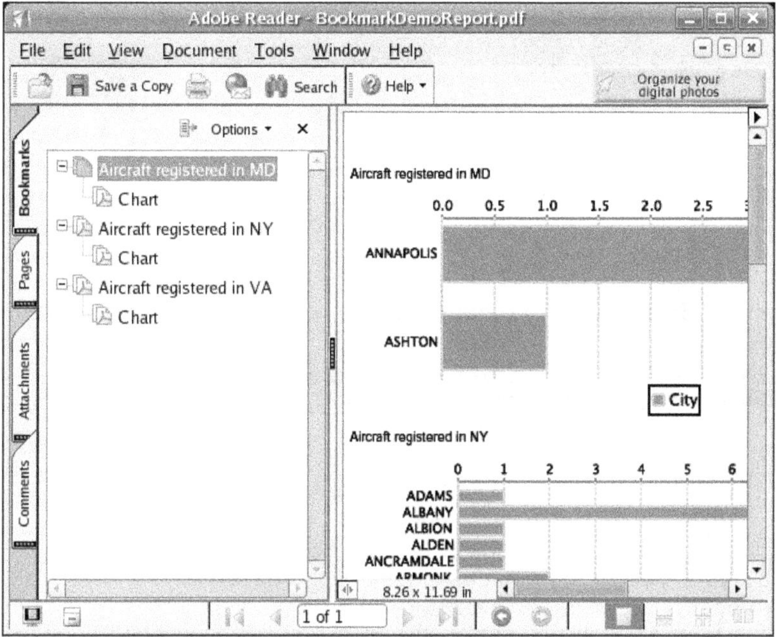

Clicking on the nodes will direct the main window to the appropriate anchor.

Handling very large reports

Sometimes, when filling a report, the report datasource may have a lot of data. In some cases, the generated report can become very large, and in some cases larger than the memory allocated for the JVM, causing an `OutOfMemoryException`.

It is possible to set up JasperReports so that it stores segments of a report on the disk in order to free some memory. This can be accomplished by using a built-in report parameter `REPORT_VIRTUALIZER`. The value for this parameter must be an instance of a class implementing `net.sf.jasperreports.engine.JRVirtualizer`. JasperReports comes with an implementation of this interface, namely `net.sf.jasperreports.engine.fill.JRFileVirtualizer`. This implementation is sufficient to handle the vast majority of the large reports. If, for some reason, this implementation is not sufficient for our needs, we can always create our own implementation of `net.sf.jasperreports.engine.JRVirtualizer`. The following example illustrates typical usage of `JRVirtualizer`:

```
package net.ensode.jasperbook;
import java.sql.Connection;
import java.sql.DriverManager;
import java.sql.SQLException;
import java.util.HashMap;
```

```
import net.sf.jasperreports.engine.JRException;
import net.sf.jasperreports.engine.JRParameter;
import net.sf.jasperreports.engine.JasperFillManager;
import net.sf.jasperreports.engine.fill.JRFileVirtualizer;
public class DbConnectionReportFill
{
  Connection connection;
  public void generateReport(String reportName)
  {
    String reportDirectory = "reports";
    JRFileVirtualizer fileVirtualizer = new JRFileVirtualizer(3,
                                                          "cacheDir");
    HashMap parameterMap = new HashMap();
    parameterMap.put(JRParameter.REPORT_VIRTUALIZER, fileVirtualizer);
    try
    {
      Class.forName("com.mysql.jdbc.Driver");
      connection = DriverManager.getConnection(
                   "jdbc:mysql://localhost:3306/flightstats?" +
                   "user=user&password=secret");
      System.out.println("Filling report...");
      JasperFillManager.fillReportToFile(reportDirectory + "/"
                                  + reportName + ".jasper",
                                  parameterMap,connection);
      System.out.println("Done!");
      connection.close();
    }
    catch (JRException e)
    {
      e.printStackTrace();
    }
    catch (ClassNotFoundException e)
    {
      e.printStackTrace();
    }
    catch (SQLException e)
    {
      e.printStackTrace();
    }
  }
  public static void main(String[] args)
  {
    new DbConnectionReportFill().generateReport(args[0]);
  }
}
```

The `JRFileVirtualizer` class has two constructors. The one we chose to use in the example takes two parameters. The first parameter is the maximum number of report pages that will be stored in primary memory (RAM) before the sections of the report are stored in virtual memory (disk). The second parameter is the directory that will be used to store the segments of the report that will be stored on disk. The other constructor takes a single parameter, an `int` indicating the maximum number of report pages that will be stored in primary memory. When using this constructor, the cached portions of the report will be stored in the working directory of the running application. We need to do nothing special in the JRXML template to be able to cache them to disk.

The process described in this section makes filling a report a much slower process than usual. Therefore, report virtualization should be used only when there is a good possibility that the report will cause the JVM to run out of memory.

Summary

In this chapter, we discussed several features that allow us to create elaborate reports. We learned to render localized reports by using the `resourceBundle` attribute of the `<jasperReport>` JRXML element. We then used scriptlets to add complex functionality to our reports, including variable value modification and performance measurement. We saw how to add cross-tabulation tables (crosstabs) to our reports by taking advantage of the `<crosstab>` JRXML element and display related charts or crosstabs for each record in a report by using subdatasets. To ease the task of report navigation, we learned how to add hyperlinks, anchors, and bookmarks to our reports. We have also seen how we can safely generate reports larger than the available memory by taking advantage of report virtualization.

9

Exporting to Other Formats

Reports can be exported to several formats. Because reports in native JasperReports format can be viewed only by using the JasperReports API (or by using the JasperViewer utility included with JasperReports), exporting reports is a common requirement. Exported reports can be viewed with readily available software like PDF viewers, word processors, and web browsers. In this chapter, we will learn how to export our reports to all of the formats supported by JasperReports.

Topics covered in this chapter include:

- Exporting reports to PDF
- Exporting reports to RTF
- Exporting reports to ODT
- Exporting reports to Excel
- Exporting reports to HTML
- Exporting reports to XML
- Exporting reports to CSV
- Exporting reports to plain text
- Directing exported reports to a browser

Exporting overview

Exporting reports is done using a series of classes that implement the `net.sf.jasperreports.engine.JRExporter` interface. This interface contains, among others, the following two methods:

- `public void setParameter(JRExporterParameter parameter, java. lang.Object value)`
- `public void exportReport()`

The `setParameter()` method is used to set the parameters needed to export the report. In most cases, two parameters need to be set: the name of the output file or output stream used to output the exported report and the JasperPrint object containing the native report. We would set the output file any time we are sure we want to save the exported report to the disk. We would set the output stream parameter to send the exported report through the network or when we are not sure if we want to save the exported report to the disk or stream it through the network. As an output stream can be easily saved to the disk or streamed through the network, the decision can be made at the runtime.

As can be seen in the signature of the `setParameter()` method, it takes an instance of `net.sf.jasperreports.engine.JRExporterParameter` as its first argument. `JRExporterParameter` contains a number of static constants that are typically used as the first argument to the `setParameter()` method. To accommodate the most common cases, the `JRExporterParameter` constants of interest are:

- `JRExporterParameter.JASPER_PRINT`: This is used to set the JasperPrint object to export.
- `JRExporterParameter.OUTPUT_FILE_NAME`: This is used to set the output filename.
- `JRExporterParameter.OUTPUT_STREAM`: This is used to set the output stream.

There are several other constants defined in `JRExporterParameter`. Consult the JavaDoc documentation for `JRExporterParameter` at `http://jasperreports.sourceforge.net/api/net/sf/jasperreports/engine/JRExporterParameter.html` for details.

As we will see in the following sections, exporting to different formats follows the same pattern in all cases. Once we are familiar with the procedure to export to one format, learning to export to other formats will be trivial.

Exporting reports functionality is done entirely in Java code; the JRXML does not need to be modified at all. For most of the examples in this chapter, we will be using the *subdatasets* example from the previous chapter.

Before moving on, it is worth mentioning that for most formats, exported reports keep their formatting (fonts, colors, and so on). The only two formats that lose their formatting are CSV and plain text because both of these are plain text files containing no formatting information.

Exporting to PDF

We have already seen the examples of exporting reports to PDF in previous chapters. However, all the examples we have seen so far stream a PDF report straight to the browser window. In the following example, we will export a report to PDF and save it to the filesystem:

```
package net.ensode.jasperbook;

import java.io.File;

import net.sf.jasperreports.engine.JRException;
import net.sf.jasperreports.engine.JRExporterParameter;
import net.sf.jasperreports.engine.JasperPrint;
import net.sf.jasperreports.engine.export.JRPdfExporter;
import net.sf.jasperreports.engine.util.JRLoader;

public class PdfExportDemo
{
  public static final String REPORT_DIRECTORY = "reports";
  public void pdfExport(String reportName)
  {
    File file = new File(REPORT_DIRECTORY + "/" + reportName +
                                                      ".jrprint");

    try
    {
      JasperPrint jasperPrint = (JasperPrint)
                                     JRLoader.loadObject(file);
      JRPdfExporter pdfExporter = new JRPdfExporter();
      pdfExporter.setParameter(JRExporterParameter.JASPER_PRINT,
                                                  jasperPrint);
      pdfExporter.setParameter(JRExporterParameter.OUTPUT_FILE_NAME,
                         REPORT_DIRECTORY + "/" + reportName + ".pdf");
      System.out.println("Exporting report...");
      pdfExporter.exportReport();
      System.out.println("Done!");
    }
```

```
        catch (JRException e)
        {
          e.printStackTrace();
        }
      }
      public static void main(String[] args)
      {
        new PdfExportDemo().pdfExport(args[0]);
      }
    }
```

As we can see in the example, the `JRExporter` implementation used to export to PDF is `net.sf.jasperreports.engine.export.JRPdfExporter`. We need to pass it to the compiled report in the native JasperReports format by setting the `JRExporterParameter.JASPER_PRINT` parameter to the appropriate instance of `net.sf.jasperreports.engine.JasperPrint`.

Because we are saving the report to disk, we set the output filename to be the report name. The only difference is that we substitute the file extension with "pdf".

The code we just wrote will generate a PDF that looks like the following screenshot:

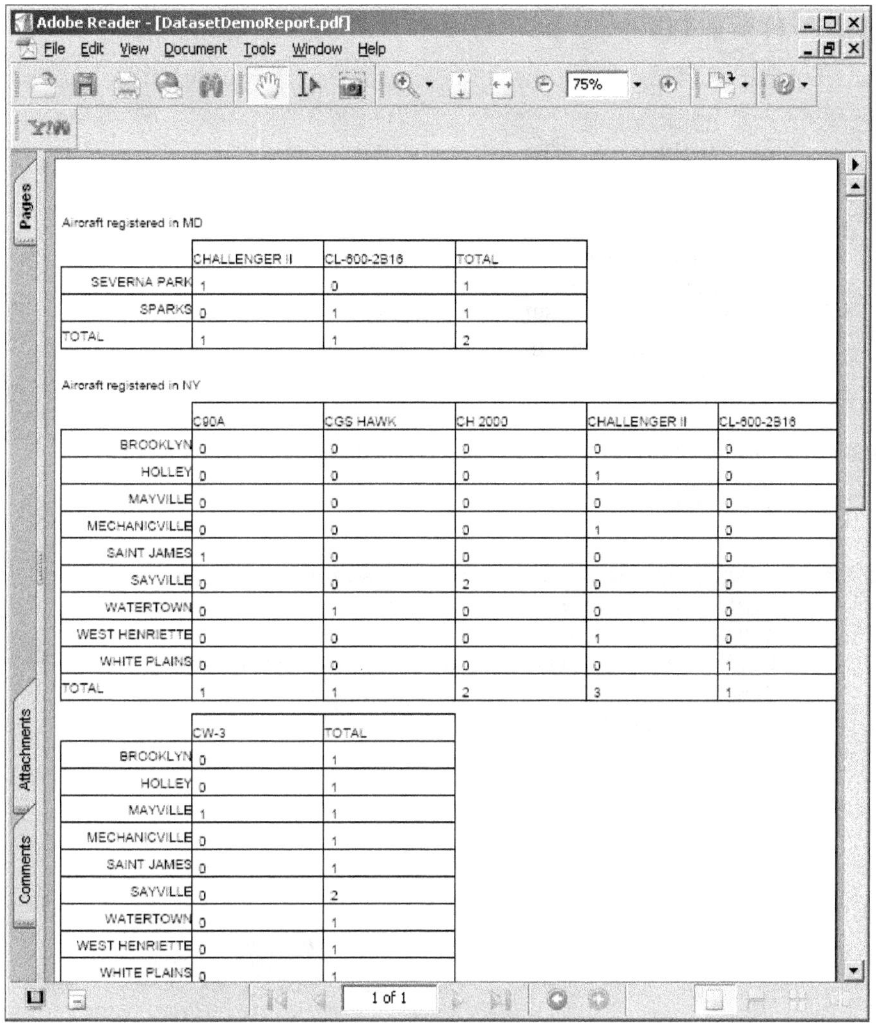

Aircraft registered in MD

	CHALLENGER II	CL-600-2B16	TOTAL
SEVERNA PARK	1	0	1
SPARKS	0	1	1
TOTAL	1	1	2

Aircraft registered in NY

	C90A	CGS HAWK	CH 2000	CHALLENGER II	CL-600-2B16
BROOKLYN	0	0	0	0	0
HOLLEY	0	0	0	1	0
MAYVILLE	0	0	0	0	0
MECHANICVILLE	0	0	0	1	0
SAINT JAMES	1	0	0	0	0
SAYVILLE	0	0	2	0	0
WATERTOWN	0	1	0	0	0
WEST HENRIETTE	0	0	0	1	0
WHITE PLAINS	0	0	0	0	1
TOTAL	1	1	2	3	1

	CW-3	TOTAL
BROOKLYN	0	1
HOLLEY	0	1
MAYVILLE	1	1
MECHANICVILLE	0	1
SAINT JAMES	0	1
SAYVILLE	0	2
WATERTOWN	0	1
WEST HENRIETTE	0	1
WHITE PLAINS	0	1

Exporting to RTF

Rich Text Format (RTF) is a document file format that is supported by most word processors. Exporting to RTF allows our documents to be read by Microsoft Word and several other word processors.

Unfortunately, RTF documents generated by JasperReports are not always readable by OpenOffice.org or StarOffice writer because these office suites are not fully compliant with the RTF specification. As we'll see in the next section, JasperReports can export to OpenDocument Text, the native format for both of these office suites.

The following example illustrates how to export a report into RTF format:

```
package net.ensode.jasperbook;
import java.io.File;
import net.sf.jasperreports.engine.JRException;
import net.sf.jasperreports.engine.JRExporterParameter;
import net.sf.jasperreports.engine.JasperPrint;
import net.sf.jasperreports.engine.export.JRRtfExporter;
import net.sf.jasperreports.engine.util.JRLoader;
public class RtfExportDemo
{
  public static final String REPORT_DIRECTORY = "reports";
  public void rtfExport(String reportName)
  {
    File file = new File(REPORT_DIRECTORY + "/" + reportName +
                                                         ".jrprint");
    try
    {
      JasperPrint jasperPrint = (JasperPrint)
                                          JRLoader.loadObject(file);
      JRRtfExporter rtfExporter = new JRRtfExporter();
      rtfExporter.setParameter(JRExporterParameter.JASPER_PRINT,
                                                      jasperPrint);
      rtfExporter.setParameter(JRExporterParameter.OUTPUT_FILE_NAME,
                       REPORT_DIRECTORY + "/" + reportName + ".rtf");
      System.out.println("Exporting report...");
      rtfExporter.exportReport();
      System.out.println("Done!");
    }
    catch (JRException e)
    {
      e.printStackTrace();
    }
  }
```

```
    public static void main(String[] args)
    {
      new RtfExportDemo().rtfExport(args[0]);
    }
  }
```

As we can see in this example, `net.sf.jasperreports.engine.export.JRRtfExporter` is the `JRExporter` implementation we need to use to export to RTF. Like the previous example, we tell the exporter what report to export by supplying an instance of `net.sf.jasperreports.engine.JasperPrint` as the value for the `JRExporterParameter.JASPER_PRINT` parameter, and we set the output file to be the report name by setting the `JRExporterParameter.OUTPUT_FILE_NAME` with the appropriate value.

This example code will generate an RTF document as shown in the following screenshot:

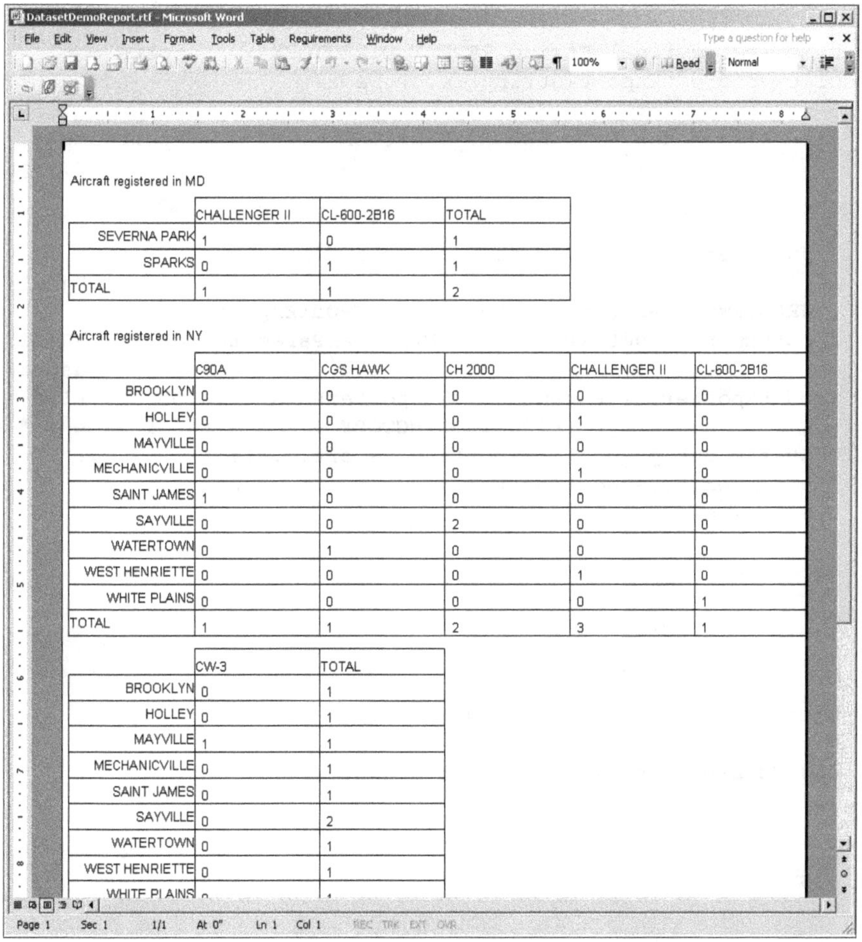

DatasetDemoReport.rtf - Microsoft Word

Aircraft registered in MD

	CHALLENGER II	CL-600-2B16	TOTAL
SEVERNA PARK	1	0	1
SPARKS	0	1	1
TOTAL	1	1	2

Aircraft registered in NY

	C90A	CGS HAWK	CH 2000	CHALLENGER II	CL-600-2B16
BROOKLYN	0	0	0	0	0
HOLLEY	0	0	0	1	0
MAYVILLE	0	0	0	0	0
MECHANICVILLE	0	0	0	1	0
SAINT JAMES	1	0	0	0	0
SAYVILLE	0	0	2	0	0
WATERTOWN	0	1	0	0	0
WEST HENRIETTE	0	0	0	1	0
WHITE PLAINS	0	0	0	0	1
TOTAL	1	1	2	3	1

	CW-3	TOTAL
BROOKLYN	0	1
HOLLEY	0	1
MAYVILLE	1	1
MECHANICVILLE	0	1
SAINT JAMES	0	1
SAYVILLE	0	2
WATERTOWN	0	1
WEST HENRIETTE	0	1
WHITE PLAINS	0	1

Exporting to ODT

OpenDocument Text (ODT) is the word processing standard for **Organization for the Advancement of Structured Information Standards (OASIS)** and the native format of several open source word processing tools, most notably OpenOffice.org Writer.

Reports can be exported to ODT by taking advantage of the `JROdtExporter` class provided with JasperReports. The following example illustrates how to do this:

```
package net.ensode.jasperbook;
import java.io.File;
import net.sf.jasperreports.engine.JRException;
import net.sf.jasperreports.engine.JRExporterParameter;
import net.sf.jasperreports.engine.JasperPrint;
import net.sf.jasperreports.engine.export.oasis.JROdtExporter;
import net.sf.jasperreports.engine.util.JRLoader;
public class OdtExportDemo
{
  public static final String REPORT_DIRECTORY = "reports";
  public void odtExport(String reportName)
  {
    File file = new File(REPORT_DIRECTORY + "/" + reportName +
                                                        ".jrprint");
    try
    {
      JasperPrint jasperPrint = (JasperPrint)
                                       JRLoader.loadObject(file);
      JROdtExporter odtExporter = new JROdtExporter();
      odtExporter.setParameter(JRExporterParameter.JASPER_PRINT,
                                                       jasperPrint);
      odtExporter.setParameter(JRExporterParameter.OUTPUT_FILE_NAME,
                    REPORT_DIRECTORY + "/" + reportName + ".ods");
      System.out.println("Exporting report...");
      odtExporter.exportReport();
      System.out.println("Done!");
    }
    catch (JRException e)
    {
      e.printStackTrace();
    }
  }
  public static void main(String[] args)
  {
    new OdtExportDemo().odtExport(args[0]);
  }
}
```

As we can see, exporting to ODT is not much different from exporting to other formats. The `JRExporter` implementation that we need to use in this case is `net.sf.jasperreports.engine.export.oasis.JROdtExporter`. Note that in the previous examples, we have specified what report to export by supplying an instance of `net.sf.jasperreports.engine.JasperPrint` as the value for the `JRExporterParameter.JASPER_PRINT` parameter. We then set the output file to be the report name by setting `JRExporterParameter.OUTPUT_FILE_NAME` with the appropriate value.

The following screenshot illustrates how the `BarChartReportDemo` example from Chapter 7, *Adding Charts and Graphics to Reports*, is rendered in OpenOffice.org Writer after being exported to ODT:

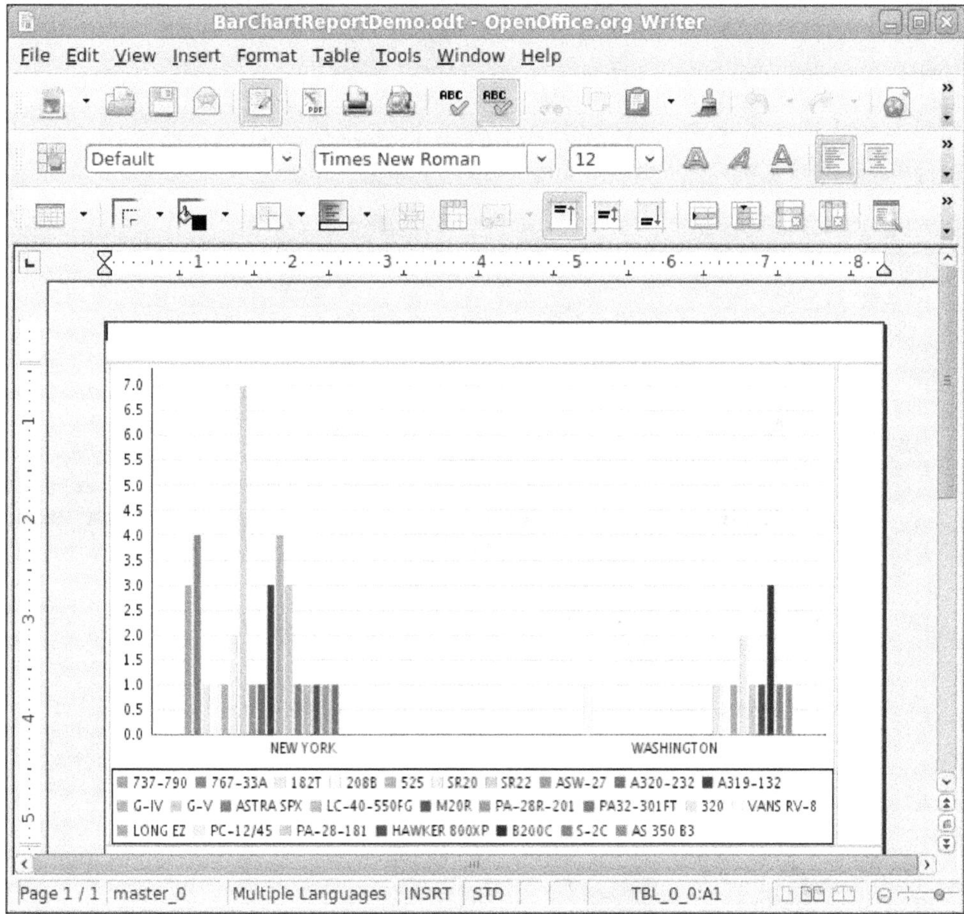

Exporting to Excel

It is not uncommon to request reports in Microsoft Excel format as Excel allows easy manipulation of report data to perform calculations. JasperReports provides built-in capability to export reports to Excel. The following example demonstrates this functionality:

```
package net.ensode.jasperbook;

import java.io.File;

import net.sf.jasperreports.engine.JRException;
import net.sf.jasperreports.engine.JRExporterParameter;
import net.sf.jasperreports.engine.JasperPrint;
import net.sf.jasperreports.engine.export.JExcelApiExporter;
import net.sf.jasperreports.engine.util.JRLoader;

public class XlsExportDemo
{
  public static final String REPORT_DIRECTORY = "reports";
  public void xlsExport(String reportName)
  {
    File file = new File(REPORT_DIRECTORY + "/" + reportName +
                                                         ".jrprint");

    try
    {
      JasperPrint jasperPrint = (JasperPrint)
                                          JRLoader.loadObject(file);
      JExcelApiExporter xlsExporter = new JExcelApiExporter();
      xlsExporter.setParameter(JRExporterParameter.JASPER_PRINT,
                                                       jasperPrint);
      xlsExporter.setParameter(JRExporterParameter.OUTPUT_FILE_NAME,
                 REPORT_DIRECTORY + "/" + reportName + ".xls");
      System.out.println("Exporting report...");
      xlsExporter.exportReport();
      System.out.println("Done!");
    }
    catch (JRException e)
    {
      e.printStackTrace();
    }
  }
  public static void main(String[] args)
  {
    new XlsExportDemo().xlsExport(args[0]);
  }
}
```

This example follows the same pattern as the previous examples in this chapter. The `JRExporter` implementation needed to export to Excel is `net.sf.jasperreports.engine.export.JExcelApiExporter`. Again, we set the report to export and the output filename by setting the appropriate parameters on `JExcelApiExporter`.

This example will generate an Excel spreadsheet that looks like the following screenshot:

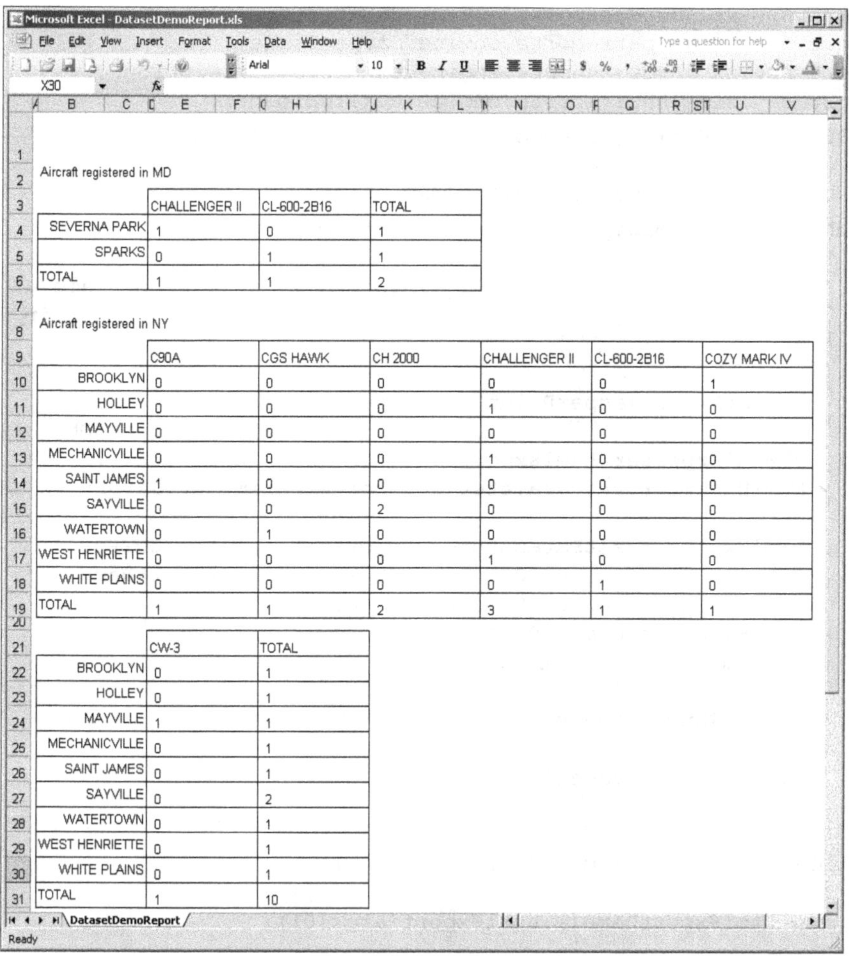

Aircraft registered in MD

	CHALLENGER II	CL-600-2B16	TOTAL
SEVERNA PARK	1	0	1
SPARKS	0	1	1
TOTAL	1	1	2

Aircraft registered in NY

	C90A	CGS HAWK	CH 2000	CHALLENGER II	CL-600-2B16	COZY MARK IV
BROOKLYN	0	0	0	0	0	1
HOLLEY	0	0	0	1	0	0
MAYVILLE	0	0	0	0	0	0
MECHANICVILLE	0	0	0	1	0	0
SAINT JAMES	1	0	0	0	0	0
SAYVILLE	0	0	2	0	0	0
WATERTOWN	0	1	0	0	0	0
WEST HENRIETTE	0	0	0	1	0	0
WHITE PLAINS	0	0	0	0	1	0
TOTAL	1	1	2	3	1	1

	CW-3	TOTAL
BROOKLYN	0	1
HOLLEY	0	1
MAYVILLE	1	1
MECHANICVILLE	0	1
SAINT JAMES	0	1
SAYVILLE	0	2
WATERTOWN	0	1
WEST HENRIETTE	0	1
WHITE PLAINS	0	1
TOTAL	1	10

JasperReports includes two Excel exporters: `JExcelApiExporter` and `JRXlsExporter`. It is preferable to use `JExcelApiExporter` because `JRXlsExporter` does not support exporting images. `JExcelApiExporter` is the newer Excel exporter. `JRXlsExporter` is still included for backward compatibility.

Exporting to HTML

Exporting to HTML is another common requirement. The following example demonstrates how to do it:

```
package net.ensode.jasperbook;
import java.io.File;
import net.sf.jasperreports.engine.JRException;
import net.sf.jasperreports.engine.JRExporterParameter;
import net.sf.jasperreports.engine.JasperPrint;
import net.sf.jasperreports.engine.export.JRHtmlExporter;
import net.sf.jasperreports.engine.util.JRLoader;
public class HtmlExportDemo
{
  public static final String REPORT_DIRECTORY = "reports";
  public void htmlExport(String reportName)
  {
    File file = new File(REPORT_DIRECTORY + "/" + reportName +
                                                        ".jrprint");
    try
    {
      JasperPrint jasperPrint = (JasperPrint)
                                      JRLoader.loadObject(file);
      JRHtmlExporter htmlExporter = new JRHtmlExporter();
      htmlExporter.setParameter(JRExporterParameter.JASPER_PRINT,
                                                     jasperPrint);
      htmlExporter.setParameter(JRExporterParameter.OUTPUT_FILE_NAME,
                     REPORT_DIRECTORY + "/" + reportName + ".html");
      System.out.println("Exporting report...");
      htmlExporter.exportReport();
      System.out.println("Done!");
    }
    catch (JRException e)
    {
      e.printStackTrace();
    }
  }
  public static void main(String[] args)
  {
    new HtmlExportDemo().htmlExport(args[0]);
  }
}
```

In this example, we generate an HTML file and save it to disk. The `JRExporter` implementation for HTML export is `net.sf.jasperreports.engine.export.JRHtmlExporter`. Like in the previous examples, we set the report to export and the filename by setting the appropriate parameters.

A common requirement when exporting to HTML is to have the exported report directed to a browser window. This technique will be covered in the last section in this chapter.

The code in the example will generate an HTML report that looks like the following:

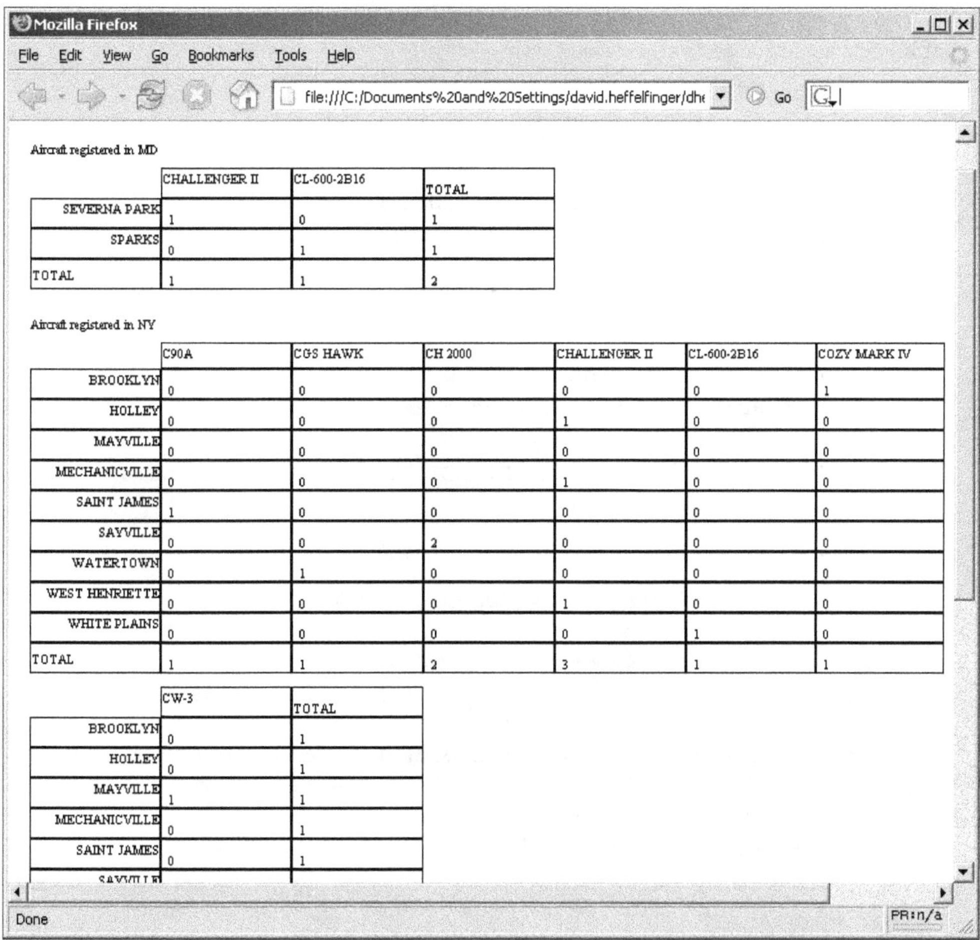

Aircraft registered in MD

	CHALLENGER II	CL-600-2B16	TOTAL
SEVERNA PARK	1	0	1
SPARKS	0	1	1
TOTAL	1	1	2

Aircraft registered in NY

	C90A	CGS HAWK	CH 2000	CHALLENGER II	CL-600-2B16	COZY MARK IV
BROOKLYN	0	0	0	0	0	1
HOLLEY	0	0	0	1	0	0
MAYVILLE	0	0	0	0	0	0
MECHANICVILLE	0	0	0	1	0	0
SAINT JAMES	1	0	0	0	0	0
SAYVILLE	0	0	2	0	0	0
WATERTOWN	0	1	0	0	0	0
WEST HENRIETTE	0	0	0	1	0	0
WHITE PLAINS	0	0	0	0	1	0
TOTAL	1	1	2	3	1	1

	CW-3	TOTAL
BROOKLYN	0	1
HOLLEY	0	1
MAYVILLE	1	1
MECHANICVILLE	0	1
SAINT JAMES	0	1

Reports exported to HTML result in a single HTML file, regardless of how many pages the original report has.

Exporting to XML

JasperReports uses a **Document Type Definition (DTD)** file to generate XML reports. XML reports can be exported back to the compiled reports by using the `net.sf.jasperreports.engine.xml.JRPrintXmlLoader` class. The following example demonstrates how to export a report to XML:

```
package net.ensode.jasperbook;

import java.io.File;

import net.sf.jasperreports.engine.JRException;
import net.sf.jasperreports.engine.JRExporterParameter;
import net.sf.jasperreports.engine.JasperPrint;
import net.sf.jasperreports.engine.export.JRXmlExporter;
import net.sf.jasperreports.engine.util.JRLoader;

public class XmlExportDemo
{
  public static final String REPORT_DIRECTORY = "reports";
  public void xmlExport(String reportName)
  {
    File file = new File(REPORT_DIRECTORY + "/" + reportName +
                                                           ".jrprint");
    try
    {
      JasperPrint jasperPrint = (JasperPrint)
                                         JRLoader.loadObject(file);
      JRXmlExporter xmlExporter = new JRXmlExporter();
      xmlExporter.setParameter(JRExporterParameter.JASPER_PRINT,
                                                       jasperPrint);
      xmlExporter.setParameter(JRExporterParameter.OUTPUT_FILE_NAME,
                   REPORT_DIRECTORY + "/" + reportName + ".jrpxml");
      System.out.println("Exporting report...");
      xmlExporter.exportReport();
      System.out.println("Done!");
    }
    catch (JRException e)
    {
      e.printStackTrace();
    }
  }
  public static void main(String[] args)
  {
    new XmlExportDemo().xmlExport(args[0]);
  }
}
```

As we can see in the example, the `JRExporter` implementation used to export to XML is `net.sf.jasperreports.engine.export.JRXmlExporter`. The same procedure used in the previous examples is used to set the report to export and to the resulting filename.

> Notice that the filename used for the exported report contains the extension `jrpxml`. Even though exported reports are standard XML files, it is customary to use this extension instead of `xml`.

The following is a partial listing of the generated XML file:

```
<?xml version="1.0" encoding="UTF-8"?>
<!DOCTYPE jasperPrint PUBLIC "-//JasperReports//DTD Report Design//EN"
  "http://jasperreports.sourceforge.net/dtds/jasperprint.dtd">
<jasperPrint name="DatasetDemoReport" pageWidth="595"
             pageHeight="842">
  <page>
    <text textHeight="13.578125" lineSpacingFactor="1.3578125"
          leadingOffset="-3.1972656">
      <reportElement x="5" y="40" width="500" height="20"/>
      <textContent>
        <![CDATA[Aircraft registered in MD]]>
      </textContent>
    </text>
    <rectangle radius="0">
      <reportElement mode="Opaque" x="5" y="60" width="782"
                     height="80" forecolor="#000000"/>
      <graphicElement pen="None" fill="Solid"/>
    </rectangle>
    <frame>
      <reportElement x="105" y="80" width="100" height="20"
                     backcolor="#FFFFFF"/>
      <box border="Thin" borderColor="#000000"/>
      <text textAlignment="Left"
            verticalAlignment="Bottom"
            textHeight="13.578125"
            lineSpacingFactor="1.3578125"
            leadingOffset="-3.1972656">
        <reportElement x="5" y="0" width="55" height="20"/>
        <textContent><![CDATA[1]]></textContent>
      </text>
    </frame>
  </page>
</jasperPrint>
```

The DTD for the XML generated when exporting to XML can be found at `http://jasperreports.sourceforge.net/dtds/jasperprint.dtd`.

Reports exported to XML can be viewed with the JasperViewer utility included with JasperReports. To view a report exported to XML, the XML argument needs to be passed to it. For example, to view this XML report, the following command needs to be typed in the command line (assuming all required libraries are already in the CLASSPATH):

```
net.sf.jasperreports.view.JasperViewer -Freports/DatasetDemoReport.jrpxml
-XML
```

Exporting reports to XML has some advantages over using the compiled report directly. For example, exported reports are human readable and editable, and they can easily be stored in a database without resorting to **Binary Large Objects (BLOBS)**.

Exporting to CSV

Comma Separated Values (CSV) files contain a number of values separated by commas. There are several software utilities that can parse CSV files. JasperReports includes built-in functionality to export reports to CSV files. The following example illustrates the process:

```
package net.ensode.jasperbook;

import java.io.File;

import net.sf.jasperreports.engine.JRException;
import net.sf.jasperreports.engine.JRExporterParameter;
import net.sf.jasperreports.engine.JasperPrint;
import net.sf.jasperreports.engine.export.JRCsvExporter;
import net.sf.jasperreports.engine.util.JRLoader;

public class CsvExportDemo
{
  public static final String REPORT_DIRECTORY = "reports";
  public void csvExport(String reportName)
  {
    File file = new File(REPORT_DIRECTORY + "/" + reportName +
                                                        ".jrprint");
    try
    {
      JasperPrint jasperPrint = (JasperPrint)
                                          JRLoader.loadObject(file);
      JRCsvExporter csvExporter = new JRCsvExporter();
```

```
        csvExporter.setParameter(JRExporterParameter.JASPER_PRINT,
                                                      jasperPrint);
        csvExporter.setParameter(JRExporterParameter.OUTPUT_FILE_NAME,
                           REPORT_DIRECTORY + "/" + reportName + ".csv");
        System.out.println("Exporting report...");
        csvExporter.exportReport();
        System.out.println("Done!");
      }
      catch (JRException e)
      {
        e.printStackTrace();
      }
    }
    public static void main(String[] args)
    {
      new CsvExportDemo().csvExport(args[0]);
    }
  }
```

Again, there is nothing earth shattering about this example. It follows the same pattern we have seen in previous examples. As can be seen in the example, the `JRExporter` implementation used to export to CSV is `net.sf.jasperreports.engine.export.JRCsvExporter`. The report to export and the filename of the exported report are set by assigning the appropriate values to the `JRExporterParameter.JASPER_PRINT` and `JRExporterParameter.OUTPUT_FILE_NAME` parameters.

This example code will generate a CSV file that looks like the following:

```
Aircraft registered in MD,,,,,,,,,,,
,CHALLENGER II,,CL-600-2B16,,TOTAL,,,,,,
SEVERNA PARK,,1,,0,,1,,,,,
SPARKS,,0,,1,,1,,,,,
TOTAL,,1,,1,,2,,,,,
Aircraft registered in NY,,,,,,,,,,,
,C90A,,CGS HAWK,,CH 2000,,CHALLENGER II,,CL-600-2B16,,COZY MARK IV,
BROOKLYN,,0,,0,,0,,0,,0,,1
HOLLEY,,0,,0,,0,,1,,0,,0
MAYVILLE,,0,,0,,0,,0,,0,,0
MECHANICVILLE,,0,,0,,0,,1,,0,,0
SAINT JAMES,,1,,0,,0,,0,,0,,0
SAYVILLE,,0,,0,,2,,0,,0,,0
WATERTOWN,,0,,1,,0,,0,,0,,0
WEST HENRIETTE,,0,,0,,0,,1,,0,,0
WHITE PLAINS,,0,,0,,0,,0,,1,,0
TOTAL,,1,,1,,2,,3,,1,,1
```

```
,CW-3,,TOTAL,,,,,,,,
BROOKLYN,,0,,1,,,,,,,,
HOLLEY,,0,,1,,,,,,,
MAYVILLE,,1,,1,,,,,,,,
MECHANICVILLE,,0,,1,,,,,,,,
SAINT JAMES,,0,,1,,,,,,,,
SAYVILLE,,0,,2,,,,,,,,
WATERTOWN,,0,,1,,,,,,,,
WEST HENRIETTE,,0,,1,,,,,,,,
WHITE PLAINS,,0,,1,,,,,,,,
TOTAL,,1,,10,,,,,,,,
Aircraft registered in VA,,,,,,,,,,,
,CL-600-2B19,,CL-600-2C10,,TOTAL,,,,,,
ARLINGTON,,18,,5,,23,,,,,,
DULLES,,4,,0,,4,,,,,,
TOTAL,,22,,5,,27,,,,,,
```

Here is how the CSV file is rendered by OpenOffice.org's spreadsheet component, Calc:

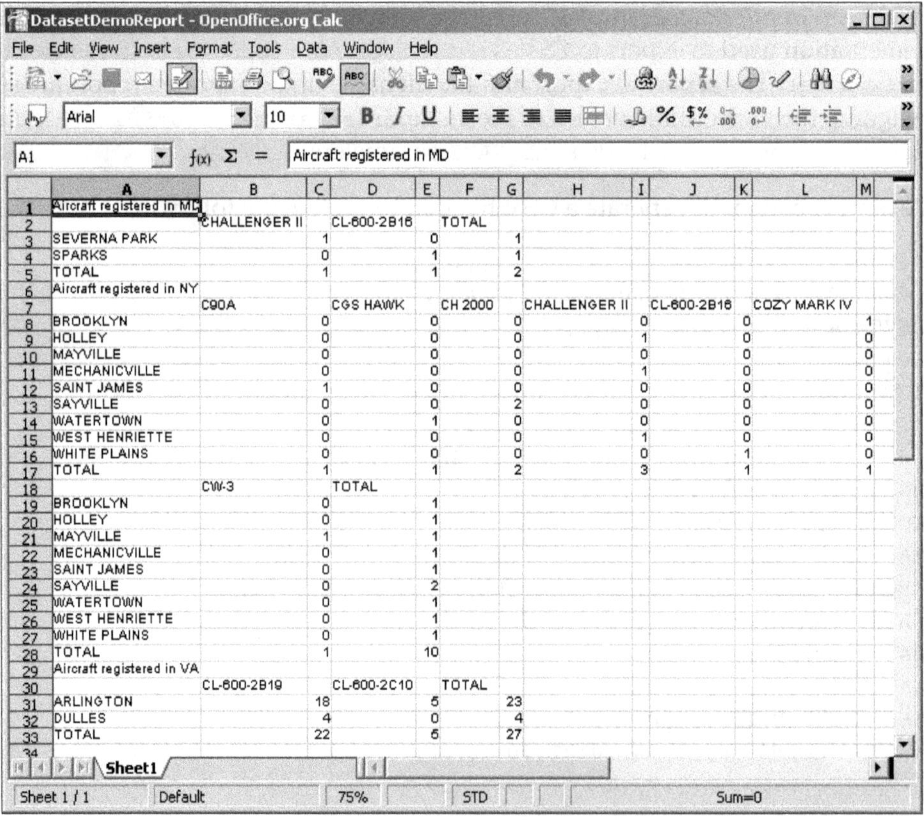

	A	B	C	D	E	F	G	H	I	J	K	L	M
1	Aircraft registered in MD												
2		CHALLENGER II		CL-600-2B16		TOTAL							
3	SEVERNA PARK		1		0		1						
4	SPARKS		0		1		1						
5	TOTAL		1		1		2						
6	Aircraft registered in NY												
7		C90A		CGS HAWK		CH 2000		CHALLENGER II		CL-600-2B16		COZY MARK IV	
8	BROOKLYN		0		0		0		0		0		1
9	HOLLEY		0		0		0		1		0		0
10	MAYVILLE		0		0		0		0		0		0
11	MECHANICVILLE		0		0		0		1		0		0
12	SAINT JAMES		1		0		0		0		0		0
13	SAYVILLE		0		0		2		0		0		0
14	WATERTOWN		0		1		0		0		0		0
15	WEST HENRIETTE		0		0		0		1		0		0
16	WHITE PLAINS		0		0		0		0		1		0
17	TOTAL		1		1		2		3		1		1
18		CW-3		TOTAL									
19	BROOKLYN		0		1								
20	HOLLEY		0		1								
21	MAYVILLE		1		1								
22	MECHANICVILLE		0		1								
23	SAINT JAMES		0		1								
24	SAYVILLE		0		2								
25	WATERTOWN		0		1								
26	WEST HENRIETTE		0		1								
27	WHITE PLAINS		0		1								
28	TOTAL		1		10								
29	Aircraft registered in VA												
30		CL-600-2B19		CL-600-2C10		TOTAL							
31	ARLINGTON		18		5		23						
32	DULLES		4		0		4						
33	TOTAL		22		5		27						
34													

Exporting to plain text

In this section, we will export a more "textual" report than the one we used for previous sections. The JRXML template for the report that we will export is as follows:

```
<?xml version="1.0" encoding="UTF-8"?>
<!DOCTYPE jasperReport PUBLIC "-//JasperReports//DTD Report Design//
  EN" "http://jasperreports.sourceforge.net/dtds/jasperreport.dtd">
<jasperReport name="PlainTextExportDemoReport" >
  <title>
    <band height="30">
      <staticText>
        <reportElement x="0" y="0" width="555" height="30" />
        <text>
          <![CDATA[Text Heavy Report]]>
        </text>
      </staticText>
    </band>
  </title>
  <detail>
    <band height="100">
      <staticText>
        <reportElement x="0" y="0" width="555" height="100" />
        <text>
          <![CDATA[Exporting to plain text makes more sense when the
             report is completely (or mostly) text.Since tables and
             graphical elements don't translate to plain text very
             well. We created this report template to demonstrate
             exporting to plain text. Exciting, isn't it?]]>
        </text>
      </staticText>
    </band>
  </detail>
</jasperReport>
```

The following Java code fragment will export the JasperReports' native report generated by this JRXML template into plain text:

```
package net.ensode.jasperbook;

import java.io.File;

import net.sf.jasperreports.engine.JRException;
import net.sf.jasperreports.engine.JRExporterParameter;
import net.sf.jasperreports.engine.JasperPrint;
import net.sf.jasperreports.engine.export.JRTextExporter;
import net.sf.jasperreports.engine.export.JRTextExporterParameter;
```

```
import net.sf.jasperreports.engine.util.JRLoader;

public class PlainTextExportDemo
{
  public static final String REPORT_DIRECTORY = "reports";
  public void plainTextExport(String reportName)
  {
    File file = new File(REPORT_DIRECTORY + "/" + reportName +
                                                       ".jrprint");
    try
    {
      JasperPrint jasperPrint = (JasperPrint)
                                          JRLoader.loadObject(file);
      JRTextExporter textExporter = new JRTextExporter();
      textExporter.setParameter(JRExporterParameter.JASPER_PRINT,
                                                       jasperPrint);
      textExporter.setParameter(
        JRExporterParameter.OUTPUT_FILE_NAME, REPORT_DIRECTORY
        + "/" + reportName + ".txt");
      textExporter.setParameter(JRTextExporterParameter
                             .CHARACTER_WIDTH, new Integer(10));
      textExporter.setParameter(JRTextExporterParameter
                            .CHARACTER_HEIGHT, new Integer(10));
      System.out.println("Exporting report...");
      textExporter.exportReport();
      System.out.println("Done!");
    }
    catch (JRException e)
    {
      e.printStackTrace();
    }
  }
  public static void main(String[] args)
  {
    new PlainTextExportDemo().plainTextExport(args[0]);
  }
}
```

After compiling and executing this code with the report generated by the JRXML template we have just written, we should have a text file with the following contents in our hard drive:

```
                    Text Heavy Report

Exporting to plain text makes more sense when the
report is completely (or mostly) text.
Since tables and graphical elements don't translate to
plain text very well.
We created this report template to demonstrate
exporting to plain text.
Exciting, isn't it?
```

Notice how, in this example, we had to set some parameters in addition to the output filename. The `JRTextExporterParameter.CHARACTER_WIDTH` and `JRTextExporterParameter.CHARACTER_HEIGHT` parameters tell JasperReports the number of pixels in the report to be mapped to a character in the exported text. This is because the text in the report is essentially a bunch of pixels, and the JasperReports engine does not directly recognize the characters in it. By specifying the `CHARACTER_WIDTH` and `CHARACTER_HEIGHT` parameters, the engine can make an educated guess on how to map the pixels to ASCII characters.

Another way to help JasperReports map report pixels to ASCII characters is to specify the page width and height of the exported report. This can be achieved by setting the `JRExportParameter.PAGE_WIDTH` and `JRExportParameter.PAGE_HEIGHT` parameters to the appropriate values in `JRTextExporter`.

Either the page width and height or the character width and height (or both) must be specified when exporting to plain text. If both page and character dimensions are specified, then character dimensions take precedence.

> Because the algorithm JasperReports uses to generate plain text reports maps pixels to ASCII characters, the conversion is not always 100% accurate. In most cases, report templates must be modified so that they can be successfully exported to text. For these reasons, we do not recommend exporting reports to plain text unless absolutely necessary.

Directing HTML reports to a browser

In previous chapters, we have seen the examples of generating a PDF report and streaming it to the browser "on the fly". Earlier in this chapter, we saw how to export reports to an HTML and store them in the filesystem. In this section, we will see how to export a report to HTML and immediately send it to the user's browser window. The following example is a servlet that exports an already filled JasperPrint object to HTML and displays the resulting exported report into the browser. As can be seen in the following code, it takes the base report name as a request parameter. Executing this report using the `BarChartDemoReport` from Chapter 7, *Adding Charts and Graphics to Reports,* results in the following page being displayed in the browser:

```
package net.ensode.jasperbook;

import java.io.File;
import java.io.IOException;
import java.io.PrintWriter;

import javax.servlet.ServletContext;
import javax.servlet.ServletException;
import javax.servlet.http.HttpServlet;
import javax.servlet.http.HttpServletRequest;
import javax.servlet.http.HttpServletResponse;

import net.sf.jasperreports.engine.JRException;
import net.sf.jasperreports.engine.JRExporterParameter;
import net.sf.jasperreports.engine.JasperPrint;
import net.sf.jasperreports.engine.export.JRHtmlExporter;
import net.sf.jasperreports.engine.export.JRHtmlExporterParameter;
import net.sf.jasperreports.engine.util.JRLoader;
import net.sf.jasperreports.j2ee.servlets.ImageServlet;

public class HtmlReportServlet extends HttpServlet
{
  public static final String REPORT_DIRECTORY = "/reports";
  protected void doGet(HttpServletRequest request, HttpServletResponse
                                                              response)
  throws ServletException, IOException
  {
    ServletContext context = this.getServletConfig()
                                                .getServletContext();
    String reportName = request.getParameter("reportName");
    File file = new File(context.getRealPath(REPORT_DIRECTORY + "/"
                                     + reportName + ".jrprint"));
    PrintWriter printWriter = response.getWriter();
    try
    {
```

```
      JasperPrint jasperPrint = (JasperPrint) JRLoader
                                  .loadObject(file.getPath());
      JRHtmlExporter htmlExporter = new JRHtmlExporter();
      response.setContentType("text/html");
      request.getSession().setAttribute(
                ImageServlet.DEFAULT_JASPER_PRINT_SESSION_ATTRIBUTE,
                jasperPrint);
      htmlExporter.setParameter(JRExporterParameter.JASPER_PRINT,
                                                        jasperPrint);
      htmlExporter.setParameter(JRExporterParameter.OUTPUT_WRITER,
                                                        printWriter);
      htmlExporter.setParameter(JRHtmlExporterParameter.IMAGES_URI,
                                                      "image?image=");
      htmlExporter.exportReport();
    }
    catch (JRException e)
    {
      // display stack trace in the browser
      e.printStackTrace(printWriter);
    }
  }
}
```

Directing the browser to the URL for this servlet will result in the report being displayed in the browser in HTML, as can be seen demonstrated in the following screenshot:

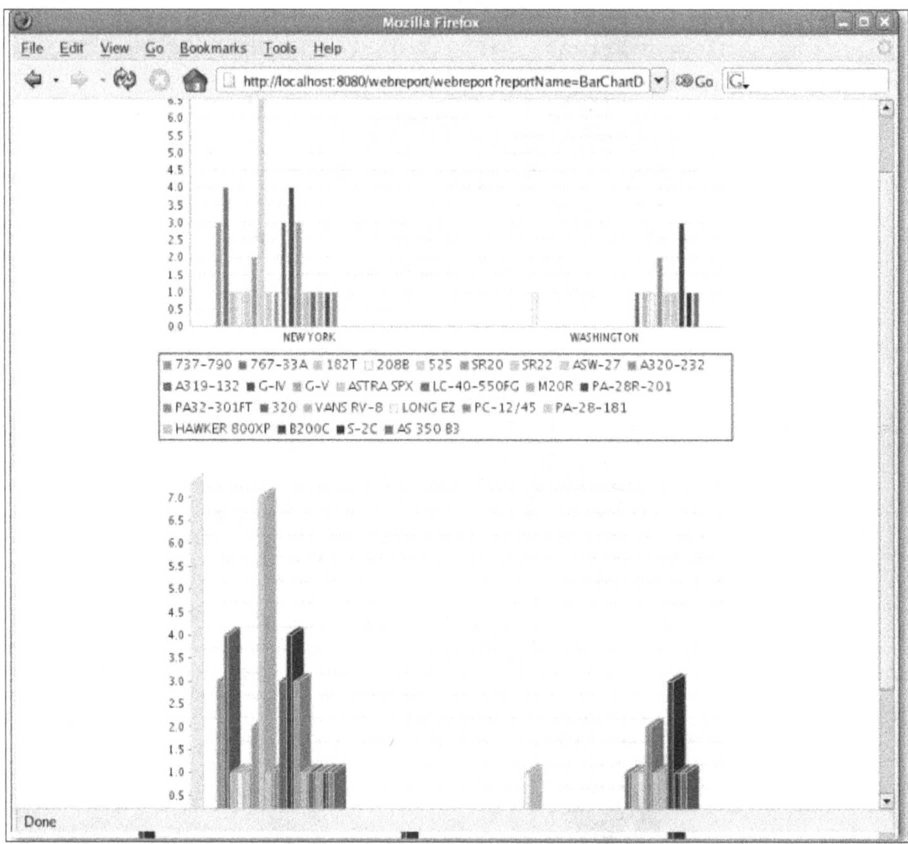

We chose to export this particular report to illustrate that the HTML exporting capability works fine for complex reports. This report generates charts at the filltime, which get translated to image files when exporting to HTML.

In order to stream a report as HTML to the browser, we need to set some parameters on an instance of `net.sf.jasperreports.engine.export.JRHtmlExporter`. The first parameter name we need to set is defined in the `net.sf.jasperreports.engine.JRExporterParameter.JASPER_PRINT` constant. Its value must be an instance of `net.sf.jasperreports.engine.JasperPrint` containing the report we wish to stream to the browser.

The next parameter we need to set is defined in the `net.sf.jasperreports.engine.JRExporterParameter.OUTPUT_WRITER` constant. As can be seen in the example, its corresponding value must be the instance of `java.io.PrintWriter` obtained by calling the `getWriter()` method on the `HttpServletResponse` object.

If the report we are exporting contains images, then there are a couple of extra steps we need to take to make sure the images are displayed correctly in the browser. We must attach the JasperPrint instance to the HTTP session. The session attribute name is defined in the `DEFAULT_JASPER_PRINT_SESSION_ATTRIBUTE` constant defined in `net.sf.jasperreports.j2ee.servlets.ImageServlet`.

We also need to set the `JRHtmlExporterParameter.IMAGES_URI` parameter in the instance of `JRHtmlExporter`; its corresponding value must be a string indicating the location of the images. In practice, this value is almost always set to the URL mapped to the `net.sf.jasperreports.j2ee.servlets.ImageServlet` included with JasperReports. In our example, we set its value to `"image?image="`, which is a typical value. Of course, the `ImageServlet` must be included in the `web.xml` for reports with images to render properly. The `web.xml` corresponding to the previous servlet deployment is as follows:

```
<!DOCTYPE web-app
    PUBLIC "-//Sun Microsystems, Inc.//DTD Web Application 2.3//EN"
    "http://java.sun.com/dtd/web-app_2_3.dtd">
<web-app>
  <servlet>
    <servlet-name>webreport</servlet-name>
    <servlet-class>
      net.ensode.jasperbook.HtmlReportServlet
    </servlet-class>
  </servlet>
  <servlet>
    <servlet-name>ImageServlet</servlet-name>
    <servlet-class>
      net.sf.jasperreports.j2ee.servlets.ImageServlet
    </servlet-class>
  </servlet>
  <servlet-mapping>
    <servlet-name>webreport</servlet-name>
    <url-pattern>/webreport</url-pattern>
  </servlet-mapping>
  <servlet-mapping>
    <servlet-name>ImageServlet</servlet-name>
    <url-pattern>/image</url-pattern>
  </servlet-mapping>
</web-app>
```

Notice that, for this example, we loaded an already filled report from the filesystem and streamed it to the browser as HTML. It is also possible to load a jasper template, fill it, export the resulting report to HTML, and then stream it to the browser. To accomplish this, we would load the jasper template from the filesystem, fill it using the `JasperFillManager.fillReport()` method, and then export the resulting JasperPrint object to HTML. The following example is a modified version of the previous servlet, and the new version illustrates this procedure:

```
package net.ensode.jasperbook;

import java.io.IOException;
import java.io.InputStream;
import java.io.PrintWriter;
import java.sql.Connection;
import java.sql.DriverManager;
import java.sql.SQLException;
import java.util.HashMap;

import javax.servlet.ServletException;
import javax.servlet.ServletOutputStream;
import javax.servlet.http.HttpServlet;
import javax.servlet.http.HttpServletRequest;
import javax.servlet.http.HttpServletResponse;

import net.sf.jasperreports.engine.JRException;
import net.sf.jasperreports.engine.JRExporterParameter;
import net.sf.jasperreports.engine.JasperFillManager;
import net.sf.jasperreports.engine.JasperPrint;
import net.sf.jasperreports.engine.export.JRHtmlExporter;
import net.sf.jasperreports.engine.export.JRHtmlExporterParameter;
import net.sf.jasperreports.j2ee.servlets.ImageServlet;

public class HtmlReportServlet2 extends HttpServlet
{
  public static final String REPORT_DIRECTORY = "/reports";
  protected void doGet(HttpServletRequest request, HttpServletResponse
                                                              response)
  throws ServletException, IOException
  {
    Connection connection;
    String reportName = request.getParameter("reportName");
    PrintWriter printWriter = response.getWriter();
    InputStream reportStream = getServletConfig().getServletContext()
                  .getResourceAsStream("/" + REPORT_DIRECTORY + "/"
                  + reportName + ".jasper");
    JasperPrint jasperPrint;
    try
```

```
      {
        Class.forName("com.mysql.jdbc.Driver");
        connection = DriverManager.getConnection("jdbc:mysql://
              localhost:3306/flightstats?user=root&password=password");
        jasperPrint = JasperFillManager.fillReport(reportStream, new
                                              HashMap(), connection);

        JRHtmlExporter htmlExporter = new JRHtmlExporter();
        response.setContentType("text/html");
        request.getSession().setAttribute(
                 ImageServlet.DEFAULT_JASPER_PRINT_SESSION_ATTRIBUTE,
                 jasperPrint);
        htmlExporter.setParameter(JRExporterParameter.JASPER_PRINT,
                                                        jasperPrint);
        htmlExporter.setParameter(JRExporterParameter.OUTPUT_WRITER,
                                                        printWriter);
        htmlExporter.setParameter(JRHtmlExporterParameter.IMAGES_URI,
                                                     "image?image=");
        htmlExporter.exportReport();

        connection.close();
      }
      catch (Throwable t)
      {
        // display stack trace in the browser
        t.printStackTrace(printWriter);
      }
    }
  }
```

The main difference between this example and the previous one is that, instead of loading the JasperPrint object from the filesystem, we are loading the jasper template, filling it, and storing the filled report in a JasperPrint object. This instance is then used as the value for the `JRExporterParameter.JASPER_PRINT` parameter.

Summary

In this chapter, we learned how to export reports to all of the formats supported by JasperReports. We learned to export reports to PDF by taking advantage of the `JRPdfExporter` class. We also saw how to export reports to RTF/Microsoft Word by taking advantage of the `JRRtfExporter` class. Additionally, we saw how reports can be exported to OpenDocument format (the native format for OpenOffice.org and StarOffice) using the `JROdtExporter` class. Similarly, to export reports to Microsoft Excel, HTML, and CSV formats we used the `JExcelApiExporter`, `JRHtmlExporter`, and `JRCsvExporter` classes, respectively. The `JRXmlExporter` class of JasperReports provided us with the functionality to export our reports to the XML format. Finally, we learned to export reports to plain text by taking advantage of the `JRTextExporter` class. The chapter also gave us an insight on how to direct HTML reports to a browser.

10
Graphical Report Design with iReport

So far, we have been creating all our reports by writing JRXML templates by hand. JasperSoft, the company behind JasperReports, offers a graphical report designer called iReport. iReport allows us to design reports graphically by dragging report elements into a report template and by using its graphical user interface to set report attributes.

iReport started as an independent project by Giulio Toffoli. JasperSoft recognized the popularity of iReport and, in October 2005, hired Giulio Toffoli and made iReport the official report designer for JasperSoft. Like JasperReports, iReport is also open source. It is licensed under the **GNU Public License (GPL)**.

In 2008, iReport was rewritten to take advantage of the NetBeans platform. It is freely available both as a standalone product and as a plugin to the NetBeans IDE.

In this chapter, we will be covering the standalone version of iReport; however, the material is also applicable to the iReport NetBeans plugin.

By the end of this chapter, you will be able to:

- Obtain and set up iReport
- Quickly create database reports by taking advantage of iReport's Report Wizard
- Design reports graphically with iReport
- Add multiple columns to a report
- Group report data
- Add images and charts to a report

Obtaining iReport

iReport can be downloaded from its home page at `http://jasperforge.org/projects/ireport` by clicking on the **Download iReport** image slightly above the center of the page.

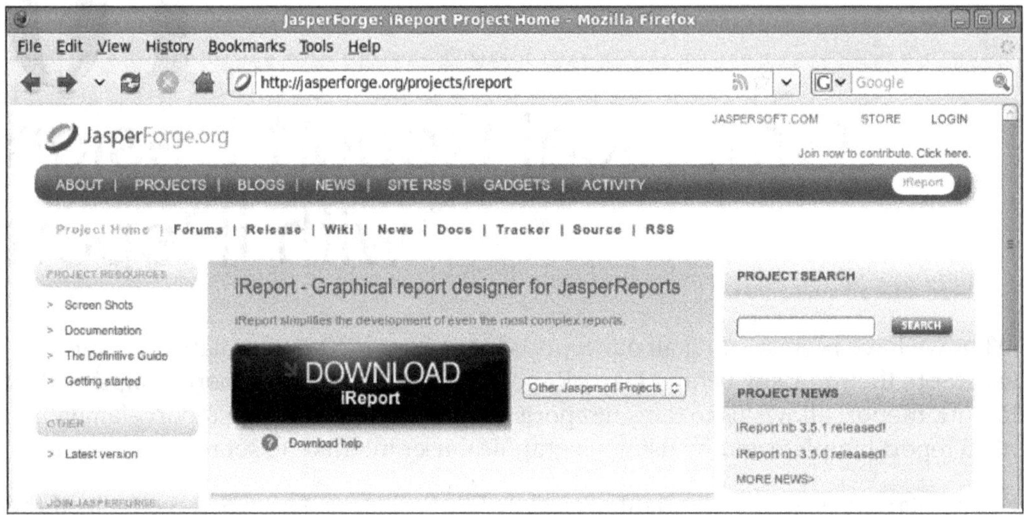

Once we click on the image, we are directed to an intermediate page where we can either log in with our JasperForge account or go straight to the download page.

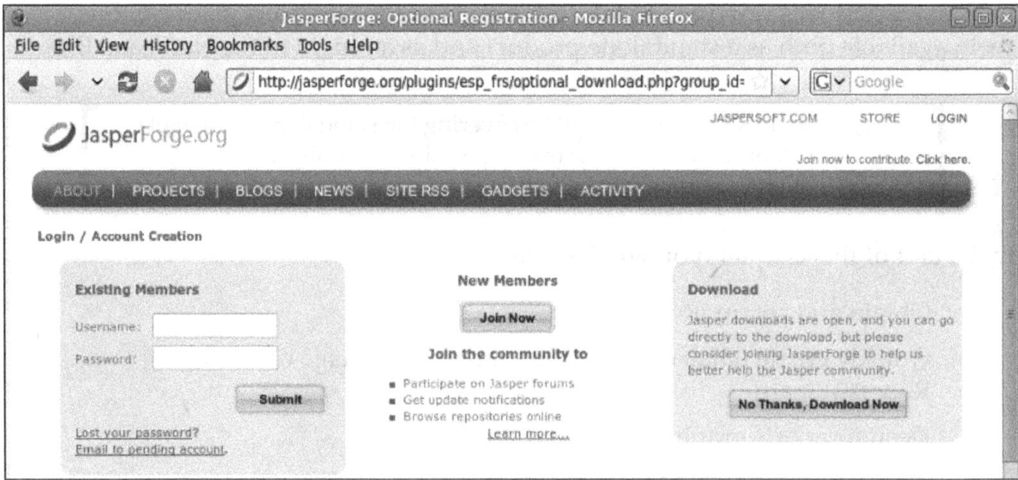

Either logging in or clicking on the **No Thanks, Download Now** button takes us to the iReport download page.

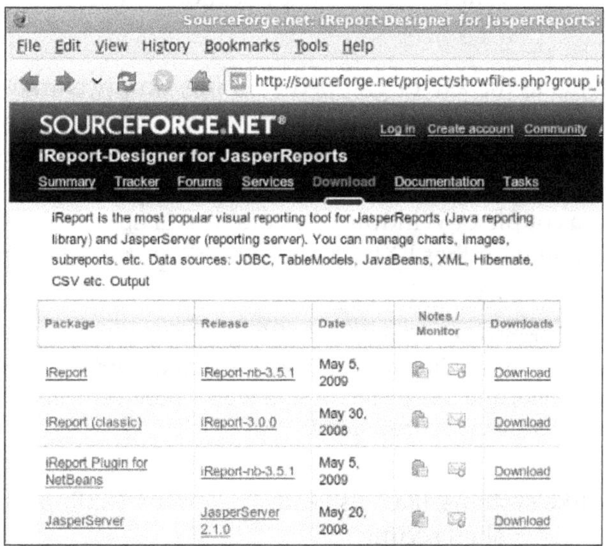

The standalone iReport product is in the first row of the table on the page. To download it, we simply click on the **Download** link in the last column. Other downloads on the page are for older versions of JasperReports, iReport NetBeans plugin, and other JasperSoft products.

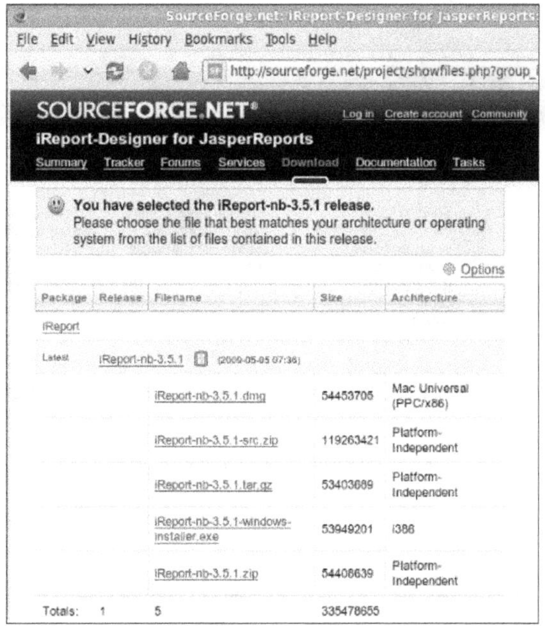

iReport can be downloaded as a DMG file for Macintosh computers, as a Windows installer for Windows PCs, as a source file, as a ZIP file, or as a gzipped TAR file. To install iReport, simply follow the usual application installation method for your platform.

If you chose to download the ZIP or gzipped TAR file, simply extract it into any directory. A subdirectory called something like `iReport-nb-3.5.1` will be created. (The exact name will depend on the version of iReport that was downloaded.) Inside this directory, you will find a `bin` subdirectory containing an executable shell script called `ireport` and a couple of Windows executables, `ireport.exe` and `ireport_w.exe`. On Windows systems, either EXE file will start iReport.

> The difference between the two Windows executables is that the `ireport.exe` will display a command-line window when iReport is executed, and `ireport_w.exe` won't. Both versions provide exactly the same functionality.

On Unix and Unix-like systems, such as Linux and Mac OS, iReport can be started by executing the `ireport` shell script.

The following screenshot illustrates how iReport looks when it is opened for the first time:

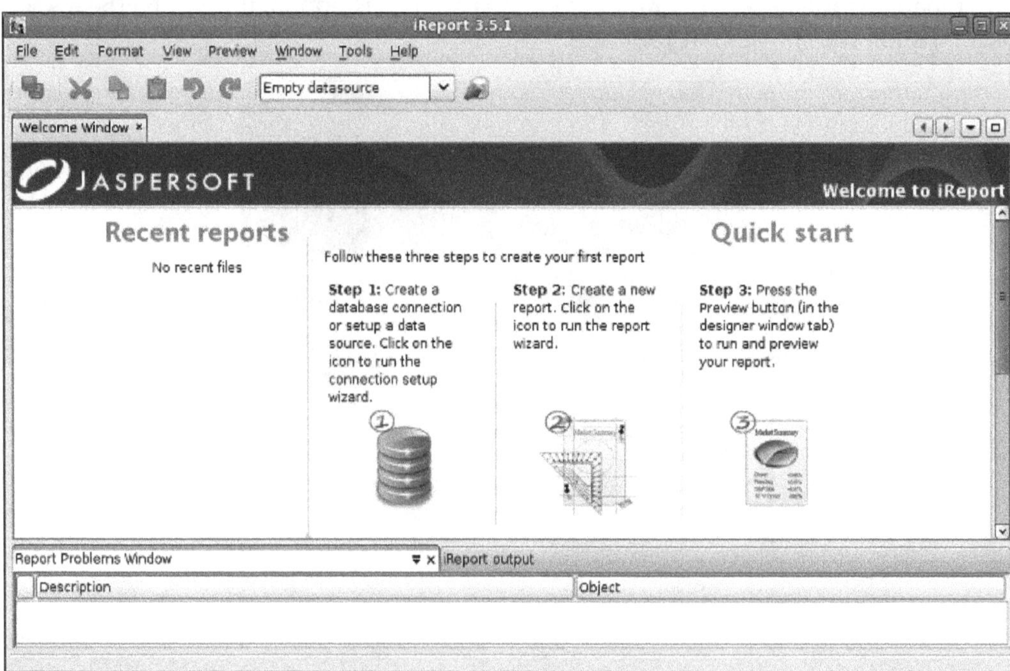

Setting up iReport

iReport can help us quickly generate database reports. To do so, we need to provide it with the JDBC driver and connection information for our database.

iReport comes bundled with JDBC drivers for several open source relational database systems, such as MySQL, PostgreSQL, HSQLDB, and others. If we want to connect to a different database, we need to add the JDBC driver to iReport's CLASSPATH. This can be done by clicking on **Tools** | **Options** and then selecting the **Classpath** tab.

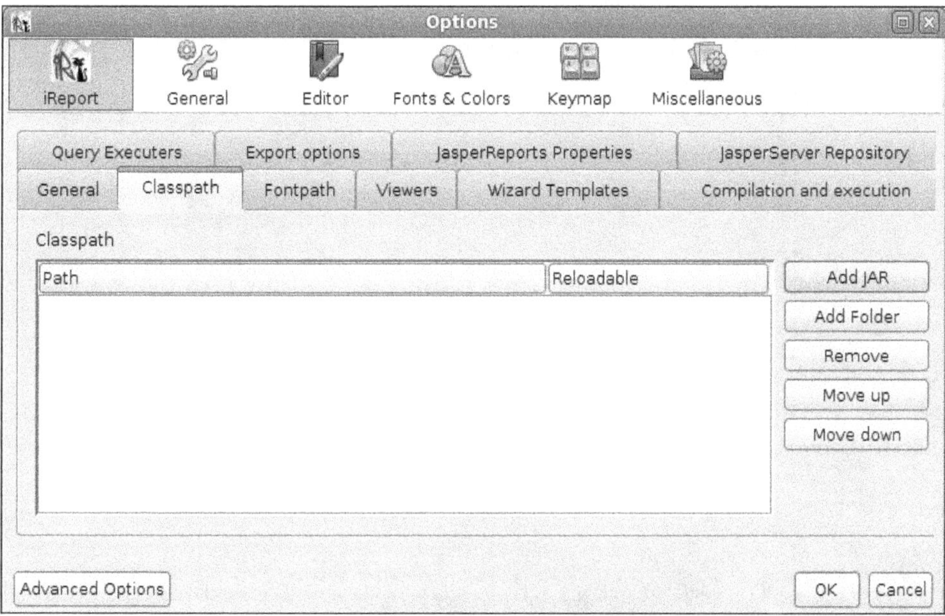

To add the JDBC driver to the CLASSPATH, click on the **Add JAR** button, and then navigate to the location of the JAR file containing the JDBC driver. Select the JAR file and click on the **OK** button at the bottom of the window.

We won't actually add a JDBC driver, as we are using MySQL for our examples, which is one of the RDBMS systems supported out of the box by iReport. The information just provided is for the benefit of readers using an RDBMS system that is not supported out of the box.

Before we can create reports that use an RDBMS as a datasource, we need to create a database connection. In order to do so, we need to click on the **Report Datasources** icon in the toolbar:

After doing so, the **Connections / Datasources** configuration window should pop up.

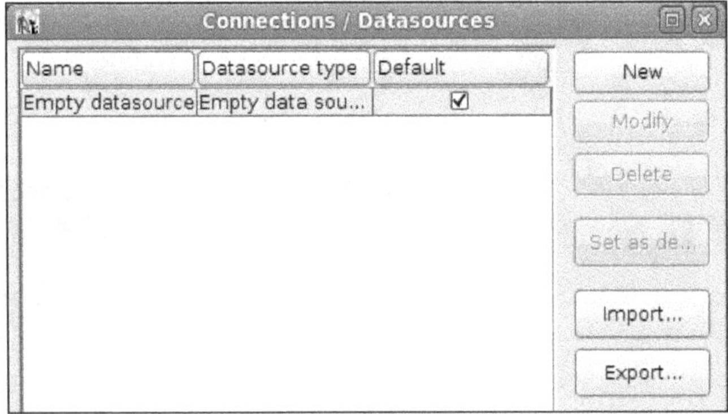

To add the connection, we need to click on the **New** button, select **Database JDBC connection**, and then click on the **Next>** button.

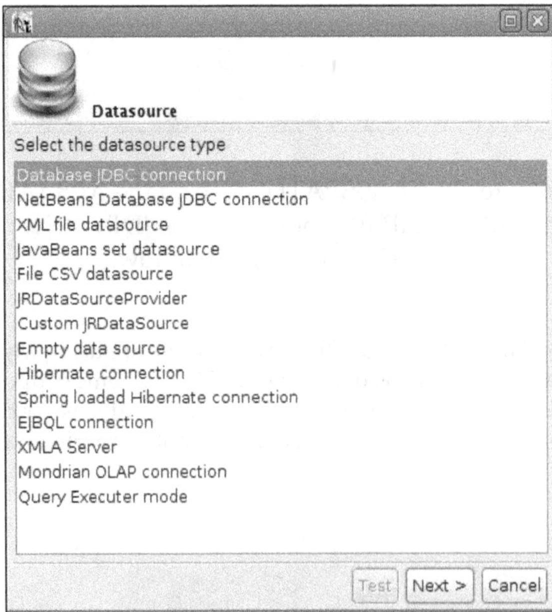

We then need to select the appropriate JDBC driver, fill in the connection information, and click on the **Save** button.

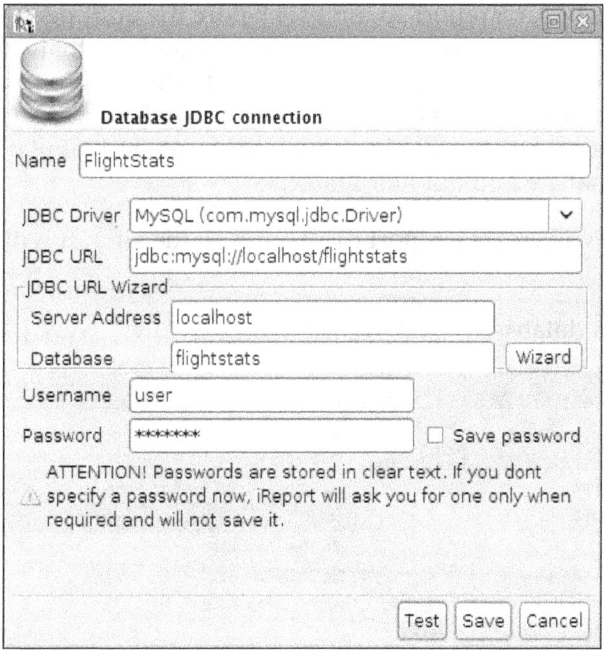

Before saving the database connection properties, it is a good idea to click on the **Test** button to make sure we can connect to the database. If we can, we should see a pop-up window like the following:

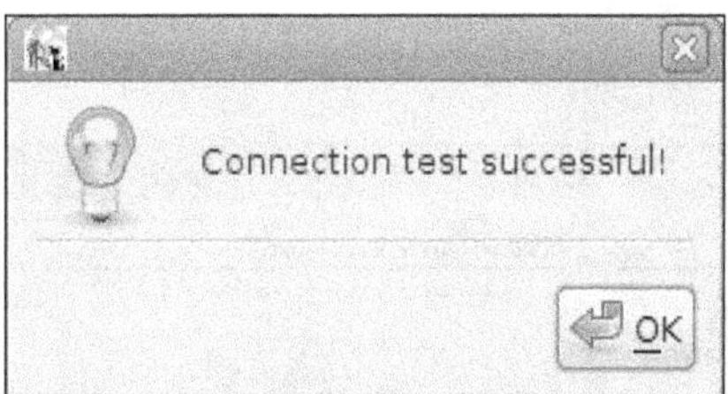

After verifying that we can successfully connect to the database, we are ready to create some database reports.

Creating a database report in record time

iReport contains a wizard that allows us to quickly generate database reports (very useful if the boss asks for a report 15 minutes before the quitting time on a Friday!). The wizard allows us to use one of the predefined templates that are included with iReport. The included report templates are divided into two groups: templates laid out in a "columnar" manner and templates laid out in a "tabular" manner. Columnar templates generate reports that are laid out in columns, and tabular templates generate reports that are laid out like a table.

In this section, we will create a report displaying all the aircraft with a horsepower of 1000 or more.

To quickly create a database report, we need to go to **File | New | Report Wizard**.

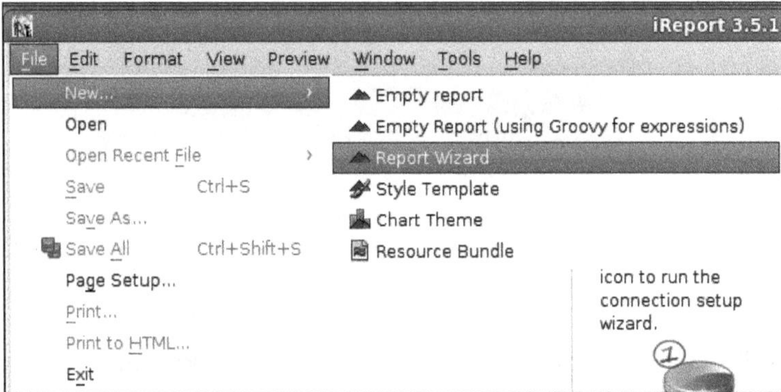

We should then enter an appropriate name and location for our report and click on **Next>**.

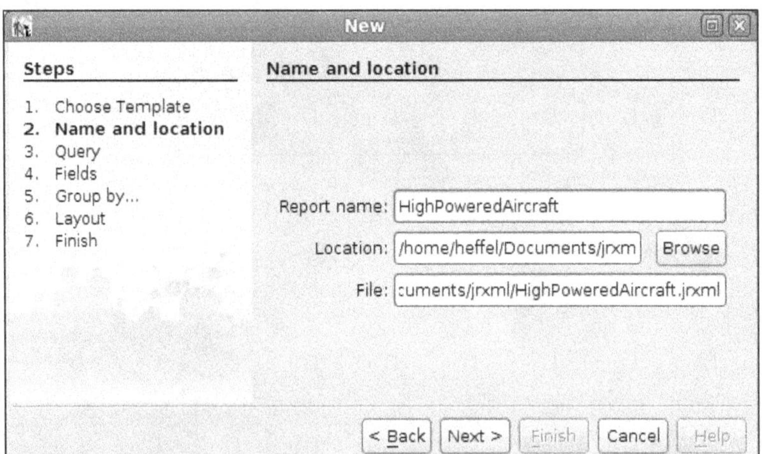

Next, we need to select the datasource or database connection to use for our report. For our example, we will use the JDBC connection we configured in the previous section. We can then enter the database query we will use to create the report. Alternatively, we can use the iReport query designer to design the query.

For individuals with SQL experience, in many cases it is easier to come up with the database query in a separate database client tool and then paste it in the **Query** text area than using the query designer.

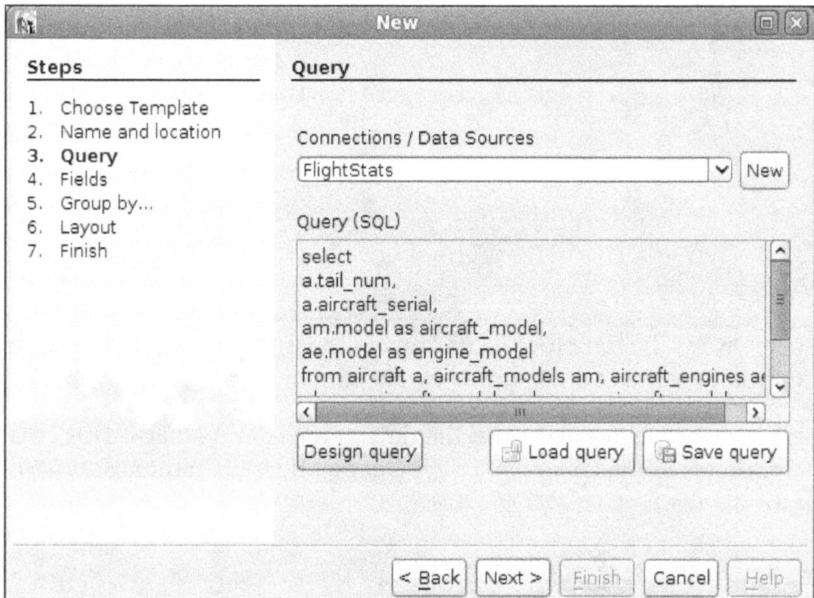

The complete query for the report is:

```
select
a.tail_num,
a.aircraft_serial,
am.model as aircraft_model,
ae.model as engine_model
from aircraft a, aircraft_models am, aircraft_engines ae
where a.aircraft_model_code = am.aircraft_model_code
and a.aircraft_engine_code = ae.aircraft_engine_code
and ae.horsepower >= 1000
```

The following window shows a list of all the columns selected in the query, allowing us to select which ones we would like to use as report fields:

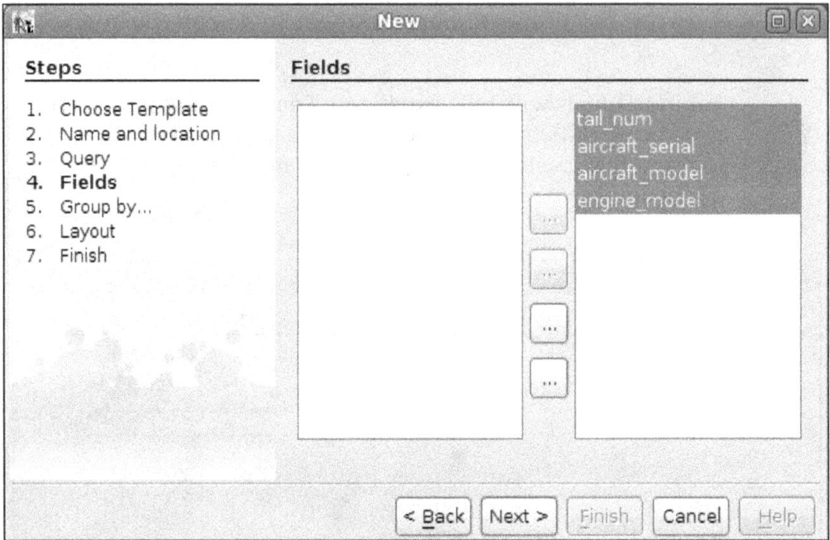

In this case, we want the data for all columns in the query to be displayed in the report. Therefore, we select all columns by clicking on the second ... button.

We then select how we want to group the data and click on **Next>**. This creates a report group. (Refer to the *Grouping Report Data* section in Chapter 6, *Report Layout and Design* for details.)

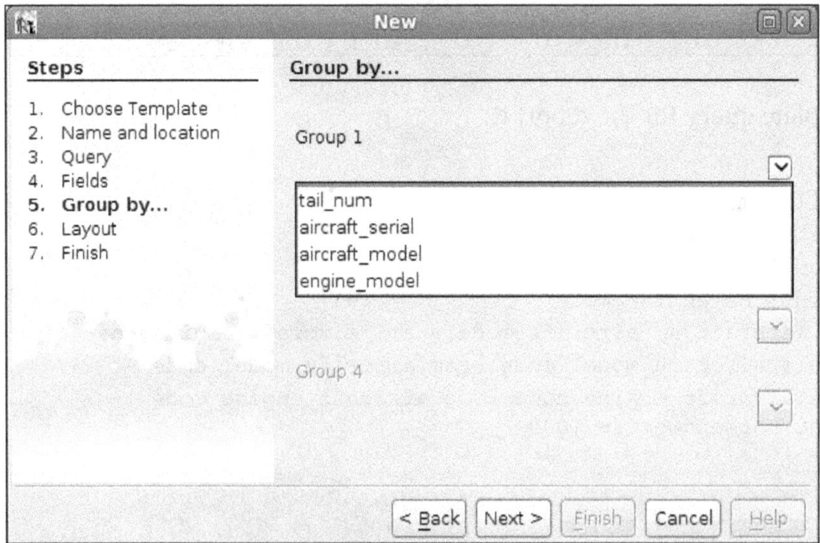

In this example, we will not group the report data. The screenshot illustrates how the drop-down box contains the report fields selected in the previous step.

We then select the report layout (Columnar or Tabular). In this example, we will use the **Tabular Layout**.

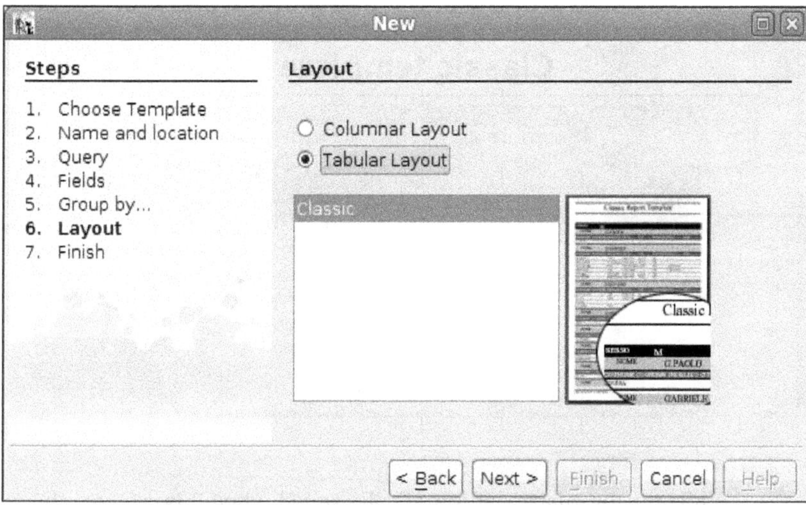

After selecting the layout, we click on **Next>** to be presented with the last step.

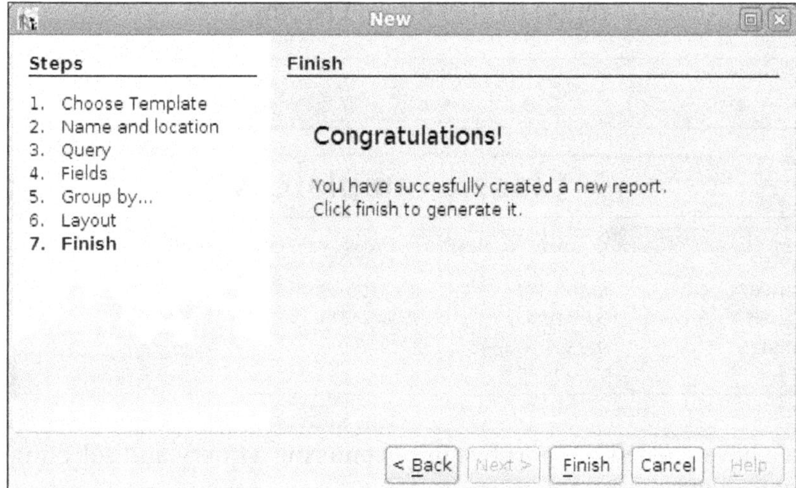

We then click on **Finish** to generate the report's JRXML template.

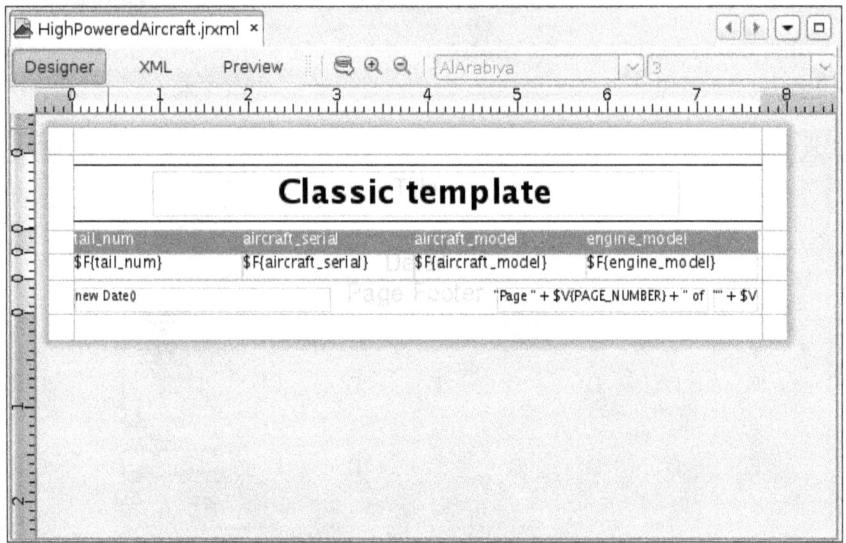

While the template is automatically saved when it is created, the report generated by the **Preview** button is not automatically saved.

We can then preview our report by clicking on **Preview**.

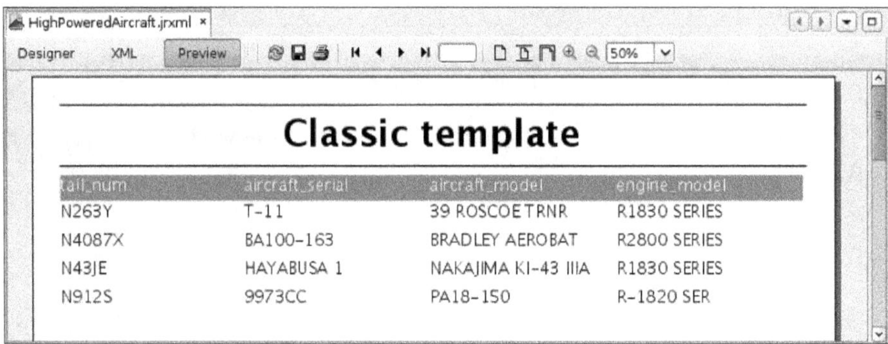

That's it! We have created a report by simply entering a query and selecting a few options from a wizard.

Tweaking the generated report

Admittedly, the report title and column headers of our report need some tweaking. To modify the report title so that it actually reflects the report contents, we can either double-click on the report title on iReport's main window and type an appropriate report title, or we can modify the value of the **Text** property for the title static text in the **Properties** window at the lower righthand side.

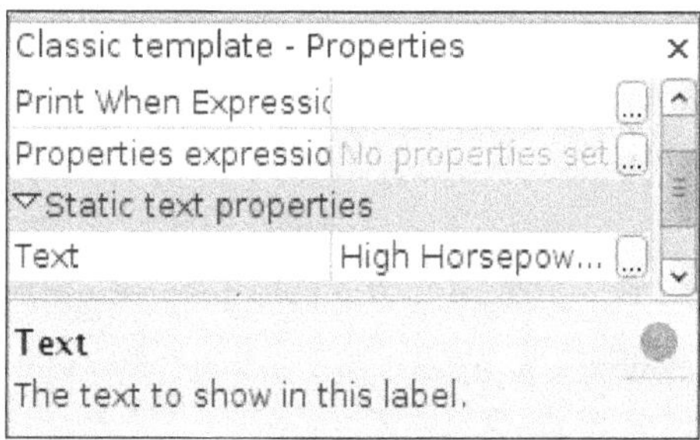

Double-clicking on the title is certainly the fastest way to modify it. However, the Properties window allows us to modify not only the text, but also the font, borders, and several other properties.

We can follow the same procedure for each column header. The following screenshot shows the resulting template as displayed in iReport's main window:

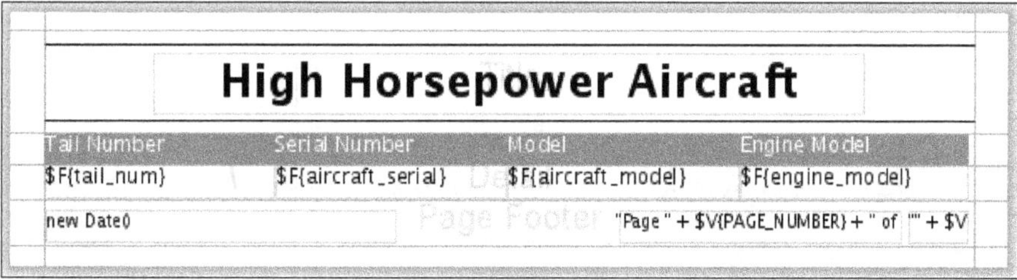

We'll preview the report one more time to see the final version.

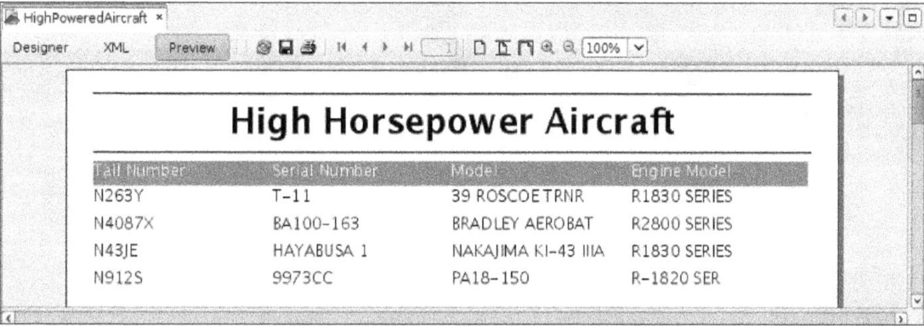

There you have it! The boss can have his or her report, and we can leave work and enjoy the weekend!

Creating a report from scratch

In the previous section, we discussed how to quickly generate a database report by using iReport's Report Wizard. The wizard is very convenient because it allows us to create a report very quickly. However, its disadvantage is that it is not very flexible. In this section, we will learn how to create a report from scratch in iReport. Our report will show the tail number, serial number, and model of every aircraft in the `FlightStats` database.

To create a new report, we need to go to the **File | New | Empty report** menu item.

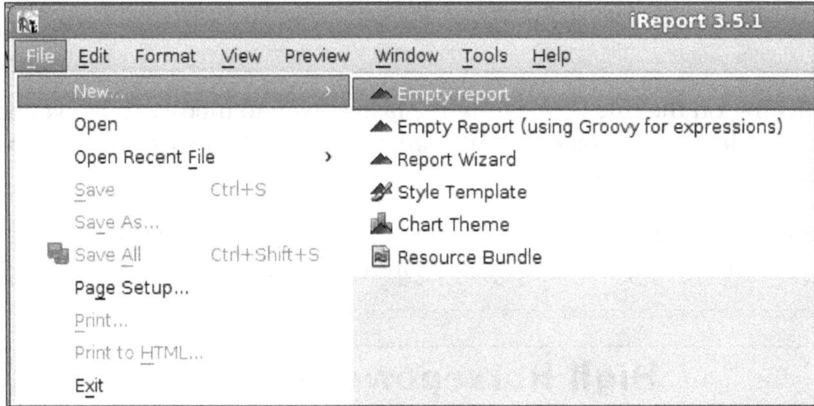

At this point, we should enter a **Report name** and **Location**.

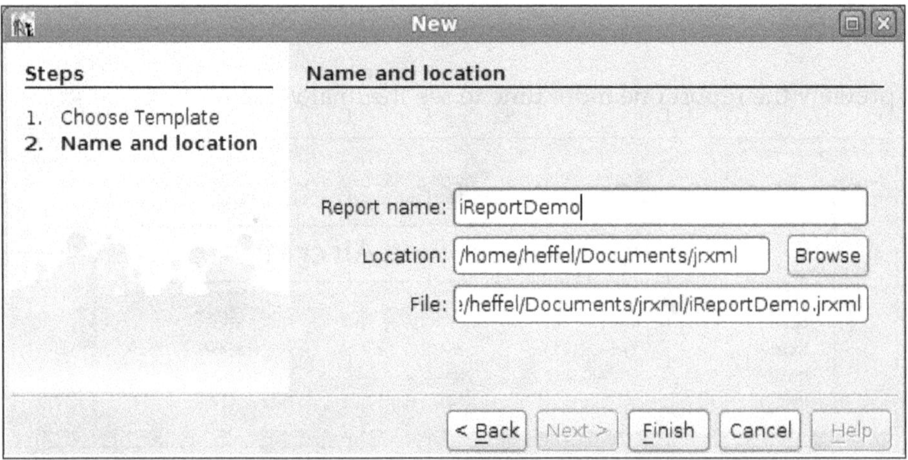

In this example, we will set the report name to **iReportDemo** and accept all the other default values. After clicking on the **OK** button, iReport's main window should look like this:

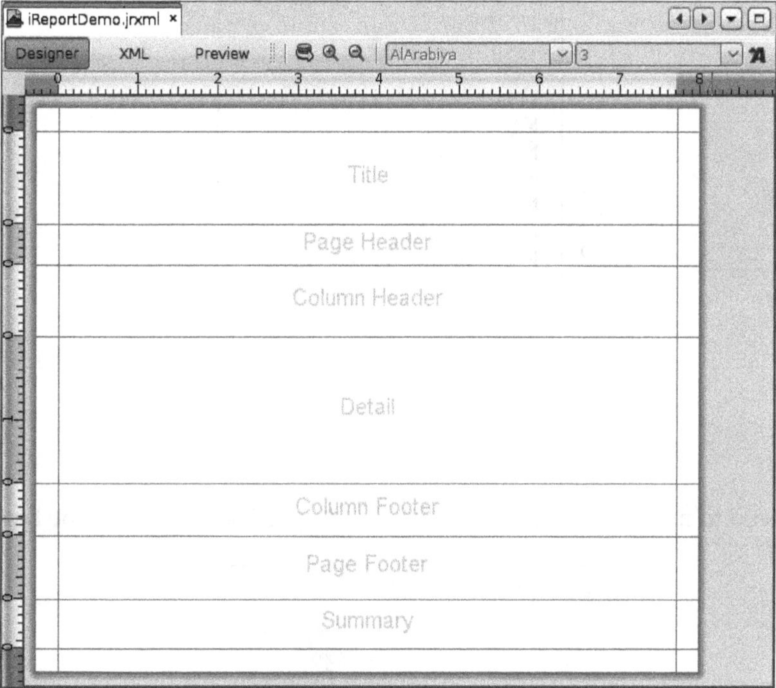

The horizontal lines divide the different report sections. Any item we insert between any two horizontal lines will be placed in the appropriate report section's band. Horizontal lines can be dragged to resize the appropriate section(s).

The vertical lines represent the left and right report margins. It is not possible to drag the vertical lines. To modify the left and right margins, we must select the report in the **Report Inspector** window at the top left.

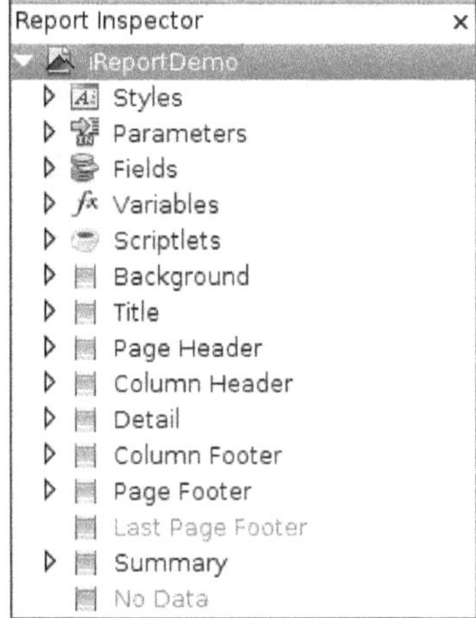

Then, we need to modify the margins from the Properties window at the bottom right.

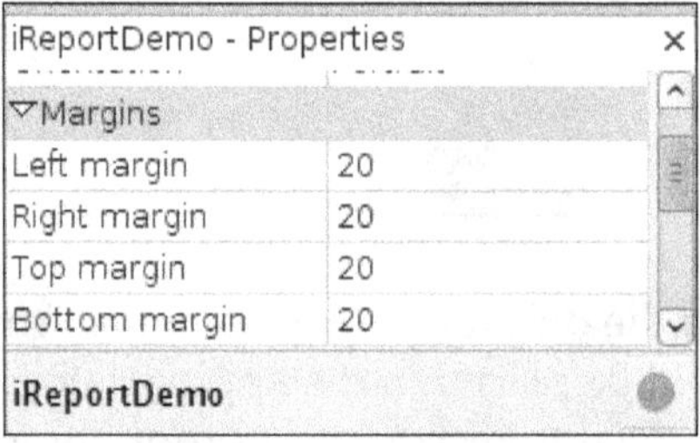

Properties for all the report sections and elements, such as variables, scriptlets, title, background, detail, and so on, can be modified by following the approach described here.

Going back to our empty report template, let's add a report title. For this, we will use the static text **Aircraft Report**. To add the static text, we need to use the **Static Text** component in the **Palette**.

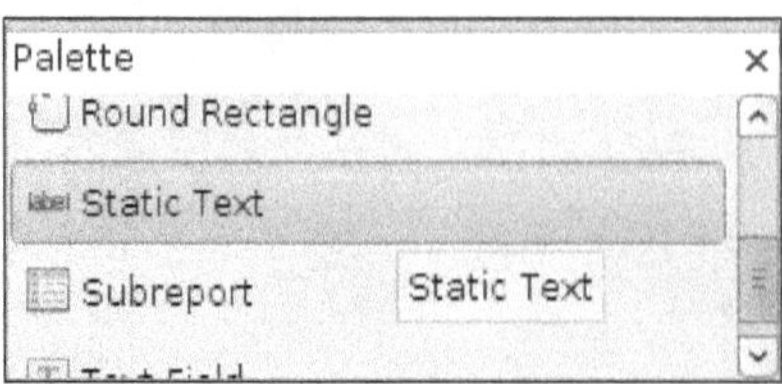

We then need to drag the **Static Text** component to the Title area of the report. iReport, by default, inserts the text **Static text** inside this field. To modify this default text, we can double-click anywhere inside the field and type in a more appropriate title. Alternatively, we can modify the **Text** property for the static text field in the Properties window at the lower righthand side.

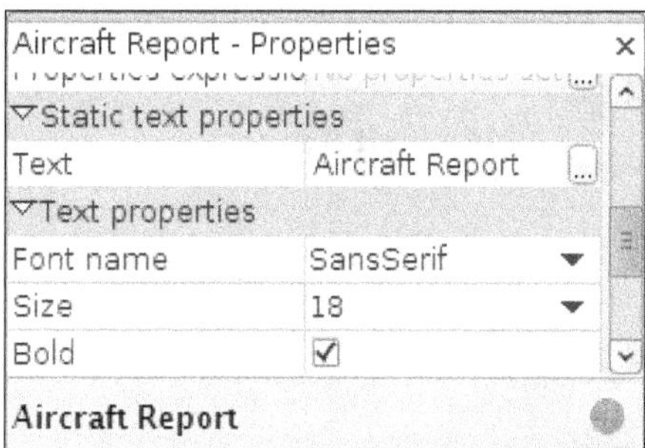

In the Properties window, we can modify other properties for our text. In the above screenshot, we modified the text size to be **18** pixels, and we made it bold by clicking on the checkbox next to the **Bold** property.

We can center the report title within the Title band by right-clicking on it, selecting **Position**, and then **Center**.

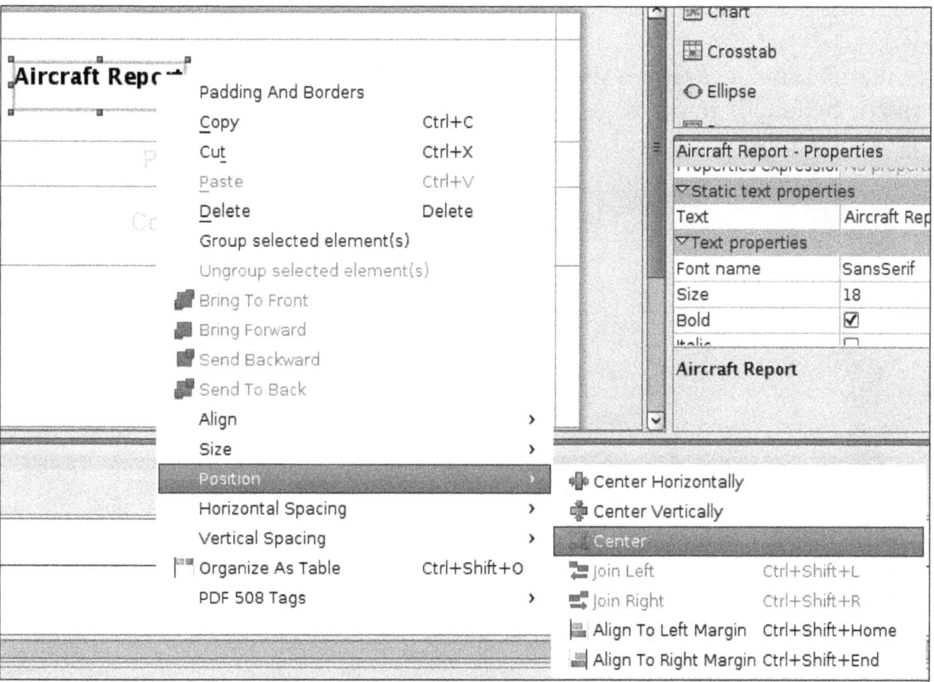

After following all of these steps, our report should now look like this:

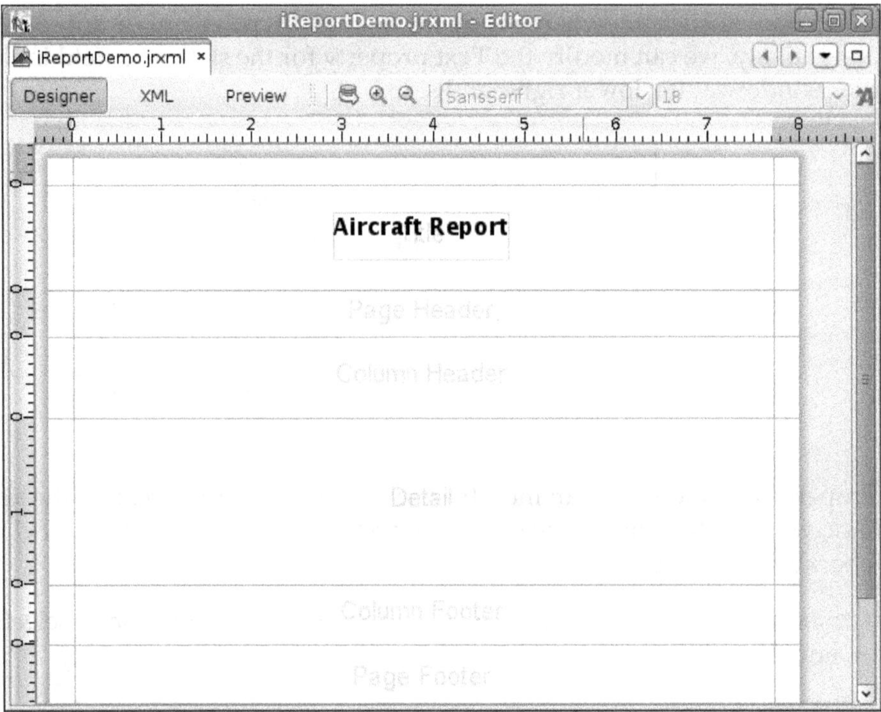

Applying the same techniques used for adding the report title, we can add some more static text fields in the page header. After adding the page header, our report now looks like this:

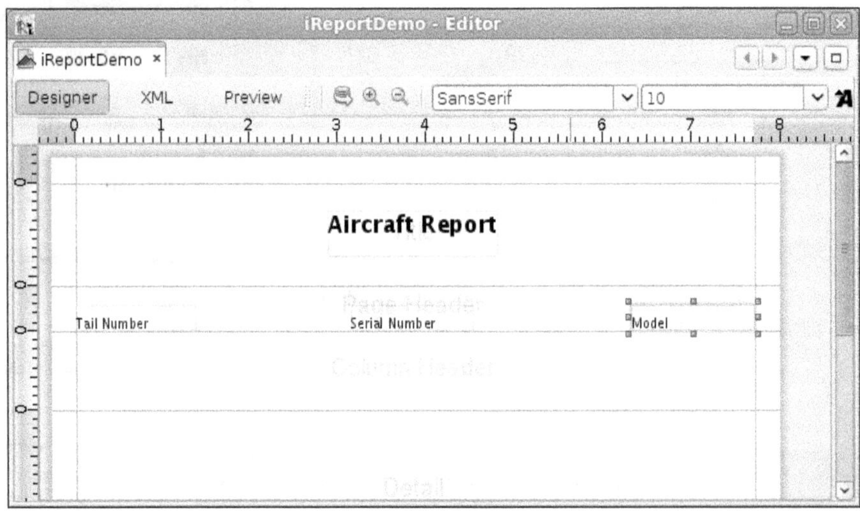

We modified the **Vertical Alignment** of all three text fields in the page header by selecting the appropriate values in the Properties window for each one of them.

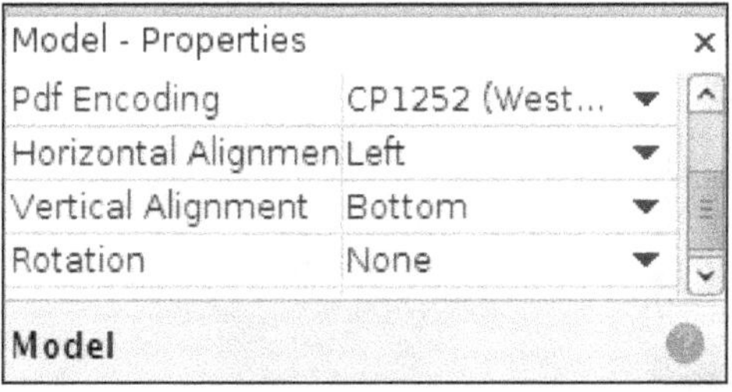

Now it is time to add some dynamic data to the report. We can enter a report query selecting the report node in the Report Inspector window and then selecting **Edit Query**.

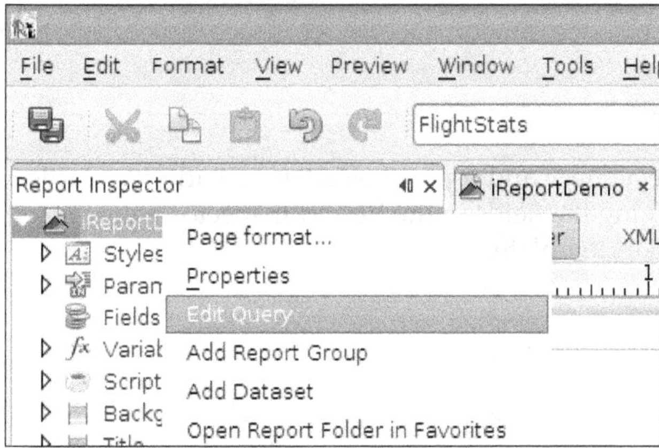

As we type the report query, by default iReport retrieves report fields from it. This query will retrieve the tail number, serial number, and model of every aircraft in the database.

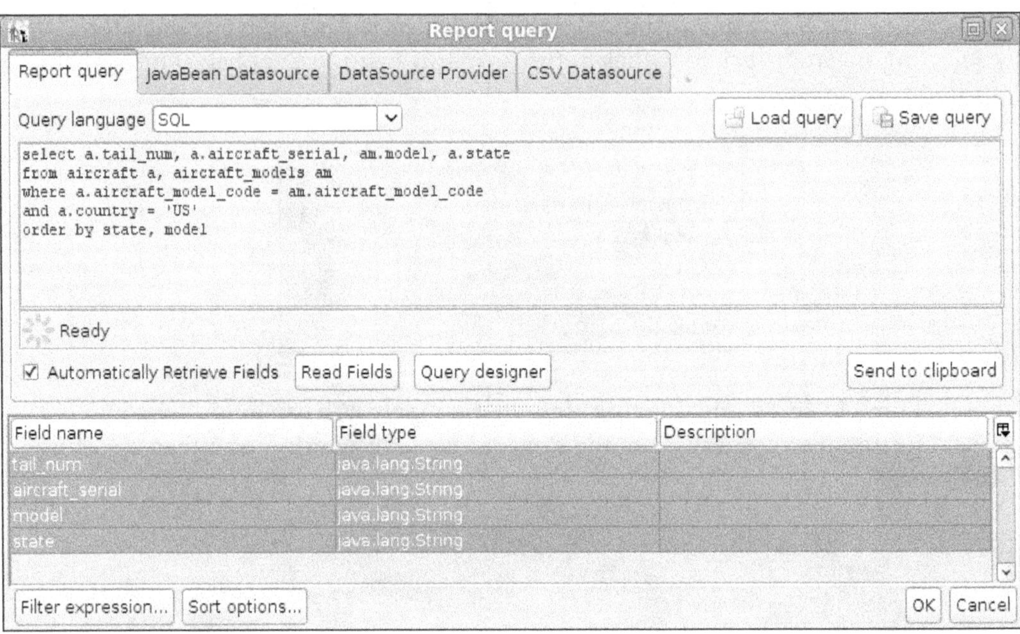

Now that we have a query and report fields, we can add text fields to the report. We can do so by dragging the fields in the Report Inspector window to the appropriate location in the report template.

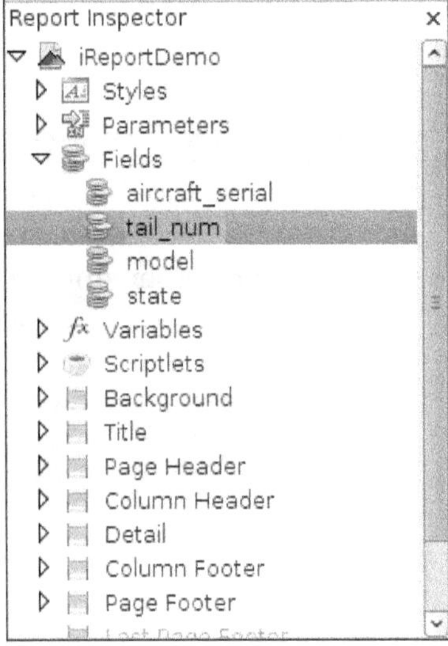

After aligning each text field with the corresponding header, our report should now look like this:

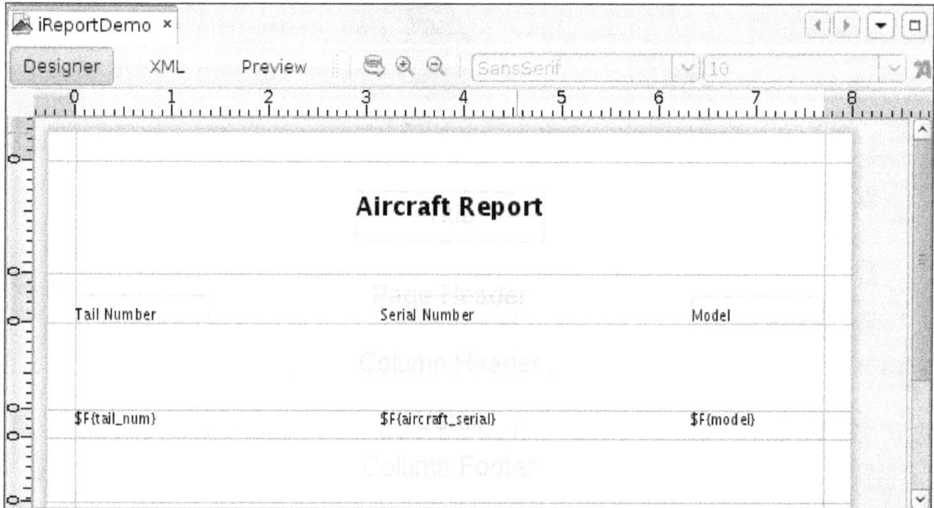

To avoid extra vertical space between records, we resized the Detail band by dragging its bottom margin up. The same effect can be achieved by double-clicking on the bottom margin.

Notice that we have an empty **Column Header** band in the report template. This empty band will result in having some whitespace between each header and the first row in the Detail band. To avoid having this whitespace in our report, we can easily delete this band by right-clicking on it in the Report Inspector window and selecting **Delete Band**.

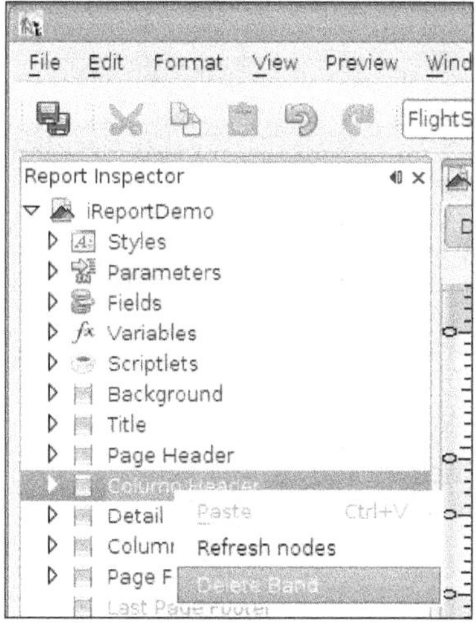

We now have a simple but complete report. We can view it by clicking on **Preview**.

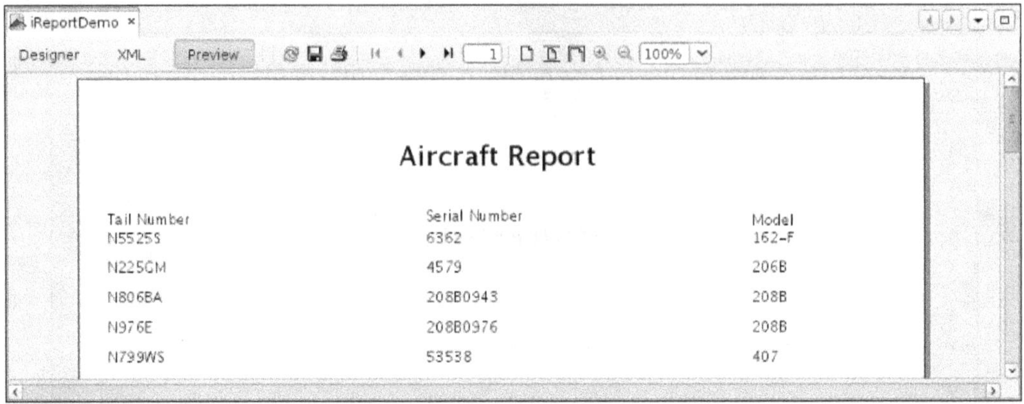

That's it! We have created a simple report graphically with iReport.

Creating more elaborate reports

In the previous section, we created a fairly simple database report. In this section, we will modify that report to illustrate how to add images, charts, and multiple columns to a report. We will also see how to group report data. We will perform all of these tasks graphically with iReport.

Adding images to a report

Adding static images to a report is very simple with iReport. Just drag the **Image** component from the Palette to the band where it will be rendered in the report.

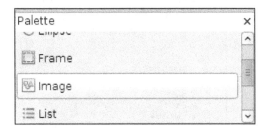

When we drop the image component into the appropriate band, a window pops up asking us to specify the location of the image file to display.

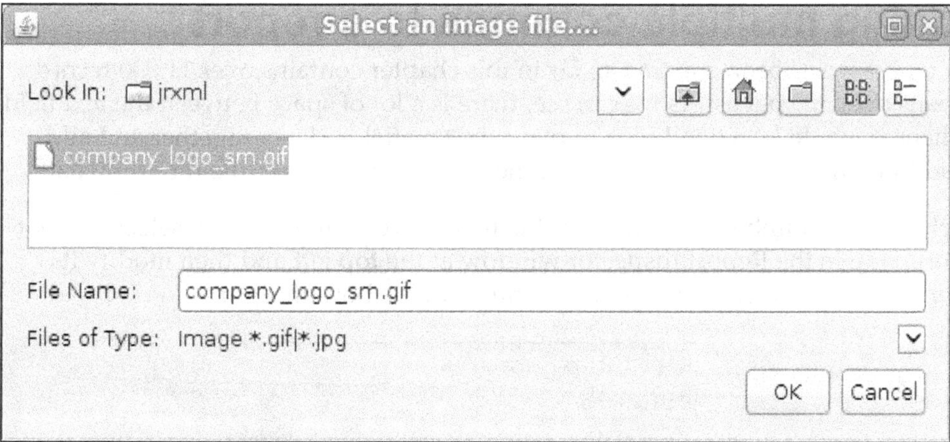

After we select the image, we can drag it to its exact location where it will be rendered.

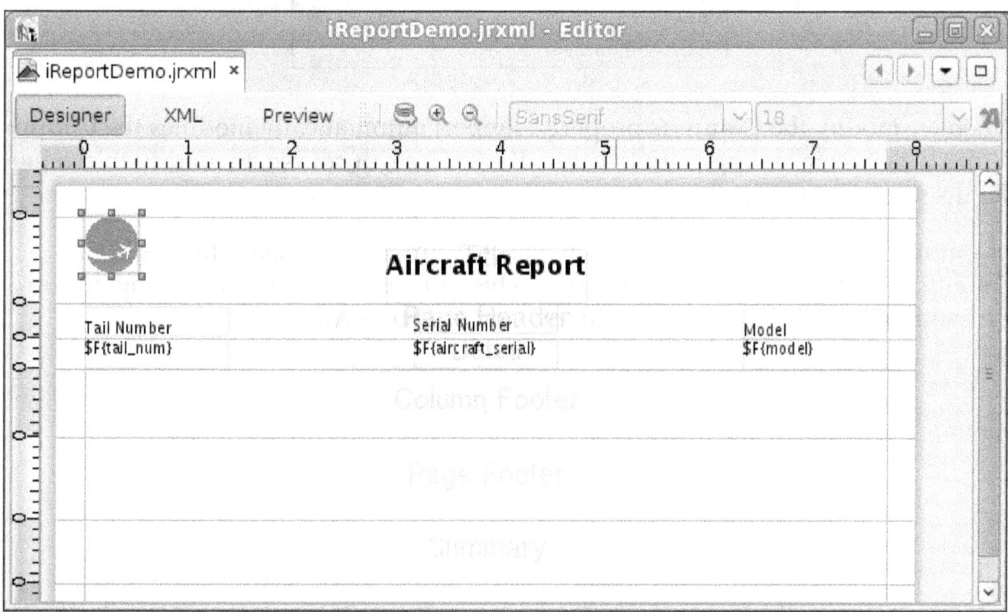

As we can see, adding images to a report using iReport couldn't be any simpler.

Adding multiple columns to a report

The report we've been creating so far in this chapter contains over 11,000 records. It spans over 300 pages. As we can see, there is a lot of space between the text fields. Perhaps it would be a good idea to place the text fields closer together and add an additional column. This would cut the number of pages in the report by half.

To change the number of columns in the report, we simply need to select the root report node in the Report Inspector window at the top left and then modify its **Columns** property in the Properties window at the bottom right.

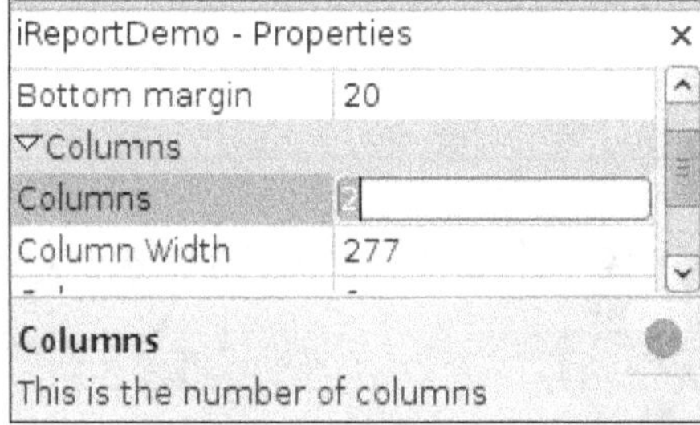

When we modify the **Columns** property, iReport automatically modifies the **Column Width** property to an appropriate value. We are free, of course, to modify this value if it doesn't meet our needs.

As our report now contains more than one column, it makes sense to re-add the Column Header band we deleted earlier. This can be done by right-clicking on the band in the Report Inspector window and selecting **Add Band**.

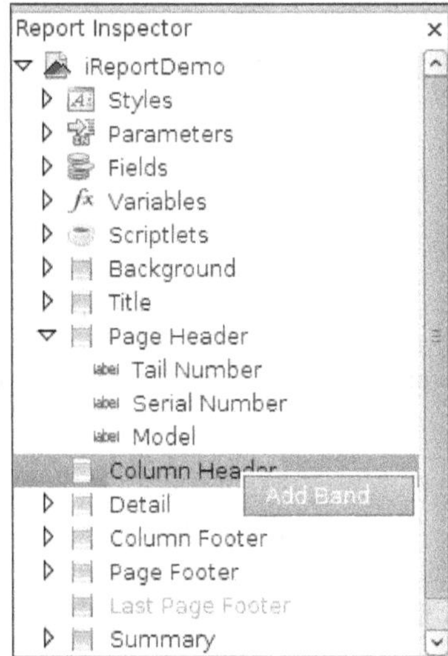

Next, we need to move the static text in the page header to the Column Header band. To move any element from one band to another, all we need to do is drag it to the appropriate band in the Report Inspector window.

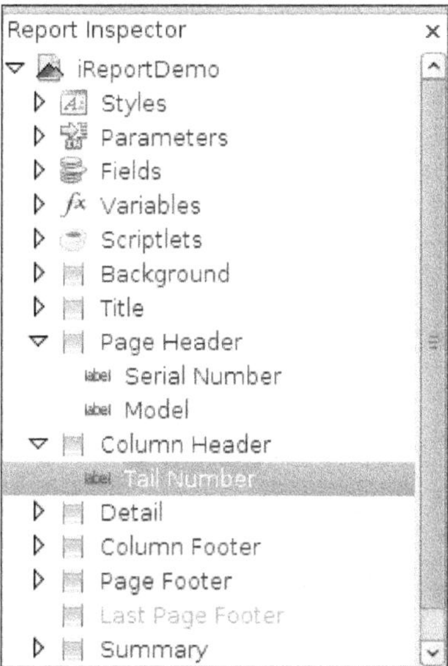

Next, we need to resize and reposition the text fields in the Detail band and the static text elements in the Column Header band so that they fit in the new, narrower width of the columns. Also, resize the Column Header band to avoid having too much whitespace between the elements of the Column Header and Detail bands. Our report now looks like this:

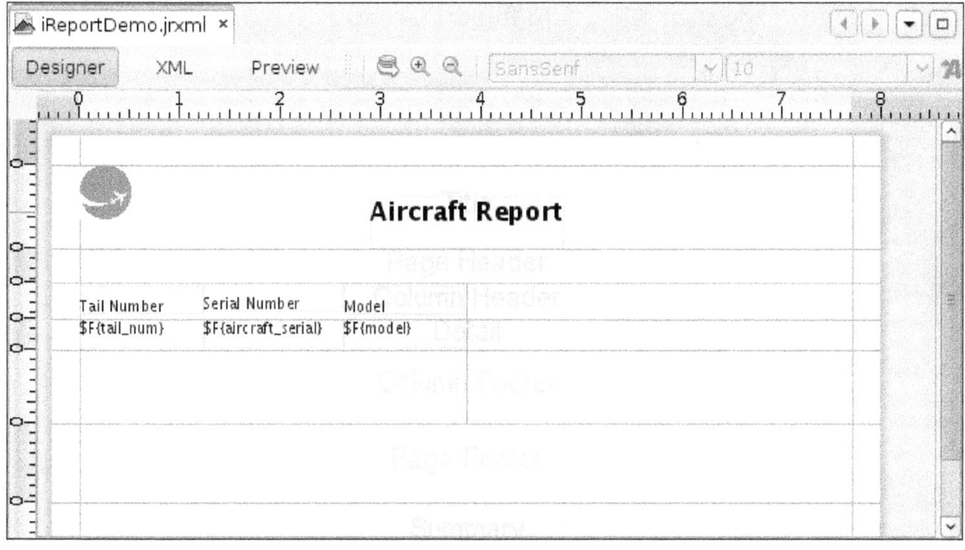

We can see the resulting report by clicking on **Preview**.

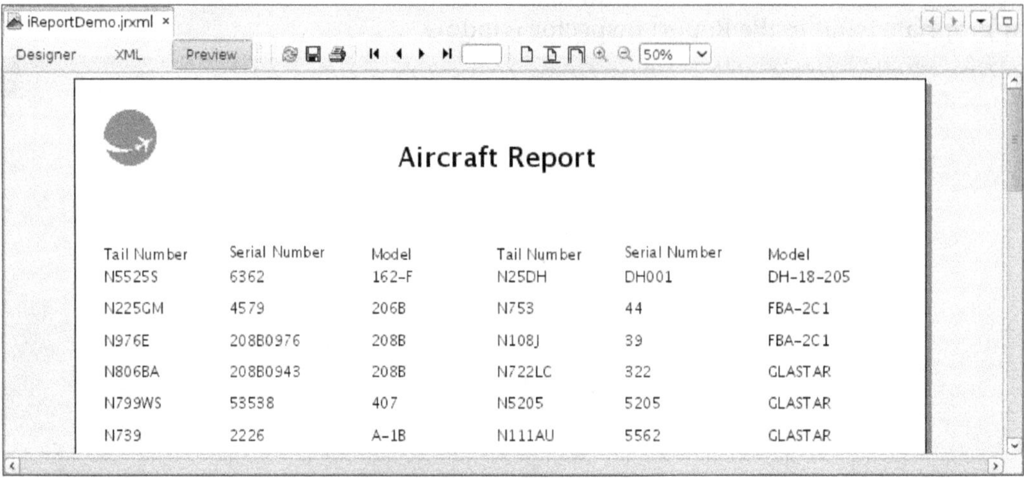

Grouping report data

Suppose we are asked to modify our report so that data is divided by the state where the aircraft is registered. This is a perfect situation to apply report groups. Recall from Chapter 6, *Report Layout and Design*, that report groups allow us to divide report data when a report expression changes. Recall that our report query limits the result set to aircraft registered in the United States, and one of the columns it retrieves is the state where the aircraft is registered.

To define a report group, we need to right-click on the root report node in the Report Inspector window, and then select **Add Report Group**.

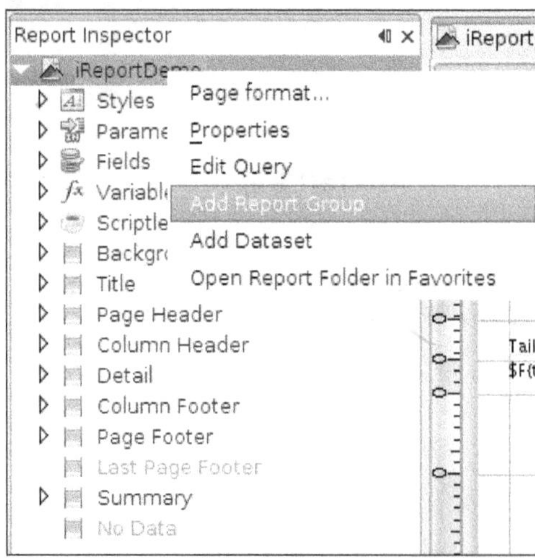

Then, enter the **Group name** and indicate whether we want to group by a field or by a report expression. In our case, we want to group the data by `state` field.

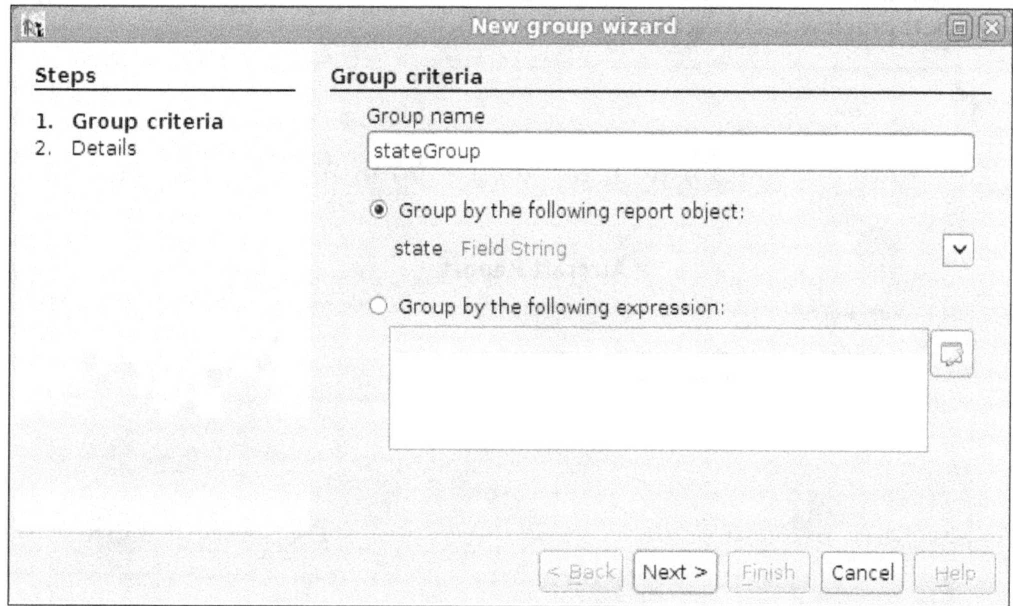

After clicking on **Next>**, we need to indicate whether we want to add a group header and/or footer to our report.

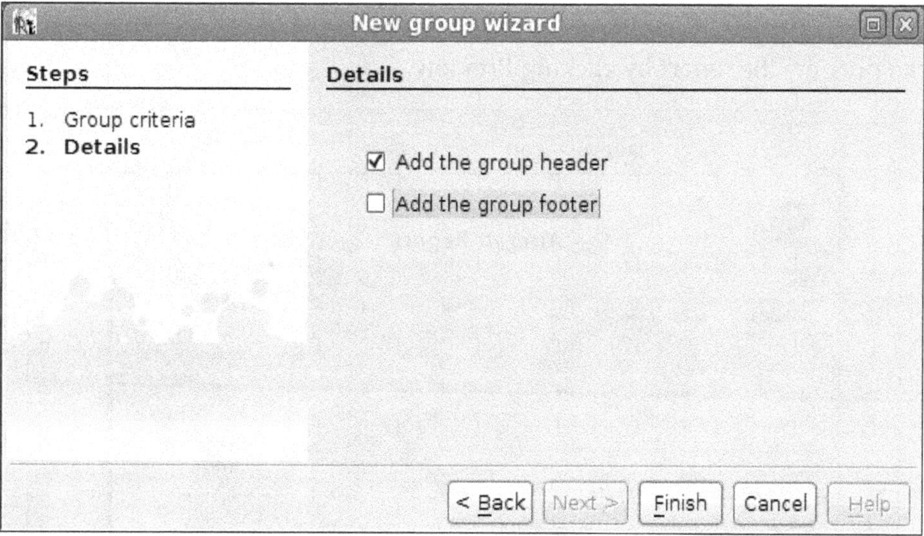

For aesthetic purposes, we move the static text fields in the Column Header band to the Group Header band, remove the column and page header bands, and add additional information to the Group Header band. After making all of these changes, our report preview will look like this:

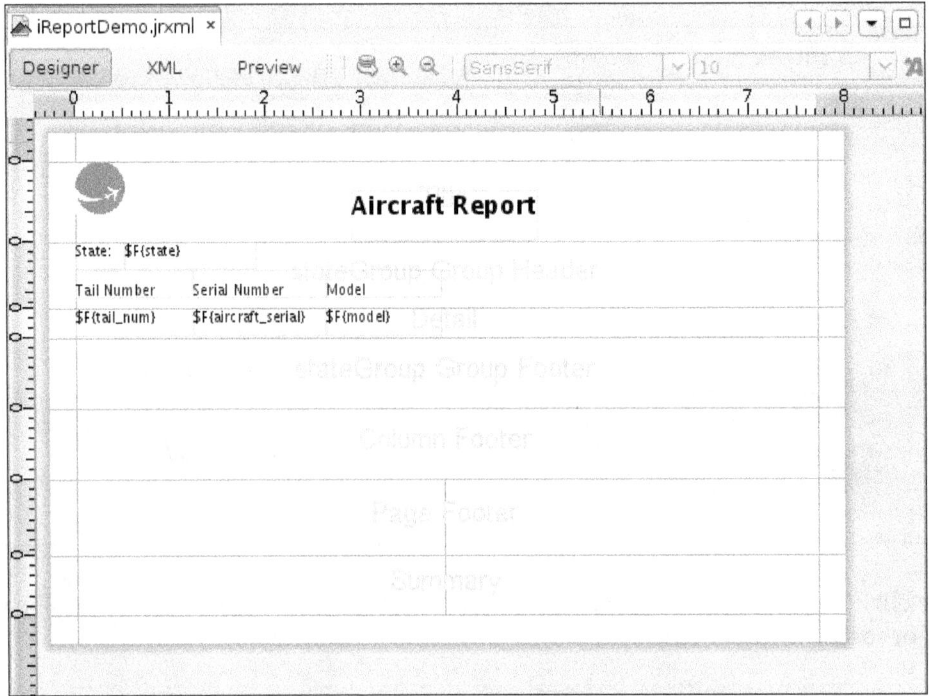

We can preview the report by clicking **Preview**.

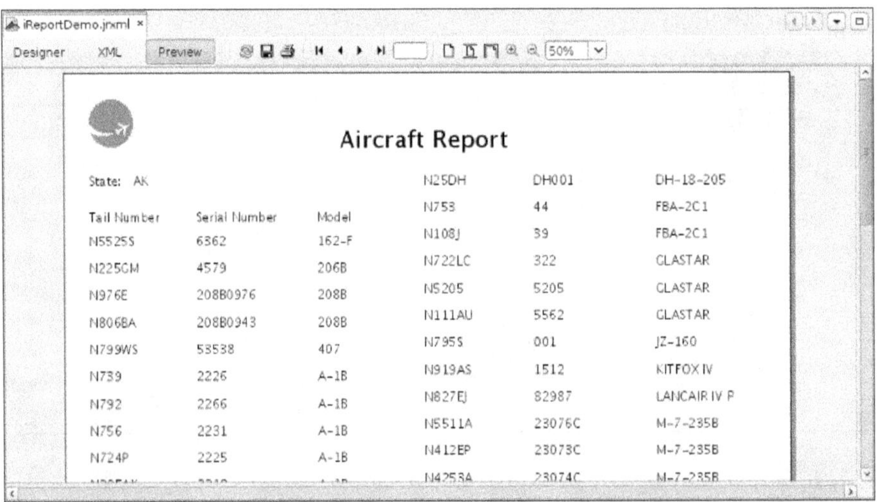

Adding charts to a report

To add a chart to a report, we need to drag the **Chart** component from the Palette into the approximate location where the chart will be rendered in the report.

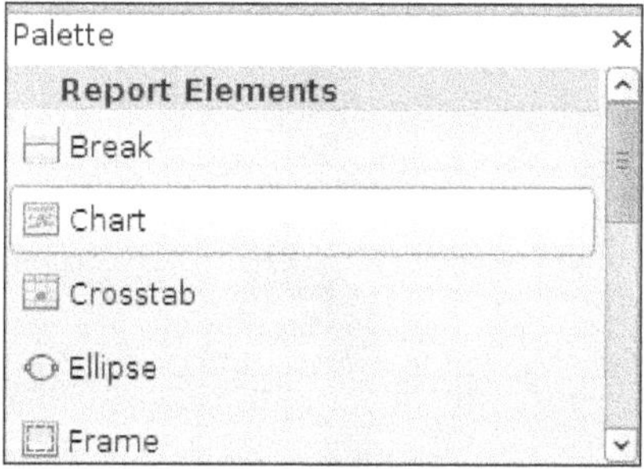

When dropping the chart component into the report, the following window will pop up, allowing us to select the type of chart we want to add to the report:

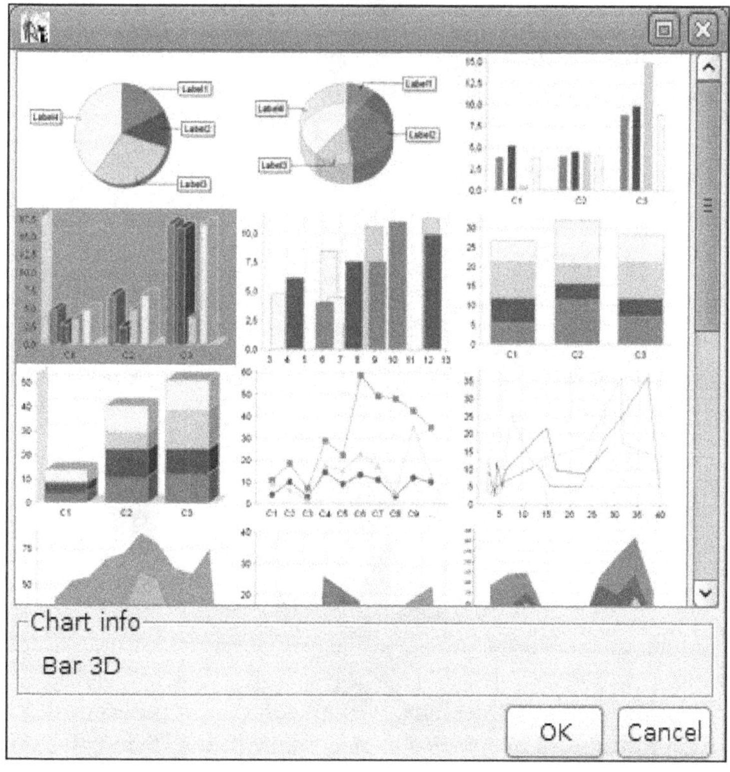

For this example, we will add a 3D bar chart to the report. All that needs to be done is to click on the appropriate chart type, and then click on the **OK** button.

Our chart will graphically illustrate the number of aircraft registered in each state of the United States. (We will explain how to have the chart display the appropriate data later in this section.) We will place the chart in the Summary band at the end of the report. As the chart will illustrate a lot of data, we need to resize the Summary band so that our chart can fit. After resizing the Summary band, outlining the area of the report to be covered by the chart, and selecting the chart type, the Summary section of our report preview looks like this:

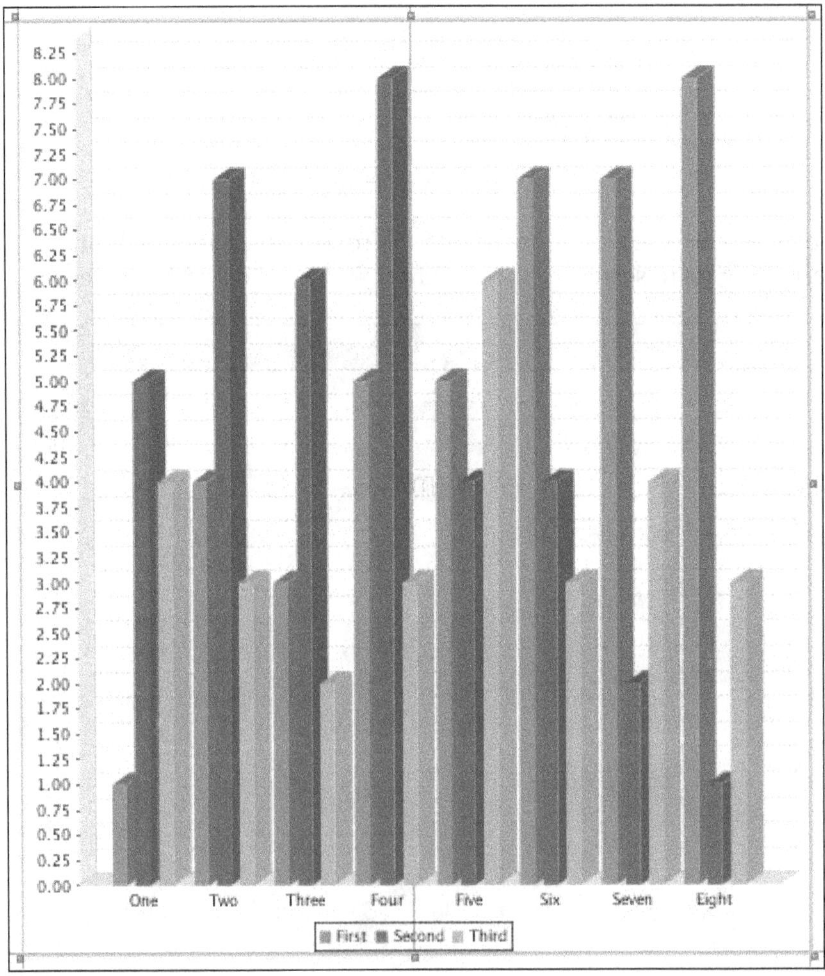

To fine-tune the appearance of the chart, we can select it in the Report Inspector window and then modify its properties as necessary in the Properties window.

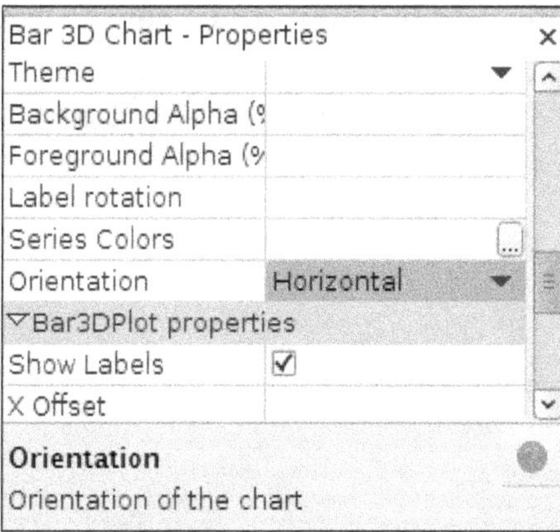

To specify the data that will be displayed in the chart, we need to right-click on the chart in the Report Inspector window and select **Chart Data**. We then need to click on the **Details** tab in the resulting pop-up window.

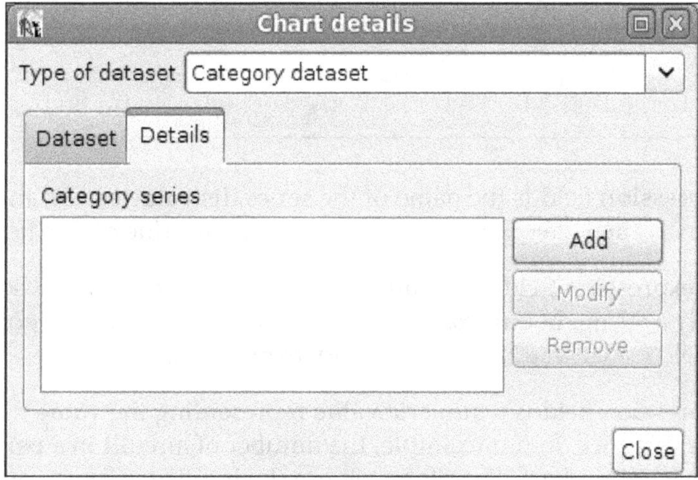

We then need to click on the **Add** button to add a new **Category series**.

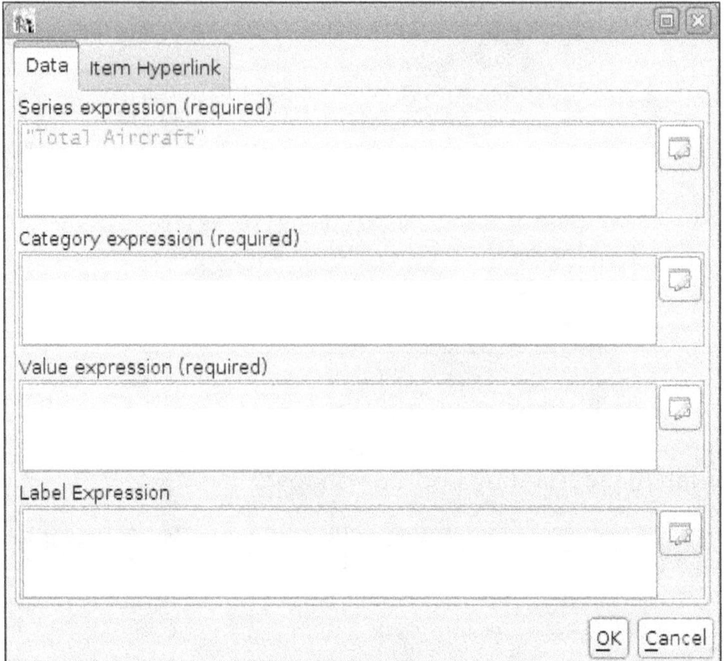

The **Series expression** field is the name of the series. Its value can be any object that implements `java.lang.Comparable`. In most cases, the value of this field is a string.

The **Category expression** field is the label of each value in the chart. The value of this field is typically a string. In our example, each state is a different category, so we will use the state field (`$F{state}`) as our category expression.

The **Value expression** field is a numeric value representing the value to be charted for a particular category. In our example, the number of aircraft in a particular state is the value we want to chart. Therefore, we use the implicit `stateGroup_COUNT` variable (`$V{stateGroup_COUNT}`) as our value expression.

The optional **Label Expression** field allows us to customize item labels in the chart.

> Every time we create a group in a report template, an implicit variable named `groupName_COUNT` is created, where `groupName` is the name of the group.

We can either type in a value for the **Series expression**, **Category expression**, and **Value expression** fields, or we can click on the icon to be able to graphically select the appropriate expression using iReport's **Expression editor**.

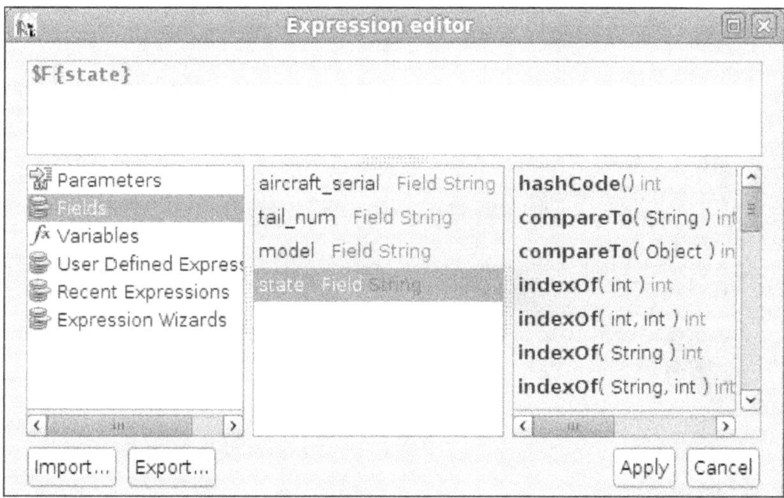

Using the **Expression editor**, we can select any parameter, field, or variable as our expression. We can also use user-defined expressions to fill out any of the fields that require a valid JasperReports expression.

After selecting the appropriate expressions for each of the fields, our chart details are as follows:

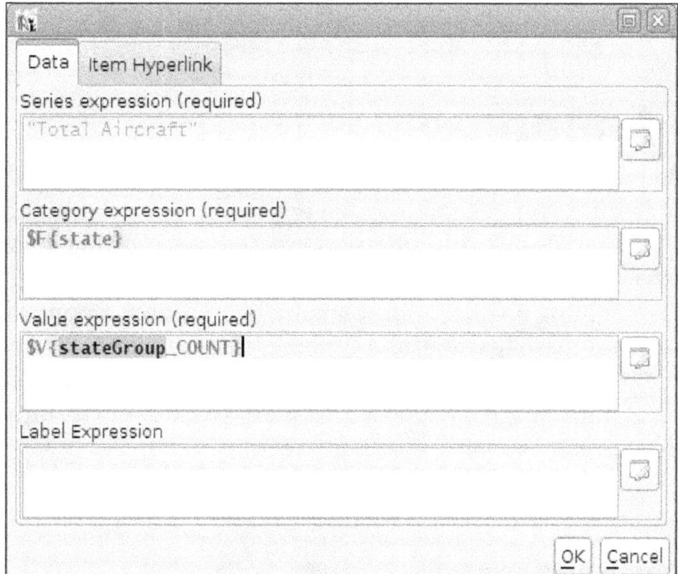

After clicking on **OK** and closing the **Chart details** window, we are ready to view our chart in action, which can be done simply by clicking on **Preview**.

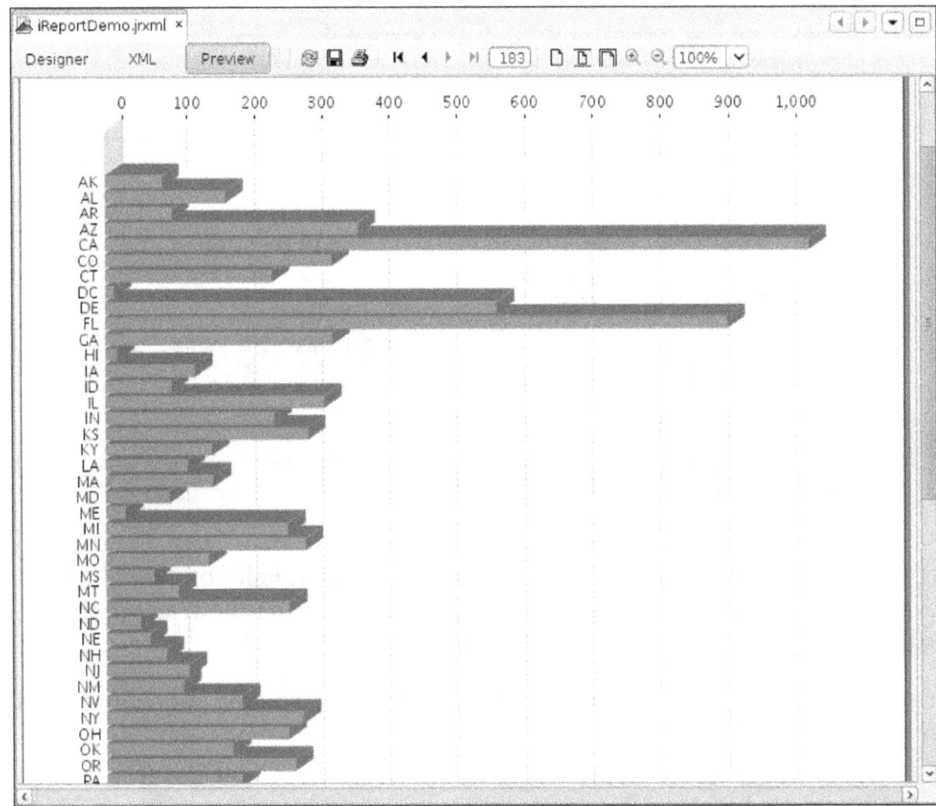

Help and support

Although this chapter didn't discuss every iReport feature, I'm confident that iReport is intuitive enough after you get comfortable with it. Some of the iReport features not covered in this chapter include subreport creation and adding crosstabs, lines, ellipses, and rectangles to a report. However, we have learned all these features the "hard" way by creating a JRXML template by hand. For someone familiar with JasperReports, adding these features to a report created by iReport should be trivial. If more help is needed, JasperSoft provides additional documentation for iReport, and lots of knowledgeable people frequent the iReport forums at `http://jasperforge.org/plugins/espforum/browse.php?group_id=83&forumid=101`.

Summary

This chapter taught us how to install and set up iReport, use iReport's Report Wizard to quickly generate a report, and graphically design custom reports. Moreover, we learned how to group report data graphically with iReport, to add multiple columns to a report, and to add images and charts to a report graphically with iReport.

iReport is a very powerful tool that can significantly reduce report design time. To use all of the features of iReport effectively, however, an iReport user must be familiar with basic JasperReports concepts, such as bands, report variables, report fields, and so on.

11
Integrating JasperReports with Other Frameworks

In previous chapters, we have seen several examples of web-based applications generating reports and streaming them to the browser. In those examples, we have been using "raw" servlets to generate reports. Most modern web-based Java applications are written using one of several web application frameworks. In addition to using a web application framework, most modern Java projects use an **object-relational mapping (ORM) tool** for database access. In this chapter, we will cover how to integrate JasperReports with several popular web application frameworks and ORM tools. We will cover the following topics:

- Integrating JasperReports with Hibernate
- Integrating JasperReports with the Java Persistence API (JPA)
- Integrating JasperReports with Spring
- Integrating JasperReports with Java Server Faces (JSF)
- Integrating JasperReports with Struts

Please note that this chapter assumes some familiarity with the above frameworks. Feel free to skip to the sections that apply to the frameworks used in your project.

Integrating JasperReports with Hibernate

Hibernate (`http://www.hibernate.org`) is a very popular ORM tool. JasperReports (version 1.2 and newer) includes native support for Hibernate integration. This integration consists of allowing embedded report queries to be written in the **Hibernate Query Language (HQL)**. The following JRXML template illustrates how to do this:

```
<?xml version="1.0" encoding="UTF-8"?>
<jasperReport
  xmlns="http://jasperreports.sourceforge.net/jasperreports"
  xmlns:xsi="http://www.w3.org/2001/XMLSchema-instance"
    xsi:schemaLocation="http://jasperreports.sourceforge.net
        /jasperreports http://jasperreports.sourceforge.net/xsd
        /jasperreport.xsd"
  name="HibernateQueryDemoReport" pageWidth="595" pageHeight="842"
        columnWidth="555" leftMargin="20" rightMargin="20"
        topMargin="30" bottomMargin="30">
  <parameter name="countryCode" class="java.lang.String"/>
  <queryString language="hql">
    <![CDATA[from Aircraft aircraft
       where country = $P{countryCode} order by aircraft.id]]>
  </queryString>
  <field name="id" class="java.lang.String"/>
  <field name="aircraftSerial" class="java.lang.String"/>
  <field name="yearBuilt" class="java.lang.String"/>
  <title>
    <band height="30">
      <textField>
        <reportElement x="0" y="0" width="555" height="30"/>
        <textElement/>
        <textFieldExpression class="java.lang.String">
          <![CDATA["Aircraft Registered in Country Code: " +
                   $P{countryCode}]]>
        </textFieldExpression>
      </textField>
    </band>
  </title>
  <pageHeader>
    <band height="30">
      <staticText>
        <reportElement x="0" y="0" width="100" height="30"/>
        <textElement/>
        <text>
          <![CDATA[Tail Number]]>
```

```
          </text>
        </staticText>
        <staticText>
          <reportElement x="100" y="0" width="100" height="30"/>
          <textElement/>
          <text>
            <![CDATA[Serial Number]]>
          </text>
        </staticText>
        <staticText>
          <reportElement x="200" y="0" width="100" height="30"/>
          <textElement/>
          <text>
            <![CDATA[Year Built]]>
          </text>
        </staticText>
      </band>
    </pageHeader>
    <detail>
      <band height="30">
        <textField>
          <reportElement x="0" y="0" width="100" height="30"/>
          <textElement/>
          <textFieldExpression class="java.lang.String">
            <![CDATA[$F{id}]]>
          </textFieldExpression>
        </textField>
        <textField>
          <reportElement x="100" y="0" width="100" height="30"/>
          <textElement/>
          <textFieldExpression class="java.lang.String">
            <![CDATA[$F{aircraftSerial}]]>
          </textFieldExpression>
        </textField>
        <textField>
          <reportElement x="200" y="0" width="100" height="30"/>
          <textElement/>
          <textFieldExpression class="java.lang.String">
            <![CDATA[$F{yearBuilt}]]>
          </textFieldExpression>
        </textField>
      </band>
    </detail>
  </jasperReport>
```

This JRXML template does not look much different from other JRXML templates we have seen before. The only difference is that its embedded report query is written in the HQL. To let JasperReports know that it should interpret the query as HQL (as opposed to SQL), the `language` attribute of the `<queryString>` element must be set to `hql`.

There is nothing special we need to do in order to compile a report using HQL as its query language. We can either use standard ANT tasks or compile it programmatically, just like any other JRXML template.

The HQL query in this template retrieves data in the `aircraft` table for all the aircraft registered in the country specified by the `countryCode` parameter. Hibernate uses **Value Objects** that map to database tables. In order to make the HQL query in the JRXML template work, we need to create a Value Object that maps to the `aircraft` table.

To develop the example for this section, we have used an Eclipse plug-in called **Hibernate Synchronizer**. Hibernate Synchronizer generates Hibernate Java source code and XML configuration from the database schema. It greatly speeds up development of the Data Access Layer of an application using Hibernate for database access. Hibernate Synchronizer can be downloaded from `http://hibernatesynch.sourceforge.net`.

The code for this Value Object is as follows:

```
package net.ensode.jasperbook.dbaccess;
import net.ensode.jasperbook.dbaccess.base.BaseAircraft;
public class Aircraft extends BaseAircraft
{
  private static final long serialVersionUID = 1L;
  /* [CONSTRUCTOR MARKER BEGIN] */
  public Aircraft()
  {
    super();
  }
  /**
   * Constructor for primary key
   */
  public Aircraft(java.lang.String id)
  {
    super(id);
  }
  /**
   * Constructor for required fields
```

```
     */
    public Aircraft(java.lang.String id,
                    java.lang.String aircraftSerial,
                    java.lang.String aircraftModelCode,
                    java.lang.String aircraftEngineCode,
                    java.lang.String yearBuilt,
                    java.lang.String aircraftTypeId,
                    java.lang.String aircraftEngineTypeId,
                    java.lang.String registrantTypeId,
                    java.lang.String name, java.lang.String address1,
                    java.lang.String address2, java.lang.String city,
                    java.lang.String state, java.lang.String zip,
                    java.lang.String region, java.lang.String county,
                    java.lang.String country,
                    java.lang.String certification,
                    java.lang.String statusCode,
                    java.lang.String modeSCode,
                    java.lang.String fractOwner,
                    java.util.Date lastActionDate,
                    java.util.Date certIssueDate,
                    java.util.Date airWorthDate)
    {
      super(id, aircraftSerial, aircraftModelCode, aircraftEngineCode,
      yearBuilt, aircraftTypeId, aircraftEngineTypeId,
      registrantTypeId, name, address1, address2, city, state, zip,
      region, county, country, certification, statusCode, modeSCode,
      fractOwner, lastActionDate, certIssueDate, airWorthDate);
    }
    /* [CONSTRUCTOR MARKER END] */
  }
```

Notice that this class extends a class called `BaseAircraft`, and its source code is as follows:

```
package net.ensode.jasperbook.dbaccess.base;

import java.lang.Comparable;

public abstract class BaseAircraft implements Comparable, Serializable
{
  public static String REF = "Aircraft";
  public static String PROP_AIRCRAFT_SERIAL = "AircraftSerial";
  public static String PROP_AIRCRAFT_TYPE_ID = "AircraftTypeId";
  public static String PROP_STATE = "State";
  public static String PROP_REGISTRANT_TYPE_ID = "RegistrantTypeId";
  public static String PROP_ADDRESS1 = "Address1";

  //remaining property constants removed for brevity
  //constructors omitted for brevity
```

```
protected void initialize()
{
}

private int hashCode = Integer.MIN_VALUE;
// primary key
private java.lang.String id;
// fields
private java.lang.String aircraftSerial;
private java.lang.String aircraftModelCode;
private java.lang.String aircraftEngineCode;
private java.lang.String yearBuilt;
private java.lang.String aircraftTypeId;
private java.lang.String aircraftEngineTypeId;
private java.lang.String registrantTypeId;
private java.lang.String name;
private java.lang.String address1;
private java.lang.String address2;
private java.lang.String city;
private java.lang.String state;
private java.lang.String zip;
private java.lang.String region;
private java.lang.String county;
private java.lang.String country;
private java.lang.String certification;
private java.lang.String statusCode;
private java.lang.String modeSCode;
private java.lang.String fractOwner;
private java.util.Date lastActionDate;
private java.util.Date certIssueDate;
private java.util.Date airWorthDate;

//Getters, setters, equals() and hashCode() methods
//omitted for brevity

public int compareTo(Object obj)
{
  if (obj.hashCode() > hashCode())
    return 1;
  else if (obj.hashCode() < hashCode())
    return -1;
  else
    return 0;
}

public String toString()
{
```

```
        return super.toString();
    }
}
```

In order to let Hibernate know that the preceding class maps to the `aircraft` table, we need to write an XML configuration file, and its source code is as follows:

```
<?xml version="1.0"?>
<!DOCTYPE hibernate-mapping PUBLIC
 "-//Hibernate/Hibernate Mapping DTD//EN"
 "http://hibernate.sourceforge.net/hibernate-mapping-3.0.dtd">
<hibernate-mapping package="net.ensode.jasperbook.dbaccess">
  <class name="Aircraft"
         table="aircraft">
    <id name="Id"
        type="string"
        column="tail_num">
    </id>
    <property name="AircraftSerial"
              column="aircraft_serial"
              type="string"
              not-null="true"
              length="20"/>
    <property name="AircraftModelCode"
              column="aircraft_model_code"
              type="string"
              not-null="true"
              length="7"/>
    <property name="AircraftEngineCode"
              column="aircraft_engine_code"
              type="string"
              not-null="true"
              length="5"/>
    <property name="YearBuilt"
              column="year_built"
              type="java.lang.String"
              not-null="true"
              length="4"/>
    <property name="AircraftTypeId"
              column="aircraft_type_id"
              type="java.lang.String"
              not-null="true"
              length="3"/>
    <property name="AircraftEngineTypeId"
```

```
                    column="aircraft_engine_type_id"
                    type="java.lang.String"
                    not-null="true"
                    length="3"/>
          <property name="RegistrantTypeId"
                    column="registrant_type_id"
                    type="java.lang.String"
                    not-null="true"
                    length="3"/>
          <property name="Name"
                    column="name"
                    type="string"
                    not-null="true"
                    length="50"/>
          <property name="Address1"
                    column="address1"
                    type="string"
                    not-null="true"
                    length="33"/>
          <property name="Address2"
                    column="address2"
                    type="string"
                    not-null="true"
                    length="33"/>
          <property name="City"
                    column="city"
                    type="string"
                    not-null="true"
                    length="18"/>
          <property name="State"
                    column="state"
                    type="string"
                    not-null="true"
                    length="2"/>
          <property name="Zip"
                    column="zip"
                    type="string"
                    not-null="true"
                    length="10"/>
          <property name="Region"
                    column="region"
                    type="string"
                    not-null="true"
                    length="1"/>
```

```
    <property name="County"
              column="county"
              type="string"
              not-null="true"
              length="3"/>
    <property name="Country"
              column="country"
              type="string"
              not-null="true"
              length="2"/>
    <property name="Certification"
              column="certification"
              type="string"
              not-null="true"
              length="10"/>
    <property name="StatusCode"
              column="status_code"
              type="string"
              not-null="true"
              length="1"/>
    <property name="ModeSCode"
              column="mode_s_code"
              type="string"
              not-null="true"
              length="8"/>
    <property name="FractOwner"
              column="fract_owner"
              type="string"
              not-null="true"
              length="1"/>
    <property name="LastActionDate"
              column="last_action_date"
              type="date"
              not-null="true"
              length="10"/>
    <property name="AirWorthDate"
              column="air_worth_date"
              type="date"
              not-null="true"
              length="10"/>
  </class>
</hibernate-mapping>
```

This XML file lets Hibernate know that the `Aircraft` class maps to the `aircraft` table, and also defines the mapping between the table's columns and the class fields.

Hibernate needs another XML configuration file, which allows it to know the database connection information and the XML files to be used to map database tables to Java classes. This XML configuration file is called `hibernate.cfg.xml`, and its source code is as follows:

```
<?xml version='1.0' encoding='UTF-8'?>
<!DOCTYPE hibernate-configuration PUBLIC
  "-//Hibernate/Hibernate Configuration DTD 3.0//EN"
  "http://hibernate.sourceforge.net/hibernate-configuration-3.0.dtd">

<hibernate-configuration>
  <session-factory>
  <!-- local connection properties -->
    <property name="hibernate.connection.url">
      jdbc:mysql://localhost:3306/flightstats
    </property>
    <property name="hibernate.connection.driver_class">
      com.mysql.jdbc.Driver
    </property>
    <property name="hibernate.connection.username">user</property>
    <property name="hibernate.connection.password">secret</property>
  <!-- property name="hibernate.connection.pool_size"></property -->
  <!-- dialect for MySQL -->
    <property name="dialect">
      org.hibernate.dialect.MySQLDialect
    </property>
    <property name="hibernate.show_sql">false</property>
    <property name="hibernate.transaction.factory_class">
      org.hibernate.transaction.JDBCTransactionFactory
    </property>
    <mapping resource="Aircraft.hbm.xml" />
    <mapping resource="AircraftEngines.hbm.xml"/>
    <mapping resource="AircraftEngineTypes.hbm.xml"/>
    <mapping resource="AircraftModels.hbm.xml"/>
    <mapping resource="AircraftTypes.hbm.xml"/>
  </session-factory>
</hibernate-configuration>
```

The following code fragment illustrates how to fill a report using HQL as its query language:

```
package net.ensode.jasperbook;

import java.util.HashMap;
import java.util.Map;

import net.sf.jasperreports.engine.JRException;
import net.sf.jasperreports.engine.JasperFillManager;
import net.sf.jasperreports.engine.query.
JRHibernateQueryExecuterFactory;
import org.hibernate.Session;
import org.hibernate.SessionFactory;
import org.hibernate.cfg.Configuration;

public class HibernateQueryDemo
{
  Session session;
  SessionFactory sessionFactory;
  public static void main(String[] args)
  {
    new HibernateQueryDemo().fillReport(args[0]);
  }
  public void fillReport(String countryCode)
  {
    String reportDirectory = "reports";
    session = createSession();
    Map parameterMap = new HashMap();
    parameterMap.put(JRHibernateQueryExecuterFactory
                           .PARAMETER_HIBERNATE_SESSION, session);
    parameterMap.put("countryCode", countryCode);

    try
    {
      System.out.println("Filling report...");
      JasperFillManager.fillReportToFile(reportDirectory
              + "/HibernateQueryDemoReport.jasper", parameterMap);
      System.out.println("Done!");
    }
    catch (JRException e)
    {
      System.out.println("There was an error filling the report.");
      e.printStackTrace();
    }
  }

  private Session createSession()
```

```
    {
      SessionFactory sessionFactory = new Configuration().configure()
                                              .buildSessionFactory();
      return sessionFactory.openSession();
    }
  }
```

Once again, there is not much difference between filling a report using an embedded HQL query and filling a report using an embedded SQL query or a datasource. The main difference is that an instance of `org.hibernate.Session` must be passed to the report through a parameter named `JRHibernateQueryExecuterFactory.PARAMETER_HIBERNATE_SESSION`. Executing this code will generate a report similar to the following:

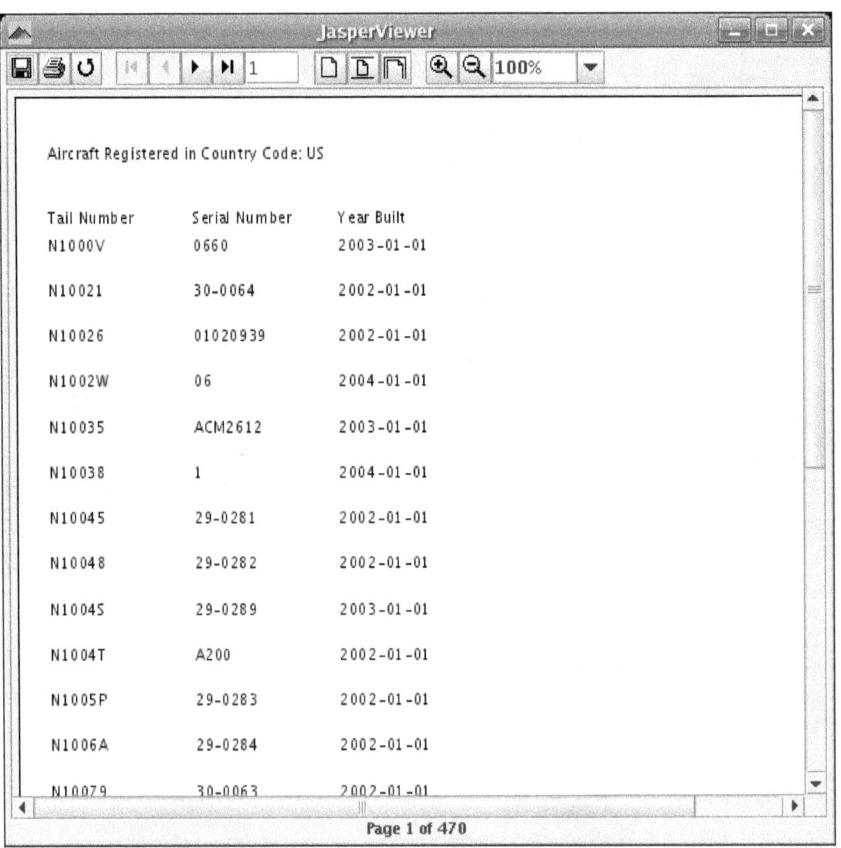

Aircraft Registered in Country Code: US

Tail Number	Serial Number	Year Built
N1000V	0660	2003-01-01
N10021	30-0064	2002-01-01
N10026	01020939	2002-01-01
N1002W	06	2004-01-01
N10035	ACM2612	2003-01-01
N10038	1	2004-01-01
N10045	29-0281	2002-01-01
N10048	29-0282	2002-01-01
N1004S	29-0289	2003-01-01
N1004T	A200	2002-01-01
N1005P	29-0283	2002-01-01
N1006A	29-0284	2002-01-01
N10079	30-0063	2002-01-01

Of course, in order for this procedure to work, Hibernate must be configured properly so as to connect to the database from which the report data will be retrieved. Refer to the online Hibernate documentation at `http://hibernate.org/5.html` for details on configuring Hibernate for your environment.

As we can see, integrating JasperReports and Hibernate is trivial. Because Hibernate is a very popular ORM tool, this integration was a welcome addition to JasperReports 1.2.

Integrating JasperReports with JPA

Hibernate is just one of many available ORM tools. The proliferation of the ORM tools motivated Sun Microsystems to come up with a standard ORM tool for Java. Out of this initiative, the **Java Persistence API (JPA)** was born.

It is possible to integrate JasperReports with JPA by writing report templates that use JPA's query language as opposed to using SQL. The following JRXML template illustrates this:

```
<?xml version="1.0" encoding="UTF-8"?>
<jasperReport
  xmlns="http://jasperreports.sourceforge.net/jasperreports"
  xmlns:xsi="http://www.w3.org/2001/XMLSchema-instance"
  xsi:schemaLocation= "http://jasperreports.sourceforge.net
      /jasperreports http://jasperreports.sourceforge.net/xsd
      /jasperreport.xsd"
  name="JpaQueryDemoReport" pageWidth="595" pageHeight="842"
  columnWidth="555" leftMargin="20" rightMargin="20"
  topMargin="30" bottomMargin="30">
  <parameter name="countryCode" class="java.lang.String"/>
  <queryString language="ejbql">
    <![CDATA[select a from Aircraft a
           where a.country = $P{countryCode}
           order by a.tailNum]]>
  </queryString>
  <field name="tailNum" class="java.lang.String"/>
  <field name="aircraftSerial" class="java.lang.String"/>
  <field name="name" class="java.lang.String"/>
  <title>
    <band height="30">
      <textField>
        <reportElement x="0" y="0" width="555" height="30"/>
        <textElement/>
        <textFieldExpression class="java.lang.String">
          <![CDATA["Aircraft Registered in Country Code: " +
                  $P{countryCode}]]>
        </textFieldExpression>
      </textField>
    </band>
```

```
    </title>
    <pageHeader>
      <band height="30">
        <staticText>
          <reportElement x="0" y="0" width="100" height="30"/>
          <textElement/>
          <text>
            <![CDATA[Tail Number]]>
          </text>
        </staticText>
        <staticText>
          <reportElement x="100" y="0" width="100" height="30"/>
          <textElement/>
          <text>
            <![CDATA[Serial Number]]>
          </text>
        </staticText>
        <staticText>
          <reportElement x="200" y="0" width="100" height="30"/>
          <textElement/>
          <text>
            <![CDATA[Name]]>
          </text>
        </staticText>
      </band>
    </pageHeader>
    <detail>
      <band height="30">
        <textField>
          <reportElement x="0" y="0" width="100" height="30"/>
          <textElement/>
          <textFieldExpression class="java.lang.String">
            <![CDATA[$F{tailNum}]]>
          </textFieldExpression>
        </textField>
        <textField>
          <reportElement x="100" y="0" width="100" height="30"/>
          <textElement/>
          <textFieldExpression class="java.lang.String">
            <![CDATA[$F{aircraftSerial}]]>
          </textFieldExpression>
        </textField>
        <textField isBlankWhenNull="true">
          <reportElement x="200" y="0" width="100" height="30"/>
```

```
        <textElement/>
        <textFieldExpression class="java.lang.String">
          <![CDATA[$F{name}]]>
        </textFieldExpression>
      </textField>
    </band>
  </detail>
</jasperReport>
```

Just like with Hibernate, writing a JRXML template using the **Java Persistence Query Language (JPQL)** is not much different from writing a standard JRXML template using SQL. All we need to do is specify `ejbql` as the value of the `language` property for the `<queryString>` element of our JRXML template.

> Originally, JPA was going to be a part of the EJB 3.0 specification; however, the expert group decided to separate JPA from EJB. When JPA was part of the EJB specification, the query language was called EJBQL. When JPA separated from the EJB specification, the query language was renamed to JPQL. JasperReports still uses the old EJBQL name as the value of the `<queryString>` JRXML element.

As far as the code is concerned, we need to pass an instance of `javax.persistence.EntityManager` as a report parameter. Behind the scenes, JasperReports uses this `EntityManager` object to execute the JPQL query. The following example illustrates this:

```
package net.ensode.jasperbook.jpa;

import java.util.HashMap;
import java.util.Map;
import javax.persistence.EntityManager;
import javax.persistence.EntityManagerFactory;
import javax.persistence.Persistence;
import net.sf.jasperreports.engine.JRException;
import net.sf.jasperreports.engine.JasperFillManager;
import net.sf.jasperreports.engine.query.JRJpaQueryExecuterFactory;

public class JpaDemo
{
  public static void main(String[] args)
  {
    EntityManagerFactory entityManagerFactory = Persistence
                         .createEntityManagerFactory("flightstatsPU");
    EntityManager entityManager = entityManagerFactory
                                              .createEntityManager();
    Map parameterMap = new HashMap();
```

```
        parameterMap.put(JRJpaQueryExecuterFactory
                        .PARAMETER_JPA_ENTITY_MANAGER, entityManager);
        parameterMap.put("countryCode", args[0]);
        try
        {
          JasperFillManager.fillReportToFile("reports/
                             JpaQueryDemoReport.jasper", parameterMap);
        }
        catch (JRException ex)
        {
          ex.printStackTrace();
        }
        finally
        {
          if (entityManager != null && entityManager.isOpen())
          {
            entityManager.close();
          }
          if (entityManagerFactory != null &&
                                   entityManagerFactory.isOpen())
          {
            entityManagerFactory.close();
          }
        }
      }
    }
```

In order to be able to run JPQL queries from within a report template, we need to obtain an instance of `javax.persistence.EntityManager` as usual. When working in standalone Java applications like our example, we obtain an instance of `EntityManager` by invoking the `createEntityManager()` method on an instance of `javax.persistence.EntityManagerFactory`.

When working with Java EE applications that are deployed to an application server, an instance of `EntityManager` can be injected into the code. My book "*Java EE 5 Development Using GlassFish Application Server*", *Packt Publishing* explains how to do this.

Once we have an instance of `EntityManager`, we need to pass it as a report parameter by adding it to the `java.util.Map` instance that we pass to JasperReports when filling a report. There is a predefined constant that JasperReports will use to retrieve the `EntityManager`. The constant name is `PARAMETER_JPA_ENTITY_MANAGER` and, it is defined in `net.sf.jasperreports.engine.query.JRJpaQueryExecuterFactory`. All we need to do to pass the `EntityManager` instance is use this constant as its key in the Map.

After adding the `EntityManager` instance to the map, we fill the report as usual. In the example we just saw, we filled the report to a JRPRINT file by invoking `JasperFillManager.fillReportToFile()` and passing the report template location and `parameterMap` as parameters.

Once the report has been filled, we need to close the `EntityManager` and `EntityManagerFactory` instances as we usually do when working with JPA.

JPA requires us to develop entity classes (denoted by the `@Entity` annotation) that map to the database tables. JPQL queries refer to JPA entities as opposed to database tables. In our example, we are using an `Aircraft` entity that maps to the `Aircraft` table in our database.

```
package net.ensode.jasperbook.jpa.entities;

import java.io.Serializable;
import java.util.Date;
import javax.persistence.Basic;
import javax.persistence.Column;
import javax.persistence.Entity;
import javax.persistence.Id;
import javax.persistence.NamedQueries;
import javax.persistence.NamedQuery;
import javax.persistence.Table;
import javax.persistence.Temporal;
import javax.persistence.TemporalType;

@Entity
@Table(name = "aircraft")
public class Aircraft implements Serializable
{
  private static final long serialVersionUID = 1L;
  @Id
  @Basic(optional = false)
  @Column(name = "tail_num")
  private String tailNum;
  @Basic(optional = false)
  @Column(name = "aircraft_serial")
```

```
    private String aircraftSerial;
    @Basic(optional = false)
    @Column(name = "aircraft_model_code")
    private String aircraftModelCode;
    @Basic(optional = false)
    @Column(name = "aircraft_engine_code")
    private String aircraftEngineCode;
    @Basic(optional = false)
    @Column(name = "year_built")
    @Temporal(TemporalType.DATE)
    private Date yearBuilt;
    @Basic(optional = false)
    @Column(name = "aircraft_type_id")
    private short aircraftTypeId;
    @Basic(optional = false)
    @Column(name = "aircraft_engine_type_id")
    private short aircraftEngineTypeId;
    @Basic(optional = false)
    @Column(name = "registrant_type_id")
    private short registrantTypeId;
    @Basic(optional = false)
    @Column(name = "name")
    private String name;
    @Basic(optional = false)
    @Column(name = "address1")
    private String address1;
    @Basic(optional = false)
    @Column(name = "address2")
    private String address2;
    @Basic(optional = false)
    @Column(name = "city")
    private String city;
    @Basic(optional = false)
    @Column(name = "state")
    private String state;
    @Basic(optional = false)
    @Column(name = "zip")
    private String zip;
    @Basic(optional = false)
    @Column(name = "region")
    private char region;
    @Basic(optional = false)
    @Column(name = "county")
    private String county;
```

```
    @Basic(optional = false)
    @Column(name = "country")
    private String country;
    @Basic(optional = false)
    @Column(name = "certification")
    private String certification;
    @Basic(optional = false)
    @Column(name = "status_code")
    private char statusCode;
    @Basic(optional = false)
    @Column(name = "mode_s_code")
    private String modeSCode;
    @Basic(optional = false)
    @Column(name = "fract_owner")
    private char fractOwner;
    @Basic(optional = false)
    @Column(name = "last_action_date")
    @Temporal(TemporalType.DATE)
    private Date lastActionDate;
    @Basic(optional = false)
    @Column(name = "cert_issue_date")
    @Temporal(TemporalType.DATE)
    private Date certIssueDate;
    @Basic(optional = false)
    @Column(name = "air_worth_date")
    @Temporal(TemporalType.DATE)
    private Date airWorthDate;

    public Aircraft()
    {
    }
    public Aircraft(String tailNum)
    {
      this.tailNum = tailNum;
    }
  //Other constructors, methods and getters and setters omitted for //
  brevity.
  }
```

The JPA entities are configured through annotations. The `@Entity` annotation at the class level marks the above class as a JPA entity. The `@Table` annotation, also at the class level, specifies what database table the entity maps to. The `@Column` annotation specifies what column in the table each field in the entity maps to.

JPA requires an XML configuration file called `persistence.xml`. The format of `persistence.xml` will vary slightly depending on the JPA implementation we are using, and also on whether we are working on a standalone application, or an application that needs to be deployed to an application server. The `persistence.xml` configuration file for our example looks like the following:

```
<?xml version="1.0" encoding="UTF-8"?>
<persistence version="1.0"
  xmlns="http://java.sun.com/xml/ns/persistence"
  xmlns:xsi="http://www.w3.org/2001/XMLSchema-instance"
  xsi:schemaLocation="http://java.sun.com/xml/ns/persistence
         http://java.sun.com/xml/ns/persistence/persistence_1_0.xsd">
  <persistence-unit name="flightstatsPU"
                    transaction-type="RESOURCE_LOCAL">
    <class>net.ensode.jasperbook.jpa.entities.Aircraft</class>
    <properties>
      <property name="toplink.jdbc.user"
                value="user"/>
      <property name="toplink.jdbc.driver"
                value="com.mysql.jdbc.Driver"/>
      <property name="toplink.jdbc.password"
                value="secret"/>
      <property name="toplink.jdbc.url"
                value="jdbc:mysql://localhost:3306/flightstats?
                       zeroDateTimeBehavior=convertToNull"/>
    </properties>
  </persistence-unit>
</persistence>
```

In our example, we are using `toplink` as our JPA implementation. Therefore, we need to use some `toplink` specific properties to specify the JDBC URL, driver, and credentials. The property names will vary depending on the JPA implementation being used. For Java EE applications, database credentials and URL should not be specified, instead, we should specify the **JNDI (Java Naming and Directory Interface)** name for a connection pool in the application server.

After running our code, a report similar to the following is generated:

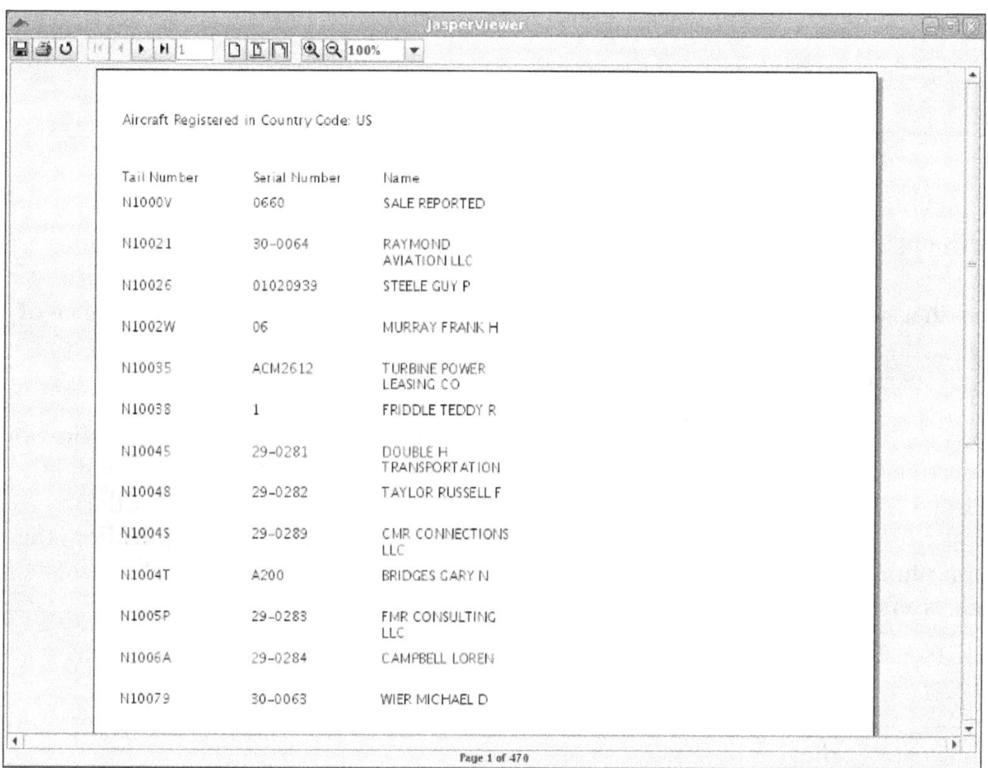

Aircraft Registered in Country Code: US

Tail Number	Serial Number	Name
N1000V	0660	SALE REPORTED
N10021	30-0064	RAYMOND AVIATION LLC
N10026	01020939	STEELE GUY P
N1002W	06	MURRAY FRANK H
N10035	ACM2612	TURBINE POWER LEASING CO
N10038	1	FRIDDLE TEDDY R
N10045	29-0281	DOUBLE H TRANSPORTATION
N10048	29-0282	TAYLOR RUSSELL F
N10049	29-0289	CMR CONNECTIONS LLC
N1004T	A200	BRIDGES GARY N
N1005P	29-0283	FMR CONSULTING LLC
N1006A	29-0284	CAMPBELL LOREN
N10079	30-0063	WIER MICHAEL D

Integrating JasperReports with Spring

Spring (`http://www.springframework.org`) is a very popular framework that helps simplify the development of Java EE applications. The Spring Framework integrates nicely with JasperReports. In this section, we will develop a simple web application using Spring Web MVC, which is Spring's native web application framework.

The `web.xml` for our simple application is as follows:

```
<?xml version="1.0" encoding="ISO-8859-1"?>
<!DOCTYPE web-app PUBLIC
    "-//Sun Microsystems, Inc.//DTD Web Application 2.3//EN"
    "http://java.sun.com/dtd/web-app_2_3.dtd">
<web-app>
  <servlet>
    <servlet-name>jasperSpring</servlet-name>
    <servlet-class>
      org.springframework.web.servlet.DispatcherServlet
```

```
        </servlet-class>
        <load-on-startup>1</load-on-startup>
    </servlet>
    <servlet-mapping>
        <servlet-name>jasperSpring</servlet-name>
        <url-pattern>/jasperSpring/*</url-pattern>
    </servlet-mapping>
</web-app>
```

As can be seen in this `web.xml` code, there is only one servlet in our application, `DispatcherServlet`. This servlet is provided by the `springframework`. Please note that we named our servlet `jasperSpring` to make it clear that this instance of `DispatcherServlet` will be used to generate reports. However, `DispatcherServlet` is not specific to JasperReports functionality.

Each application developed with the Spring framework must contain an application context, which is usually an XML file containing additional configuration. For Spring Web MVC applications, the application context file is named after the servlet, following the `servletname-servlet.xml` pattern. For our application, the application context file is named as `jasperSpring-servlet.xml`, and its source code is as follows:

```
<?xml version="1.0" encoding="UTF-8"?>
<!DOCTYPE beans PUBLIC "-//SPRING//DTD BEAN//EN" "http://www.
 springframework.org/dtd/spring-beans.dtd">
<beans>
  <bean id="dataSource"
        class="org.springframework.jdbc.datasource
                    .DriverManagerDataSource" destroy-method="close">
    <property name="driverClassName">
      <value>com.mysql.jdbc.Driver</value>
    </property>
    <property name="url">
      <value>jdbc:mysql://localhost:3306/flightstats</value>
    </property>
    <property name="username">
      <value>user</value>
    </property>
    <property name="password">
      <value>secret</value>
    </property>
  </bean>
  <bean id="publicUrlMapping"
        class="org.springframework.web.servlet.handler
                                        .SimpleUrlHandlerMapping">
```

```
        <property name="mappings">
          <props>
            <prop key="report">jasperController</prop>
          </props>
        </property>
      </bean>
      <bean id="jasperController"
            class="net.ensode.jasperbook.spring.JasperSpringController">
        <property name="dataSource">
          <ref local="dataSource"/>
        </property>
      </bean>
      <bean id="viewResolver"
            class="org.springframework.web.servlet.view
                                        .ResourceBundleViewResolver">
        <property name="basename" value="views"/>
      </bean>
    </beans>
```

One of the main features of the `springframework` is that it allows applications to be very loosely coupled by allowing the dependencies to be defined in XML configuration files. This allows changing dependencies without having to change a single line of code.

In the `jasperSpring-servlet.xml` file, we define a dependency on the datasource of the database by declaring the bean with an `id` of `datasource` and setting it up as a property of the `jasperController` bean. The bean with the `id` of `publicUrlMapping` maps the URL ending in `report` (for example, `http://localhost/jasperSpring/report`) to our controller. The bean with the `id` of `viewResolver` is an instance of `org.springframework.web.servlet.view.ResourceBundleViewResolver`. Its purpose is to look up values in a resource bundle to determine what view to use. Its `basename` property defines the name of the property file containing the keys to look up. In this case, the property file must be named `views.properties`.

```
report.class=org.springframework.web.servlet.view.jasperreports
.JasperReportsPdfView
report.url=reports/DbReportDS.jasper
```

Notice that the base name of the keys (`report`, in this case) must match the name of the controller property defined in the application context for `SimpleUrlHandlerMapping`. It is in this property file where we actually declare that JasperReports will be used to render the data.

In this example, we are using the `JasperReportsPdfView` class to export to PDF. The Spring framework also supports exporting to CSV, HTML, and Excel. To export to one of these formats, the classes to use would be `JasperReportsCsvView`, `JasperReportsHtmlView`, and `JasperReportsXlsView` respectively. All of these classes are in the `org.springframework.web.servlet.view.jasperreports` package.

The `report.url` property defines where to find the compiled report template. In order for the `JasperReportsPdfView` class to find the compiled report template, it must be located in a directory matching the value of this property. The report template we will use for this example is the one we discussed in the *Database reporting through a datasource* section of Chapter 4, *Creating Dynamic Reports from Databases*.

Just as with most MVC frameworks, we never code our servlets directly when writing web applications using Spring MVC; instead, we write controller classes. In this example, our controller class implements the `org.springframework.web.servlet.mvc.Controller` interface. This interface defines a single method called `handleRequest()`.

```
package net.ensode.jasperbook.spring;

import java.io.IOException;
import java.sql.Connection;
import java.sql.ResultSet;
import java.sql.SQLException;
import java.sql.Statement;
import java.util.HashMap;
import java.util.Map;

import javax.servlet.ServletException;
import javax.servlet.http.HttpServletRequest;
import javax.servlet.http.HttpServletResponse;
import javax.sql.DataSource;

import net.sf.jasperreports.engine.JRResultSetDataSource;

import org.springframework.web.servlet.ModelAndView;
import org.springframework.web.servlet.mvc.Controller;

public class JasperSpringController implements Controller
{
  private DataSource dataSource;
  public ModelAndView handleRequest(HttpServletRequest request,
                                    HttpServletResponse response)
  throws ServletException, IOException, ClassNotFoundException,
         SQLException
  {
    return new ModelAndView("report", getModel());
```

```
    }
    private Map getModel() throws ClassNotFoundException, SQLException
    {
      Connection connection;
      Statement statement;
      ResultSet resultSet;
      HashMap model = new HashMap();

      String query = "select a.tail_num, a.aircraft_serial, "
        + "am.model as aircraft_model, ae.model as engine_model from
            aircraft a, "
        + "aircraft_models am, aircraft_engines ae where "
        + "a.aircraft_engine_code in ("
        + "select aircraft_engine_code from aircraft_engines "
        + "where horsepower >= 1000) and am.aircraft_model_code = "
        + "a.aircraft_model_code "
        + "and ae.aircraft_engine_code = a.aircraft_engine_code";

      connection = dataSource.getConnection();
      statement = connection.createStatement();
      resultSet = statement.executeQuery(query);

      JRResultSetDataSource resultSetDataSource = new
                                      JRResultSetDataSource(resultSet);
        model.put("datasource", resultSetDataSource);
      return model;
    }
    public void setDataSource (DataSource dataSource)
    {
      this.dataSource=dataSource;
    }
  }
```

Note that our implementation of the `handleRequest()` method is very simple. It returns a new instance of `org.springframework.web.servlet.ModelAndView`. We pass the view name (defined in the application context) and a map containing the data to be displayed to the constructor of `ModelAndView`, and return it.

The `getModel()` method of `JasperSpringController` executes an SQL query in the database and populates an instance of `JRResultSetDataSource` with the results.

Finally, we need to write a JSP that will invoke `JasperSpringController`.

```
<%@ page language="java" contentType="text/html;
        charset=UTF-8" pageEncoding="UTF-8"%>
<!DOCTYPE HTML PUBLIC "-//W3C//DTD HTML 4.01 Transitional//EN">
<html>
  <head>
    <meta http-equiv="Content-Type" content="text/html;
          charset=UTF-8">
    <title>Generate Report</title>
  </head>
  <body>
    Click on the button to generate the report.
    <form name="reportForm" action="jasperSpring/report"
          method="post">
      <input type="submit" name="submitButton" value="Submit"/>
    </form>
  </body>
</html>
```

Notice that no special JSP tag libraries are needed to integrate with Spring. After we deploy our web application and direct our browser to `http://localhost:8080/jasperspring/generate_report.jsp`, we should see a web page like the following:

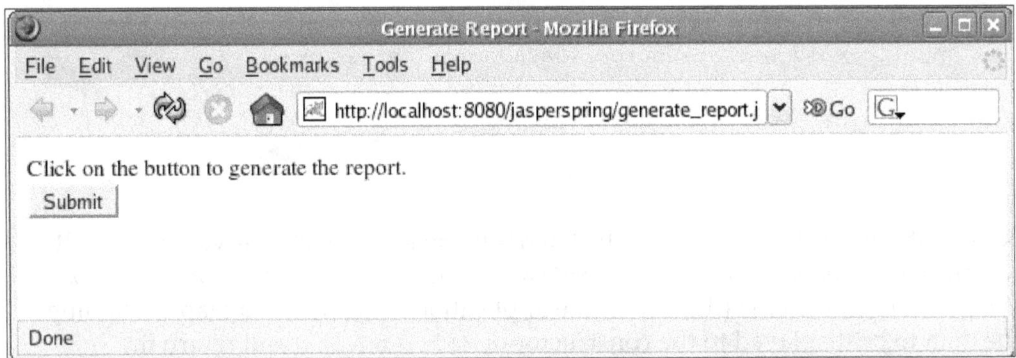

After clicking on the **Submit** button, the report will be generated and displayed in the browser in PDF format.

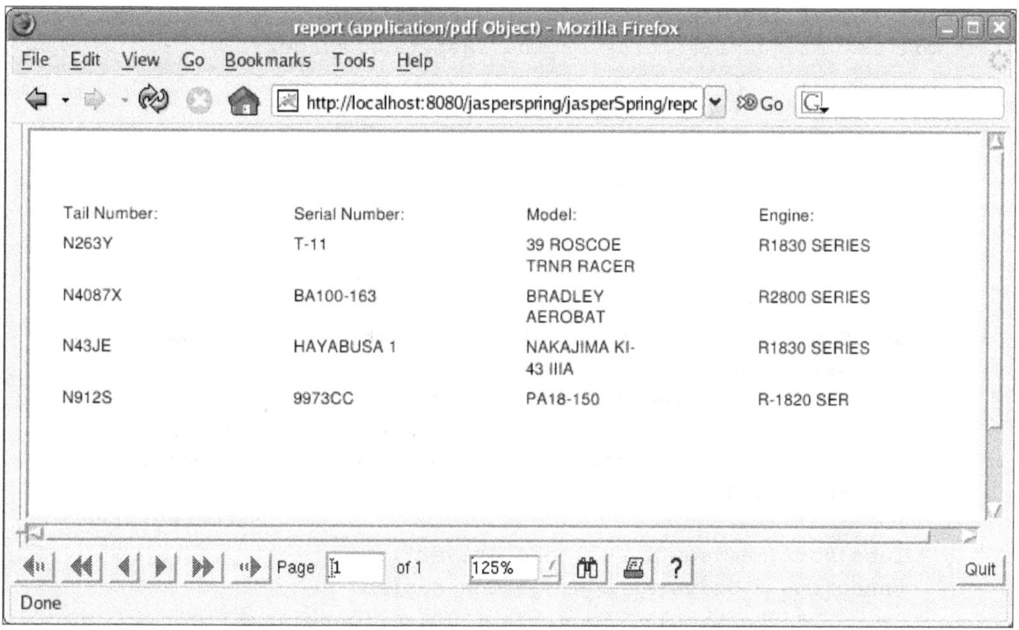

Integrating JasperReports with JSF

JavaServer Faces (JSF) is the standard technology for developing user interfaces for Java server applications. In theory, JSF is view technology agnostic (that is, it can be used to develop user interfaces for a variety of technologies). However, in practice, JSF is almost always used to develop web applications.

JSF applications typically consist of JSP and backing beans, with the latter serving as controllers for the former. JSF and JasperReports integration can be accomplished by creating a backing bean that will generate a report. The following example illustrates this technique:

```
package net.ensode.jsf;

import java.io.IOException;
import java.io.InputStream;
import java.sql.Connection;
import java.sql.DriverManager;
import java.sql.SQLException;
import java.util.HashMap;

import javax.faces.context.FacesContext;
import javax.faces.event.ActionEvent;
import javax.servlet.ServletOutputStream;
import javax.servlet.http.HttpServletResponse;
```

```
import net.sf.jasperreports.engine.JRException;
import net.sf.jasperreports.engine.JasperRunManager;

public class ReportGenerator
{
  public void generateReport(ActionEvent actionEvent)
  throws ClassNotFoundException, SQLException, IOException,
        JRException
  {
    Connection connection;
    FacesContext facesContext = FacesContext.getCurrentInstance();
    HttpServletResponse response = (HttpServletResponse)
                    facesContext.getExternalContext().getResponse();
    InputStream reportStream = facesContext.getExternalContext()
                   .getResourceAsStream("/reports/DbReport.jasper");
    ServletOutputStream servletOutputStream = response
                                            .getOutputStream();
    Class.forName("com.mysql.jdbc.Driver");
    connection = DriverManager.getConnection(
           "jdbc:mysql://localhost:3306/flightstats?" +
           "user=user&password=secret");
    facesContext.responseComplete();
    response.setContentType("application/pdf");
    JasperRunManager.runReportToPdfStream(reportStream,
                    servletOutputStream, new HashMap(), connection);
    connection.close();
    servletOutputStream.flush();
    servletOutputStream.close();
  }
}
```

JasperReports does not natively integrate with JSF. The trick to getting them to work together is to use the JSF API to obtain objects from the servlet API, as JasperReports integrates nicely with these objects. The `HttpServletResponse` object is of particular interest.

As can be seen in the preceding example, we can obtain the `HttpServletResponse` object by calling the `FacesContext.getExternalContext().getResponse()` method. We can then obtain an instance of `ServletOutputStream` from the `response` object as usual, by calling the `HttpServletResponse.getOutputStream()` method.

In order to know what report to compile, we need to load the compiled report template as a stream. This is accomplished by calling the `FacesContext.getExternalContext().getResourceAsStream()` method, as illustrated in the code. For this example, we will use the report template discussed in the *Embedding SQL queries into a report template* section of Chapter 4, *Creating Dynamic Reports from Databases*.

Once we have obtained the `HttpServletResponse` and `servletOutputStream` objects, and loaded the report template into memory, then all we need to do in order to generate the report is execute the `JasperRunManager.runReportToPdfStream()` method, passing the appropriate parameters. This, of course, assumes that we want to render the report as a PDF. To render the report in other formats, we need to substitute with the appropriate call.

Notice that we call `facesContext.responseComplete()` before invoking `JasperRunManager.runReportToPdfStream()`. The reason for this is to interrupt the JSF processing cycle. If we don't call this method, JSF will try to apply a navigation rule and render the page as HTML. By interrupting the cycle and taking over, we are able to display the report as a PDF.

In order to execute the `generateReport()` method in the backing bean, we need to bind it to a JSP action. The following JSP illustrates how to do this:

```
<%@ page language="java" contentType="text/html; charset=UTF-8"
 pageEncoding="UTF-8"%>
<%@ taglib uri="http://java.sun.com/jsf/html" prefix="h"%>
<%@ taglib uri="http://java.sun.com/jsf/core" prefix="f"%>
<!DOCTYPE HTML PUBLIC "-//W3C//DTD HTML 4.01 Transitional//EN">
<html>
  <head>
    <meta http-equiv="Content-Type" content="text/html;
          charset=UTF-8">
      <title>Generate Report</title>
  </head>
  <body>
    <f:view>
      <h:outputText value="Click on the link below to generate the
                           report."/>
      <h:form>
        <h:commandLink action="generate_report"
                 actionListener="#{reportGenerator.generateReport}">
          <h:outputText value="Generate Report"/>
        </h:commandLink>
      </h:form>
    </f:view>
  </body>
</html>
```

This JSP links the action of clicking on a `commandLink` component (basically an HTML hyperlink) to the `generateReport()` method on the `ReportGenerator` backing bean. This JSP file is rendered as follows:

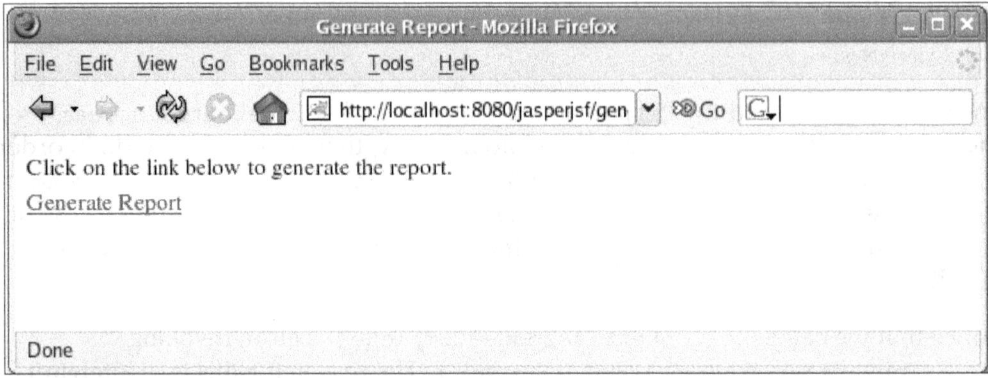

Clicking on the **Generate Report** link results in the report template being filled, exported to PDF, and displayed to the user.

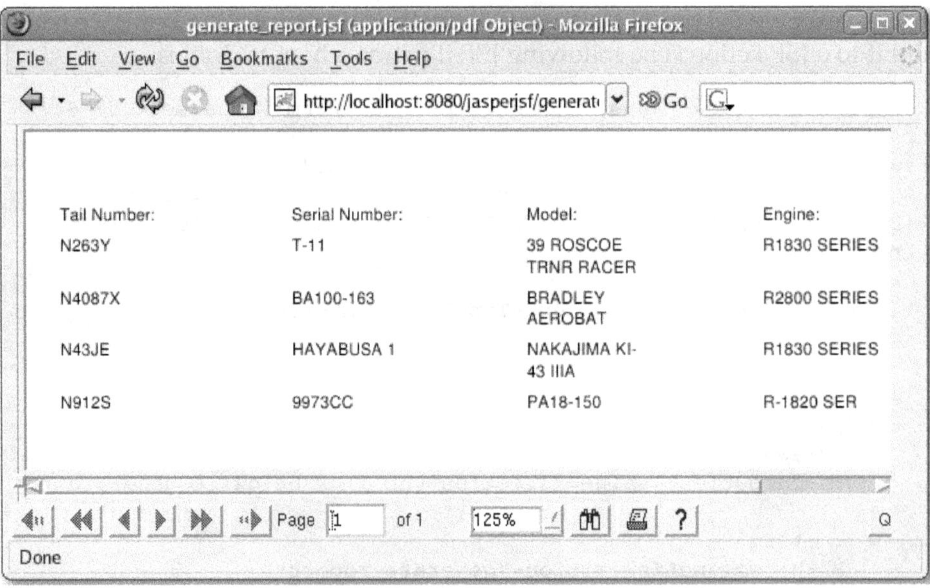

In order for this to work as expected, some configuration needs to be done behind the scenes. The `faces-config.xml` file must be configured properly to let JSF know that `ReportGenerator` is a backing bean.

```
<?xml version="1.0"?>
<faces-config version="1.2"
              xmlns="http://java.sun.com/xml/ns/javaee"
              xmlns:xi="http://www.w3.org/2001/XInclude"
              xmlns:xsi="http://www.w3.org/2001/XMLSchema-instance"
              xsi:schemaLocation="http://java.sun.com/xml/ns/javaee
                  http://java.sun.com/xml/ns/javaee
                  /web-facesconfig_1_2.xsd">
  <managed-bean>
    <managed-bean-name>reportGenerator</managed-bean-name>
    <managed-bean-class>
      net.ensode.jsf.ReportGenerator
    </managed-bean-class>
    <managed-bean-scope>request</managed-bean-scope>
  </managed-bean>
</faces-config>
```

This file must be placed in the `WEB-INF` directory inside the `war` file used to deploy the application.

The last step needed to make this technique work properly is to set up the `web.xml` file to use JSF.

```
<?xml version="1.0" encoding="ISO-8859-1"?>
<web-app xmlns="http://java.sun.com/xml/ns/j2ee"
         xmlns:xsi="http://www.w3.org/2001/XMLSchema-instance"
         xsi:schemaLocation="http://java.sun.com/xml/ns/j2ee
             http://java.sun.com/xml/ns/j2ee/web-app_2_4.xsd"
         version="2.4">
  <servlet>
    <servlet-name>Faces Servlet</servlet-name>
    <servlet-class>
      javax.faces.webapp.FacesServlet
    </servlet-class>
    <load-on-startup>1</load-on-startup>
  </servlet>
  <servlet-mapping>
    <servlet-name>Faces Servlet</servlet-name>
    <url-pattern>*.jsf</url-pattern>
  </servlet-mapping>
</web-app>
```

This tells the web container to use the `javax.faces.webapp.FacesServlet` servlet to process any requests for filenames ending in `.jsf`.

Integrating JasperReports with Struts

The **Struts** framework is the most popular Java web application framework. Typically, Struts applications consist of JSP's, **action classes** that serve as the controller component of MVC, **form beans** that map HTML form elements, and an XML configuration file. For more information on the Struts framework take a look at "*Learning Jakarta Struts 1.2*", *Stephan Wiesner, Packt Publishing*. JasperReports and Struts integration consists of writing a controller that will generate a report when executed.

The following action class demonstrates this technique:

```
package net.ensode.jasperbook.struts;

import java.io.InputStream;
import java.sql.Connection;
import java.sql.DriverManager;
import java.util.HashMap;

import javax.servlet.ServletOutputStream;
import javax.servlet.http.HttpServletRequest;
import javax.servlet.http.HttpServletResponse;
import net.sf.jasperreports.engine.JasperRunManager;
import org.apache.struts.action.Action;
import org.apache.struts.action.ActionForm;
import org.apache.struts.action.ActionForward;
import org.apache.struts.action.ActionMapping;

public class GenerateReportAction extends Action
{
  public ActionForward execute(ActionMapping mapping,
                               ActionForm form,
                               HttpServletRequest request,
                               HttpServletResponse response)
  throws Exception
  {
    Connection connection;
    ServletOutputStream servletOutputStream = response
                                              .getOutputStream();
    InputStream reportStream = getServlet().getServletConfig()
                             .getServletContext().getResourceAsStream(
                                         "/reports/DbReport.jasper");
    response.setContentType("application/pdf");
    Class.forName("com.mysql.jdbc.Driver");
```

```
        connection = DriverManager.getConnection("jdbc:mysql://localhost:
                     3306/flightstats?user=user&password=secret");
        JasperRunManager.runReportToPdfStream(reportStream,
                            servletOutputStream, new HashMap(), connection);
        connection.close();
        servletOutputStream.flush();
        servletOutputStream.close();
        return mapping.getInputForward();
    }
}
```

All the action classes must extend the `org.apache.struts.action.Action` class. Typically, the `execute()` method is overridden to implement custom logic for servicing a request. As can be seen in this code, the `execute()` method takes an instance of `HttpServletResponse` as one of its parameters. This makes it easy to write action classes that generate reports.

The technique illustrated in the preceding example is not much different from what we have seen in various earlier examples throughout the book. In most examples, we used standard Java servlets to generate web reports, implementing the report logic in the servlet's `doGet()` method. As both the `HttpServlet.doGet()` and `Action.execute()` methods take an instance of `HttpServletResponse` as one of their parameters, the technique to generate a report from an action class is virtually identical to the technique used when employing a servlet.

Let us take a look at the JSP that will invoke the `GenerateReportAction.execute()` method.

```
<%@ taglib uri="http://struts.apache.org/tags-html" prefix="html"%>
<!DOCTYPE HTML PUBLIC "-//W3C//DTD HTML 4.01 Transitional//EN">
<html>
  <head>
    <title>Generate Report</title>
  </head>
  <body>
    <p>Click on the button to generate the report.</p>
    <html:form action="/generate_report">
      <html:submit />
    </html:form>
  </body>
</html>
```

This JSP will generate a very simple HTML form with a **Submit** button as its only input field.

Next, let us take a look at the form bean for this JSP.

```
package net.ensode.jasperbook.struts;

import org.apache.struts.action.ActionForm;

public class GenerateReportForm extends ActionForm
{
}
```

As the HTML form generated by the preceding JSP has no input fields other than a **Submit** button, its corresponding form bean has no fields. We still need to write it because, when writing Struts applications, each JSP must have a corresponding form bean.

To wire the action class, the form bean, and the JSP together, we need to create a `struts-config.xml` file and deploy it in the `WEB-INF` directory of the application's war file.

```
<?xml version="1.0" encoding="ISO-8859-1"?>

<!DOCTYPE struts-config PUBLIC
 "-//Apache Software Foundation//DTD Struts Configuration 1.2//EN"
 "http://jakarta.apache.org/struts/dtds/struts-config_1_2.dtd">

<struts-config>
  <!-- ==================================== Form Bean Definitions -->
  <form-beans>
    <form-bean name="generateReportForm"
               type="net.ensode.jasperbook.struts.GenerateReportForm">
    </form-bean>
  </form-beans>
  <!-- =============================== Action Mapping Definitions -->
  <action-mappings>
    <action path="/generate_report"
            type="net.ensode.jasperbook.struts.GenerateReportAction"
            name="generateReportForm"
            scope="request"
            input="generate_report.jsp">
    </action>
  </action-mappings>
</struts-config>
```

The `<form-bean>` tag defines the `GenerateReportForm` class as a form bean and assigns the logical name `generateReportForm` to it.

The `<action>` tag maps the `GenerateReportAction` action class to the `/generate_report` path. It also specifies that the `GenerateReportForm` form bean will be associated with this action. Finally, it links the `generate_report.jsp` JSP file through the `input` attribute.

Like all server-side Java web applications, Struts applications must contain a `web.xml` file in the `WEB-INF` directory inside the application's `war` file.

```
<!DOCTYPE web-app PUBLIC
  "-//Sun Microsystems, Inc.//DTD Web Application 2.3//EN"
  "http://java.sun.com/dtd/web-app_2_3.dtd" >
<web-app>
    <display-name>Struts JasperReports Application</display-name>
    <servlet>
      <servlet-name>action</servlet-name>
      <servlet-class>
        org.apache.struts.action.ActionServlet
      </servlet-class>
      <init-param>
        <param-name>config</param-name>
        <param-value>/WEB-INF/struts-config.xml</param-value>
      </init-param>
      <init-param>
        <param-name>debug</param-name>
        <param-value>2</param-value>
      </init-param>
      <init-param>
        <param-name>detail</param-name>
        <param-value>2</param-value>
      </init-param>
      <load-on-startup>2</load-on-startup>
    </servlet>
  <!-- Standard Action Servlet Mapping -->
    <servlet-mapping>
      <servlet-name>action</servlet-name>
      <url-pattern>*.do</url-pattern>
    </servlet-mapping>
</web-app>
```

This `web.xml` file simply defines the Struts `ActionServlet` to process all the URLs ending in `.do`. The Struts `ActionServlet` calls the appropriate JSP and action class behind the scenes for the appropriate URL.

Following the standard procedure for deploying web applications, we create a WAR file with the preceding files and required dependencies, deploy it to a servlet container, and point the browser to the corresponding URL. We should then see a web page similar to the following:

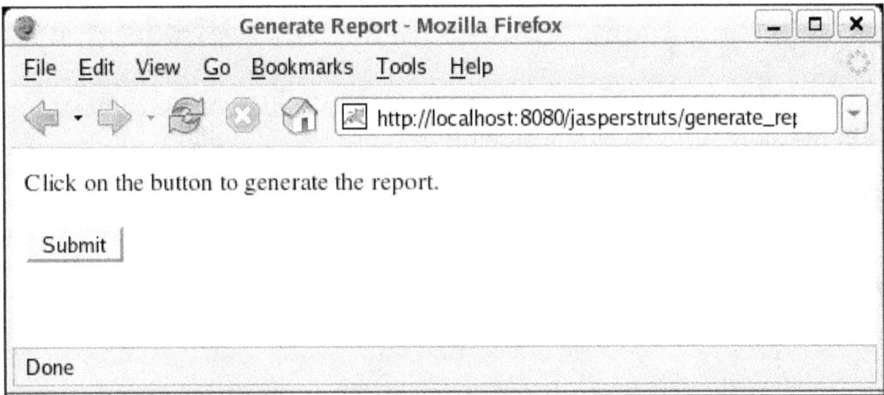

Clicking on the **Submit** button generates the report, exports it to PDF, and displays it in the browser.

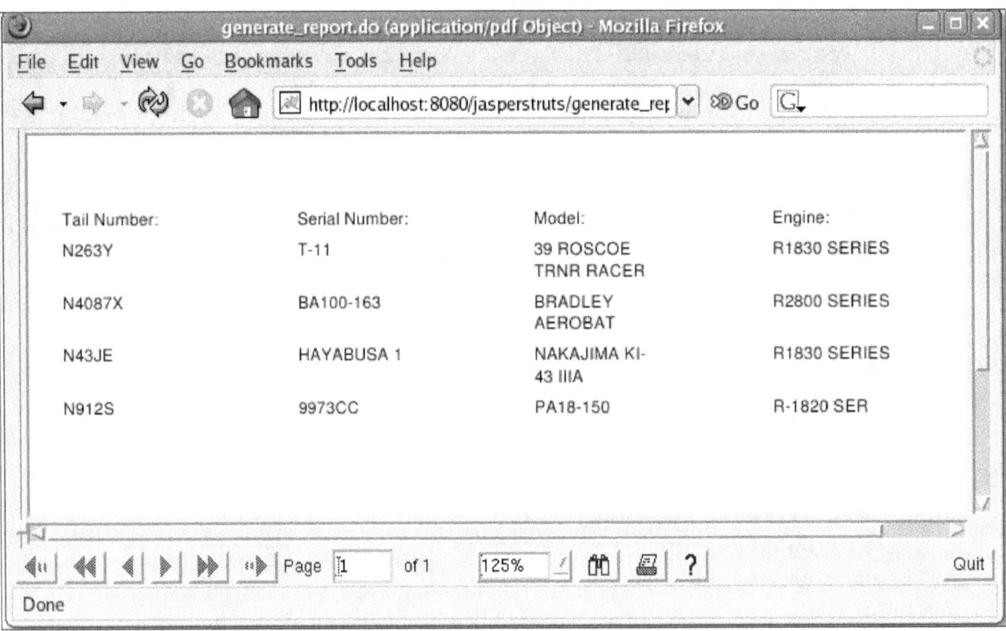

Summary

The chapter started with integrating JasperReports with Hibernate by writing embedded report queries in the HQL. JasperReports with HQL queries is similar to reports containing SQL queries except that the `language` attribute of the `<queryString>` element must be set to `hql`. Next, we saw how to integrate JasperReports with the JPA. As with Hibernate, JPA integration requires that the `language` attribute of the `<queryString>` element be modified. For JPA, the value of this attribute must be set to `ejbql`. Following our discussion of JPA, we saw how to integrate JasperReports with the Spring framework by taking advantage of Spring's built-in support for JasperReports integration.

The chapter also dealt with JSF and JasperReports integration and illustrated how to write backing beans that fill a report and display it in the browser. Finally, the chapter illustrated the integration of JasperReports with Struts by explaining how to write action classes that fill a report and display it in the browser.

Index

Symbols

A

B

L

M

N

O

P

R

S

T

U

V

W

X

Y

Packt Open Source Project Royalties

When we sell a book written on an Open Source project, we pay a royalty directly to that project. Therefore by purchasing JasperReports 3.5 for Java developers, Packt will have given some of the money received to the JasperReports project.

In the long term, we see ourselves and you—customers and readers of our books—as part of the Open Source ecosystem, providing sustainable revenue for the projects we publish on. Our aim at Packt is to establish publishing royalties as an essential part of the service and support a business model that sustains Open Source.

If you're working with an Open Source project that you would like us to publish on, and subsequently pay royalties to, please get in touch with us.

Writing for Packt

We welcome all inquiries from people who are interested in authoring. Book proposals should be sent to `author@packtpub.com`. If your book idea is still at an early stage and you would like to discuss it first before writing a formal book proposal, contact us; one of our commissioning editors will get in touch with you.

We're not just looking for published authors; if you have strong technical skills but no writing experience, our experienced editors can help you develop a writing career, or simply get some additional reward for your expertise.

About Packt Publishing

Packt, pronounced 'packed', published its first book "Mastering phpMyAdmin for Effective MySQL Management" in April 2004 and subsequently continued to specialize in publishing highly focused books on specific technologies and solutions.

Our books and publications share the experiences of your fellow IT professionals in adapting and customizing today's systems, applications, and frameworks. Our solution-based books give you the knowledge and power to customize the software and technologies you're using to get the job done. Packt books are more specific and less general than the IT books you have seen in the past. Our unique business model allows us to bring you more focused information, giving you more of what you need to know, and less of what you don't.

Packt is a modern, yet unique publishing company, which focuses on producing quality, cutting-edge books for communities of developers, administrators, and newbies alike. For more information, please visit our website: `www.PacktPub.com`.

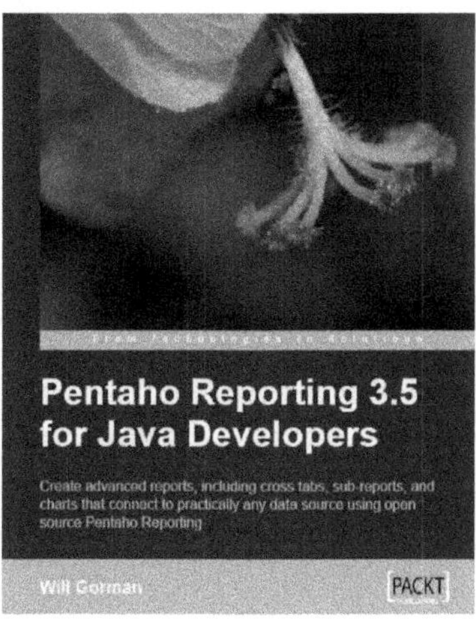

Pentaho Reporting 3.5 for Java Developers

ISBN: 978-1-847193-19-3 Paperback: 300 pages

Create advanced reports, including cross tabs, sub-reports, and charts that connect to practically any data source using open source Pentaho Reporting.

1. Create great-looking enterprise reports in PDF, Excel, and HTML with Pentaho's Open Source Reporting Suite, and integrate report generation into your existing Java application with minimal hassle
2. Use data source options to develop advanced graphs, graphics, cross tabs, and sub-reports

---

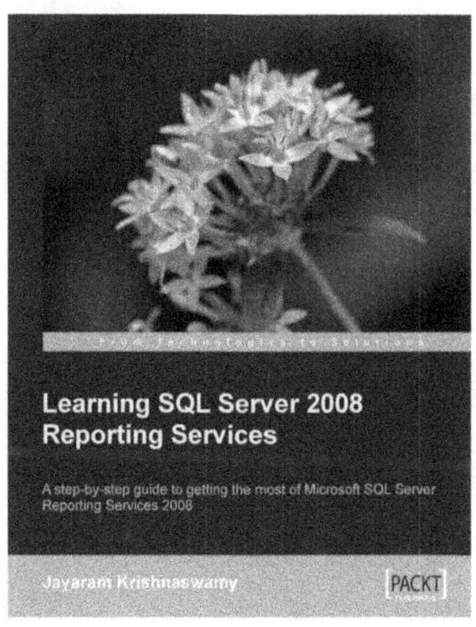

Learning SQL Server 2008 Reporting Services

ISBN: 978-1-847196-18-7 Paperback: 512 pages

A step-by-step guide to getting the most of Microsoft SQL Server Reporting Services 2008

1. Everything you need to create and deliver data-rich reports with SQL Server 2008 Reporting Services as quickly as possible
2. Packed with hands-on-examples to learn and improve your skills
3. Connect and report from databases, spreadsheets, XML Data, and more

Please check **www.PacktPub.com** for information on our titles

www.ingramcontent.com/pod-product-compliance
Lightning Source LLC
Chambersburg PA
CBHW062051050326
40690CB00016B/3054

* 9 7 8 1 8 4 7 1 9 8 0 8 2 *